ISBN: 9781799054436

Manufactured in the U.S.A.

Dedicated to William Peyton Foster

and all the soldiers of the Revolutionary War

Seedlings of William Foster

Book II

By Flavius Milton Foster (1909-2006)

Updated and revised in 2016
by Adrienne Foster Potter

INTRODUCTION

**Note: Birthdates of living persons have been omitted in order to protect them from identity theft—a problem that didn't exist during Flavius' lifetime but which is now a major concern.

Includes additional notes, sources and names added by Adrienne Foster Potter (cousin of Flavius—both are direct descendants of Harrison Foster b. 1776 and Anna Margaret Bartlett. Harrison--son of William b. 1747, the Revolutionary War Patriot who served six years). Harrison Foster was a great-grandson of William Foster "The Elder," for whom "Seedlings" Book I is named. Spelling is left largely as written to retain the original warmth and humor of the authors and for historical value, except in cases where clarification is needed. Book I -- which was revised earlier -- is a history of the descendants of William Foster "The Elder" b. 1686, son of Robert Foster and Elizabeth Garnett, the Virginia Fosters who first came to Northumberland Co., parent of Stafford Co. from which Prince William County was formed in Virginia. Book II is a history of their great-grandson William Foster b. 1747, the Revolutionary War Hero, and his descendants. He was the son of George Foster and Margaret Grigsby, who was the son of William Foster "The Elder" b. 1686 mentioned above. *Note from Adrienne: There is another William Foster who settled in Amelia, Virginia, who many families claim is the son of Robert and Elizabeth, but I believe he is the son of our William "The Elder" and therefore the grandson of Robert and Elizabeth, because of the age difference. The Amelia County William Foster was born 16 Jul 1714 in Northumberland, VA, and married another Elizabeth (last name unknown). He is found in "Seedlings" Bk. I.*

This book is by no means an indication that Foster research is "finished," since that word means little to a genealogist. In spite of all the combined research of many Foster descendants there are still many people in this book on whom more research is needed, and many who are not yet included. Special thanks to Flavius, Gen. Ivan Leon Foster, Vivian L. Snyder, LeNora Thomas Foster, Gloria Thompson Foster, Katherine Foster Shepherd, Gertie Wilson, now deceased, and Charles Leary, Julie Richards, Denise Dunn, Wiggi Dietz, and others who contributed years of their lives to this effort.

Note: The book is not indexed because Internet Explorer and Google Chrome both have a "find" feature to use when searching for a name or word in digital books.

FOREWARD

Flavius Foster was an ordinary man who did an extraordinary work. Though not flawless, it is a relentless, detailed, compilation of thousands of Fosters and their forefathers. Flavius listed few sources and so I have traced historical facts family-by-family for much of his book and found that his work is in most cases, correct. I added a few families from family trees without sources because their names, locations, and dates connect smoothly with existing data. There are minor spelling and grammatical errors that even an English major sometimes commits, but keep in mind that many men who invented jet engines and surgical tools could not spell perfectly.

Flavius was the son of a farmer and a survivor of the Great Depression. He did a tour of duty in the Navy in 1930, was honorably discharged, and did another tour in the army in WWII. He was in the invasion of North Africa and saw 31 months of combat in a division that suffered 34,000 casualties. After WWII he made a good living as a mechanic. When the Korean War started he moved his family westward to Washington and at age 40, joined the Navy again as an auto mechanic. He compiled his family data after work, on weekends, and after he retired, with no fortune, no office, no desk, no library, no computer, no internet—only the kitchen table that had to be cleared for dinner every night.

I'm grateful to Flavius' wife Marie for sharing her kitchen with Flavius for so many years, and for indulging him in his hobby. They didn't live a flashy life but chose instead to use any extra cash for mailing costs and trips to cemeteries and libraries. He corresponded with hundreds of private families and government agencies, sniffed out family mysteries like a bloodhound, and instinctively connected family lines.

I also honor Flavius' grandfather, Flavius Josephus Foster, who compiled numerous family records and motivated his grandson to do the same, and to the great-grandfather, Silas Jackson Foster, who also kept a family history and no doubt inspired his son to follow. Their exceptional work will not be forgotten.

* WILLIAM PEYTON FOSTER *
REVOLUTIONARY WAR VETERAN

From the following account by William's grandson we learn that William's middle name was Peyton: "ACCOUNT OF AN EARLY SETTLER OF THE MACKINAW, as given by his son, Silas Jackson Foster - A short account of the life and times of an old settler on the Mackinaw, which is not given in the history of McLean County: Aaron Foster was born in the month of May, 1804, Kentucky being his native state. His father, whose name was Harrison Foster, was born in the state of Virginia, and his grandfather, PEYTON FOSTER, was a soldier of the Revolution from that state. I have a lock of his hair and from its appearance it was clipped from his head when he was yet a young man. My conjecture is that his mother clipped it when her son left home for the seat of war. Of course this is only conjecture, but it was a fitting occasion for doing so when we consider that her boy was about to start on a perilous expedition from which he might never return, and so she wished to have a lock of his hair as a memento. It is needless to add that my great-grandfather fought through the war and returned home in safety, otherwise there would have been no sketch to write and I would not have been here to write it." We can surmise that because there were so many "Williams" in the Foster family, it was logical for our veteran to go by his middle name instead of his first.

There are many connections between the Foster and Peyton families, and the name "Peyton" is used as a given name for many generations. William's friend Timothy Peyton and Timothy's family emigrated with William from Prince William Co., VA to Bourbon Co., KY, where Timothy was killed by Indians. William led the group who went to retrieve Timothy's body, and who knows in what condition it was found?)

WILLIAM PEYTON, eldest son of GEORGE & MARGARET (GRIGSBY) FOSTER (source below under "Additional notes" proves parentage), was born in Prince William Co., Virginia. By the time William reached manhood, relations between the Colonists and the mother country were in a turmoil and growing worse. It was during this period that William met and married SALLIE SLADE, and their two oldest children were born. (Note: William has an 88-page Revolutionary Pension File—No. W2986-- found in the National Archives that details the information found below)

The situation came to a boil, when shots were exchanged between British troops and angered farmers in far-off Massachusetts Colony. News of how local citizens – with their privately owned arms had sent a large British force fleeing, created quite a stir. It wasn't long till the whole country was rising up in arms, and recruiting squads appeared in every village.

Brought up during a period of almost continual warfare, first with the French and Indians, then with unnumbered stories of Indian attacks along the not-too-distant frontier, it is doubtful that William thought war romantic. Despite this, and the face he had a wife and family, William couldn't resist the call to arms.

During early February of 1777, William Foster and a group of his neighbors went to Fauquier Co., Virginia, where they signed up with John Green's Company of Artillery. While skirmishing around Philadelphia in the fall of 1777, John Green was wounded and Thomas Baytop took over the company. Later John Green was made Colonel of Artillery with his own unit.

Among those who signed up for William Foster's battery were his neighbors:- John Hopper, Philip and Gideon Johnson, John Roach, Dale Carter, Sylvester Welch Sr., Edward Shacklett, and James Bailey. (An artillery batter consisted of 20 men.)

"William Foster, bombardier, appointed Feb. 8, 1777. Wm. Foster served out his enlistment and returned to his family, then reenlisted and finished out the war. Wm. Foster was on the lists of Company 9 at Valley, June 3, 1778, Thomas Baytop Capt. Of Col. Charles Harrison's Virginia Regiment of Artillery, as it stood from Nov. 30 1776 to Apr. of 1783. Wm. Foster served with this regiment till the end of the war. ("Sheffell's Record of the Rev. War," pg. 25)

In his pension application, William stated that he reenlisted "In Jersey, about 50 miles from Philadelphia," and that he was discharged, "May 18, 1783, on Larner Island, a few miles from Charleston, South Carolina."

As stated earlier, William's unit was in the skirmishing when the British took Philadelphia. His unit was with the army in Valley Forge during the winter of 1777-78. Here the troops hungered, froze, and often left bloody prints in the snow due to lack of shoes. Here, too Baron Stueben, a German army officer, joined the American army as drillmaster. Despite the inhuman living conditions, and the good Baron's outrageous English, the Americans learned to maneuver and use the principal infantry weapon of the day—the bayonet. Many troops died of exposure, others deserted, but those who remained became the backbone of the American army and carried the war to its triumphant conclusion.

Meanwhile, the British army in Philadelphia was living off the fat of the land. A break for the Americans came in the spring of 1778, when a French fleet sailed up Chesapeake Bay and the British found they had urgent business in New York City. Near Monmouth, New Jersey the pursuing Americans caught up with the British rear guard and were well on the way to destroying it. At the most crucial point in the fighting, Gen. Charles Lee disobeyed Gen. Washington's orders by retiring with his troops. The British guard escaped, and Gen. Lee was drummed out of the army.

William Foster remained with Washington's army near New York City, where they engaged in a few minor skirmishes, but the war in that area had reached a stalemate. Early in 1780, William went home to his family, then returned to the army. Meanwhile, the seat of war had shifted to the southern Colonies, where Gen. Cornwallis' British army was overrunning all opposition. To counter this invasion, Gen. Washington detached all his Virginia and Maryland troops and sent them south under Baron DeKalb. Here, they were joined by Virginia and North Carolina militia, and formed into an army.

Over the strong objections of Gen. Washington, Congress placed Gen. Gates in command of this army. During the battle of Saratoga, N.Y. Gen. Gates had remained in his tent, wringing his hands, while the British got set for an attack. Without orders, Gen. B. Arnold and other American officers in Gates' command met and defeated the British, so decisively they were forced to surrender. After the firing ceased, Gen. Gates emerged from his tent and claimed all the glory.

As Gen. Washington feared, Gates walked into a trap, and the British scattered his troops like chaff. Gen. Nathaniel Greene was then given command of the army, which he reorganized into two units. Gen. Greene took one unit and went after Gen. Cornwallis, and sent Gen. Daniel Morgan after Col. Tarleton's British cavalry. (Gen. Tarleton was known as "The Butcher," because of his inhumane treatment of American prisoners.)

Gen. Morgan met Tarleton Jan. 17, 1781 at a place where drovers held stock sales, called Cowpens. The General placed his troops with the militia in the front lines, backed by the Continental Line and artillery. The militia gave the attacking British two volleys, then retired behind the regular troops, who bore the brunt of the British attack. The British charge was broken, then the Americans attacked in their turn.

After a fierce struggle, the Americans got the upper hand. Tarleton got a bad sword cut in his hind end and barely escaped with a few troops. He did so by firing his cannon through the backs of his own infantrymen, who were fighting a desperate bayonet duel with the Continental troops.

The British losses at Cowpens caused Gen. Cornwallis to retire to the cover of his fleet at Wilmington, N.C. Keeping enough troops to cover the British in Wilmington, Gen. Greene sent detachments to clear British troops from South Carolina and Georgia. During this cleanup campaign, William Foster was at the battles of Ft. Ninety-six and Eutaw Springs, S.C.

William Foster's unit then rejoined Gen. Green, who followed Gen. Cornwallis into Virginia. Here, at a place he called "Little York," Gen. Cornwallis was trapped between American and French armies, with a French fleet behind the British. William's artillery battery was emplaced to help reduce the British fortifications, and soon Gen. Cornwallis was forced to surrender. With the loss of one third of the British troops in America the war was practically over.

William Foster's uniform was described thusly: A blue coat with red facing, lining, cuffs, lapels and collar. The skirts of the coat6 were turned back to show the red lining. The britches and waistcoat, white with yellow buttons. There were also yellow buttons on the front and cuffs of the coat. The rest of the uniform consisted of a white, ruffled shirt, black gaiters, and a black cocked hat with yellow braid.

The war years hadn't been kind to William. All he had to show for his six years of service was an arm shattered by a musket ball, and a handful of "not worth a

Continental" paper money. His father and wife had died and his children were living with his mother, who had children of her own to support. William had inherited 100 acres of land from his father, but it was mortgaged to the hilt.

WILLIAM FOSTER, was born, grew to manhood and married SALLIE, daughter of WILLIAM & ELIZABETH SLADE in Prince William Co., Virginia. They were married in late 1772 or early 1773, and Sallie died after 1780 and before March of 1783. After Sallie's death William's children went to live with his mother, Margaret. When Margaret died, Lettice Foster, the eldest child, took care of her brothers till of age. William took son Harrison to Kentucky with him and his new wife, and was joined there by son Aaron in 1799.

Additional notes and sources on William Foster:

Loyalist claims during the years 1784-1803 against the citizens of Virginia
(Reel 041, Public Record Office 122, Volume VI, No. 79,
British Manuscripts Project, Library of Congress): p. 199,
William Foster, son of George, of Prince William.
Debt due in 1776 Ð15.5.9 1/2.
Removed to Kentucky fourteen years ago; "poor".

His death date is from the Revolutionary War Pension Files, National Archives. He is in "Seedlings of William Foster," by Flavius Foster, Bk II, pgs. 2-7. Flavius Foster wrote in a letter to Kathie Foster Shepherd (sister of Adrienne Foster Potter), "DAR (Daughters of American Revolution) Lineage Book given; William Foster b. 1747 d. 2-7-1824, Md. 1st Sallie Slade; 2nd Sarah Hart."

DAR RECORD: FOSTER, WILLIAM
Ancestor #: A041904
Service: VIRGINIA Rank: PRIVATE
Birth: 1747 VIRGINIA
Death: 2-7-1824 CLARK CO KENTUCKY
*Pension Number: S*W2986*
*Service Source: S*W2986*
Service Description: 1) ARTILLERY, MATROSS IN COL CHARLES HARRISON'S CO
Residence 1) County: PRINCE WILLIAM CO - State: VIRGINIA
Spouse Number Name
1) SALLIE SLADE
2) SARAH HART

Associated Applications and Supplementals

Nat'l Num	***Child***	***Spouse***
PEYTON	[1] POLLY DANIEL	
MARGARET	[1] HAMILTON HISLE	
HARRISON	[1] ANNA MARGARET BARTLETT	
GEORGE	[1] SARAH MILLER	

Based on the data available in his day Gen. Ivan Leon Foster believed that Mildred was a daughter of William Foster and Sallie Slade. In truth, Mildred was the first child of William Foster and his 2nd wife, Sarah Hart. Mildred m. Minor Hart 27 May 1811 Bath, KY.

"Kentucky Pensioners of the War of 1812" *- ancestry.com*
William Foster, Virginia Line, of Clarke, KY, placed on pension 11 Feb 1819

*He is in the **1820 Census of Clark, KY**, with 14 members in the household. On the same page is his son, Paten Foster (Peyton). Flavius Foster wrote, "I learned today from National Archives that William Foster was discharged from the army May 18, 1783." He was in the company of Col. Harrison for two years." (Note: William named one of his sons Harrison, after this man)*

William's war record states, "I was in the battle of Monmouth and was at the battle of Little York when Cornwallis was taken, and at the Battle of Eutaw Springs and at the battle of ninety-six in South Carolina, also at Charleston Virginia but had no fighting in this last place." He wrote that he had 100 acres of land in Clark? North Township with all of its improvements worth $200, his horses were worth $40, his cattle $20, his sheep $11, hogs and pigs $25, household furniture $30, and farming utensils $12, for a total of $338. Record # W2986, Roll 332, Image 596, B.L.Wt 462-100, 269-60-55. Benjamin Grigsby signed one of the pages. This war record also shows Williams date of death as 7 Feb 1824. (There were many marriages and transactions between the Grigsbys and Fosters of Prince William, Virginia)

Burial place is from http://www.rootsweb.com/~kyclark3/family/fr071-foster.htm (Judith H. Martin)
Judith's email: martin5581@bellsouth.net

Prince William County, Virginia, Tax List, 1782:
Foster, William, 0 white polls.
Foster, William, 1 white poll.

***Land Tax List of Prince William County, VA 1784:** Margaret, William, and James Foster.*

***"Southern Lineages, Records of Thirteen Families,"** by A. Evans Wynn, p. 254:*
William and his wife, Sarah, deed land in Prince William County to John THOMAS, "109 acres at the corner of Howson Hooe, James FOSTER, Redmond FOSTER."

The following shows sources for the Peyton family. William migrated to Bourbon, Kentucky with his friend Timothy Peyton (also of Prince William, VA), who was later killed by Indians:

Virginia Personal Property Tax 1787, Bourbon County Tax List C:
PEYTON Sarah, self, [one unnamed male under age 21], 4 blacks above 16, 4 blacks under 16, 4 horses mares colts & mules, 7 cattle.

Extracts of Kentucky Assembly Records (1792-1799):
29 June 1792
Concerning property of Timothy PEYTON, Bourbon Co., who died "some time in the year of our Lord one thousand seven hundred and 87." Trustees appointed: James Garrard, John Allen, John Walker.

More sources for William Foster b. 1747
1800 Kentucky Taxpayers:
FORSTER, William, Bourbon County.
On February 27, 1807 William sold his land in Prince William County, Virginia, which had been given to him by his father. The land was sold to John Thomas of Rockingham County, North Carolina, who, as records indicate, was buying up the land of William and his relatives. The deed was for 109 acres 'at the corner of Howson Hooe, James Foster and Redmon Foster.' Redmon Foster was a witness to the deed. 'William Foster of Clark County, Kentucky' and Sarah, his wife, signed the deed, so they must have both been on a visit at the time

***1810 US Census, Clark County, Kentucky**, p. 129:*
William FOSTER, one male age 0-9, one male age 10-15, one male age 45+, three females age 0-9, two females age 10-15, one female age 26-44.

In 1811, William purchased 100 acres of land on which he was then living, from John Rankin and wife of Clark County, Kentucky. William's son, Peyton, was one of the witnesses to the deed. This land was near Lulbegrud, Clark County, Kentucky.

John Frederick Dorman,Virginia Revolutionary pension applications, abstracted (Washington, 1958-), *[with additions from Southern Lineages, Records of Thirteen Families, by A. Evans Wynn]:*
22 June 1818. Clark Co., Ky. William FOSTER of said county, aged 71, declares he enlisted in Prince William Co., Va., in the company of Capt. John GREEN in the 1st Regiment of Artillery of Col. Charles HARRISON on 8 Feb. 1777, served three years, re enlisted for the war in Jersey about 60 miles from Philadelphia, and continued until 18 May 1783 when he was discharged on James Island near Charleston, S.C. He was in the battles of Monmouth and Eutaw Springs and several skirmishes.

22 June 1818. Clark Co., Ky. Benja. GRIGSBY declares he was acquainted with William FOSTER during the Revolutionary War. He was in service for several years.

1820 US Census, Clark County, Kentucky, p. 86:
William FOSTER, one male age 10-15, one male age 16-25, one male age 45+, two females age 10-15, two females age 16-18, one female age 25-44, 6 persons engaged in agriculture.

More from his Revolutionary Pension file: 6 Oct. 1821. Clark Co., Ky. William FOSTER of said county, aged 73, makes similar statement of service but adds he was at the battle of Little York when Cornwallis was taken, at the battle of Ninety Six, S.C., and was at Charlestown, Va., but had no fighting in that place. He has a claim for nine Negroes which are in North Carolina, which claim originated in 1778 and he does not know whether he will ever get any. He has 100 acres of poor land worth $200 and horses, cattle, sheep, hogs and pigs, household and kitchen furniture, valued with the land at $338.00.

His family consists of his wife, aged about 54, and five children, Polly, aged 11, Nancy, aged 17, Sally, aged 18, Susan, aged 22, and Lenard, aged 14. He is a farmer which he cannot pursue having received two wounds in his right arm which disabled it.

Later William was obliged to bring suit against John Thomas of Rockingham, NC, who had purchased his Prince William, VA land, for the return of some Negro slaves. He employed Levi Hart, of Lexington, Kentucky, as his attorney. (Levi Hart was probably a relative of Sarah Hart Foster).
1822
"Know all men by these presents, that I, William Foster, of the County of Clark and State of Kentucky, having special confidence and trust in Levi Hart of Lexington, Kentucky, do nominate and appoint him my attorney in fact, for me in my name to ask for, demand, receive or sue for, or compromise, if he thinks fit so to do, a Negro woman named "Molla", her increase and descendants, supposed to be at this time in possession of John Thomas of Rockingham County, North Carolina and to which I am justly entitled, say about fifteen in number, hereby ratifying all his acts in the premises as fully as if I were present myself personally and had done the same.
Witness my hand this 22nd day of January 1822
William Foster

On February 7, 1824, William died from diabetes at his home on the land which he had purchased from John Rankin thirteen years before. He was buried near Lulbegrud in Clark County. His life of 77 years had been an eventful one. Had he chosen to write and leave behind some written record of his life, how interesting we should now find it.
Clark County, Kentucky, Records:
In obedience to an order from the worshipful County Court of Clarke at their October Term 1825, Appointing Shelton C. WATKINS, William THORNTON, Richard GROOMS and John WILLIAMS or any three of them being sworn to appraise the Estate of William FOSTER decd. Mr. Richard GROOMS, William THORTON and John WILLIAMS having met at the late dwelling house of said William FOSTER decd and after being first sworn as the Law directs proceed to make the following Valuation and report to Court To wit ($ /cts)
Clarke County May Court 1826

This Inventory and appraisement of the Estate of William FOSTER decd was produced in Court approved and ordered to be recorded Teste James F. Bullock, C.C.C.
P. G. Wardell, Virginia/West Virginia Genealogical Data from Revolutionary War Pension and Bounty Land Warrants, Vol. 2, p. 138:

FOSTER, William; query 1896 from great grandson J. M. Greenwood, Kansas City, Mo.; states he is grandson of soldier's son, Peyton, who died 1872.

Kentucky Pension Roll for 1835, p. 28:
Statement, &c. of Clarke county, Kentucky.
William FOSTER; Private; Annual allowance $96.00; Sums received $171.43; Virginia line, placed on the pension roll, Feb. 11, 1819; Commencement of pension, June 22, 1818; Age 73; Dropped under act of May 1, 1820.

Notes for SARAH HART:
***U.S. and International Marriage Records, 1560-1900** about Sarah Hart*
Name: Sarah Hart
Birth Year: 1766
Spouse Name: William Foster
Spouse Birth Year: 1747
Marriage Year: 1783
Marriage State: VA

William & Sarah decided that their best bet for a better future lay in Kentucky. So in 1784 or 1785, they joined a few neighbors under the leadership of Timothy PEYTON and headed west. William & Sarah FOSTER landed in Bourbon Co., Kentucky.

Due to the many, bloody Indian raids, Kentucky settlers lived in fortified settlements and farmed the surrounding land. William and Sarah were living in the William THOMAS station when their eldest child was born. Soon after they moved to Timothy PEYTON's station, where they were living when Timothy was killed and scalped by Indians. William organized a party to recover the body. William & Sarah lived on the Peyton station till 1805, when they moved to Clark County, Ky.

After William died of diabetes, Sarah married (2nd.) Moses BAKER, who died in 1844. At his death, Sarah applied for a pension as widow of William FOSTER. At that time, the above 100 acres was sold to their daughter Susan and her husband, who paid off the other heirs. [Clark County Deed Book 31, pp. 380-381.]

In 1844, Sarah was living with her youngest child, Polly HULSE, in Montgomery Co., Ky., and remained there till her death. Sarah is buried in Montgomery County, Ky. .
Reference: rin#-267

***From William Foster's Revolutionary Pension File, National Archives:** 9 July 1844. Montgomery Co., Ky. Sarah BAKER of said county, aged 78, declares she is the widow of William FOSTER who was a soldier from Prince William Co., Va. She was married to William FOSTER 6 March 1783 in Prince William County and he died 7 Feb. 1825 in Clark Co., Ky. She married Moses BAKER on 6 July 1826 and he died 31 Jan. 1844. She had a family record but it was destroyed by water leaking through the roof of the house and was rotten and spoiled before any of the family knew it. She had eleven children while married to William FOSTER. She is unable to give the age of any of her children. Her eldest child Milly HART resides in Fayette Co., Ky., and was born 20 April 1785.*

12 July 1844. Bourbon Co., Ky. Ann T. MALLORY of said county, aged 69, declares she was at the marriage of William FOSTER and Sarah FOSTER, now Sarah BAKER. She was 6 or 7 years old and had been going to school before their marriage. She and Sarah BAKER were raised in the same neighborhood in Prince William Co., Va. After the marriage her father Timothy PEYTON and William FOSTER with his wife Sarah moved to Kentucky together in 1784 and 1785 and the next year after they came to Kentucky their first child was born. Her father and William FOSTER settled in Bourbon County in the same neighborhood. They lived there until they had five or six children and then William FOSTER and his wife Sarah moved from Bourbon County to Clark County where he was living when he died. She frequently heard William FOSTER speak of being in the Revolutionary War. [She further states that the said Sarah FOSTER is a lady of truth.]

***31 July 1844. Bourbon Co., Ky. Ann T. MALLORY** of said county, aged about 68, declares she was born in Prince William Co., Va., and was raised there until she was ten years old. One of her neighbors Leonard HART had a daughter Sarah HART who married William FOSTER in the fall of 1784. She was at the marriage and saw them married. The next spring in June 1785 her father and his family and Sarah and William FOSTER all came together to Bourbon Co., Ky., and settled not far apart. Sarah FOSTER had a child twelve or thirteen months after she was married and her name was Mildred FOSTER and she married Minor HART and now lives in Fayette Co., Ky., and must be 58 years of age. Afterward Sarah FOSTER had several children; some live in Illinois, Missouri and others in Kentucky. She has her father's account book starting the day they started to Kentucky and it states 2 June 1785. Sarah HART was married to William FOSTER the year before, she thinks in the fall of 1784. They lived together until William FOSTER died, about 17 years past. Sarah married Moses BAKER and she has understood that BAKER died last winter or spring. William and Sarah lived on her father's farm for many years and when her father, T. PATIN, was killed by the Indians, William FOSTER was one of the men that went and brought him home.*

***31 July 1844. Bourbon Co., Ky. Sarah D. SCOTT** of said county, aged about 67, declares she lived with her father William JAMES [or THOMAS] in his station when William FOSTER [who was a Revolutionary soldier] and his wife Sarah came about 1785 or 1786. In the station she had her first born, Mildred FOSTER, and another before they left the station and moved to T. PATAN's where they lived and had several children before William FOSTER died. Sarah married Moses BAKER who died last winter or spring.*

***15 Aug. 1844. J. WILLIAMS** writes from Brentsville, Prince William Co., Va., that he has examined the records of his office from 1780 to 1790 and has not found the marriage bond or certificate of marriage of William FOSTER. He has enquired of Mr. Redmon FOSTER of this county but has not been able to get any material fact in relation to said marriage.*

***22 Aug. 1844. Montgomery Co., Ky. Mrs. Polly M. HULSE** of said county, aged about 33, declares she is the youngest child of William FOSTER and Sarah his wife. After the death of her father her mother married Moses BAKER who died 31 Jan. 1844. Her mother now lives with her.*

***12 Sept. 1844. Fayette Co., Ky. Mrs. Milly HART** of said county, aged about 57, declares she is the oldest child of William FOSTER, late of Clark County. Her father and mother lived together until the death of William FOSTER about 1821 to 1826 (cannot recollect). Her mother Sarah FOSTER remained a widow eighteen months or two years and then married Moses BAKER of Montgomery County who died about the last of January or first of February 1844. [She further states that her father was dropped from the pension roll on account of his being worth more that the law allowed to draw a pension, etc.]*

***2 Aug. 1855. Montgomery Co., Ky. Sarah BAKER** of Mount Sterling in said county, aged 87, declares she was allowed a pension for the services of her late husband William FOSTER of Clark Co., Ky.*

***Sarah BAKER**, formerly widow of William FOSTER who died 7 Feb. 1824, matross in the regiment of Col. Harrison in the Virginia line for two years, was placed on the Kentucky pension roll at $100 per annum. Certificates 8944 under the Act of 1838 and 6517 under the Acts of 1843-44 were issued 14 Dec. 1844 and 3181 under the Act of 1848 was issued 19 Jan. 1849. Bounty land warrant 269 for 60 acres was issued 4 Aug. 1856.*

Kentucky Death Records, 1852-1953 about Sarah Baker
Name: Sarah Baker [Sarah Hart]
Death Date: 27 Dec 1858

Death Location: Montgomery
Residence Location: Montgomery
Age: 98
Birth Date: abt 1760
Father's name: Leonard Hart
Mother's name: Sarah Hart

Sylvester Welch *states in his pension file that William Foster was in his regiment (Col. Harrison's). Sylvester Welch said the Artillery was commanded by Gen. Knox and that he enlisted from Northumberland County (later Fauquier), and then marched to Yorktown and from there to Valley Forge, crossing through Fredericksburg, Leesburg, and Frederick Town, Md, Lancaster, Pennsylvania, that he was in the battle of Monmouth, and marched from thence to the white plains and sundry other places. Others in his regiment were John Reach, Cale Carter, James Bailey, John Hopper, and Gideon Johnson.*

Gen. Ivan Foster believed that William Peyton Foster b. 1747 was the son of William Foster b. 1720, but the research of Flavius Foster points toward George being the actual father, and William b. 1720 was probably the brother of George. ***The following land transaction positively links our William b. 1747 to George Foster b. 1723:*** *"On Feb. 27, 1807 William & wife #2 Sarah (Hart) Foster had immigrated to Kentucky and released their claims to the above land to his brother-in-law John Thomas. John & Ann Thomas then sold the land to Rutland Johnson and used the money to pay off the estate debt on July 4, 1808." Seedlings, Grigsby Connection III." John Thomas was the husband of Ann, daughter of George Foster.*

WILLIAM FOSTER b. 1747 Prince William Co., VA d. Feb. 7, 1824 Clark, KY
SALLIE (SLADE) b. abt 1747 PW, VA d. before 1783 PW, VA
Were married 1772 Virginia

U.S. and International Marriage Records, 1560-1900 *about Sallie Slade*
Name: Sallie Slade
Spouse Name: William Foster
Spouse Birth Place: VA
Spouse Birth Year: 1747
Marriage Year: 1772
Marriage State: VA

CHILDREN BY 1st WIFE SALLIE SLADE:

1. LETTICE b. 1773 Prince William, Virginia, d. Prince William, Virginia
2. HARRISON b. 1774 d. June 27, 1819 m. ANNA MARGARET BARTLETT
3. AARON b. 1777 or early 1778, based on 1st tithing m. SUSANNA BRAMBLETT
4. WILLIAM b. 1780 or early 1781, based on 1st tithing
   (Tithing, "Free, White and 21," that old over-worked phrase.)

AARON (#3 above) was in Bourbon, Kentucky in 1799 when he witnessed his brother Harrison's marriage license. He met SUSANNA BRAMBLETT there and married her on Aug. 2, 1800 in Bourbon, Co., KY. On May 17, 1815 he is listed as a Private in the U.S. Dragoons commanded by Capt. A. Cummings. His height is shown as 5' 6 1/4" with hazel eyes, brown hair, and brown complexion. He is 37 years old. Occupation is farmer, and he was born in Prince William, Virginia. He was enlisted by Lt. Parch at Carlisle for 5 years. Under remarks it states: " Capt: Haynes Co. Aug 31, 1813 to present - a fit subject for discharge... July 11/1815, Joined from Dragoons - Transfd to Inf. Unfit for service, disease -Gravel & lameness - Book 553, Discharged July 12/1815,

Invalid. Source: U.S. Army, Register of Enlistments, 1789 - 1914, 1798 May 17 - 1815, F-G." www.ancestry.com.

WILLIAM FOSTER b. 1747 of Prince William, Virginia, married #2, SARAH, daughter of LEONARD & SARAH HART. After much debating and considering the prospects of their area, William & Sarah decided that their best bet for a better future lay in Kentucky. So in 1784 of 1785, they joined a few neighbors under the leadership of Timothy Peyton and headed west. William & Sarah Foster landed in Bourbon Co., Kentucky.

Due to the many bloody Indian raids, Kentucky settlers lived in fortified settlements and farmed the surrounding land. William and Sarah were living in the William Thomas station when their eldest child was born. Soon after they moved to Timothy Peyton's station, which is where they were living when Timothy was killed and scalped by Indians. William organized a party to recover the body. William & Sarah lived on the Peyton station till 1804, when they moved to Clark County, Ky., probably because there were more settlers there and it offered better protection from Indian raids and wolves.

In 1811, William & Sarah bought 100 acres of land from John & Sarah Rankin, on Lulbegrud Creek. This stream bears the name of a character from "Gulliver's Travels," a book that was being read by a member of Daniel Boone's survey party when they camped on the creek. On Feb. 11, 1819 William applied for and received a war pension, and lost it two years later because he was worth over $300 in land and stock.

After William died of diabetes, Sarah married #2, MOSES BAKER, who died in 1844. At his death, Sarah applied for a pension as widow of William Foster. At that time, the above 100 acres was sold to their daughter Susan and her husband, who paid off the other heirs. In 1844 Sarah was living with her youngest child, Polly Hulse, in Montgomery Co., Ky., and remained there till her death. Sarah is buried in Montgomery County, Ky.

According to one of William & Sarah Foster's descendants who has spent her entire life in Kentucky, William is buried on Lulbegrud Creek. The cemetery is on the opposite side of the Creek from the Tennessee Gas Plant, in what is known as "Foster's Hole." But no tombstone was found among the other graves. (It is hard for us today to conceive the hardships and frustration our ancestors endured for the barest necessities of life.)

WILLIAM FOSTER b. 1747 Prince William, VA d. Feb. 7, 1824 Clark, KY
SARAH (HART) b. 1766 d. Dec. 27, 1858 Mt. Sterling, Montgomery, KY

Were married Mar. 6, 1783, Virginia.

U.S. and International Marriage Records, 1560-1900
William Foster m. Sarah Hart 1783
William b. 1747
Sarah b. 1766

To this union were born:

1. MILDRED b. Apr. 20, 1785 William Thomas Station, Bourbon, KY d. 1885 Fayette, KY
2. JEANETTE b. 1788 William Thomas Station, Bourbon, KY d. Aug. 27, 1870 Macon, MO
3. PEYTON b. Oct. 18, 1791 Bourbon, KY d. Sep. 5, 1872 La Plata, Macon, MO
4. MARGARET M. b. Apr. 27, 1794 Bourbon, KY d. 1885 Clark, Kentucky
5. BABY b. 1796
6. SUSAN b. 1798 Bourbon, KY, d. abt 1880 Clark, KY
7. GEORGE b. 5 Jul 1800 Bourbon, KY d. 7 May 1837 Auburn, Sangamon, Illinois
8. SARAH (SALLIE) b. 1802, Bourbon, KY d. abt 1880 Shelby, KY
9. NANCY b. Mar. 13, 1804 Clark, KY d. Oct. 8, 1844 Clark, KY
10. LEONARD b. 1806 Clark, KY d. May 11, 1877 Clark, KY
11. POLLY (MARY) b. 1809 KY

MILDRED or MILLIE (#1 above) eldest child of WILLIAM & SARAH FOSTER, was born on the Wm. Thomas Station, Bourbon Co., Kentucky, In 1806, she went with her parents to Clark County, where she met and married MINOR HART. Doubtlessly, Minor was relative of Sarah's. Some time after marriage, Minor & Mildred joined other Hart families in Fayette Co., Ky. Here, they lived out their lives and are buried.

According to the 1830-40 census, Minor & Mildred had a son, ca. 1814, a daughter ca. 1817, and a daughter ca. 1826, but I have no names for any of them. Children:

1. LEVI b. 1819 d. aft 1900
2. JOHN b. 1821 d. abt 1846
3. ANNA b. 1823
   Other children:
4. SUSANNAH HART b. 1821
5. N C HART b. 1825 m. "E. D." and had 1) M. A., 2) M. D., 3) Elizabeth, 4) Sally A, 5) and Edwin

LEVI HART married LYDIA and lived in Fayette Co., KY., where all of their children were born:

1. JOSEPHINE b. 1846 M. HENRY BOONE

2. NAPOLEAN, later changed to Levi Jr. b.1847
3. CHINA b. 1850
4. STEPHEN b. 1854
5. ELENOR b. 1857
6. MINOR b. 1857
7. ROBERT R b. 1859 M. ELLEN
8. EDWIN OR EDWARD b. 1861

JOSEPHINE (#1 above) married Henry Boone in Fayette Co., Ky., where all their children were born: 1) EMMA 1868, 2) WILLIAM APR. 1870, 3) MOLLIE, 4) LUCY,5) WALLACE, AND 6) LEVI.

ROBERT R. (#7 above) married ELLEN and had 1) MARY, 2) PEARL, 3) DENNIS GEORGE, 4) LENA E, 5) LYDIA, 6) NANNIE, 7) TILLIE, 8) ROBERT W, 9) KINNIARD, 10) and JOE T.)

JOHN HART, son of MINOR HART and MILDRED FOSTER married his cousin Martha Armstrong Rankins, a widow with three children. Nancy's first family is given on p. 19. John and Martha Hart's children: 1) Nancy E 1860, 2) John M 1862, 3) Martha 1864, 4) Thomas J 1868.

JEANETTE, 2nd child of William & Sarah (Hart) Foster, was born in Bourbon Co, Kentucky and went with her parents to Clark County. Here, she grew to adulthood, met and married #1, JOHN H. PATRICK. Soon after their children were born, John went to Mississippi on business and died there. John was born Nov. 1, 1789.

Jeanette married #2 JOHN ARMSTRONG, and in 1827 they went to Sangamon Co., ILL, (where her brothers George W. and Peyton, had arrived the previous year), and settled what is now Loami Township; There were no known children born to this marriage. Armstrong died before Jeanette, but I don't know where. Jeanette died in her daughter's home in Macon Co., Missouri.

Both of her husbands served in the War of 1812 and she drew a pension after they died, as the widow of John Armstrong, until her death. Her birthplace is stated in the Revolutionary pension file of her father William, in a testimony given by Sarah Scott, daughter of William Thomas or James.

Marriage Records Fayette County, Kentucky Volume II 1810-1814
Name: John Patrick
Spouse: Jane Foster
Marriage Date: 17 Jan 1810
Leonard Hart, B.; Peyton Foster, W.; Sarah Patrick, M. for groom

John Patrick and Jeanette Foster's children:

1. SOPHIA b. 1823 KY who married WILLIAM EASLEY in 1828 in Illinois. In 1838, they moved to Macon Co., Mo., where he was a noted judge.

2. MARGARET F. b. 5 Jan 1815, who married ALBERTES BARGER,
3. LAVICA b. 1817 who married JOSEPH BURCH and moved to Lafayette Co., Missouri.

MARGARET F (in the paragraph above)., born Jan. 5, 1815 married ALBARTES BARGER in Sangamon Co., Ill. Dec. 23, 1829. He was born May 26, 1811. Both lived out their lives in Illinois. Their children: 10 JOHN A. b. July 21, 1831, 2) MAJOR E, 3) JEANETTE b. June 2, 1834, 4) SOPHIA b. Feb. 10, 1836, 5) WILLIAM b. Dec. 19, 1838, 6) JULIA b. Dec. 18, 1840, 7) JAMES N. b. Mar. 20, 1842, 8) CHARLES H. b. Nov. 18, 1845 9) LEROY b. Feb. 20, 1847, 10) GEORGE b. June 10, 1849, 11) ALBERT, 12) LUCINDA J., 13) HARRIET E.

PEYTON, 3rd child of WILLIAM & SARAH FOSTER, born in Bourbon Co., Kentucky, went to Clark County with his parents. Here, he grew to manhood, met and married POLLY DANIEL, and their first six children were born. In 1826, Peyton sold his holdings in Kentucky and migrated to Sangamon Co., Illinois, where his last children were born. On Nov. 8, 1852,Peyton, his brother George and sister Jeanette moved to Adair Co., Missouri. Peyton and Polly are buried in La Plata, Missouri.

Peyton was a veteran of the War of 1812, a farmer and hotel keeper.

Descendant Jodi Bond wrote: "He inherited all of his father's land as oldest living son. He also served in the Mexican War and enlisted in Illinois." ***He was (a Colonel) in Company D*** *of the Illinois 4th Infantry Regiment. Source: http://www.ilsos.gov/GenealogyMWeb/MexicanWarSearchServlet*

Source: ***"History of the Early Settlers of Sangamon, Illinois: Centennial Record,"*** *by John Carroll Power, assisted by his wife, Mrs. S. A. Power, Springfield, Illinois, Edwin A Wilson & Co. 1876; pg. 308. PEYTON FOSTER, was born about 1799 near Winchester, Scott county, Ky, and was married there to Polly Daniels, a native of the same county. They had six children in Kentucky, and moved to Sangamon County, Ill., with his brother George, arriving in the year 1826, and settled in what is now Loami township, where four children were born.*

Gen. Ivan Leon Foster wrote: "In 1826 Peyton, in company with his brother, George W. and their sister, Jeanette, (usually called Jane or Jennie) and their respective families, [immigrated] to the State of Illinois. They settled first near the present town of Loami in Sangamon County. Peyton and his brother, George, both took part in the Indian Wars. Except for short visits back in Kentucky, Peyton remained in Illinois until 1852 when he moved to the State of Missouri. He died in Commerce, Scott County, Missouri in 1872. His wife, Polly, preceded him in death by one year."

COL. PEYTON FOSTER b. Oct. 18, 1791 d. Sept. 5, 1872
POLLY (DANIEL) b. May 5, 1794 d. Jan. 30, 1871
Were married May 21, 1812, Kentucky. To this union were born:

1. JEANETTE B. Feb. 21, 1813 d. May 30, 1897
2. WILLIAM HARRISON b. 1815
3. GEORGE W. b, 1817
4. JOHN D. b, 1820 d. 1901
5. RUTH N. b. 1822
6. PEYTON JR. b. 1825
7. LEONARD b. 1829 d. 1897

8. HIRAM BYRD b. July 30, 1832 d. Mar. 30, 1904
9. Three sons and a daughter died young.

JEANETTE, born in Clark Co., Kentucky went with her parents to Sangamon Co., Illinois. Here she met and married EDMOND GREENWOOD. In 1852 they went to Missouri with her parents. In later life, Jeanette was totally blind. Both are buried near Brashear, Adair Co., Missouri, where they lived on a farm.

EDMUND GREENWOOD b. Jan. 8, 1814 d. Aug. 26, 1903
JEANETTE (FOSTER) b. Feb. 21, 1813 d. May 30, 1897
Were married 1835, Illinois. To this union were born:

1. JAMES M b. Nov. 15, 1837 d. Aug. 1, 1914
2. RUTH E. b. 1838
3. PEYTON FOSTER B. Feb. 12, 1840 d. Apr. 6, 1918
4. SARAH ELIZABETH b. Oct. 4, 1852 d. Nov. 13, 1881
5. MARY ANN b. May 5, 185? D. Nov. 28, 1948

JAMES M., born in Illinois, came with his parents to Adair Co., Missouri. Here he grew to manhood, met and married in 1859, AMANDA McDANIEL. She was born in 1840 d. July 19, 1904. Their children: HAVER, JEANETTE, and ADDIE G., who married MacLAUGHLIN and lived in Kansas City, Missouri.

RUTH E. married JAMES HATFIELD and had: 1) EDMUND, 2) JEANETTE, 3) JAMES, AND 4) WAYNE.

As noted, the names Peyton, Edmund and Jeanette have followed the family to this day.

PEYTON FOSTER GREENWOOD was born in Sangamon Co., Ill. and made the migration to Missouri. Here he married #1, FANNIE FOSTER, Sept. 5, 1861, who died in a short time. Peyton then married #2, JULIA A. BRYAN. Peyton F. spent all his adult life as a lawyer in Adair Co., Missouri. Both he and his wife are buried in Kirksville Cemetery."

"History of the Early Settlers of Sangamon County, Illinois: Centennial Record" *p. 337--Peyton was born 12 Feb 1840 in Sangamon Co, attended district school with his brother, James, M. in his native county, and private schools in Kirksville, MO. He also spent one year in the Baptist College at Lagrange, MO. He was married Sept. 1861 to Frances M. (Fannie) Foster, who died six weeks after marriage. In April 1864, he married Julia Bryan and has three children, Eva, Samuel E and Grace. Peyton F. Greenwood is a practicing lawyer and resides in Kirksville, Mo.*

PEYTON F. GREENWOOD b. Nov. 15, 1837 d. Aug. 1, 1914
JULIA A. (BRYAN) b. Sept. 1844 Indiana d. Mar. 17, 1928
Were married Mar. 3, 1864, Missouri. To this union were born:

1. EVALINE b. 1865
2. SAMUEL E. b. 1867 d. 1877
3. GRACE M b. 1847 d. 1892
4. JEANETTE b. 1876 m. JOHN C. CASEBOLT

5. HELEN b. 1878 m. DR. MORRIS TAYMAN
6. JAMES M. b. 1881 d. 1904
7. MARY C. b. 1882 m. SANFORD J> MILLER
8. CARL PEYTON b. 1884 d. Oct. 5, 1969

MARY C. (above) married #2 ARTHUR COLLETT in Seattle, Wash. Both her husbands are dead, but Mary C., Collett still lives in Seattle – (Oct. 1971).

MARY ANN (POLLY) GREENWOOD, 5th child of Jeanette Foster and Edmund Greenwood, was born in Adair Co., Missouri. Here she grew to adulthood, met and married VINCENT H. KING Nov. 23, 1881. To this union was born: NORMA, who married WILLARD SUMMERS. Norma Summers is now widowed, but she was a son: Dr. HAROLD SUMMERS, who lives in Excelsior Springs, MO. MARY ANN married #2, JAMES SPITLER but there were no children born to this union. Mary Ann is buried in the Kirksville Cemetery. Note: It is possible that Mary Ann Greenwood has a 2nd child, Mary Ann b. abt 1884.

Before going on to the last child of EDMUND & JEANETTE GREENWOOD, (not youngest), I wish to add a bit on their eldest son. James M. was Superintendant of Schools for Kansas City, Missouri for over 40 years and was highly thought of as an educator.

SARAH ELIZABETH GREENWOOD, 4th child of EDMUND GREENWOOD and JEANETTE (FOSTER) was born on Lick Creek, Sangamon, Illinois, and made the migration to Adair Co., Missouri. Here she grew to adulthood and met and married Thomas Preston Wiseman, a medical doctor. He was a widower with at least one child, and after Sarah E. died Dr. Wiseman married a widow with a child.

THOMAS P. WISEMAN
SARAH (GREENWOOD)
Were married Nov. 12, 1878 Missouri. To this union were born:

1. JEANETTE
2. CHILD WISEMAN who died in infancy

Jeanette (Sarah's daughter) was taken from her mother at birth because Sarah E was in the last stages of TB. Jeanette was raised by her grandparents Edmund and Jeanette Greenwood, till she was 15 years old. At that time Jeanette visited relatives in Sangamon Co., Illinois, where she met and married #1 Morris Blair. Morris is buried in Adair Co., Missouri, Jeanette in Spokane, Washington.

MORRIS BLAIR b. 1870 d. 1905
JEANETTE (WISEMAN) b. June 13, 1880 d. Feb. 7, 1959
Were married 1895 Illinois. To this union were born:

1. RALPH b. 1896 d. 1919
2. GUY and RUTH, who died in infancy

Ralph (#1 above) was so badly afflicted with asthma, his grandfather Dr. T. P. Wiseman suggested his mother take him to a dryer climate. Jeanette did so, moving in with her half-sister on her ranch near Almira, Washington. Here Ralph grew to manhood, and was drafted into the Army during WWII. Coming home again, Ralph contracted WWI-type flu and died. Ralph was married, but I have no wife's name, however, they had a daughter, ARLINE, Mar. 13, 1918.

While living in Washington, Jeanette met and married #2, HARRY R. ELSDON. He was born in Halifax, Nova Scotia, Canada, and took out his American citizenship papers in Spokane, Wash. Both Jeanette and Harry Elsdon are buried in Spokane, Wash.

HARRY R. ELSDON b. Jan. 25, 1876 d. Nov. 7, 1948
JEANETTE (WISEMAN) b. June 13, 1880 d. Feb. 7, 1959.
Were married Mar. 14, 1908, Washington. To this union were born:

1. JAMES H. b. Feb. 17, 1909
2. NORMA b. July 29, 1911
3. VIRGINIA b. Nov. 25, 1916

JAMES H. ELSDON (#1 above) was born in Medical Lake, Wash., got his Ph.D. at the Univ. of California, and became an officer in the U.S. Navy. He is now retired, and living in Washington D.C. with his wife, FRANCIS (JECHLINGER). They have no children.

VIRGINIA E. ELSDON (#3 above) was born in Spokane, met, married and divorced #1:
JAMES W. SIMONTON b. Jan. 29, 1899
VIRGINIA (ELSDON) b. Nov. 25, 1916
Were married Feb. 2, 1935, Washington. To this union were born:

1. HAROLD LELAND b. Jan. 12, 1936
2. LAWRENCE TEMPLE b. Mar. 24, 1938

HAROLD L. married BARBARA JO LARA September of 1957. Their children: MICHAEL B., MARK.

In Portland, Ore., Virginia E. met, married, and divorced #2: BENJAMIN E. WOLFE. Marriage date was Sept. 3, 1943. He was born, Aug. 19, 1899. They had one child: NORMA CONSTANCE.

After her second marriage ended Virginia took a contract as an organist-vocalist in Fairbanks, Alaska. Here she met and married #3 GORDON L. SCHROEDER Jan. 4, 1954.

GORDON L. SCHROEDER was born in Grants Pass, Oregon, Jan. 17, 1921. He is a WWII Navy veteran and is now working for the government in Fairbanks, Alaska. They have no children of their own, but he adopted Norma CONSTANCE WOLFE., who now lives near them in Fairbanks.

NORMA CONSTANCE WOLFE, daughter of Virginia and Benjamin E. Wolfe, went to Alaska with her mother. Here she met and married a soldier, who soon deserted:

GIOVENNA CANALE. Norma C. had a daughter whom the father has not seen, and lives in Fairbanks: VIRGINIA MARIE b. July 18, 1965.
****

WILLIAM HARRISON, 2nd child of Peyton & Polly Foster, was born in Clark Co., KY and went with his parents to Sangamon Co., Illinois. Here, he met and married Margaret Greenwood, sister of Edmund, pg. 9. All their children were born in Illinois.

This was during the page in our history when the Pacific coast was the promised land, and long treks by wagon train were the plan of the day. In 1852, William H. got the urge to go to California. They must have started late in the season, because they had to winter near Salt Lake City.

Margaret sickened and died in Nebraska, and was buried beside the trail. The rest of the family continued on to California, and settled in Napa County, where some of their descendants still live.

New source: WILLIAM H. (Foster), born in Kentucky, married Margaret Greenwood and she died in Nebraska, on the road to the Pacific. He and his children live in California. Source: ***"History of the Early Settlers of Sangamon, Illinois: Centennial Record,"*** *by John Carroll Power, assisted by his wife, Mrs. S. A. Power, Springfield, Illinois, Edwin A Wilson & Co. 1876; pg. 308.*

WILLIAM H. FOSTER b. 1815
MARGARET (GREENWOOD) b. 1820
Were married 1836 Illinois. To this union were born:

1. MARY JANE b. July 14, 1837 d. May 4, 1924
2. GEORGE b. 1838
3. ELIZABETH b. 1841
4. JEANETTE b. 1843
5. SARAH FRANCES b. Apr. 17, 1846 d. June 28, 1922
6. MARGARET b. 1860

MARY JANE FOSTER (#1 above) married her father's 1st cousin, PEYTON FOSTER. Their family is given on pg. 20.

ELIZABETH FOSTER (#3 above) married ALEXANDER AYERS, and lived on Haight St., San Francisco, Calif.

SARAH FRANCES (#5 above) was born in Sangamon Co., Illinois, went with her parents to California. Here, she grew to adulthood and met and married JAMES JOSHUA PRIEST. They made their 1st home in Solano County, later moving to Napa County. In 1869 James J and his brother J. L. Priest bought 747 acres of land in Napa County, where they farmed and ranched. In late 1800s or early 1900s, they set up a bottling works in St. Helena where they bottled and sold soda water from the springs on their ranch.

After James died, his son Daniel C. leased the land and plant from his mother, Sarah Priest. Both James J. & Sarah Priest are buried in or near St. Helena, California.

JAMES J. PRIEST b. Feb. 14, 1826 d. Nov. 11, 1896
SARAH FRANCES (FOSTER) b. Apr. 17, 1846 d. June 28, 1922
Were married Nov. 20, 1862, California. To this union were born:

1. KATIE Feb. 14, 1864 d. 1883
2. WILLIAM H. b. Dec. 31, 1866
3. DANIEL CHURCHILL b. Dec. 22, 1867
4. JAMES L. b. Dec. 22, 1869
5. DAVID Q. b. Jan. 29, 1871
6. ALONZO b. 1874
7. CHARLES H. b. 1877
8. GEORGE L. b. 1879
9. MARION W. b. 1882
10. REUBEN F. b. 1884

(Note: Sarah F's birth date is given as 1846 in two sources, but on her death certificate it is given as 1848. However death certificate are famous for having information that isn't quite accurate.)

GEORGE W. FOSTER, 3rd child of PEYTON & POLLY FOSTER (and grandson of WILLIAM FOSTER b. 1747) was born in Clark Co., Ky., and went with his parents to Sangamon Co., Illinois. Here he grew to manhood and met and married #1 LUCILE SHORT, and their children were born. After her death, George moved to Louisiana, Missouri. He remarried and had another family, but I have no names.

*GEORGE W., born in KY, married in Sangamon County to Lucille Short. She had four children and died. He married again, and resides in Louisiana, Mo. Source: **"History of the Early Settlers of Sangamon, Illinois: Centennial Record,"** by John Carroll Power, assisted by his wife, Mrs. S. A. Power, Springfield, Illinois, Edwin A Wilson & Co. 1876; pg. 308.*

GEORGE W. FOSTER b. 1817
LUCILE (SHORT) b. 1823
Were married 1839, Illinois. To this union were born:

1. FRANCES B. 1841
2. SARAH b. 1847
3. JOHN b. 1850

COL. JOHN D. FOSTER, 4th child of Peyton & Polly Foster, was born in Clark Co., KY, and went with his parents to Sangamon Co., Illinois. Here, he met and married #1 Eunice Miller, and their children were born. In 1862, John D joined his parents in their move to Adair Co., Missouri. Later, John D. took his family to Scott Co., Missouri. Here John D and Eunice separated, and Eunice returned to Illinois where she spent the rest of her life with her daughter, Leonora. John D. married twice afterwards, and these families will be given after we have finished with this one (family chart, pg. 8)"

While living in Illinois John D served in the Mexican War, in the 4th Illinois Infantry, under Col. E.D. Baker. During the Civil War John D commanded the 22nd Regiment Missouri Volunteer Infantry.

COLONEL JOHN D. FOSTER, son of Peyton Foster, was born in 1820 in Clark County, Kentucky. In 1826, he came to Illinois with his parents, whose arrival in Sangamon County in 1826 has been mentioned before. He lived near the present town of Loami for many years. He was service in two wars, the Mexican War and the Civil War. In 1846, he was commissioned 2nd Lieutenant of Company D of Colonel E.D. Baker's Fourth Illinois Infantry. This Regiment was at Tampico, Matamoras and Jalapa. Lieutenant John D. took part in the attack on Vera Cruz March 9, 1847 and was in the Battle of Cerro Gordo on April 18, 1847. He fought with credit and distinction throughout the war.

After the war he returned to Springfield, Illinois and took up the study of law. He was admitted to the bar in that city. He moved to Kirksville, Adair County, Missouri in 1851 and from 1852 to 1856, he represented Adair County in the state legislature. From 1856 to 1860 he was a member of the State Senate. He was also a member of the State Convention from 1861 to 1864 and helped to form the Provisional Government during that time.

In 1861 he left his law practice in order to take part in the Civil War. He helped organize the 10th and 22nd Missouri Volunteer Infantry, was Lieutenant Colonel of each and later Colonel of the 86th Enrolled Militia of the State of Missouri. All of his sympathies and all of his efforts were on the side of the Union. He was mustered out in 1864 on October 31.
In 1865, he went to Commerce, Missouri to practice law. In 1880, he was elected Circuit Judge of the 10th Judicial District of Missouri by an overwhelming majority.

Colonel Foster was married three times. His first wife was Eunice Miller, a daughter of Jacob Miller, who was a brother of Sarah (Miller) Foster. Their marriage occurred on February 22, 1839 and their children were:
i. George W., born ________, died ________, married Mary M. Scott. Their children were:
1. Emma D.
2. William F.
3. Ada
4. John D.
5. Dora B.
ii. Emily M., born ______, died ______, married to Joseph P. Ringo.
iii. Peyton F., born ______, died ______, married Martha F. Dunn
iv. Lucina, born ________, died ______, married James C. Smith and now living in Kirksville, Missouri.
v. James H. born _______, died ______.
vi. Leonora Polly, born about 1800, married 1st, William Canham of Springfield. Their children were:
1. William Edward
2. Jennie
3. Robert Earl
4. James H.
5. B __________ E ___________
She was married a second time in 1926 to J. I. DeVaney and they live in Goodland, Kansas.
Colonel Foster's second wife was Losetta Knowles. They had one child.
Addie Earle.
His third wife was Mary A. Williams. They had no children. Judge Foster, as the colonel was often called, was one the largest land owners in Southeast Missouri. He died in 1901. The sword which he carried through two wars is now in my possession and is one of my most valued treasures. I also have a copy of his Mexican War record furnished by the Adjutant General of the State of Illinois and a copy of his Civil War record furnished by the Adjutant General of the State of Missouri.
FOSTER'S AND THEIR ANCESTRY
Prepared from various sources, a list of which will be given at the end.
By: Lieutenant Ivan Leon Foster, Field Artillery, U.S. Army

1927

Colonel Foster's second wife was Losetta Knowles. They had one child: Addie Earle. His third wife was Mary A. Williams. They had no children. Judge Foster, as the colonel was often called, was one the largest land owners in Southeast Missouri. He died in 1901. The sword which he carried through two wars is now in my possession and is one of my most valued treasures. I also have a copy of his Mexican War record furnished by the Adjutant General of the State of Illinois and a copy of his Civil War record furnished by the Adjutant General of the State of Missouri. – Source: Gen Ivan Leon Foster

JOHN D. FOSTER b. 1820 d. 1901
EUNICE MILLER b. 1821
Were married Feb. 21, 1839, Illinois. To this union were born:

1. GEORGE W. b. 1839
2. EMILY M. b. 1841
3. PEYTON F. b. Nov. 28, 1843
4. LUCINDA b. 1845
5. LEONORA P. b. 1848
6. JAMES HIRAM BYRD b. 1851

GEORGE W. (#1 above) remained in Illinois, where he met and married MARY M. SCOTT. Their children: EMMA D, WILLIAM F., ADA, JOHN D., DORA. *GEORGE W. served as Quartermaster Sergeant in the 22d Mo. Inf., of which his father was Colonel. He was afterwards Orderly Sergeant in Co. E, 39th Mo. Inf. He married Mary M. Scott, has five children, EMMA D, WILLIAM F. , ADA, JOHN D. and DORA B., and resided in Loami township. Source: "History of the Early Settlers of Sangamon, Illinois: Centennial Record," by John Carroll Power, assisted by his wife, Mrs. S. A. Power, Springfield, Illinois, Edwin A Wilson & Co. 1876; pg. 308.*

EMILY (#2 above) went to Missouri with her parents, where she married in Adair County to JOSEPH P. RINGO, who was born in Indiana in 1835. Later they moved to Oregon, and had at least 6 children, but I have no more data on this family, except: REBECCA A., b. 1849.

EMILY M. married Joseph P. Ringo in Adair county, Mo., has six children, and resides in Oregon. Source: "History of the Early Settlers of Sangamon, Illinois: Centennial Record," by John Carroll Power, assisted by his wife, Mrs. S. A. Power, Springfield, Illinois, Edwin A Wilson & Co. 1876; pg. 308.

LUCINDA (#4 above): *Lucina, ... married James C. Smith and now living in Kirksville, Missouri. --Gen. Ivan Leon Foster*
"History of the Early Settlers of Sangamon, Illinois: Centennial Record," by John Carroll Power, assisted by his wife, Mrs. S. A. Power, Springfield, Illinois, Edwin A Wilson & Co. 1876; pg. 308. LUCINA, is married and resides in Adair county, Missouri.

LEONORA P. (#5 above) remained in Illinois, where she met and married WILLIAM CANHAM. In 1876 her mother Eunice was living with them, as was her youngest brother. This brother (James H.) was farming an adjacent plot of land. Leonora's children: WILLIAM E., JEANETTE (JENNIE). Seedlings pg. 15

PEYTON F. like his father, married more than once, and did a lot of moving around, as you will see. Marriage #1, MARTHA J. DUNN, took place in Sangamon County, Illinois.

We've Dunn all we can on this page, so don't just set there, turn to page 16 and we'll continue our quest.

PEYTON F. FOSTER b. Nov. 28, 1843
MARTHA J. (DUNN) b. Feb. 17, 1843 d. Jan. 3, 1917
Were married May 14, 1863, Illinois. To this union were born:

1. SARLLDA ALICE b. Feb. 20, 1865 d. Aug. 19, 1952
2. OSCAR b. Oct. 1, 1870 d. Dec. 20, 1950
3. Twin sons died in infancy

SARLLDA A. (#1 above was born in Illinois, and married ALEXANDER McCORD.

OSCAR (#2 above) was born in Vernon Co., Missouri, and married HATTIE HARPER. Both of these children lived in Liberal, Kansas, where their mother Martha J. joined them when she separated from Peyton Foster.

In Hennepen, Minn. Peyton F. married #2 SARAH E. PAINTER, who died after the births of these children: LEONARD, JESSIE, CORA, MARY, PANZIE.

Peyton F. married wife #3 SADIE GUINN, in California. And in Oregon he married #4 MARTHA E. McCUISTON. I have no data on these last two marriages.

Now back to JOHN D. FOSTER, who married in Scott Co., Missouri to #2 ADDIE. They had at least one child: PEARL. JOHN D. FOSTER married #3 MARY ANN STANLEY, and had a child: ALICE E. (Chart p. 8)

PEYTON Jr., 5th child (actually the 7th) of PEYTON & POLLY FOSTER, was born in Clark Co. KY and went with his parents to Sangamon Co., Illinois. Here he met and married MARIE COLBURN. After the birth of their children (2 named), they moved to Kansas. They had at least 5 children but I have names of only two.

PEYTON FOSTER JR. b. 2825
MARIE (COLBURN) b. 1826
Were married 1845 Illinois. To this union were born:

1. MARY m. ALFRED C. CAMPBELL
2. SARAH

Note: Ancestry.com lists Peyton Foster III as a child of Peyton and Marie. Sadly, other children born to this couple are listed only by their initials in this census.

1860 US Federal Census, Subdivision 17, Sangamon, Illinois

P Foster age 35 b. KY, farmer
M Foster age 34 b. IL
P Foster age 14, female b. IL
SJ Foster age 12, female b. IL
E Foster age 9, female b. IL
B Foster age 7, female b. IL
A Foster age 4, female b. IL
C Foster age 3 mos. female b. IL

I've been sitting here too long. See you tomorrow on top of page 17.

HIRAM BYRD, 7th child of PEYTON & POLLY FOSTER, was born in Sangamon Co., Illinois. In the fall of 1852, he moved to Adair Co., Missouri with his parents, where he became a well-known lawyer. Here, too he met and married Martha Jeanette Ferguson, and lived in LaCrosse, Missouri, where both are buried (Chart pg. 8).

Hiram B. served in the 22nd Missouri Regiment as Captain of Infantry, under his brother John D. In the same regiment, John D's son, George W. served as quartermaster sergeant, and later in Co., E, 39th Missouri Infantry Regiment.

HIRAM B. FOSTER b. July 30, 1832 d. Mar. 30, 1904
MARTHA FERGUSON b. Aug. 9, 1838 d. July 3,1919
Were married Jan. 22, 1861, Missouri. To this union were born:

1. JAMES MANROE b. Nov. 22, 1861 d. Mar. 12, 1926
2. JOHN PEYTON b. May 9, 1866 d. Sept. 29, 1938
3. JEANETTE b. 1868
4. EVERETT BYRD b. 1878
5. EMMETTO. B. July 21, 1879 d. May 15, 1924

Two unnamed children died in infancy.

HIRAM B., born in Sangamon county, married Martha Ferguson, have two children, and reside in Macon county, Mo. Source: "History of the Early Settlers of Sangamon, Illinois: Centennial Record," by John Carroll Power, assisted by his wife, Mrs. S. A. Power, Springfield, Illinois, Edwin A Wilson & Co. 1876; pg. 308.

1900 US Federal Census, Dist. 84, Richland, Macon, Missouri
Bird Foster (Hiram Bird) b. Jul 1832 KY, age 67, both parents b. KY
Martha J, wife b. Aug 1838 Missouri, age 61, father b. KY, mother b. IN
James M, son, b. Nov 1861 MO, age 38, father b. KY, mother b. IN
Ernst O, son, b. Aug 1880 MO, age 20, father b. KY, mother b. IN
Lana Powers, boarder, b. Dec 1882 MO, age 18
Next door to them is:
John P Foster, b. May 1866 Missouri, age 34, father born KY, mother born IN
Rachel, wife, Apr 1867 Missouri, age 33, both parents born Canada
James Greenwood, cousin, b. Jan 1880 Missouri, age 20, father b. IL, mother b. MO, son of Peyton Foster Greenwood, and grandson of Jeanette Foster, the sister of Hiram Bird Foster.

1890 Veterans Schedules
Hiram B Foster, 22nd Missouri Infantry, Enl. 1861, Disch. 1862, served 10 months 3 days. Rank: Adjutant

Hiram B., wife, Martha and most of their children are buried in the cemetery, Kirksville, MO.
JOHN F. FOSTER became a well-known M.D. in Kirksville, Mo. Here, too he met and married CLARIBEL GILLELAND, Oct. 1, 1895. She was born April 12, 1867 and d. Oct. 31, 1952.

JEANETTE FOSTER b. 1868 (#3 above) married JOHN TELFORD FARMER in 1895 in Kirksville, MO., where he was born in 1864. They had children, but I have no material on their family.

This concludes the family lines of PEYTON & POLLY FOSTER. Now we will backpedal to family chart on page 7.

MARGARET M., 4th child of WILLIAM (b. 1747) & SARAH (HART) FOSTER, was born in Bourbon Co., Kentucky, and went with her parents to Clark County 1806. Here she grew to adulthood, met and married HAMILTON G. HISLE. They lived out their lives and are buried in Clark Co., Ky.

HAMILTON HISLE b. Jan. 28, 1800 d. Oct. 8, 1842
MARGARET (FOSTER) b. Apr. 27, 1794 d. 1885
Were married Mar. 2, 1824, Kentucky. To this union were born:

1. EVALINE B. Jan. 28, 1825 d. Oct. 12, 1864 m. RAMEY
2. WILLIAM A. b. July 19, 1826
3. GEORGE W. b. May 10, 1828 d. Feb. 25
4. WICKLIFF b. Oct. 5, 1830 d. Mar. 13, 1836
5. JONAS G. b. Feb. 11, 1833 d. Mar. 7, 1836
6. MINOR HART b. Dec. 21, 1835 d. Jan. 30, 1913
7. HAMILTON G. Jr. b. Nov. 3, 1837 d. June 13, 1924

MINOR HART HISLE married ELIZABETH ANN STRODE, and spent his life in Clark Co., Ky., where both are buried.

Additional notes: Minor H. HISLE was educated in the common schools of Kiddville, acquiring only an ordinary knowledge of the English branches. He began farming for himself near Indian Fields, on his father's land, where he remained for twenty-five years. He then purchased a farm near Schoolsville, where he labored for fourteen years, and in 1879 he purchased the farm he still owns, which contains 280 acres of fine blue grass land; he also owns 40 acres on Howard's Creek and 112 acres in Powell County. Within the last five years he has devoted special attention to buying and selling tobacco, in which he has achieved a marked success.

December 2, 1857, he married Miss Elizabeth A. Strode, a native of Clark County, a daughter of Nelson and Elvina (Rash) Strode, natives of the same county. The birth of two sons followed their union, James N. and George H. Mr. Hisle is a member of William H. Cunningham's Lodge, No. 512, F. & A.M., and has attained the third degree.
He is a Democrat in politics, and is a consistent member of the Methodist Episcopal Church South.

1860 US Federal Census, Clark Co., KY - District 1 - Post Office, Winchester
284-284
Minor H. Hisle - age 25 - Farmer
Elizabeth Hisle - 20
Leonard Foster - age 54 - Stock Driver - (Uncle)
Mary Martin - age 17

MINOR HART HISLE
ELIZABETH (STRODE)
Were married Dec. 2, 1857 Kentucky. To this union were born:

JAMES N. b. Oct. 17, 1859
GEORGE HAMILTON b. Mar. 4, 1866
One child died in infancy

JAMES N. HISLE (above) b. Oct. 17, 1859
ROXIE ANN (SPHAR) b. Mar. 4, 1859
Were married May 24, 1882, Kentucky. To this union were born:

1. VERNON STRODE B. May 1, 1883 d. Dec. 21, 1919 who married ILLA QUISENBERRY STEWART on Apr. 27, 1910 and had a son, MONOR (Minor?) HART b. Dec. 26, 1911.
2. ANNA MAE, b. July 24, 1885, who married OSCAR L. LYNE, Oct. 27, 1909
3. OTHO GRAVES b. Feb. 4, 1888 who married MARGUERITE ANGELIN MATHEWS Feb. 4, 1920.

GEORGE H. HISLE (son of Minor Hart Hisle and Elizabeth Strode):
GEORGE H. HISLE b. Mar. 4, 1866
LUCIE (SPHAR) b. abt 1867
Were married Mar. 24, 1897 Kentucky. To this union were born:

1. ELGIN SPHAR b. Feb. 23. 1899
2. MINNIE RUTH b. Sept. 12, 1900 m. EDWIN ARNOLE Aug. 6, 1922
3. ANNA BELLE S b. June 19, 1906

SUSAN, 5th child of WILLIAM & SARAH (HART) FOSTER, born in Bourbon Co., Kentucky, went with her parents to Clark County. Here, she grew to adulthood, met and married ALLEN ARMSTRONG. On Feb. 11, 1844 Allen and Susan bought the other heirs' interest in the land her father had bought from John Rankins (DB #31, pgs. 380-381, Clark Co., Ky.)

Peyton, George Foster, and Jeanette (Foster) Patrick-Armstrong, all of whom then lived in Sangamon Co., Illinois, made separate Deed of Release, Allen and Susan Armstrong are buried near Winchester, Kentucky. (Note. In earlier versions of this history, Martha and her families were mistakenly given to Leonard Foster.)

ALLEN ARMSTRONG b. 1797 d. 187?
SUSAN (FOSTER) b. 1796 d. 188?
Were married Apr. 9, 1823, Kentucky. To this union were born:

1. MARTHA b. 1834

MARTHA married #1 JOHN RANKINS. They lived in Clark Co., Ky., where their children were born, and John died.

1. ALLEN ARMSTRONG b. 1848
2. SUSAN b. 1853
3. WILLIAM b. 1860

ALLEN ARMSTRONG RANKINS married LENORA and lived in Clark Co., Ky., where their children were born:

1. ELLEN b. 1867
2. WALLER b. Mar 1870
3. FRANK b. 1872
4. ELBERT b. 1874
5. ALLEN A. Jr. b. 1875

ALLEN ARMSTRONG Jr. (1875-1943) married FANNIE STAFFORD, 18929-1963. They lived near Winchester, Ky., where they are buried. Children:

1. ALLEN III 2. WILLIAM 3. CLAUDE S. 4. WALLER 5. ALVIN 6. JUNE 7. FRED (Family chart p. 7)

GEORGE, 6th child of WILLIAM & SARAH (HART) FOSTER, was born in Bourbon Co., Kentucky and went with his parents to Clark County. Here he grew to manhood, met and married SARAH MILLER. In 1826, George & Sarah joined his brother Peyton and sister Jeanette in the migration to Sangamon Co., Illinois. Here, George and Sarah Foster lived out their lives and are buried.

GEORGE W., second son of William and Sarah Hart Foster, was born in 1800 on May 7th, in the State of Kentucky. On August 8, 1821 he married Miss Sarah Miller, daughter of Abraham Miller of Clark County, that state. She was born in Clark County on February 17, 1797.

In those days, people usually married quite young. On the day of the wedding, the groom and his friends met at his father's house quite early in the morning. When they set out for the house of the bride, which place they had to reach well before noon, as the whole community would be assembled there, and the ceremony must, without fail, be completed before twelve o'clock. After a heavy dinner of venison, bear meat, etc., came dancing (reels, square dances, jigs, etc.) which continued far into the night or even until the next morning. A few days later came the house-raising on a piece of land belonging to one of the parents of the couple. Everyone helped on this and then followed an all night housewarming dance. After that the young couple [was] allowed to move into their new log cabin.

As mentioned before, George and his family came to Illinois in 1826 in company with his brother, Peyton, and their sister, Mrs. Jeanette Armstrong, and settled near the site of the present town of Loami. George later moved to a farm which he purchased in 1832, and spent the rest of his life thereon. When the Foster's first came to Illinois, the state presented a much different appearance than it now does. At that time there were no well established trails leading into the Illinois country and a limitless expanse of rolling prairie stretched in every direction as far as the eye could see. Indians (friendly ones) were to be seen quite often, and deer, prairie chickens and other game swarmed on all sides. One had only to be a good shot in order to keep the family larder well stocked with venison, wild turkey, bear meat, etc. And, of course, practically every man and boy was by necessity, compelled to be a good shot.

One old settler of Sangamon County, describing things as he saw them in 1828, said: "Riding along the gently rolling prairie, now you descend into a valley and your vision is limited to a narrow circle. That herd of deer has taken flight at your coming and quits its grazing on the tender grass of the valley, and following that old buck as a leader, runs off with heads erect, horns thrown back, their white tails waving in the air, has circled around until yonder hillock is reached. When turning toward you, they gaze with their dark bright eyes, as if inquiring why you have invaded their free pastures. As you ride along, the rattle snake is stretched across the road (way or path) sunning itself, and the prairie wolf takes to his heels and gallops off much like a dog, but slowly, as if to show you that he is not frightened. That flock of prairie chickens has taken wings, and with a whirr flies away and now has alighted yonder." Then all around was unbroken prairie, the home of the wolf, the deer and the prairie fowl, unmarked by civilization or cultivation, except the scattering farms and houses along the timber.

Such were the sounds witnessed by George W. Foster, and so might he have written of them had he chosen to do so.
In the winter of 1830-31 came the famous Deep Snow. This snow was an accumulation of several snowfalls followed by a storm of unusual severity and very intense cold.

As a result the snow became crusted over so heavily that dogs and men could walk upon it in many places, although it sometimes broke through with a man. Due to his small sharp hoofs, a deer could not run over the snow but broke through, and so was easily caught by man or dogs. Game of all sorts suffered severely and died in great numbers. Deer, prairie chickens, etc. never again became plentiful.

Many of the settlers were lost in the big snow storm itself or fell through the crusted snow later and several thus lost their lives, their bodies being found in the Spring after the snow had melted. On the day on which the last big storm of the series began, George Foster went deer hunting, taking with him his two eldest sons, William and Peyton. The storm began before any success had attended the hunters' efforts. Thinking the weather too bad for boys of seven and eight years of age to be out, George sent his sons home. This act undoubtedly saved their lives. It was the last they saw of him for many days.

The storm grew worse and worse and at last it dawned upon George that he was lost. Fortunately, he had his dog with him. This faithful friend was a great comfort to him during the trying time that followed, and eventually the animal helped to save his master's life. Four or five nights later Mr. Wilcoxon, a neighbor who lived about five miles from the Foster log cabin heard, late one night, weird sort of cries or sound. While considering what to do and waiting for it to be repeated, he heard a scratching at the cabin door. He found there, the faithful dog, which led him out into the night through two or three hundred yards of the unbelievably deep snow to a man more dead than alive. Mr. Wilcoxon managed to get George into his cabin and by patient and careful labor, saved his life. A few days later he took him home. Imagine the joy in the Foster household when the scratching and whining of the dog caused them to open the door, and they beheld coming across the crusted snow, the loved one whom they had given up as dead. George Foster's life was saved. He was to live over six years longer but the man who had been acknowledged as the strongest man in the county was never fully restored to health.

The depth of the snow is the best illustrated by repeating the undoubtedly true statement that stumps of trees cut for fuel during that time in some cases stood eight and ten feet high after the snow melted in the Spring. Is it any wonder then, that the man who fell through the top crust of that snow seldom, if ever, escaped?

In 1832, Black Hawk, still in the pay of the British, organized the Indians along the Mississippi River to resist the encroachments of the Whites of Illinois and Wisconsin. Indian depredations and atrocities were given considerable publicity in the Sangamon Journal of that period. A song calculated to aid in recruiting was printed in the same paper. It is here quoted in part:

"Brave Sangamon hath armed,
All to defend her right –
Arouse, ye bold Kentucky boys,
The foremost in the fight!
Away! Away! Away!
The flames of war are burning red,
The naked frontier needs your aid.
Huzza for old Kentuck!
Away! Away! Away!"

George W. Foster, a man with a family and plenty to do at home, felt the urge to help protect this country, his family and his neighbors against the savage Redmen and enlisted at Michland, Illinois on April 21, 1832 as a Sergeant in the company which was to be commanded by Captain Abraham Lincoln, elected by the men to lead them against the Indians. George was transferred at his own request, to the company commanded by Captain Jacob Ebey on April 29, 1832. Neither company saw any very active service, although the latter was at Dixon's Ferry when Stillman's Defeat occurred.

Thus it was that George Foster happened to be among those who calmed the survivors of that ignominious repulse after they had fled posthaste for some thirty miles. The Battle is frequently referred to as Stillman's Run. Captain Ebey's Company was discharged on May 25, 1832, along with Captain Lincoln's Company. A great many of these men from both companies went to the mouth of the Fox River where new companies were being organized and reenlisted in new outfits. Thus it happened that we next find George W. Foster a corporal over Private Abraham Lincoln, his former captain. Captain Elijah Iles was elected to the command of this company and it was mustered in to service by a regular army officer, Lieutenant Anderson, later Major Anderson of Fort Sumpter fame in 1861. This company saw a little more service than the other two we have mentioned but it took part in no real serious engagements. Each man was equipped for instant and prolonged service against the Indians. This equipment consisted of a horse, blanket, gun, powder-flask, (well filled) pouch of balls, canteen of water, some coffee, side meat and bread.

Evidently George W. Foster did not enjoy his Indian War service. Perhaps it was because he saw no real hand-to-hand fighting, or it may have been due to a natural reticence to discuss his adventures, that we have no stories in the family concerning what he did during the war.

George Foster bought a great deal of land in Sangamon County directly from the United States Government. He, at one time, probably owned well over 1,000 acres of find land. At the time of his death this had been reduced to approximately 600 acres. He was a kind hearted man and disposed to help his fellowman at every opportunity. His habit of acting as security for people less fortunate than himself cost him a great many acres of land during his lifetime. On December 30, 1834 he purchased the land now known as the Foster Farm, north of Sugar Creek and west of the present town of Thayer, Illinois. At that time the property was heavily wooded but it has been cut off until now it is practically all under cultivation. This farm has been continuously in the possession of the Foster Family for nearly 100 years. It was next owned by Leonard, son of George, and then by William E. Another adjoining farm, which belonged to George W., next owned by his son John, and finally sold out of the family. Still another 200 or 300 acres of land west of Chatham, Illinois went to William, eldest son of George, and is now owned in turn by his son, John Douglas, of Chatham, Illinois.

George W. Foster died on May 7, 1837, as a result of typhoid fever. He was taken away while in the prime of life and the inscription on his tombstone is particularly fitting and suitable:

"Remember me as you pass by,
As you are now, so once was I.
As I am now so you must be.
Prepare in time to follow me."

Sarah (Miller) Foster lived nearly sixty years after her husband's death. She died on August 1, 1895 when she was over 98 years of age. They lay side by side in West Grove Cemetery about one mile form their old home.

The site of their old log cabin can still be determined by the small stones scattered from the foundation and fireplace of the old home. It stood just north of the fine big barn originally built by George's son, Leonard, and later improved and enlarged by William E., the present owner of the land. A big modern house begun by Leonard and completed by William E. stands about 100 yards east of the site of the old log cabin.

George and Sarah Miller Foster had eight children:

i. William, born on March 15, 1823 in Kentucky, and died on November 22, 1910 (see later)
ii. Elizabeth, born 1825 in Kentucky and died ________ in Kansas. She married William Roach.
iii. Peyton, born in 1829 in Illinois. Married Mary J. Foster, a daughter of ________ Foster. Peyton served with his brother, William during the Mexican War, and died in California about 1920, leaving two children:
iv. Leonard, born March 17, 1830, died May 8, 1880 (see later).
v. Polly, born 1829, died ________, married George Organ and they had five children:

1. Minerva J., married Wesley Lowdermilk
2. Sarah F., married James Lowdermilk
3. William, married ____________ Bumgarner
4. Ida, married August White
5. Leslie, married ____________
vi. Sarah, born 1833, died ________, married Alexander Orr.
vii. Matilda, born Feb. 2, 1834, died April 24, 1876, married Micajah Treadway. A son, George, was born March 31, 1855 and died on September 4, 1856. They lived in Henry County, Missouri, for a time. She is buried in West Cemetery in Auburn Township, Sangamon County, Illinois.
viii. John, born in 1837 (see later)
FOSTER'S AND THEIR ANCESTRY
Prepared from various sources, a list of which will be given at the end.
By: Lieutenant Ivan Leon Foster, Field Artillery, U.S. Army
1927
Source: "History of the Early Settlers of Sangamon, Illinois: Centennial Record," by John Carroll Power, assisted by his wife, Mrs. S. A. Power, Springfield, Illinois, Edwin A Wilson & Co. 1876; pg. 308.

GEORGE FOSTER b. July 5, 1800 d. May 7, 1837
SARAH (MILLER) b. Feb. 17, 1797 d. Aug. 1, 1895
Were married Aug. 8, 1821 Kentucky. To this union were born:

1. WILLIAM b. Mar. 15, 1823 d. Nov. 22, 1910
2. ELIZABETH b. 1825 m. WM. ROACH
3. PEYTON b. Jan. 11 1827 d. Oct. 19, 1919
4. POLLY (MARY) b. 1829
5. LEONARD b. Mar 7, 1830 d. May 8, 1880
6. SARAH b. 1833 m. ALEXANDER ORR
7. MATILDA b. 1834 d. Apr. 24, 1876
8. JOHN b. 1837

WILLIAM (b. 1823) was born in Clark Co., Ky., and went with his parents to Sangamon Co., Illinois. Here, he grew to manhood, met and married ELIZABETH J. SHUTT. Their children: 1) EVA J. 2) JOHN 3) WILLIAM 4) SARAH E. 5) LEONARD G. 6) GEORGE R. 7) MARIAN E. 8) CHARLES H.

Notes for WILLIAM FOSTER:
He came to Sangamon County, Illinois with his parents in 1826. He with his brother, Peyton, served [during] the Mexican War in the same company in which John D. Foster was a Lieutenant. (Company D. Fourth Ill. Inf.) They had many interesting experiences during the war. William and Peyton either actually captured or assisted in capturing General Santa Anna's personal baggage at the time he so narrowly escaped the American forces. His wooden leg, captured at that time is now in the Illinois State Museum at Springfield, Illinois. On another occasion William's knowledge of Spanish enabled him to understand the plotting of some Mexicans and so saved the lives of several of his comrades as well as his own. "History of Sangamon County, Illinois"

1870 US Federal Census, Chatham, Sangamon, Illinois (pg. 19)
William Foster age 46 b. KY, farmer, land $12,000, property $1500
Elizabeth Foster age 37 b. IL
George Foster age 20 b. IL
William P Foster age 18 b. IL
Jacob S or F Foster age 15 b. IL
Elizabeth Foster age 13 b. IL
Douglas Foster age 12 b. IL

Leonard Foster age 10 b. IL
Marion Foster (male) age 6 b.IL
Eva Foster age 3 b. IL
Charles Foster age 1 b. IL

PEYTON, 2nd son of GEORGE FOSTER and SARAH (MILLER), born in Clark Co., KY, went with his parents to Sangamon Co., Ill, where he grew to manhood. In 1852 Peyton joined his cousin, William H. Foster, pg. 13, in a wagon train bound for California. They must have set out late in the season, or had tough luck, because Peyton and William wintered near Salt Lake City.

During the layover in Utah, Peyton married his cousin's daughter, Mary Jane Foster. Peyton and Mary went on to California, back to Illinois, Missouri, and returned to California, where they ended their lives (their lives ended). They are buried in Woodland, CA. Family Chart:

PEYTON FOSTER b. Jan. 11, 1827 d. Oct. 19, 1919
MARY JANE (FOSTER) b. July 14, 1837 d. May 4, 1924
Were married Dec. 13, 1852, Utah. To this union were born:

1. IDA ELLA b. Aug. 15, 1862 d. Nov. 13, 1943
2. HETTY BELLE b. Oct. 10, 1867 d. Jan. 8, 1892 m. MR. TOWNES
3. CARRIE AGNES b. Nov. 15, 1874 d. Feb. 2, 1898 m. ROBERT EASTHAM
4. CHARLES LESLIE b. Jan. 10, 1879 d. Mar. 14, 1953
5. WILLIAM b. 1856 d. in infancy
6. GEORGE b. 1857 d. in infancy

IDA Ella, born in Cordelia, Calif. Made the swing to the mid-west and returned to California, where she is buried. She married #1, HARLAN WILBER ROBERTS and had: HARLAN W. Jr. Ida Ella married #2, GEORGE PRITCHETT.

CHARLES LESLIE FOSTER was born and lived in Henry Co., Missouri till 1889, at which time his parents took him to California. Here he grew to manhood, met and married CRYSTA KATHLEEN BAKER of Healdsburg, Calif. Charles L. was a carpenter, who plied his trade in Yolo and Napa Counties, Calif. Charles L. is buried with his parents and sisters in Woodland, California.

CHARLES LESLIE FOSTER b. Jan. 10, 1879 d. Mar. 14, 1953
CRYSTA KATHLEEN BAKER b. Aug. 22, 1885 d. Dec. 10, 1965
Were married June 10, 1913 California. To this union were born:

1. ROSAMOND KATHLEEN b. Apr. 12, 1914
2. THEO ELAINE b. July 31, 1915
3. DOROTHY RUTH b. Nov. 12, 1920

ROSAMOND KATHLEEN, above, born in Woodland, Calif., married ARON FINCHER, and had four children: 1) PHYELIS, who died, 2) BARBARA, 3) DARREL, 4) KAREN.

THEO ELAINE, born in Healdsburg, Calif. Married CARL F. NELSON, and had three children: 1) LINDA LEE, 2) ALLEN, 3) STEPHEN.

DOROTHY RUTH, born in Willits, Calif., married GEORGE 2. FOWLER, and lives in Napa, Calif. It is through Dorothy's research that this material on the Peyton & Mary J. (Foster) Foster family is written here. Dorothy is still trying to locate other members of Mary J's family in California. Let's hope she has a lot of luck.

GEORGE W. FOWLER
DOROTHY RUTH (FOSTER) b. Nov. 12, 1920
Were married in California. To this union were born:

1. JON ALLYN (NELSON - child by former mar.)
2. JUDITH KATHLEEN (FOWLER)

Family chart pg. 20

POLLY was the first child of GEORGE & SARAH (MILLER) FOSTER to be born in Illinois. Here she grew to adulthood, met and married GEORGE L. ORGAND. He was born in Kentucky Dec. 29, 1820. His mother was Susanna Donner, sister to George & Jacob Donner of the ill-fated Donner-Reed Party, whose immigrant train got stranded in Donner's Pass, Calif., where many died of starvation and exposure.

George & Polly Organd lived out their lives in Illinois, where they are buried. Children: 1) SARAH, 2) MINERVA, 3) WILLIAM, 4) IDA, 5) LESLIE.

Polly died and George married #2, MARY WYATT, and had: JACOB.

POLLY (Foster), born in Sangamon county, and married George Organ. See his name. Source: "History of the Early Settlers of Sangamon, Illinois: Centennial Record," by John Carroll Power, assisted by his wife, Mrs. S. A. Power, Springfield, Illinois, Edwin A Wilson & Co. 1876; pg. 308.

LEONARD, 5th child of GEORGE & SARAH (MILLER) FOSTER WAS BORN AND GREW TO MANHOOD IN Sangamon Co., Illinois. Here, too he met and married ELVIRA GATES, and their children were born. Both are buried near Thayer, Illinois. He was killed during a snow storm by a train.

LEONARD, third son of George W. and Sarah (Miller) Foster, was born on March 17, 1830. He was too young to go to the Mexican War with his brothers, William and Peyton in 1846. Most of his life was spent on his father's farm near Sugar Creek in Sangamon County, Illinois, although he sometimes made trips to Kentucky to see relatives in that state. One such trip was made in 1857 for the purpose of bringing back his chosen life-partner whose home was in Muhlenburg County, Kentucky. Leonard met Miss Elvira Gates, daughter of John and Lucinda (Groves) Gates, while she was visiting her uncle, __________ Gates, in Sangamon County, Illinois. After a long and patient suit in the face of considerable competition, he finally won out and in December, 1857, they were married. She was born near Greenville, Muhlenburg County, Kentucky on April 24, 1834.

When the Civil War broke out, Leonard made preparations to take part in it. While engaged in felling a tree a few days before he was to have left, he was so badly injured as to be physically incapacitated for military service. As a result he had no military experience whatsoever.

In April, 1880, he was fatally injured in a railway accident and died on May 8, 1880. He left his family in very comfortable circumstances on a farm of two hundred and ten acres, now valued at some _______________ per acre. In a History of Sangamon County, published in 1881, by the Inter-State Publishing Company, we find, among other things written of Leonard, the following:
"He was a kind and good husband and father, and was respected by all who knew him. He died, leaving the family in comfortable circumstances, with a farm of two hundred and ten acres of land valued at $60 per acre." The huge barn and house begun by Leonard in his lifetime have been mentioned elsewhere.
I have a picture of Leonard which plainly shows his character. A handsome man, he was with firmness and honesty of purpose written large upon his face.

Elvira (Gates) Foster died on November 26, 1901. I can dimly remember her, a severe and plain appearing lady, austere but kind, and looking always as if she had known far more sorrow than joy during her more than sixty years of life. She is buried in West Cemetery beside her husband who preceded her in death by more than twenty years. Source: FOSTER'S AND THEIR ANCESTRY
Prepared from various sources, a list of which will be given at the end. --By: Lieutenant Ivan Leon Foster, Field Artillery, U.S. Army
1927

LOENARD FOSTER, born in Sangamon county, married Elvira Gates, has several children, and reside in Auburn township. Source: "History of the Early Settlers of Sangamon, Illinois: Centennial Record," by John Carroll Power, assisted by his wife, Mrs. S. A. Power, Springfield, Illinois, Edwin A Wilson & Co. 1876; pg. 308.

Family Chart:
LEONARD FOSTER b. May 8, 1830 d. Mar. 8, 1880
ELVIRA GATES B. Mar. 25, 1835 d. Dec. 26, 1901
Were married Dec. 12, 1857, Illinois. To this union were born:

1. ALICE b. June 9, 1859 d. Mar. 23, 1910
2. FLORA E. b. Sept. 6, 1860 d. Jan. 13, 1961 m. L. M. BUMGARNER
3. GEORGE EDGAR b. Nov. 4, 1861 d. Jan. 15, 1939 M. CECELIA MOORE
4. MARY OLIVE b. Feb. 3, 1865 d. Apr. 17, 1940 m. ABE. MILLER
5. WILLIAM EDWIN b. May 30, 1867 d. Oct. 18, 1960
6. MINNIE b. Jan. 12, 1870 d. 1936 m. FRANK KESSLER
7. ETTA b. Aug. 5, 1873 d. 1949 m. OTIS BARBEE

Last minute material on the family of Leonard & Elvira Foster, pg. 22: *(Note from Adrienne: I moved this from pg. 25 to its proper place with the rest of his family. Computers allow me to do things that Flavius couldn't do with typewriter.)*
GEORGE EDGAR (#3 above), was born, grew to manhood, met and married CECELIA JOANNA MOOR in Sangamon Co., Ill. She was born in Haymaker Town, Virginia, and came to Sangamon County with her parents, Hayden & Charlotte (Bigler) Moor. Soon after marriage, George and Cecilia went to Kansas, and homesteaded near Grainfield. Here, their first two children were born, before they sold their claim and moved to Fillmore Co., Nebraska, near Strang. Here their last children were born. The family ended up in western Nebraska, NW of Sidney, where George and Cecilia Foster are buried, in the Greenwood Cemetery.

GEORGE FOSTER b. Nov. 4, 1861 d. Jan. 15, 1939
CECELIA (MOOR) b. Nov. 8, 1861 d. Oct. 3, 1952
Were married Feb. 10, 1886, Illinois. To this union were born:--

1. EVERETT LESLIE b. Aug. 23, 1887 d. Aug. 22, 1958
2. HERBERT AUSTIN b. Apr. 25, 1890 d. Aug. 1, 1890
3. ALMA ALETTA b. Dec. 24, 1892 d. 196? m. Art LeSueur
4. GRACE MARIE b. Sept. 24, 1895 d. June 15, 1980
5. VERA IVA b. Nov. 16, 1897 d. Dec. 19, 1918 m. John Cox

EVERETT LESLIE was born near Grainfield, Kansas and went with his parents to Fillmore Co., Nebraska, then in 1904 to the homestead NW of Sidney. He attended the Beatrice, Neb. Business School, and held jobs with the U.P. (Union Pacific) Railroad, and with the Nebraska Agriculture Department, where he was stricken with a heart attack, in 1940. After this illness, Everett moved to Redondo Beach, California, where he died.

Everett Leslie married DORA GRACE, daughter of EDWIN & GRACE TOWNE, in Council Bluffs, Iowa. All their children were born near Sidney Neb., before Everett and Dora moved to California, where both are buried in Pacific Crest Cemetery, Redondo Beach, Calif. (Nora married #2, Merle L. Cole. No children.)

EVERETT LESLIE FOSTER b. Aug. 23, 1887 d. Aug. 23, 1958
DORA (TOWNE) b. Sept. 23, 1901 d. Dec. 10, 1976
Were married Apr. 24, 1917, Iowa. To this union were born:

1. IRIS b. Apr. 7, 1918
2. IVAN LESLIE b. June 24, 1920
3. HELEN MAXINE b. Feb. 22, 1922
4. JOHN WILLIAM b. Aug. 6, 1927

IRIS (#1 above) was born and grew to adulthood in Sidney, Nebraska, where she met IVAN ROBERT PAYNE. They married in Julesburg, Colorado. Their children were born in Nebraska. Iris worked for the state of Nebraska, then for the federal government, during which she moved from job to job. She ended up in California, working for the Tuna Research Foundation. When this job was phased out Iris retired.

Due to events beyond her control, Iris' "matrimonial history has been a disaster." Her first three marriages all went onto the rocks, and she is now married to #4, JAMES W. KALB. They live in San Pedro, Calif., where James is employed by Hughes Space Division. They were married Mar. 15, 1958, Calif. No children.

IRIS and IVAN ROBERT PAYNE married Jan. 18, 1936, divorced in 1939. Children: 1) FREDRICK b. May 30, 1937 d. in June; 2) SHARON born and died May of 1939; 3) ROBERT LESLIE b. Aug. 29, 1938.

ROBERT LESLIE PAYNE, son of IRIS & IVAN PAYNE was born in Sidney Nebraska and traveled around the USA with his mother as she moved from one Civil service job to the next. In California he met and married PATRICIA WONG Jan. 5, 1962. After a hitch in the army, Robert took up the trade of draftsman. Patricia has a daughter from a former marriage, but she and Robert have no children of their own. Patricia's child: ROBIN.

IVAN LESLIE FOSTER, son of EVERETT and DORA (TOWNE) FOSTER, was born, grew to manhood, met and married BERNICE M. TOMPKINS in Sidney, Nebraska. Ivan, a veteran of WWII, is about to retire from his job with North American Aviation, El Segundo, Calif. Children: 1) CONSTANCE LEE; 2) KIM THOMPKINS, 3) VICTORIA DORA.

CONSTANCE LEE FOSTER, daughter of IVAN LESLIE & BERNICE (THOMPKINS) FOSTER above, married #1 her cousin DAN JOHN SELLERS, Dec. 7, 1956. He was killed in an auto accident. Child: JORI MARIE. (Note pg. 28)

Constance L. married #2, RODNEY HENDERSON, Sept. 17, 1962. They live in Walnut Creek, Calif, where they own a real estate business. Children: 1) RODNEY IVAN; 2) DAWN MARIE.
KIM THOMPKINS FOSTER, 2nd daughter of IVAN LESLIE and BERNICE FOSTER, was born in Redondo Beach, Calif., and married while in the army in the Panama Canal Zone to TERRI LOMBRIA Dec. 20, 1962. They later divorced. Child: TROY THOMPKINS.

Kim married #2, DIXIE HENRY Apr. 18, 1981.

VICTORIA DORA, 3rd daughter of IVAN LESLIE & DORA FOSTER (above) was born in Gardena, Calif., and married #1 RICHARD HARDY ON Apr. 14, 1967. Children: 1) FAITH CHRISTINE; 2) TIFFANY ANN.

They divorced and Victoria married #2 DOUGLAS PARKER Nov. 28, 1975. He is a postman in Missouri. Child: ROBERT BRIAN.
Family Chart pg. 26

HELEN MAXINE FOSTER, 3rd child of EVERETT & DORA (TOWNE) FOSTER, was born near Sidney, Nebraska, where she grew to adulthood, met and married ORVILLE S. JACKSON on Nov. 15, 1938. She is now retired from Hughes Aircraft Co., after many years of traveling around on this job. She divorced Orville, remarried and divorced again, and is now married to #3 WILLIAM McMAHON, and lives in Marina Del Rey, Calif. (No children to last marriages).

Helen & Orville's children: 1) NINA JELENA; 2) NANCY JEAN. NINA JELENA married RAYMOND VIRGIL KENDRICK Feb. 8, 1958. He was born June 2, 1934. Children: 1) STEPHEN RAYMOND ; 2) RONALD RAYMOND; 3) JERAY MICHEL. STEVEN RAYMOND married (unknown) and had: RAYMOND E..

NANCY JEAN JACKSON, daughter of HELEN MAXINE FOSTER & ORVILLE S. JACKSON, married STEVEN LORENZ on Jan. 1, 1961 and lives in Thousand Oaks, Calif. Children: 1) STEVEN; 2) DANNY. Family chart pg. 26.

JOHN WILLIAM FOSTER, 4th child of EVERETT & DORA (TOWNE) FOSTER, was born in Sidney Nebraska and went to California where he met and married MATILDA GEROW on Sept. 4, 1948. Her father changed his name from GOLUBSKI to Gerow upon immigrating from Germany. Her mother, CAROLINE KARALUS, was born in Warsaw, Poland. Matilda was born, Mar. 3, 1924 in Dayton, Ohio. After three years with the army in Korea, John went to work with North American Aviation. He is now retired and is a contractor with his son, building homes in the Redondo Beach, California area. Children: 1) CYNTHIA DENISE; 2) GEORGE CURTIS.

CYNTHIA DENISE FOSTER (directly above) was born in Redondo Beach, Calif. And married BRADLEY BROWN. Children: 1) JOSHUA IAN; 2) NATHANIEL JOSIAH.

GEORGE CURTIS FOSTER, 2nd child of JOHN WILLIAM & MATILDA (GEROW) FOSTER, was born in Inglewood, Calif. And married and divorced ARAH? He is now working with his father in the building trade. Children: NIECIA RAE.

GRACE MARIE FOSTER, daughter of GEORGE & CECELIA (MOOR) FOSTER, was born and grew to adulthood near Sidney, Neb. Married JOHN NEWTON SELLERS in Sterling, Colorado. They lived out their lives in Sidney and are buried in the Greenwood Cemetery. John was a carpenter by trade.

JOHN N. SELLERS b. July 3, 1891 d. May 20, 1980
GRACE (FOSTER) b. Sept. 24, 1895 d. June 15, 1980
Were married June 24, 1915, Colorado. To this union were born:

1. MARJORIE LAVONNE b. Jan. 29, 1917 d. June 15, 7 m. EARL BLACK
2. ESTHER VERA b. Feb. 28. 1920 m. ASA CLASSBURN
3. JENNIE JOAN b. Jun 8, 1921 m. JOHN GUENTHER
4. BETTY JANE b. Apr. 1, 1923 d. Apr. 25, 1949 m. BERNARD STIBLEY
5. RUTH MARIE b. June 4, 1926 m. RAYMOND SLAMA
6. DAN JOHN b. May 25, 1932 d. Nov. 7, 1960 m. CONSTANCE FOSTER (pg. 26—daughter of Ivan Leslie Foster, son of Everett Foster—Constance was Dan's cousin)
7. LEE ALFRED b. May 13, 1934 m. JOAN CLEMENTS

****

WILLIAM EDWIN (5th child of Leonard and Elvira (Gates) Foster above) married ANNETTE GOODPASTURE, Jan. 8, 1895. She was born Dec. 17, 1868 d. Feb. 12, 1933. They had six children: 1) IVAN LEON b. Apr. 23, 1896 d. Nov. 26, 1965.

WILLIAM EDWIN, second son of Leonard and Elvira (Gates) Foster, was born on May 30, 1867. William spent his early youth on his father's farm. When he was but 13 years of age, his father died; and he and his brother, George, some seven years older, were left to care for the family. Strangely enough, Leonard's father too, died when Leonard was only seven years of age.

In 1895, on January 8th, William E. was married to Annette Goodpasture who was born December 17, 1868, daughter of Andrew Seymour Goodpasture, who lived on his own farm about three miles north of the Foster farm. Her mother was Mary Jane Fletcher Goodpasture. The Goodpasture family is an old

Virginia family which came to Menard County, Illinois by way of Overton County, Tennessee. It has been traced to Captain James Goodpasture who was born about 1750 and lived in Washington County, Virginia. He is said to have built the first court house in Richmond. The Fletcher family is also well traced out. Mary Jane Fletcher's great-uncle, Job Fletcher, was a state senator with Abraham Lincoln and was one of those who are known in history as "The Long Nine". Both of these families are traced out elsewhere among my papers.

Shortly after their marriage, William E. and Annette moved to Missouri where the writer was born on April 23, 1896. While there they lived near Yates in Randolph County, on a farm owned by Mr. John A. Pitts, Sr. In 1899 when my Grandmother Foster decided to move to Virden, Illinois, my father and mother returned to Illinois to live on the old Foster homestead, where they have lived ever since.

WILLIAM E. has served the public in a small way for a good part of his life. He has been a member of the local school board for over twenty five years and has twice been elected Township Commissioner. He is highly respected by all who know him.—"Fosters and Their Ancestry," by Gen. Ivan Leon Foster

IVAN LEON, son of WILLIAM EDWIN FOSTER, (b. 1896) was a West Pointer who ended up as a Major General during WWII and is buried in Arlington National Cemetery. He married #1 IRMA M. Von HOLZ, Nov. 5, 1919. She was born Dec. 10, 1895. They divorced. To them was born: IVAN LEON Jr. Jan. 30, 1925. *Note: Maj. Gen. Ivan Leon Sr. did a significant amount of research on the Foster family and wrote the book "Fosters and Their Ancestry," which is often used as a source for Foster genealogy.*

IVAN Jr. is a retired Lt. Col., jet pilot, and is now (in 1962) teaching school at Ft. Bragg, N.C. Ivan Jr. married & divorced #1, ALLIE J. Oct. of 1947 and had: 1) BARBARA A., 2) MARILYN A., 3) MARIANNE E.

IVAN L. Sr. married #2 FRANCES KENNEDY IN 1948 and had: ELIZABETH. Both wives and the daughter live in California.

MABLE LOUISE (2nd child of WILLIAM EDWIN FOSTER & ANNETTE GOODPASTURE) was b. Dec. 29, 1899 and married EARL T. GIBERSON, in 1926 and had: MARY LOUISE.

Mabel Louise, born December 29, 1899, on the Foster farm, as were all the rest of my brothers and sisters. She is a graduate of the Auburn Township High School and completed two years of work at the Chicago Art Institute. She has received many honorable mentions and prizes because of her paintings. On June 27, 1925 she married Earl T. Giberson of Virden, Illinois. The wedding was one of the prettiest and largest ever seen in West Grove neighborhood. She and her husband moved soon thereafter to their beautiful new home in Stuart, Florida. WILLIAM E. has served the public in a small way for a good part of his life. He has been a member of the local school board for over twenty five years and has twice been elected Township Commissioner. He is highly respected by all who know him. "Fosters and Their Ancestors," by Gen. Ivan Leon Foster

WILLIAM ANDREW (3nd child of WILLIAM EDWIN FOSTER & ANNETTE GOODPASTURE) b. Dec. 15, 1900, who resides on the old home place near Auburn, Ill. He married GRACE CLOYD, June 16, 1928 and had: 1) STEPHEN CLOYD, 2) NANCY JANE (SHEHAN), 3) JUDITH ANN (KRAMER), 4) CHARLES WILLIAM.

JAMES MERVIN (4th child of WILLIAM EDWIN FOSTER & ANNETTE GOODPASTURE) b. Jan. 10, 1902 d. Dec. 28, 1956. He married #1 MARIAN MANN in

1927 and had: 1) ANN, 3) ALICE (MacDONALD). James married #2 MARGARET MEYERS – no children.

MARY LUCILE (5th child of WILLIAM EDWIN FOSTER & ANNETTE GOODPASTURE) b. Mar. 2, 1904, who married EVERETT INGERSOLL in 1930 and had: 1) CAROL YVONE (DUFF), 2) DANIEL.

GEORGE BRITTIN (6th child of WILLIAM EDWIN FOSTER & ANNETTE GOODPASTURE) b. July 3, 1910. He lives in Springfield, Illinois, and it was he who gave me this material on the Leonard Foster family. George B. married #1 MARGARET BARTOSH, Dec. 21, 1932, and had: DONALD GEORGE.

GEORGE BRITTIN married #2, WILMA ILENE GIBBS, Oct. 13, 1944 in Brownwood, Texas and had: 1) ANNETTE ILENE (BECK), 2) GEORGE DOUGLAS. This entire family lives in Springfield, Illinois, where George Jr. has an electronic business.

MATILDA, 7TH child of GEORGE b. 1800 & SARAH (MILLER) FOSTER, was born in Sangamon Co., Ill., where she met and married MICAJAH TREADWAY. They lived in Henry Co., Missouri, where she died, and is buried near Verden, Illinois. Children: 1) TRUDY, 2) HETTIE. (Family chart p. 20)

Matilda, born Feb. 2, 1834, died April 24, 1876, married Micajah Treadway. A son, George, was born March 31, 1855 and died on September 4, 1856. They lived in Henry County, Missouri, for a time. She is buried in West Cemetery in Auburn Township, Sangamon County, Illinois. Source: FOSTER'S AND THEIR ANCESTRY, Prepared from various sources, a list of which will be given at the end. By: Lieutenant Ivan Leon Foster, Field Artillery, U.S. Army, 1927

MATILDA, born in Sangamon county, married Micajah Cudaway (sp), and reside in Henry county, Mo. Source: "History of the Early Settlers of Sangamon, Illinois: Centennial Record," by John Carroll Power, assisted by his wife, Mrs. S. A. Power, Springfield, Illinois, Edwin A Wilson & Co. 1876; pg. 308.

JOHN, last child of GEORGE & SARAH (MILLER) FOSTER, was born in Sangamon Co., Illinois, where he met and married #1, FANNY BOGG, but seems to have had no children. They lived in Kansas where she died. John returned to Illinois where he met and married #2 FANNY WRIGHT, and had two children, but I have no names. Family chart p. 7.

JOHN, youngest son of George W. and Sarah (Miller) Foster was born February 15, 1837. He married Fanny Bogy on _______________. She died in Kansas. He married secondly, Fanny Wright on _______________, who is now dead. For many years they lived on the farm adjoining that of his brother, Leonard. As mentioned elsewhere, both of these farms had been inherited from George W. Later John sold his Illinois farm and moved to Fort Scott, Kansas. John Foster died April 30, 1920 in Craig, Colorado. He had only one child, and that by his second wife:
*i. **William A.**, born November 1, 1867, married Dora Powers. They had the following children:*
*1. **Arthur**, born _________________, died April 27, 1947.*
*2. **Estill**, born _________________*
Source: Gen. Ivan Leon Foster

JOHN, born in Sangamon county, married Fanny Bogy. She died in Kansas, and he married Fanny Wright. They have two children, and live in Sangamon county, near Virden, Ill. Source: "History of the

Early Settlers of Sangamon, Illinois: Centennial Record," by John Carroll Power, assisted by his wife, Mrs. S. A. Power, Springfield, Illinois, Edwin A Wilson & Co. 1876; pg. 308.

* * * *

SALLY (or SARAH), 7th child of WILLIAM b. 1747 & SARAH (HART) FOSTER, born in Bourbon Co., Kentucky, went with her parents to Clark County. Here, she grew to adulthood, met and married BENJAMIN R. GRIGSBY in 1823 (note: He is no doubt a descendant of the Virginia Grigsbys who married in to the Foster family many times.). Later they moved to Shelby Co., Ky., where they lived in 1844, when her sister Susan & Allen Armstrong bought the other heirs' share of William Foster's estate. After that event, they got "lost."

BENJAMIN GRIGSBY b. abt 1800 Kentucky
SARAH (SALLY) FOSTER b. 1803 Bourbon, KY
Were married 6 May 1822 in Clark Co., Ky. (*Kentucky Marriages, 1802-1850)*
To this Union were born:

1. JAMES b. 1834
2. ALICE b. 1842

William's Revolutionary war record states that (daughter) Sallie was age 18 in 1821, when he applied for his war pension in Clark Co., Kentucky. Sarah Sallie's children are from ancestry.com.

SARAH FOSTER, b. Abt. 1802, Bourbon Co., KY; d. Abt. 1880, Shelby Co., KY; m. BENJAMIN GRIGSBY, 05 May 1823, Clark Co., KY; b. Abt. 1800, KY; d. Bef. 1860, Shelby Co., KY.

Notes for SARAH FOSTER:
1860 Census - Shelby Co., KY - District 2
516-480
Sarah Grigsby - age 56 - Farmer
James - age 26 - Laborer
Alice - age 18
Lucie Amman - age 7
Benj. Grigsby - age 84 - b. VA

1870 Census - Shelby Co., KY - Christiansburg
197-199
Grigsby, Sarah - age 60
James - age 35
Alice - age 30
Porten, Mary - age 33
Porten, Victoria - age 17

U.S. Federal Census Mortality Schedules, 1850-1880 about Sarah Grigsby
Name: Sarah Grigsby
Gender: Female
Marital Status: Married
Place of Birth: Kentucky
Estimated birth year: abt 1810
Age: 70
Month of Death: Dec

Place of Death: (City, County, State)
Kentucky
Census Year: 1880

NANCY, 8th child of WILLIAM & SARAH (HART) FOSTER, born in Bourbon, Co., Kentucky, went with her parents to Clark County, where she grew to adulthood, met and married THOMAS CLAIBORNE. ADAMS, 18 Jan. 1826. She died after signing the land transfer in 1844, *(Note: several sources say she died after being thrown from horse 8 Oct. 1845)* and is buried in the Hisle Cemetery, Winchester, Kentucky. The last I can find on Thomas was a land sale in 1846. They had two daughters and four sons, no names *(see new data below).* Family chart pg. 7.

Additional Notes: Thomas was born 28 May 1797 in Pittsylvania Co., Virginia. He died 7 Nov 1877 in Madison Co., KY. 28 November 1849, Jane DUNCAN wife of John DUNCAN of Madison County, KY to ***Thomas ADAMS*** *of Clark Co., KY, $150, 25 acres on Red River in Clark Co., conveyed by James LOWREY to Jane DUNCAN then Jane KENNEDY by deed 8 August 1840.*
(MAD: see 29-552) (FHL film 183 181)

1850 Census - Madison Co., KY - 488-490
Adams, Thomas - age 50 – Farmer, (No wife listed)
Thomas - age 23 years - son
Patin - age 18 years - son
Elisha - age 17 years - son
Mary - age 13 years - daughter
William - age 10 years - son
Alexander - age 8 years - son
Straudin - age 6 years - son

1860 Census - Madison Co., KY - Division 1, *268-265*
Thomas C. Adams - age 60 - Farmer
Almanza - age 19 - Farmer
Strother - age 17 - Farmer

1870 Census - Madison Co., KY - Elliston
Adams, Thomas - age 73 - Farmer
Elizabeth - age 40 - Keeping house – Wife

New data:

THOMAS CLAIBORNE ADAMS b. 28 May 1797 Clark, KY d. 8 Nov 1877 Madison, KY
NANCY FOSTER b. 13 Mar 1805 Clark, KY d. 8 Oct 1845 Madison, KY
Were married 18 Jan 1826 in Clark Co., Ky. (Marriage Records of Madison County, Kentucky Letters - A and B 1790-1843 Volume I)
The following children were born in Madison County, Kentucky:

1. THOMAS CLAIBORNE RANKIN ADAMS 22 Feb. 1827 d. 14 Nov 1914
2. AMANDA JANE ADAMS 25 Feb. 1829 d. Mclean, Illinois
3. PEYTON FOSTER ADAMS 5 Feb 1831 d. 21 Jun 1911 Madison, KY
4. ELISHA GOFF ADAMS 22 Dec 1833 d. 3 May 1869 Madison, KY
5. LYNCH PROCTOR ADAMS 12 Jul 1835 d. 29 Jul 1836 Madison, KY
6. MARY HULSE ADAMS 24 May 1837 d. 27 Dec 1903 Madison, KY

7. WILLIAM SIMPSON ADAMS 12 Mar 1840 d. 14 Jul 1897 Madison, KY
8. ALEXANDER WILLS ADAMS abt 1841 d. 11 Mar 1915 Fayette, KY
9. STROTHER ADAMS 7 Apr 1843 d. 21 Oct 1926 Madison, KY

THOMAS CLAIBORNE RANKIN ADAMS (#1 above) m. #1 ELIZABETH J. BOGGS 9 Jul 1853 in Madison Co., Ky., It is unknown if there were children by this marriage. He married #2 MARTHA ANN CHRISTIAN and had: 1) James Warfield, 2) Thomas Branch, 3) Lourena b. 6 May 1864, 4) Robert Peyton b. 24 Oct. 1868.

AMANDA JANE ADAMS, 2nd child of THOMAS CLAIBORNE ADAMS and NANCY FOSTER, m. JESSE T. COBB 19 Feb 1849 in Madison Co., Ky., and had: 1) JOHN F. b. abt 1849, 2) MARY K. b. 1 Jan. 1853, 3) NANCY b. 1855, 4) EMILY b. 30 Jan 1859, 5) LINEUS B. 1863, 6) HARVEY b. 1867, 7) MINOR b. 1870 8) MARIE b. 1874. MARY K. COBB (above) m. DILLARD H. COX 1 Mar 1870 in Madison Co., Ky. Dillard was born 27 May 1845 and died 24 Sep 1905 in Oklahoma, where Mary K. died 28 Apr 1911. JESSE T. COBB was the son of ZENA COBB b. abt 1800 and PROVIDENCE TEVIS b. abt 1820.

PEYTON FOSTER ADAMS, 2nd child of THOMAS CLAIBORNE ADAMS and NANCY FOSTER, m. #1 CATHERINE EMBREE 4 Jan 1851 in Madison Co., Ky., and had EMILY abt 1851. He married #2 JULIET JARMAN RUCKER abt 1853 and had: 1) CATHERINE P. b. abt 1857, 2) LAWRENCE b. 21 Mar 1859, 3) JOHN BRUCE b. 3 Apr 1860, 4) CHARLES RUCKER b. 1863, 5) ALTHUSA b. 1865 6) COLEMAN LINCOLN b. 1868, 7) THOMAS B. 1869 8) CURTIS b. 1871, 9) PARKER b. 1873, 10) LUCY b. 17 Feb 1875, 11) PEYTON FOSTER JR. b. 1878.

JOHN BRUCE ADAMS, son of PEYTON FOSTER ADAMS (above) and JULIET JARMAN RUCKER, m. CANDIS FREEMAN (b. 25 Apr 1866 Madison, KY d. 9 Dec 1947 Amelia, Clermont, OH). Their children: 1) RUSSEL F. b. 1894, 2) WILLIAM RUCKER b. 25 Sep 1899, d. 31 Dec 1962 Amelia, Clermont, OH, m. NANCY SNEAD 3) PARKER S. b. 15 Jan 1905, d. 30 Jan 1991 Amelia, Clermont, OH, m. VIOLA P, 4) ONEIDA B. b. abt 1910 d. 21 Mar 1986 Palmetto, Manatee, FL, m. #1 EDWIN WILLIAM CARR, m. #2 TOBIAS unknown.

PEYTON FOSTER ADAMS Jr., son of PEYTON FOSTER ADAMS and JULIET JARMAN RUCKER, married Unknown and had PEYTON FOSTER ADAMS III.

ELISHA GOFF ADAMS, 4th child of THOMAS CLAIBORNE ADAMS and NANCY FOSTER m. EMILY JANE OWENS, 1 Aug 1854 in Madison Co., Ky. (Emily b. 23 Sep. 1835 in Madison and d. 13 Nov. 1901 also in Madison.) Children: 1) NANCY b. 1856, 2) MARY b. 1858. Mary m. PENDLETON TRACY abt 1857 in Madison and had: 1) ELLA M, m. WILLIAM H BABER and had LEOLA P, 2) WILLIS, 3) GOFF m. EDNA SHEARER, 4) ELIZABETH, 5) LOULA, 6) DILLARD, m. MAUDE, 7) JOHN, m. IDA B. WHITE, 8) JULINA. PENDLETON TRACY was the son of LEE TRACEY and JULIA.

MARY HULSE ADAMS, 6th child of THOMAS CLAIBORNE ADAMS and NANCY FOSTER m. SOCRATES PARRISH abt 1857 and had: 1) MATTIE b. abt 1860, 2) MILTON abt. 1862, 3) JACOB b. 1864, 4) JULIE b. 1866, 5) ELISHA b. 1877, 6) ROBERT CURTIS b. 1877.

WILLIAM SIMPSON ADAMS, 7th child of THOMAS CLAIBORNE ADAMS and NANCY FOSTER m. BATHSHEBA DOUGLAS 26 Sep 1867 in Madison, KY and had: 1) RICHARD CLAIBORNE, 2) LENORA G, 3) MARY, 4) ALGIN—see below, 5) MILLY, 6) WILLARD.

ALGIN ADAMS, (#4 above) son of WILLIAM SIMPSON ADAMS, was born abt 1873 and m. REBECCA METCAF 17 Oct 1895 Madison, KY. Their children:

1) GERTRUDE b. 28 Jul 1899 d. 26 Apr. 1874 m. COLEMAN CHRISTOPHER FRITZ;
2) SHERMAN b. 3 Aug 1901 d. 22 Apr 1972 Butler, OH, m. ALMA HURT (b. 26 Sep 1902, d. 12 Jan 1996 Butler, OH);
3) WOODARD b. 16 Mar 1903 d. 10 Mar 1998 m. LUCILLE LANTER in 1924 (b. 19 Oct 1907 d. 13 Apr 1997);
4) VIOLA b. 20 Feb 1906 d. 6 Jun 1998 m. MR. TIPTON;
5) LUCILE CLAIBORN b. 14 Feb 1907 d. 26 Nov 1979 Sarasota, FL, m. WILBUR CURTIS FOSTER (b. 26 Oct 1909 Butler, OH, d. 3 Dec 1966 Butler, OH).

ALEXANDER WILLIS ADAMS, 8th child of THOMAS CLAIBORNE ADAMS and NANCY FOSTER m. MARY ELIZABETH CRAIG who died 26 Jun 1901. Their children:

1) EMMA b. abt 1868
2) MARY ELIZABETH b. 1869
3) THOMAS CLAYBORN b. abt 1870
4) JOHN W b. 2 Feb 1872 d. 8 Apr 1948 d. 8 Apr 1948
5) FRANCIS b. abt 1874
6) SARAH EVERT b. 10 Sep 1879 d. 26 Sep 1920 Estill, KY.

JOHN W ADAMS (#4 above) m. NELLIE J (surname unknown) who died 14 Jul 1962. SARAH EVERT (#6 above) m. CHARLES DILLARD WALTERS b. 19 Jul 1870 d. 18 Nov 1963 Cincinnati, OH.

STROTHER ADAMS, 9th child of THOMAS CLAIBORNE ADAMS and NANCY FOSTER m. ELIZABETH ANN PORTWOOD 19 Feb 1866 in Madison, KY. She was born 12 Jul 1849 in Madison and died 2 Jun1930, also in Madison. Their children:

1) AMANDA b. abt 1870 m. NEVILLE GRAY 17 Nov 1897 in Madison and had WILLIAM b. 1911.

2) JOHN married SALLIE and had: WILLIAM J who married KATE, 2) LAURA M, 3)NANNIE B, 4) DILLARD P, 5) NEVEL C, 6) LUCY, 7) SALLIE C, 8) ROBERT B.

3) LULA m. JOSEPH GILBERT TIPTON 24 Nov 1892 in Estill, KY and had:

   a) CYRUS b. 8 Aug 1893 m.
   b) EVERETT b. 27 Nov 1894 m. #1 CORA, m. #2 MOLLIE
   c) EDGAR b. 13 Jul 1896 m. PAULINE
   d) LEMUEL b. 7 Dec 1898 m. GRACE
   e) ROY b. 10 Jun 1901 m. MARY
   f) MARY ANN b. abt 1904 m. ORA STEELE
   g) NORA MAE b. 17 Jan 1906 m. MR. WINKLER

4) GEORGE R m. JESSIE E. POWELL abt 1904 (Jessie b. 1884 d. 1992?)
5) DILLARD m. IDA abt 1899
6) MARTHA m. JAMES ROBERT "BOB" MARSHALL in 1902. Bob b. 9 Mar 1881 Madison, KY d. 21 Apr 1937, Madison, KY.
7) MOLLIE m. CLARENCE MARSHALL (son of Charles Marshall and Amanda Barnes) in 1907 and had: 1) HUBERT, 2) ELIZABETH, 3) RHODA, 4) GLADYS, 5) EDWARD, 6) ELLENDER b. 22 Jun 1908, 7) VERNON b. 15 Jun 1910 d. 8 Sep 1983 m. SUSIE HACKWORTH 16 Oct 1934. Susie b. 1917 d. 15 Oct 1980, 8) GLENARD BUSH b. 2 Jul 1921 d. 18 Dec 1977 m. ANNA MARGARET HUNTER.
8) LAURA b. 22 Nov 1884 Madison, KY d. 2 Dec 1975 Madison, KY, m. LUTHER HACKWORTH 22 Dec 1908. Luther b. Apr 1885 Clark, KY d. 9 Sep 1928 Red House, Madison, KY. Children:
   1) ELEANOR, 2) THOMAS HENRY b. 29 Nov 1909, 3) LONA b. 13 Sep 1911, 4) ZELIA b. 3 Apr 1913, 5) JERRY b. 27 Jan 1816, 6) SUSIE b. 1917, 7) GENEVA b. 1919, 8) BESSIE E b. 9 May 1920, 9) LUTHER WILLIAM b. 15 Feb 1923 10) LEWIS b. 14 Mar 1925.
9) GOFF married CECIL Unknown and had NAOMI abt 1915.

****

LEONARD, 9th child of WILLIAM b. 1747 & SARAH (HART) FOSTER, was born in Clark Co., Ky. He was a cattle buyer and drover. After an ill-fated marriage (to Margaret Ketchens) Leonard moved to Fayette County where he lived with his sister, Margaret Hisle, or her son, Minor. When he died, Leonard left his land to his nephew, Minor Hisle and Minor's son, James H.

xiii. LEONARD FOSTER, b. Abt. 1806, Clark Co., KY; d. 10 May 1877, Clark Co., KY; m. MARGARET KETCHENS, KY.
Notes for LEONARD FOSTER:
Sources: Old Graveyards of Clark Co., KY by Katheryn Owen; Hisle Family Bible by M. H. and E. A. Hisle;
His Will is found in the FOSTER BOOK on page 29
BIOGRAPHY: Leonard Foster was a Drover, who bought & sold cattle. He married, left her with one of her brother's family while he built & furnished a suitable home for her. Returning to fetch her, to his surprise, dismay, hurt & anger, she refused to occupy her new home. He walked away, never to return. He lived from then, to his death, with his sister, Margaret Hisle & later with her son, Minor Hisle. During his lifetime Leonard acquired much land, which he Willed to Minor & his son James H. Hisle.

POLLY, last child of WILLIAM & SARAH (HART) FOSTER, was born in Clark Co., Ky., where she grew to adulthood, met and married WILLIAM HULSE. Later, they moved to Montgomery County, where her mother joined them after the death of her 2nd husband.

WILLIAM HULSE b. 1799
POLLY (FOSTER) b. 1809
Were married Oct. 15, 1839, Kentucky. To this union were born:

1. AMANDA b. 1832
2. NANCY A. b. 1837
3. MARY b. 1839
4. MARGARET b. 1842
5. HANNAH b. 1847
6. EDWARD b. 1849

Except for my sire, HARRISON, this brings to an end the family of WILLIAM FOSTER and #1 SALLIE SLADE AND #2, SARAH HART.

RECORD PAGE #6
Land purchased in 1811 by William & Sarah (Hart) Foster, and passed down to their son, Peyton , as the surviving eldest son, by Law of Descent. Allen Armstrong married Peyton's sister, SUSAN, who was Harrison's Foster's half-sister.

"Indenture made 22nd of April 1844 between Peyton Foster of Sangamon Co., Illinois of the first part and Allen Armstrong of Clark County, Kentucky of the other part. For the sum of one dollar, Peyton Foster conveys all his undivided interest, right, title, and claim to a tract of land in Clark County on waters on Lulbegrud Creek, supposed to contain100 acres, it being the same land conveyed to William Foster, now deceased, who was the father of said Peyton Foster, by John Rankins & Ann Rankins his wife, by deed bearing date of March 1811 and recorded in clerk's office of Clark Co. Court in Deed book #7 p. 640. The interest hereby sold and conveyed to said Allen Armstrong is the undivided interest which the said Peyton Foster has in said tract by Law of Descent from the aforesaid William Foster."
Deed book #31, Pg. 224, Clark Co., Kentucky
***
On Feb. 2 & 7, 1765 George Foster mortgages 100 acres of land in Prince William Co., Virginia, to John Glassford & James Douglas for Lb. 47:1:51/2, Deed book Q, pgs. 252 & 254-255.
***
On Feb. 27, 1807, William & Sarah Foster, of Clark Co., Kentucky relinquished all claim to 100 acres of land in P.W. Co., Va., to John Thomas. On Nov. 21, 1807, John Thomas sells same land to Rutland Johnson for $513.

May 7, 1798 George Foster to Glassford & Henderson:--To balance due them this date, including interest in full, as secured by mortgage in Prince William Co., Va. Lg. 24:5:4.

Received from John Thomas the above sum; payment in full of mortgage and every other claim of Glassford & Henderson against George Foster or his estate. Recorded July 4, 1808. Db. 3, pgs. 387-389, Prince William Co., Virginia.

****** THE BARTLETTS *******

ANNA MARGARET BARTLETT, wife of HARRISON FOSTER Sr., was a "lost" name for over 125 years as far as her descendants were concerned. Anna died between the birth of her last child in 1813, and before Harrison wrote his will in 1819. The eldest daughter had married before Harrison's death, at which time the next–to-youngest child was adopted out. The rest of their children remained together till parted by death. In the pages ahead, each of their seven children and descendant will be allotted a separate chapter.

Aaron Foster, head of my branch (3rd child of Harrison and Anna Foster), moved to Indiana, where he met John Patton and married his daughter. This attachment with John Patton and family lasted over 35 years. During those years, John and Margaret Patton replaced nearly forgotten parents in his affections. By the time Aaron's son, Silas J. Foster became interested in family history, the name of his grandmother had become just a, "It runs in my mind, that her name was Ann or, maybe Anna Margaret."

"It runs in my mind," and "Aunt so-and-sp says" are often signposts leading down blind paths, yet enough of them are based on fact, none can be completely ignored. So, for many moons, I probed this trail and that one, pushing aside many musty curtains of time, till, at last I unexpectedly stumbled into the clearing where lay Anna Margaret Bartlett's secret.

WILLIAM BARTLETT of Virginia first settled on Stoner's Creek, Bourbon Co., Kentucky. On Jan. 4, 1802, William bought 1,200 acres or land from H. Marshall. Later, he purchased the James Buchanan estate from the widow, Nancy, and her son, James Jr., who later married one of William's daughters.

The land now owned by William Bartlett included Blue Lick Springs, which had a long history of death and violence, long before the coming of the white men. Here, in three encounters with Indians, Daniel Boone lost a son, a brother, and was taken captive. Here, too, was fought the Battle of Blue Licks, when both Indians and Whites lost heavily, and other Whites taken prisoner to die at the stake.

These bitter feuds between Indian and Indian, and Whites and Indian were caused by a small word – salt. William Bartlett built a salt-making plant on the site and housing for his workers, after the Indians were subdued. However, at his death, the bickering began anew although of a less violent kind.

After the births of his children, William Bartlett's wife died and he remarried. Shortly before his death, William made out a Will but failed to have it properly witnessed, and it was disallowed. At the time, William's children tried to buy the widow's share of the estate. At first she agreed to a price, then changed her mind and took the children to court.

During their disagreement with their step-mother, the children of William Bartlett made out a written agreement. From this, "Bartlett Heirs Agreement," we have learned the names of his children and their spouses., Also, the name of our Grandmother, Anna Margaret Foster. (Abstracts from this agreement can be found in D.B. H, pg. 368, Nicholas, Kentucky.)

William Bartlett Sr. is buried on his estate, in Nicholas Co., Ky., about four miles from Blue Licks Springs, now known (1975) as the "Hammond Farm." On his tombstone: -- "William Bartlett, Pioneer, died 1820."

William Bartlett's children by his first wife, as taken from the "Agreement." No children were born to 2nd marriage: EBENEZER, SAMUEL, DORCAS (WILSON), ANNA*, POLLY (PRATHER), NANCY (BUCHANAN), PHOEBE (DUNCON sp?).

From Bartlett Heirs Agreement: Anna, deceased, wife of Harrison Foster, "Left 7 children, who are eligible for their mother's share, namely: POLLY, WILLIAM, AARON, HARRISON Jr., PHOEBE, LETTICE, and DORCAS FOSTER."

The reader of this history will note two things: 1) The three sons and Lettice are Foster family names and the other three girls bear Bartlett names; 2) Here Polly is listed first instead of second, as I have done in this history. I have yet to learn which is correct.

ADDITIONAL BARTLETT INFORMATION

Numerous Bartlett descendants participated in a Bartlett DNA study completed in 2009 in order to straighten out the heritage of the numerous New England Bartletts. Although our family didn't participate directly in the study we have benefited greatly from it because we have a paper trail that links us directly to Team 6, DNA Group G, which is the Bartletts of Connecticutt. The paper trail is:

1) DAR (Daughters of the American Revolution) Patriot Index: "William Bartlett b. 1750 d. KY m. #2 Phoebe Buchanan, Sgt. VA."
2) After the birth of his children, William Bartlett's first wife (Anna Hildreth) died, and he remarried. Shortly before his death William made out a will but failed to have it properly witnessed, and it was disallowed. At that time William's children tried to buy the widow's (#2 Phoebe Hildreth Buchanan, sister of Anna) share of the estate. At first she agreed to a price, then changed her mind and took the children to court. During their disagreement with their step-mother the children of William Bartlett made out a written agreement. From this, "Bartlett Heir's Agreement," we have learned the names of his children and their spouses***. Also, the name of our Grandmother, Anna Margaret (Bartlett) Foster***. (Abstracts from this agreement can be found in D.B. H, pg. 368 Nicholas Co., KY.

Other Bartlett descendants wrote to me after the DNA study expressing dismay that we claimed a relationship without having DNA evidence. They requested proof that we were descendants of the Connecticutt Bartletts. Thanks to Flavius research I was able to respond immediately by supplying the "Bartlett Heirs Agreement" and we have been welcomed into the CT Bartlett fold. The ancestry is as follows:

ANNA MARGARET BARTLETT, wife of HARRISON FOSTER b. 1776 is the daughter of WILLIAM BARTLETT (B. 11 Oct 1750 New Canaan, Fairfield, CT d. Feb 1820 Blue Lick Springs, Bourbon, KY) and ANNA HILDRETH (b. 1759 Orange, NY d. 1809 Blue Lick Springs). Married 1777 Virginia.

William Bartlett b. 1750 is the son of SAMUEL BARTLETT (b. 1721 Norwalk, CT d. 16 Nov 1762 Goshen, Orange, NY) and MERCY or MARYANN SEELEY (b. 19 Apr 1723 Stamford, Fairfield, CT d. 1776 Stamford). Married 1750 Goshen, Orange, NY. Mercy or Mary Ann Seeley is the daughter of Ebenezer Seeley (b. 16 Jan 1696 Stamford, CT d. 7 Mar 1767 Goshen) and Mercy Dean (b. abt 1700 d. 1744). Ebenezer b. 1696 is the son of Jonas Seeley (b. 1652 d. 1703) and Mary Wicks (b. 1660 d. 1738).

Anna Hildreth b. 1759 is the daughter of JOSEPH HILDREH III (b. 21 Feb 1724 Chelmsford, Middlesex, MA d. 4 Jul 1796 Dummerston, VA) and SALLY HILDRETH (b. 1724 NY). Married abt 1744.

Samuel Bartlett b. 1721 is the son of JOHN BARTLETT (b. 5 Oct 1678 England d. 5 Aug 1761 Norwalk, CT) and ELIZABETH HAINES (b. 5 Oct 1685 Kingston, Ulster, NY d. 25 Feb 1724 Norwalk, Fairfield, CT. Married 20 Feb 1706 Norwalk, CT.

John Bartlett b. 1676 is the son of BENJAMIN BARTLETT (b. 26 Mar 1643 Windsor, Hartford, CT d. 25 Oct 1678 Windsor) and DEBORAH BARNARD (b. abt 1647 Windsor, CT d. 21 Feb 1719 Windsor). Married 8 Jun 1664.

Benjamin Bartlett b. 1643 is the son of JOHN BARTLETT (b. 9 Nov 1613 Windsor, CT d. 14 May 1670 Windsor) and MARTHA Unknown (b. 1619 Windsor, CT d. 20 Apr 1674 Windsor).

John Bartlett b. 1613 is the son of JOHN BARTLETT Sr. b. 1575 and Agnes Unknown b. 1591.

HILDRETH LINE:

Joseph Hildreth b. 1724 (father of Anna Hildreth b. 1759) is the son of JOSEPH HILDRETH II (b. 30 Nov 1695 Chelmsford, Middlesex, MA, d. 4 Jan 1780 Westford, Middlesex, MA) and PHOEBE FLETCHER (b. 24 Nov 1700 Chelmsford, Middlesex, MA d. 21 Jan 1743 Westford, MA. Married 29 Mar 1720 in Chelmsford.

- Phoebe Fletcher (above) is the daughter of WILLIAM FLETCHER (B. 21 Feb 1657 Chelmsford d. 23 May 1712 Chelmsford) and SARAH RICHARDSON (b. 25 Mar 1659 Chelmsford d. 30 Jan 1748 Tyngsboro, Middlesex, MA). Married 19 Sep 1677.

- William Fletcher b. 1657 is the son of WILLIAM FLETCHER Sr. (b. 1622 Concord, Middlesex, MA d. 6 Nov 1677 Chelmsford) and LYDIA FAIRBANKS (B. 13 Jun 1622 Boston, , Lincolnshire, England d. 12 Oct 1704 Chemlsford). Married 7 Oct 1645 Concord, MA.

- Joseph Hildreth II b. 1695 is the son of JOSEPH HILDRETH I (b. 16 Apr 1658 Chelmsford d. 28 Jan 1706 Woburn, Middlesex, MA) and ABIGAIL WILSON (b.8 Aug 1666 Woburn d. 27 Nov 1747 Chelmsford). Married 25 Feb 1683 Cambridge, Middlesex, MA.

Joseph Hildreth I b. 1658 is the son of RICHARD HILDRETH Jr.(b. 1605 Chelmsford, MA d. 23 Feb 1693 Chelmsford) and Elizabeth Hinchman (1625 Chelmsford d. 3 Aug 1693 Malden, MA). Married 31 Dec 1645 Cambridge, MA.

Richard Hildreth Jr. b. 1605 is the son of RICHARD HILDRETH Sr. (b. 1583 England d. 1645 Gainford, Durham, England) and Elizabeth (b. 1583 East, , England d. 1645 East, , England). Married 1645.

***** HARRISON FOSTER *****

HARRISON, eldest son of WILLIAM & SALLIE (SLADE) FOSTER, chart pg. 5, was born in 1776 in Prince William Co., Virginia. After his mother's death Harrison's father remarried, and in 1784 migrated to Kentucky. Of Sallie's four children Harrison was the only one to accompany his father to Kentucky.

NEW DATA ON HARRISON FOSTER:
Harrison Foster served with Robert Foster (b. 1770) in the Northwest Indian War's Battle of Fallen Timbers at the Maumee River, Maumee, Ohio, near present-day Toledo. This battle was a decisive victory for the Americans and resulted in the treaty granting them the right to inhabit the Northwest Territory. This is the first record ever found (by 2014) that shows Robert and Harrison Foster knew each other before the marriages of their children. Robert's son Dennis married Harrison's daughter, Mary Polly; Robert's daughter Ellender married Harrison's son, Harrison Jr., and Robert's son George Archie's first wife was Phebee, another daughter of Harrison. Robert's son James married another Phebee who was a granddaughter of Harrison. Robert's brothers-in-law, William and Rawleigh Williams, were also in this war, with William in the same battalion. They were brothers of Robert's first wife Bathsheba.

"Harrison Foster pg. 46 - Private - - Major General Charles Scott's Command, Major Notley Conn 's Battalion, Capt. Joseph Colvin's Company: Muster Roll of a Company of Mounted Volunteers, July 10 to Oct 23, 1794 , lost horse Sept. 3." Source: AMERICAN

MILITIA IN THE FRONTIER WARS, 1790-1796, by Murtie June Clark, published by Clearfield.

Harrison Foster is shown in "Military Records, U.S. Army, Register of Enlistments, 1798-1914 - 1798 May 17 - 1815 F-G. His birthplace is Fauquier, Virginia (parent county was Prince William). Age is 23; Occupation: Farmer, Ht. 5'11 3/4", grey eyes, black hair, fair complexion. Private, 12 US Infantry under Capt. Anderson L. Madison. End of new data.

In Bourbon County, Harrison Foster grew to manhood, met and married ANNA MARGARET BARTLETT, pg. 28.

In 1806 Harrison moved his family to Nicholas County. Here, he became a member of Capt. Gillespie's company of the 13th Regiment of Militia from 1813 to 1816 (War of 1812). Here, too, Anna died between 1813 and 1816. Harrison, with his family, joined his father William in Clark Co., Kentucky, where Harrison died.

HARRISON FOSTER'S WILL, probated July 26, 1819
In the name of God, Amen, I HARRISON FOSTER of the county of Clark and the state of Kentucky, being weak in body, but sound of mind and perfect memory to make and publish this my last will and testament. First I give and bequeath to my eldest son, WILLIAM, one sixth of my estate after paying my son, AARON, twenty dollars, which I give him extra and then to my other children. I also give and bequeath to my eldest daughter, POLLY, one sixth of the appraisement and as much more of my estate as will make her equal with her brother, WILLIAM. I also give and bequeath to my son, AARON, one sixthly part of my estate with the addition of TWENTY DOLLARS. I also give and bequeath to my son, HARRISON, one sixth on my estate after paying my son, AARON, twenty dollars. I also give and bequeath to my daughter, PHEBEE, one sixth of my estate after paying my son, AARON twenty dollars. I do also give and bequeath to my daughter DORCAS, twenty shillings. I hereby appoint my brother, PEYTON FOSTER, my sole executor of this my last Will and testament. In witness whereof I have hereunto set my hand and seal this 21st day of June in the year of our Lord 1819. His X Mark, Harrison Foster, signed in the presence of Thomas Berry, WILLIAM FOSTER (Father).

HARRISON FOSTER b. 1776 d. June 27, 1819
ANNA MARGARET (BARTLETT) b. 1781 d. 1815
Marriage bond signed Oct. 5, 1799 Kentucky. Their children:

1. WILLIAM b. abt 1800 d. 1834 m. CATHERINE LINEBACK
2. POLLY (MARY) b. 1801/1802 d. 1843 m. DENNIS FOSTER
3. AARON b. Mar. 31, 1804 d. Aug. 6, 1864 m. SARAY ROYSTON PATTON
4. HARRISON Jr. b. 1806 d. 1869 m. ELLENDER FOSTER (dau. of Robert Foster b.1700 and Bathsheba Williams)
5. PHEBEE b. 1808 d. 1828 1st wife of GEORGE ARCHIBALD FOSTER (son of Robert Foster b.1700 and Bathsheba Williams)
6. LETTICE b. June 20, 1811 d. Feb. 12, 1873 m. CALEB FENTON III (son of Caleb Fenton & Sarah Lovey Etheridge)

7. DORCAS b. Oct. 22, 1813 d. May 3, 1853 m. JOHN COX Jr. (son of John Cox & Rebecca Dunn)

WILLIAM, eldest child and 1st son of HARRISON & ANNA MARGARET FOSTER, was born in Bourbon Co., Kentucky, went with his parents to Nicholas and later Clark County. When Harrison died, William, aged 15 years, became the head of family. Before this death, Polly had married and moved to Indiana. Soon after Harrisons' death, Lettice became the ward of Abraham & Mary Davenport, ending up in Missouri. (To get the full story of each of these children, one must read the headings of chapters, pgs. 55-63-105-117-131 and 143).

In 1820 William and his younger brother Aaron decided to join their sister Polly, who had moved to Switzerland Co., Indiana. Even in their youthful disregard of hardships this must have been a rough trip. They had no transportation, so they loaded their belongings onto the backs of their milk cows. Dorcas, barely 7 years old, had to be carried piggy-back for most of the 90-mile trip through Daniel Boone's woodlot.

William grew to manhood in Switzerland Co., Indiana, where he met and married CATHERINE LINEBACK and their children were born. In 1828 William's brother Aaron had moved to McLean Co., Illinois and sent back glowing accounts of the new country. In 1830 William, his brother Harrison and their families, and their unmarried sister Dorcas, migrated to Illinois.

In McLean County, William and Harrison took up land on the Mackinaw river just 1 ¼ miles apart. During the winter of 1830-31, heavy wet snow caved in the roof of Harrison's cabin, and the family nearly froze wading snow to William's cabin. Here, the two families crowded into the small cabin till Harrison could re-roof his house.

William died and is buried in McLean Co., Illinois. After his death Catherine married #2 MOSES KIRKENDAL, and moved to Missouri in about 1841, where she is buried.

WILLIAM FOSTER .b. 1800 d. 1834
CATHERINE (LINEBACK) b. 16 Jul 1805 (Stokes, NC) d.!845 to 1850, Grundy, Missouri
Were married Jan. 3, 1821, Indiana. Their children:

1. PHEBEE b. 1822 m. JAMES T. FOSTER (son of Robert Foster b. 1770)
2. WILLIAM LEONARD b. Feb. 25, 1825 d. Dec. 13, 1894 m. ELIZABETH COX (dau. of John Cox Jr. and Dorcas Foster)
3. POLLY (MARY) b. abt 1823 d. 26 Feb 1904 m. Martin Foster (believed to be the son of JAMES MARTIN PRATHER & SARAH LEWIS of OHIO—this is a new Foster family whose relationship to the Fosters of Prince William, VA and Bourbon, KY is unknown.)
4. LUCINDA b. abt 1829
5. DORCAS b. 1830 d. 28 Feb 1858 m. ALFRED L. ATTERBERRY

PHEBEE, born in Switzerland Co., Indiana, went with her parents to McLean Co., Illinois. Here she grew to adulthood, met and married JAMES T. FOSTER. Soon after their marriage they moved to Missouri with her mother. Here she and her mother got "lost."

James T. was a member of the Foster family noted on pgs. 74-75. Grandpa F. J. Foster thought they were a blood-related family, but years of research has turned up nothing to prove or disprove this assumption. However, there is such a mix-up in this 2nd Foster family any connection is possible. (Thanks Flavius)

JAMES T. FOSTER b. abt 1807 Kentucky (son of Robert Foster and #2 Bathsheba Williams)
PHEBEE Foster b. abt 1822
Were married Dec. 20, 1840 Illinois. To this union were born:

1. MARY LUCINDA b. abt 1841 d. 1880 Missouri, m. WILLIAM BRANSON
2. AARON b. 1848 McLean, Illinois d. 25 April 1910, Ft. Leavenworth, Kansas, m. LUCY SMITH.

Illinois Marriages to 1850 *<http://www.ancestry.com/*
about James T. Phebe Foster
Spouse 1: Foster, James T.
Spouse 2: Foster, Phebe
Marriage Date: 20 Dec 1840
Marriage Location: Illinois McLean County

MARY LUCINDA married WILLIAM BRANSON in Missouri. He was born about 1835 in Virginia. It is not know if this couple had children. *Note: James' son Aaron is shown in the 1860 census of Grundy, Missouri, living with a Mitchell family, (also from Illinois) so it is possible that James and Phebee died there.*

Grundy Co. Marriages 1841 to 1850*: "State of Missouri, County of Grundy, I John Evans, a licensed Minister of the Gospel, do hereby certify that on the 12th day of January A.D. 1859 I joined in the bonds of holy matrimony Mr. William Branson and Miss* ***Mary Lucinda Foster,*** *both of Grundy County, Missouri, given under my hand this 12th day of January A.D. 1859, John Evans, G. H. Hubbell, County Clerk."*
www.ancestry.com

1860 US Federal Census, Grand River, Daviess, Missouri *(Daviess is adjacent to Grundy Co., MO, where Mary and William Branson were married.*
Wm. Branson, age 25, farmer, b. VA
Mary Branson, age 18, b. IL

AARON (#2 above) spent several in the army on the frontier, then returned to McLean Co., Illinois, where he met and married his cousin, LUCY SMITH, pg. 33 (daughter of WILLIAM and MALINDA (FOSTER) SMITH). They soon parted and Aaron went to Iowa where he married another cousin, MARGARET (Maggie) Hudson. (How this second cousin relationship came about, I have been unable to learn.)

AARON B. FOSTER b. 1848
#1 LUCY SMITH were married around 1871 (they divorced)
Aaron's military record names his daughter:

NELLIE b. abt 1872

NELLIE married WILLIAM BENNETT in 1893. He was born Feb. 1870 in Missouri. Their children: 1) WILLIAM JR b. Aug. 1893, 2) CLINTON, b. Jul 1895, 3) HELEN ELIZABETH b. 18 Feb 1900, 4) ROBERT b. 1906, 5) KATHERINE b. 1912.

1900 US Federal Census, Dist 63, Bevier, Macon, Missouri
William Bennett b. Feb 1870 MO, age 30, father b. NY, mother b. OH, occupation: Cigar maker
Nellie Bennett b. Jun 1872 MO, age 27, father b. OH, mother b. MO
William Bennett, son b. Aug 1893 MO, age 6
Clinton Bennett, son b. Jul 1895 MO, age 4
Helen G Bennett, daughter b. Feb 1900 MO

Aaron B. Foster enlisted in the army 19 Mar 1872, at age 24 yrs. Source: "U.S. Army, Register of Enlistments, 1798-1914 Record for Aaron B Foster U.S. Army, Register of Enlistments, 1798-1914" ancestry.com. He enlisted in Trenton Missouri, and lived in Leon, Iowa at the time of his discharge. His reason for disability was deafness and rheumatism which began at McMinnville, TN, probably in the battle that was fought there. He is buried in Section 27, Row 6, Grave No. 3896. His daughter, Nellie Bennett who lived at 714 Washington, Kansas City, Missouri, was notified of his death

Aaron is in the 1870 census of Center, Hancock, Indiana as a single farmer, age 25, living with the Duncan family, which is very interesting because Aaron's grandmother Bathsheba Williams Foster's brother, Rawleigh Williams, was married to Rosanna Duncan. One census file on ancestry.com incorrectly lists Aaron "mulatto."

***1900 Census, Dist. 85, Delaware, Leavenworth, Kansas**. He is living in a home.*
Aaron Foster b. March 1845, age 55, married 14 years, b. IL, father b. KY, mother b. KY, occupation taylor, number of children not shown for anyone on this page.

Military Records, US National Home for Disabled Volunteer Soldiers 1866-1938
Aaron Foster
Place of Enlistment: 25 Jul 1862, Trenton, MO
Rank: Prvt
Company: B - 23rd MO Infantry
Discharge: 23 Jun 1865, Fairfax, Norfolk, VA
Cause: Expiration of service
Disability: Deafness, Rheumatism
Born: Illinois, Age: 46, Height: 5'6", Complexion: Fair, Eyes: Blue, Hair: Dark
Occupation: Laborer
Residence subsequent to discharge: Leon, Iowa
Marital Status: Married
Wife: Mrs. Maggie Foster, Leon, Iowa
Religion: Protestant
Dates of Readmission: 17 Jul 1891 to 4 Nov 1891; 14 Jan 1898 to 3 Oct 1900; 28 Aug 1901
Date of death: 25 Apr 1910
Cause of death: Pulmonary tuberculosis
*Remarks: Died at hospital 10:55 pm, location of grave: Sec 27, Row 6, Grave No. 3896, **Mrs. Nellie Bennett, dau**. 714 Washington, Funeral 2:30 pm Apr 27, 1910, Rev. James M. Payne, Chaplain, Pension $42, personal effects appraised at: $14.*

WILLIAM LEONARD FOSTER, son of WILLIAM & CATHERINE (LINEBACK) FOSTER, married his cousin Elizabeth Cox, the daughter of John Jr. and Dorcas (Foster) Cox.

Dorcas was the daughter of Harrison and Anna Margaret (Bartlett) Foster. William Leonard's family is given on pg. 118.
**** Family chart pg. 29 *****

1860 Census - Martin Township, McLean County, Illinois *- (next to William Foster, age 33), p.250:*
William L. Foster – age 22 - farmer - value of personal property 100
Elizabeth – age 19 – Keeping house
Eliza Jane - age 1 - daughter
Martin Township is in northeastern McLean County, around Colfax.

1870 Census - Martin Township, McLean County, Illinois *- (near another William Foster, age 43 who is the son of Harrison and Ellender Foster), p. 508:*
Foster Wm L. – age 38 – farmer - value of personal property 765
Elizabeth – age 28 – Keeping house
Louisa – age 11
Dorcas C. – age 9
John W. – age 8
Margaret – age 6
Joseph – age 3
Mary – age 9/12

1880 Census - Rutland Township, Montgomery County, Kansas*:*
FOSTER, W. L. – age 52 - Farmer
Elizabeth, F – age 39 - Wife
Margret, F – age 15 - Dau.
Joseph M. – age 12 - Son
Nathan E. – age 5 - Son
Francis M. – age 2 - Son

POLLY (MARY), 3rd child of WILLIAM and CATHERINE (LINEBACK) FOSTER, is believed to have married MARTIN FOSTER, whose relationship is not known. It is believed but not proved that his lineage is MARTIN (1), JAMES PRATHER FOSTER (2) b. abt 1805 OH, BENJAMIN FOSTER (3) b. 1775 MD, JOHN FOSTER (4) b. 1731 MD and ELIZABETH LEWIS.

MARTIN FOSTER b. 1825 Ohio. His relationship to our family of Fosters is unknown but he is believed to be the son of James Prather Foster b. 1805 Ohio and Sarah Lewis. James Prather was the son of Benjamin Foster b. 1775 Allegheny, MD.
POLLY MARY FOSTER b. abt 1823 Switzerland, IN d. 26 Feb 1904 Hancock, IN. They were married about 1850.
Their children:

1. MELVILLE b. abt 1852
2. JAMES ADDISON b. abt 1855 d. 1930 IA m. SARAH E. BOURNE
3. MARGARET OR MADGE b. abt 1857
4. BROOKY b. abt 1859
5. STELLA b. 1862
6. SARAH b. abt 1865
7. CALEB b. abt 1867

1870 US Federal Census (9 Jul) Madison Twsp, Jefferson, Indiana
Martin Foster age 45, b. Ohio, carpenter

Polly Foster age 43, b. Indiana
Melville Foster age 18 b. Indiana
James Foster age 15 b. Indiana
Madge Foster age 13 b. Indiana
Brooky Foster age 11 b. Indiana
Stella Foster age 8 b. Indiana
Sarah Foster age 5 b. Indiana
Caleb Foster age 3 b. Indiana

JAMES ADDISON FOSTER (#2 above) married SARAH E. BOURNE about 1879. SARAH was b. Jul 12 1859 in Moultrie, Illinois and d. 1946 Waterloo, Blackhawk, Iowa. Their children:

1. BERTHA A b. 1878
2. LOWELL ADDISON b. 24 Feb 1880
3. EDITH b. Feb 1882
4. WALTER b. Apr 1884
5. WILLIAM O. b. 14 Mar 1886
6. MABEL b. 1888
7. VICTOR b. Feb 1893

LOWELL ADDISON FOSTER (#2 above) married FLORENCE HOLLOWAY (b. 1881) and had: 1) Arnold Lowell b. 13 Sep 1918 d. 24 Jun 1990 Naples, FL, who married Rosemary Donna Bartz (1918-1995) and had John Nicholas Foster; 2) Victor Thompson.

DORCAS, 5th child of WILLIAM and CATHERINE (LINEBACK) FOSTER, B. 1830 McLean, Illinois and died 28 Feb 1858 in Edinburgh, Grundy, Missouri, married ALFRED L. ATTERBERRY (1822-1882). Their children are unknown.

POLLY (MARY) 2nd child of HARRISON & ANNA FOSTER, born in Bourbon Co., Kentucky, went with her parents to Clark County. Here she met and married Dennis Foster, half-brother to James T. They moved to Switzerland Co., Indiana, Shelby Co., KY, and then to Hancock, Indiana, where they owned land. Some of their children were born in each of these counties. In 1842, Dennis sold the Indiana land and took his family to McLean Co., Illinois. It seems the buyer of the land couldn't make the payments, and the land was resold in late 1844.

On Oct. 10, 1845, Dennis bought land from John R. Patton, pg. 139, in McLean, Ill. When Dennis died, Polly's brothers, Harrison and Aaron Foster were appointed administrators of his estate, which included 165 acres of land. Polly and Dennis are buried in the Pleasant Hill cemetery, McLean Co., Illinois, but there is no tombstone.

Despite a lot of dust-pawing, I have been able to find very little on the ancestors of Dennis Foster. Note, "2nd Family of Fosters." *(Note: Dennis is the son of Robert Foster b. 1770 and #1 Elizabeth Leary. Their history is given later on in this book.)*

DENNIS FOSTER b. 1799 Nicholas, KY d. Sept. 6, 1846 McLean, IL
POLLY (MARY) FOSTER b. 1801/1802 Bourbon, KY d. 1843 McLean IL

Were married Jan. 13, 1819, Kentucky. To this union were born:

1. RACHEL b. Apr. 23, 1820 Switzerland, IN d. Oct. 3, 1898
2. MALINDA b. 1824 Switzerland, IN d. 15 Mar 1885 McLean, IL
3. MARY ELIZABETH b. May 22, 1825, Shelby, KY d. Nov 28, 1893 McLean, IL
4. PERRY JACKSON b. Feb 15, 1827 Shelby, KY d. Apr 5, 1863 Missouri – Civil War
5. HENRY HARRISON b. Sept 13, 1828 Shelby, KY d. Dec 7, 1898 McLean, IL
6. ROBERT L. b. June 20, 1834 Switzerland, IN d. Aug. 16, 1904 Omaha, Douglas, NB
7. JOHN died as infant
8. SALLY died as infant

RACHEL (#1 above), born in Switzerland Co., Indiana, grew to adulthood while meandering around with her parents till they landed in McLean Co., Illinois. Here she met and married her cousin, John Foster, pg. 147 (son of Aaron and Sarah Royston Patton Foster). Rachel's family is given on that page.

During her lifetime the grim reaper stood at Rachel's shoulder several times. She and John had been married a little over three months, when he died of milk fever. Rachel then moved in with her sister, Elizabeth, where Rachel's daughter was born and died. When her brother, Perry's wife died and Rachel moved into his home and cared for his children till they were able to make their own way. Then, Perry too died and Rachel was left alone to care for his children. Yet, it is said of her, that Rachel's troubles did not get her down, and till the end of her life, she was known for her pastries and helpfulness to her neighbors.

After Perry's children grew old enough to care for themselves, Rachel married #2, Alexander Newman, and she outlived him by four years. Rachel & John Foster, their daughter, Sally and Alexander Newman are buried side by side in the Pleasant Hill Cemetery, in McLean Co., Illinois.

Rachel is in the 1870 census of Martin, McLean, IL, living with William Foster--son of Harrison & Ellender Foster--and his wife Elizabeth, Harrison Jr., Evaline, Jesse, and Mary. She is listed as Rachel Foster, not Rachel Newman, who was her 2nd husband.

1850 CENSUS OF MACKINAW, MCLEAN, ILLINOIS

William Foster age 23 b. Switzerland, Indiana
Elizabeth Foster age 20 b. Switzerland (Indiana)
Harrison Foster age 3 b. Illinois
John Foster age 6 mos. b. Illinois
Racheal (Rachel) Foster, age 25 b. Switzerland (Indiana)--William's mother Ellender and Rachel's father, Dennis, were step-siblings.

1860 Census, Blue Mound, McLean, Illinois

Perry J. Foster, age 33 b. KY Farmer, land value $800, estate $400
Rachel Foster, age 36 (Rachel is Perry's sister) b. KY (this birthplace differs from other Censi)
Hiram Foster, age 10 b. IL
Emela Foster, age 8 b. IL
Amanda Foster, age 6 b. IL

***The 1870 census of Martin, McLean, Illinois** shows her with William. It says she was born in Indiana, and with her family is Rachel Foster, age 50, also born in Indiana.*
William M Foster age 43 b. Ind, farm worth $5000, estate worth $1750.
Elizabeth age 44 b. IN
Harrison age 22 b. IL
Evaline age 18 b. IL
Jesse age 11 b. IL
Mary age 8 b. IL
Rachel age 50 b. IN

MALINDA, 2nd child of DENNIS and POLLY FOSTER, born in Switzerland Co., Indiana, meandered around with her parents till they ended up in McLean Co., Illinois. Here she met and married William Smith, pg. 137, (son of John Smith and Cassandra Wiley of Maryland) and their children were born. William is buried in Evergreen Cemetery, McLean Co., Ill. After his death we "lost" Malinda.

WILLIAM SMITH b. Sept 9, 1819 d. Aug 2, 1865
MALINDA FOSTER b. ? d. 1824
Were married 15 Jan 1843, Illinois. To this union were born:

1. ROYSTON b. 1846
2. MARY ELIZABETH b. 1847 m. ___Turnipseed
3. WILLIAM Jr. b. 1849
4. LUCY b. 1852 d. Leon, Iowa m. Aaron B. Foster, son of James T. and Phoebe (Foster) Foster (James T was the son of Robert Foster b. 1770 Bourbon, KY and Phoebe was the daughter of William Foster b. 1800 and Catherine Lineback). Child: NELLIE FOSTER b. abt 1872 m. WILLIAM BENNETT in 1893 and had:
    a) William Jr. b. Aug 1893
    b) Clinton b. Jul 1895
    c) Helen Elizabeth b. 18 Feb 1900
    d) Robert b. 1906
    e) Katherine b. 1912.

    *Source: Military Records, US National Home for Disabled Volunteer Soldiers 1866-1938…Remarks: Died at hospital 10:55 pm, location of grave: Sec 27, Row 6, Grave No. 3896, **Mrs. NELLIE BENNETT, dau.** 714 Washington, Funeral 2:30 pm Apr 27, 1910,*

    1900 US Federal Census, Dist 63, Bevier, Macon, Missouri
    William Bennett b. Feb 1870 MO, age 30, father b. NY, mother b. OH, occupation: Cigar maker
    Nellie Bennett b. Jun 1872 MO, age 27, father b. OH, mother b. MO
    William Bennett, son b. Aug 1893 MO, age 6
    Clinton Bennett, son b. Jul 1895 MO, age 4
    Helen G Bennett, daughter b. Feb 1900 MO

5. CLARINDA b. abt 1852 (ancestry.com)

ROYSTON married and lived near Arapaho, Nebraska in 1916.

LUCY married #1, AARON FOSTER pg. 31 (son of James T and Phebee Foster). They parted and Lucy remarried and lived near Colfax, Illinois.
Family Chart pg. 32

MARY ELIZABETH, 3rd child of DENNIS & POLLY FOSTER, born in Shelby Co., KY, made the swing to McLean Co., Illinois with her parents. Here she grew to adulthood, met and married her double cousin, WILLIAM FOSTER pg. 61 (son of Harrison Jr. and Ellender Foster). Both are buried in Pleasant Hill Cemetery.

WILLIAM FOSTER b. Feb. 16, 1827 d. Oct. 6, 1901
MARY ELIZABETH (FOSTER) b. May 22, 1825 d. Nov. 27, 1893
Were married Oct. 11, 1846, Illinois. To this union were born:

1. HARRISON III b. Dec. 10, 1847 d. Jan. 1, 1927 m. FLORA MAY OSBORN
2. JOHN b. abt 1850
3. EVALINE ELIZABETH b. Apr. 10, 1852 d. Nov. 2, 1912 m. WILLIAM BATTERTON
4. MELISSA b. 10 July 1854 d. 25 Jul 1854
5. ANDREW JACKSON b. abt 1858
6. JESSIE CRAIG b. Apr. 23, 1858 m. ADELIA GREY
7. MARY-ETTA b. Oct. 30, 1861 d. Apr. 13, 1885 m. HENRY DERRICK
8. INFANT 1 died in infancy
9. INFANT 2 died in infancy
10. INFANT 3 died in infancy

1880 CENSUS, MARTIN, MCLEAN, ILLINOIS
William age 53 b. Indiana, Farmer (both of his parents born in Kentucky)
Elizabeth age 55 b. Indiana (both of her parents born in Kentucky)
Jesse C age 22 b. Illinois
Mary E age 18 b. Illinois
Robert H Bishop age 27 b. Illinois

In 1871 Harrison (#1 above) went to Haddam, Ks., where many of his cousins lived. Here, he became engaged to Margaret Brown, who later married Madison Cox, pg. 127. Harrison then joined other cousins in Hancock Co., Indiana, where he met and married Flora Osborn. They lived in McLean Co., Ill., where their children were born, and both are buried in the Pleasant Hill Cemetery.

HARRISON FOSTER (#1 above) b. Dec. 10, 1847 d. Jan. 1, 1927
FLORA MAY (OSBORN) b. Aug. 19, 1860 d. Dec. 26, 1927
Were married Jan. 10, 1877, Indiana. To this union were born:--

1. SHIRLEY b. Dec. 12, 1877 d. Dec. 22, 1914
2. IDA E. b. Sept. 17, 1879 d. Mar. 7, 1947
3. ANDREW J. B. Aug . 31, 1881 d. Sept 10,1900
4. LUNA MAY b. Sept. 15, 1884 d. Nov.18, 1953

My wife just told me:- Get that mess off the kitchen table, so I can set it, or you'll get no supper. After picking and mumbling to myself over this "mess" for eight hours, I'm ready for my supper!!!

Notes: on Harrison Foster and Flora Osborn: "History of McLean County, Biographical History, Vol. II" pg.. 806

"Harrison Foster, now living retired in Martin Township, was a leading farmer and a member of a prominent pioneer family of McLean County. He was born on a farm in Martin Township, McLean County, Dec. 10, 1847, the son of William and Elizabeth Foster. William Foster and his wife were natives of Kentucky and were among the first settlers of Martin Township, where they entered land from the government. Mr. Foster owned 200 acres of land and was a leading stockman of the county and also an extensive grain farmer. During the early days he hauled his grain to Chicago. Mr. Foster was a Republican and a member of the Methodist Church. He died Oct. 6, 1901, and his wife died Nov. 27,1893.

They were the parents of the following children: Harrison, the subject of this sketch; John, died at the age of six years; Evelyn, married William Batterton, deceased; Craig, deceased; Mallissa, deceased; Andrew, deceased; and three children died in infancy. Harrison has always lived in McLean County. He was reared on his father's farm in Martin Township and received his education in the district schools, after which he rented land until the time of his marriage. Mr. Foster now owns 130 acres of well-improved land, and is now living retired on the farm. He was an extensive feeder of stock.

On Jan. 10, 1877, Mr. Foster was united in marriage with Miss Flora May Osbon, a native of Hancock County, Indiana, born Aug. 19, 1860, and the daughter of G. W. and Sarah (Wright) Osbon, both natives of Indiana. Mrs. Foster has three half-brothers and sisters, as follows: William, a farmer, Lawndale Township, McLean County; Morgan, a farmer; Ford County, Ill.; and Emma the widow of Stephen Curtis, lives in Indiana. Mr. Osbon served throughout the Civil War and was a member of the Grand Army of the Republic. He died in 1913.

To Harrison and Flora May (Osbon) Foster four children have been born, as follows: Shirley, born Dec. 12, 1878, died Dec. 22, 1915; Ida, born Sept. 15, 1880, married on Sept. 16, 1896 to G. E. Kelley, and they live in Chicago, Ill; Andrew, born in1881, died at the age of 19 years; and Luna May, born in 1884, married George Kennedy, a farmer, lives on the old Foster home place in Martin Township. Harrison Foster is a Republican and a member of the Methodist Church. The foster family is well known in McLean County and are highly respected among their many friends and acquaintances."

He is in the 1850, 1860, 1870, 1880, 1890, 1900, and 1920 US Censi for Martin, McLean, Illinois.

SHIRLEY, (son of Harrison and Flora (Osborne) Foster) married MINNIE FULLER, Aug. 27, 1903. She was a sister of Warren Fuller (pg. 38). Minnie, born: Oct. 28, 1880 d. June 11, 1942. Their children: 1) REX, 2) VIOLET. *Note: Some sources show that Minnie had 4 other children who either died in infancy or whose names are unknown.*

IDA ELIZABETH (dau. of Harrison and Flora (Osborne) Foster) married her cousin, GUY KELLY pg. 62

LUNA MAY (dau. of Harrison and Flora (Osborne) Foster), married GEORGE KENNEDY, Feb. 10, 1904. Children: 1) BERNICE, 2) BEATRICE, 3) WAYNE, 4) VERNON, 5) LYLE, 6) DREXEL, 7) MYRON, 8) WILBER, 9) CLAUDE. Chart pg. 33

EVALINE ELIZABETH (dau. of WILLIAM & ELIZABETH FOSTER, who was the daughter of DENNIS FOSTER) married WILLIAM BATTERTON, who was born Mar. 10,

1848 d. Dec. 25, 1927. They had 1) Lena b. May 1880, and 2) Hugh b. Jun 1889. Evaline and William Both are buried in the Pleasant Hill Cemetery McLean Co., Illinois. Family Chart pg. 33

JESSIE CRAIG married 5 times, but had a child by only one. He had a hard time keeping wives and money. His father financed Jessie during his lifetime, and left 80 acres of land to Jessie's son, which he also squandered. Jessie C. & Adelia (Della) Grey Foster had: ARTHUR *(b. abt 1881).*

1920 Census, Dist. 140, Martin, McLean, IL
Jesse Foster age 61 b. IL, both parents b. KY
Adelia Foster, age 56 b. IL, father b. PA, mother b. OH

MARY-ETTA Foster married HENRY DERRICK. They had two children who died young: 1) Cora b. 10 Nov 1884 and Unknown b. abt 1886. All are buried in the Pleasant Hill Cemetery, Mclean Co., Illinois. *Mary-Etta also died young and this little family vanished from history.*

PERRY JACKSON, 4th child of DENNIS & POLLY FOSTER, was born in Shelby Co., Kentucky and came to McLean Co., Illinois with his parents. Here he grew to manhood, met and married China Henline. After her death Perry's sister, Rachel took over the household.

On Aug 12, 1862, Perry J. Joined the Union Army, and died in Camp Lake Springs, Missouri. He is buried in an old McLean Co., Illinois Cemetery. Some sodden mass of humanity removed all the stones, and piled them under a chicken house. He then built a barn over the cemetery, using a Civil War tomb as a corner footing for the barn.

He enlisted for 3 years and was described on his enrollment form as age 36, 5'11", dark hair and dark eyes with a sandy complexion, and his occupation was farmer. His nativity is listed as Sheldon (sp—probably Shelby) Co., Kentucky. He mustered in Aug 20, 1862 from Bloomington, Illinois, and died 8 months later of a fever at Camp Lake Springs, Missouri. Source: Illinois Civil War Detail Report - http://www.ilsos.gov/genealogy/CivilWarController.

PERRY JACKSON b. Feb. 15, 1827 d. Apr. 8, 1863
CHINA (HENLINE) b. Mar. 13, 1830 d. Feb. 28, 1857
Were married Jan. 20, 1849, Illinois. To this union were born:

1. HIRAM b. Nov. 24, 1849
2. EMILY b. Aug. 10, 1854 d. 1885
3. AMANDA M. b. Jan. 15, 1856
4. JOHN b. 1857 and died in infancy

HIRAM (#1 above) married Louise J. Reynolds and moved to Missouri. AMANDA married GIDEON HORNICK. EMILY married HENRY CRUMP. Both girls lived near Colfax, Illinois.
Family Chart pg. 32.

Notes: Perry died in a Civil War battle and China died in Childbirth with her last child, John. China is buried in McLean Co. IL in the Henline family plot with her son John. It is said that Perry's oldest sister raised the two girls after the death of Perry. Source: http://www.oocities.com/mwanvlp/fosterfamily/foster.htm#foster line #2

1850 Census, Mackinaw, McLean, Illinois
Perry J Foster age 24, laborer, b. KY
China, age 19, b. Illinois
Hiram, age 1 b. Illinois

1860 Census, Blue Mound, McLean, Illinois
Perry J. Foster, age 33 b. KY Farmer, land value $800, estate $400
Rachel Foster, age 36 (Rachel is Perry's sister) b. KY
Hiram Foster, age 10 b. IL
Emela Foster, age 8 b. IL
Amanda Foster, age 6 b. IL

Children of Hiram Foster, son of PERRY JACKSON and CHINA (HENLINE) FOSTER, and Louise Jane Reynolds:
(1) Frank T Foster born 03/22/1874 in McLean Co. IL. died 06/24/1938 in Independence, OR. married 01/10/1894 to Laura Bugher born 04/10/1876 in Cerro Gerdo Co. IA. died in Arapahoe, Furnas Co. NE. buried in Cambridge, Furnas Co. NE
(2) Dora Foster born 10/11/1876 died 1878
(3) Charlie Foster born 02/22/1880 in McLean Co. IL died 09/25/1932 in OR married Angie Ellen Clark born 11/28/1879 burial date is 02/18/1954
(4) Lula Foster born 07/19/1887 died 1889
(5) Effie May Foster born 09/14/1891 died 10/17/1965 buried in Elwood, Gosper Co. NE married Roy Phillips born 08/31/1890 died 09/23/1953 and is buried in Elwood, Gosper Co. NE
Source: http://www.oocities.com/mwanvlp/fosterfamily/foster.htm#foster line #2

GIDEON HORNICK b. 1842 IN
AMANDA (FOSTER)—dau. of PERRY J. and CHINA FOSTER) b. 1853 IL
Children (all were born in Illinois):

1. EMMA b. 1871
2. WILLIAM b. 1873
3. ELDORA b. 1875
4. MINA b. 1880

Notes on Gideon and Amanda (Foster) Hornick:
1880 Federal Census, Dist, 181, Martin, McLean, Illinois
Gideon Hornick, age 38, farmhand, b. IN, both parents born in Virginia
Amanda Hornick age 27 b. IL
Emma Hornick, age 9 b. IL, at school, daughter
William Hornick, age 7 b. IL, at school, son
Eldora age 5, daughter b. IL
Mina, age 2 months, daughter b. IL
Fred Logan, age 27, b. KY, farmhand

HENRY HARRISON, 5th child of Dennis & Polly Foster, born in Shelby Co., KY, went with his parents to Hancock Co., Indiana, then to McLean Co., Illinois. Here he grew to manhood, met and married Polly Ann Chance, and their children were born. Henry,

Polly, Daniel, Rosette, Hezekiah, are all buried in the McNaugh Cemetery near Carlock, Illinois.

HENRY HARRISON FOSTER b. Sept 13, 1828 d. Dec. 7, 1898
POLLY (MARY) ANN (CHANCE) b. Aug. 1830 d. Dec. 3, 1871
Were married Apr. 9, 1848. To this union were born:

1. ZACHARIA TAYLOR b. Mar. 23, 1849 d. Dec. 31, 1927
2. HEZEKIAH b. Apr. 13, 1850 d.
3. ELLEN MALINDA b. Jam. 24, 1852 d. Dec. 25, 1914
4. CHARLOTTE b. June 23, 1854 d. Mar. 16, 1946
5. DANIEL b. Sept 1, 1858 d. 1876
6. LOUISA JANE b. July 8, 1860 d. Nov. 25, 1916
7. ROSETTA b. Mar. 1, 1862 d. 1879
8. LILLIAN MAY b. Feb. 24, 1871 d. Feb. 12, 1906

Notes:
1850 Census Mackinaw (south side), McLean, Illinois
Harrison Foster, age 21, b. North Carolina, Farmer, land $500
Mary A Foster, age 10 (this can't be right, it is actually 19) b. Indiana
Zachariah age 1 b. Illinois
Hezekiah, age 6 mos. b. Illinois

1860 Census, Gridley, McLean, Illinois
Harrison Foster age 37, b. Ohio, Farmer, land $1000, estate $500
Polly Ann Foster age 39 b. Indiana
Zacharia Foster age 11 b. IL
Ellen Foster age 8 b. IL
Charlotte Foster age 5 b. IL
Daniel Foster, age 1 b. IL

Above it says Henry Harrison was born in Ohio. This differs from the birthplace Flavius Foster listed for him in "Seedlings," which was Shelby, Kentucky. However, note that "The Falls of the Ohio," (meaning Ohio River) a place often mentioned in pioneer writings, is located in Shelby Co., KY. All of Henry Harrison's children are born in Illinois. He is a farmer with real estate valued at $1100 and personal estate at $500.

1870 Census, Gridley, McLean, Illinois
Harrison Foster age 41 b. Kentucky, Farmer, land $3000, estate $1065
Polly Foster age 40 b. IN
Zachariah age 21 b. IL, working on farm
Charlotte age 15 b. Iowa
Daniel age 11 b. IL
Louisa age 9 b. IL
Rosetta age 8 b. IL
James and Mary Chance are living nearby, who are no doubt related to Polly Mary Chance Foster.

Zachariah TAYLOR, 1st child of HENRY HARRISON AND POLLY (CHANCE) FOSTER, was born in McLean Co., Illinois, where he grew to manhood, met and married Mary Jane Manning. Their first two children were born in Illinois. Between 1875 and 1879, the family moved to cedar Co., Missouri, where the other children were born. Here Zachariah farmed till his death, and is buried with Mary in the Eldorado Springs., Missouri, Cemetery.

ZACHARIA TAYLOR FOSTER b. Mar. 23, 1849 d. Dec. 31, 1927
MARY JANE (MANNING) b. Feb. 16, 1855 d. Sept 22, 1926
Were married Mar. 14, 1872, Illinois. To this union were born:

1. FRANK ELMO b. Oct. 6, 1873
2. NANCY ANN b. Mar. 30, 1875
3. LILLY ALICE b. Oct. 27, 1879 d. June 6, 1971
4. EVERETT b. Sept 19, 1882 d. July 13, 1884
5. GRACE b. Nov. 27, 1886 d. July 14, 1968
6. ERNEST OSBORN b. Mar. 23, 1890 d. Mar. 18, 1947
7. LABAN LURALL b. Nov. 6, 1897

FRANK ELMO (#1 above), born in Gridley, Illinois, moved with his parents to Missouri where he grew to manhood, met and married, ANNA DRUIE SEXTON, June 5, 1898. She was born Mar. 28, 1875. Child: SCEATTA LOWELL b. Jan. 22, 1902, who married JAMES PRICE GITTINGER Feb. 26, 1926. They had: 1) JAMES PRICE Jr. in 1927, 2) FRANCES ANNA July 18, 1931.

NANCY ANN (#2 above), born in Gridley, Illinois, went with her parents to Missouri where she met and married HARLEY BERTRUM MILLER on Feb. 9, 1902. He was born Sept. 3, 1875 and d. Sept 20 1948. Both are buried in Eldorado Springs, Mo. They had two children:

1) BERYL LAVESTA b. Mary 24, 1903, who married JOHN WILLIAM JANES Dec. 24, 1920. He was born July 31, 1889. Children:
   a) EVELYN BERYL b. Aug. 24, 1921,
   b) LLOYD LEE b. Feb. 12, 1923,
   c) VELMA IRENE b. Oct. 12, 1925,
   d) JOHN WILLIAM Jr. b. Jan. 9, 1927.

2) ARYL FOSTER MILLER, b. July 22, 1908, who married KATHERINE LAURA MOODY on June 20, 1937. She was born Sept. 2, 1910. Their child: JUDY ANN b. July 14, 1939.

LILLY ALICE, 3rd child of ZACHARIA T. and MARY JANE (MANNING) FOSTER, was born, grew to adulthood, and wed in Cedar Co., Missouri to CLIFFORD LEROY PARRISH on Dec. 31, 1899. He was born May 2, 1880. Both are buried in Pratt, Kansas. They had three children:

1. ANNA GLADYS b. Oct. 25, 1900, who married JAMES ALBERT GARDNER on Aug. 25, 1923. He was born Nov. 13, 1898 d. May 1, 1958. Their children:
   a. BARBARA JEAN b. June 27, 1924
   b. DONALD DALE b. Nov. 19, 1927
   c. SHIRLEY JOAN b. Aug. 13, 1930
   d. JAMES LOWELL b. Feb. 22, 1932
2. INEZ MARIE PARRISH b. Dec. 20, 1901, who married ROLLEY L. KING on Apr. 5, 1924. He was born Apr. 17, 1899 d. May 1, 1968, buried in Hutchinson,

Kansas. They had: BEVERLY ANN b. Jan. 29, 1926, who married LEONARD L. SHOUP on June 8, 1947.

3. NEVA MAE PARRISH b. May 26, 1903, who married VIRGIL L. MUNGER on Apr. 24, 1926 in Boulder, Colorado. He was born June 19, 1903. Their child: PATRICIA ANN.

GRACE FOSTER, 5th child of ZACHARIA AND MARY JANE FOSTER, was born in Cedar Co., Missouri and is buried in Steubenville, Ohio. She married MARION THOMAS MAYS on June 14, 1908. He was born Jan. 21, 1887 d. Dec. 6, 1969. Their child:

1. VIVIAN LUELLA b. May 27, 1909, who married EARL GEORGE SNYDER on Oct. 14, 1928. He was born May 5, 1906. They had:
    a. WAYNE FOSTER
    b. CINDY LEE

ERNEST OSBORN FOSTER, 6th child of ZACHARIA AND MARY JANE FOSTER, born in Cedar Co., Missouri, is buried in McPherson, Kansas. He married KATE CRIPE on July 9, 1910. Their children:

1. GORDON HARRISON b. Sept. 2, 1918
2. WAYNE ORVILLE b. July 16, 1929

LABAN LURALL FOSTER, 7th child of ZACHARIA AND MARY JANE FOSTER, was born in Cedar Co., Missouri, where he met and married #1 JESSIE BLEVINS on Feb. 19, 1916, and had:

1. JACKSON b. Dec. 13, 1919
2. LABAN LURALL Jr. b. June 28, 1921 d. 1944.

Laban Lurall Sr. married #2 EMMA A. VOGEL and had:

1. LOIS JEAN
2. JOAN MARIE

Vivian L. Snyder gave me this material on the families of Zachariah Foster.
Family chart pg. 35

ELLEN MALINDA, 3rd child of HENRY HARRISON & POLLY (CHANCE) FOSTER, was born 24 Jan 1852 in McLean, IL and died 25 Dec 1914 in Lexington, IL. She married #1 JOHN W. SMARR on 28 Feb 1869 and had HENRY about 1870. Ellen Malinda married #2 BUTLER SMITH around 1872, who was born Mar. 4, 1852. They moved to Eldorado Springs, Missouri, where their children were born, and where Butler is buried.
Their children:

1. MINNIE FRANCES who married JOHN PARKER and had a son the same day her mother did, both named LONNIE.
2. DANIEL, who married CLARA LYONS,
3. ASA, who married MALISSA BURDETTE,
4. CLARA, who married WILLIAM LYONS, Clara Lyon's brother,
5. OTHA , who married ROSE HART,

6. GUY,
7. LONNIE SMITH, who married THELMA SMITH, a cousin.

After the death of Butler Smith, ELLEN MALINDA returned to Lexington, Illinois and married #3 JOHN WILLIAM HENLINE in 1903 in Lexington, Illinois. He was born June 17, 1842 in Martin,, McLean, Illinois , and died in 1910 in the same town. There were several marriages between the Foster and Henline families and so presumably, John William was some sort of cousin to Ellen.
Family chart pg. 35

CHARLOTTE, 4th child of HENRY HARRISON & POLLY FOSTER, was born in Wapello Co., Iowa, and is buried in Lexington, Illinois. She married JOSEPH POLK JANES on July 8, 1874. He was born Oct. 28, 1844 d. Aug. 21, 1904. They had one child who died young.
Family chart pg. 35.

LOUISA JANE, 6th child of HENRY HARRISON & POLLY FOSTER, was born in McLean Co., Illinois. She married JOHN D. LYONS in 1879. He was born Mar.30, 1858 d. Aug. 21, 1942, uncle to the two Lyons' above. Louisa and John are buried in the Wiley Cemetery, Colfax, Illinois. Their children:

1. JOHN D. Jr. b. 1880 d. 1919
2. JANET, who married WARREN G. FULLER and had:
   a. DORIS, who married W.A. HOFFMAN
   b. GERALDINE, who married GENE BURTON

Family chart pg. 35

LILLIAN MAY, 8th child of HENRY HARRISON & POLLY FOSTER, was born in McLean Co., Illinois, where she met and married GEORGE CRUMP.
Both are buried in Colfax, Illinois. Children:

1. DORA b. 23 Feb 1890 m. JAMES M. HARRISON 4 Sep 1912 and had five children:
   a. LILLY KATHERIN b. 18 Dec 1913 m. MR. SCHULLER
   b. IRMA HARRISON b. 16 Nov 1917 m. WALTER POPE
   c. LOLA IMOGENE b. 25 Jan 1919 m. JOSEPH W. SCOTT and had:
      1) JEFFERSON
      2) JANICE
      3) DOREEN
      4) JEANNE KAY
      5) GEORGE F.
      6) LOTTIE MAE b. Aug. 18, 1921 m. BRICE TAYLOR and had MARCIA ELLEN.

   d. GEORGE F b. abt 1920
   e. LOTTIE MAE b. 18 Aug 1921 m. BRICE TAYLOR
2. ELMER LEE b. 7 Apr 1892 m. #1 RONDA and had ELSIE; m. #2 STELLA HAWTHORN and had :

   a) IVAN RAY
   b) GERALDINE
3. DELMAR FRANKLIN b. 5 Apr 1894 m. GLADYS BATTMAN and had :
   a) GEORGE,
   b) GERALD,
   c) WARREN,
   d) DELMAR F. Jr.
4. LOTTIE VIVIAN b. 6 Mar 1902 d. 20 Sep 1921
5. JOSEPHINE IRENE b. 13 Oct 1905 m. Russell Crotty and had Mary Jo.
6. LILLIAN was raised by a family in Michigan after her mother's death. She married and had children but I have no names.
7. BABY 1
8. BABY 2
9. BABY 3

Family char pg. 32
****

ROBERT L., last child of Dennis and Polly Foster, born in Hancock Co, Indiana, went to McLean Co, Illinois with his parents. Here, he grew to manhood, met and married his cousin, Sally Ann (Sarah Ann) Cox, pg. 117. In 1859, Robert and family joined the families of his father-in-law, John Cox, and uncle, Harrison Foster in a wagon train bound for Kansas territory. Robert lived with his Uncle till Harrisons' death, near Frankfort, Kansas.

While living near Frankfort Robert enlisted in a local Militia unit and was at the battle of The Little Blue, described on pg. 208-209 (see below). In 1868, after the death of John Cox, Robert took his family to Washington Co., Kansas and settled near present-day Haddam. At that time there were three large families of Fosters and Coxes living in that area, but today, 1979, no Fosters live there.

Two and one half miles south of Haddam, on the west side of the highway, is a cemetery, the land of which was donated by one of the Foster families. Here, in an unmarked grave, Sally Ann rests. She died of tuberculosis, the "White Plague" of the period.

After the death of his first wife Robert moved to the old Solomon River settlement where many of his cousins lived. Here, he took up a homestead as a civil war veteran, which he later sold. Today this land supports several oil-producing wells. After selling his land, Robert moved back to eastern Kansas, where he met and married #2, Margaret Ellen Howard, widow of Thomas H. Smith. Robert is buried in the Laurel Hills Cemetery, Omaha, Nebraska.

Notes:
***Kansas, Civil War Enlistment Papers**, 1862, 1863, 1868 <http://www.ancestry.com/*
Name: Robert Foster
Birth Year: abt 1834
Birth Location: Hancock, Indiana
Enlistment Date: 29 Aug 1862
Enlistment Town: Vermillion

Military unit: 13th Kansas Volunteer Infantry Company G

***1850 Census, Union, Hancock, Indiana**, living with the Hutson family because his parents are both dead and he is just 16.*
1850 US Federal Census, Union, Hancock, Indiana
Richard Hutson age 66 b. VA
Elizabeth Hutson age 64 b. VA
Elizabeth Hutson age 25 b. KY
Phebe Hutson age 20 b. KY
Matilda Hutson age 18 b. KY
Robert L Foster age 15 b. IN
Jonas Foster age 13 b. IN (this is probably the son of George and Tabitha Foster--he's the right age)

***1860 Census, Vermillion Township, Marshall, Kansas**. Pg. 28 (living with Harrison Foster, their Uncle)*
This census shows Harrison as born in Ohio.
Harrison Foster, age 53 b. OH, Farmer, land value $800, estate value $350
Robert Foster, age 26 b. KY, farm laborer
Sarah Foster, age 17 b. IL
Clarissa Foster age 5 mos. b. Kansas

***1870 Census, Mill Creek, Washington, Kansas,** Pg. 5 No. 319*
Robert Foster age 36, b. Indiana, farmer, land $300
Sarah age 35 b. Illinois
Clarissa age 10 b. Kansas
Malinda age 8 b. Kansas
Daniel age 4 b. Kansas
Harrison age 2, b. Kansas

1880 Census, Independence, Nodaway, Missouri
Robert age 45 b. Indiana, farmer, mother born in Kentucky
Sarah A age 45 b. Illinois, father b. Virginia, mother b. Kentucky
Malinda age 17 b. Kansas
David (Daniel) age 13 b. Kansas
Dorcas age 9 b. Kansas
Joseph age 6 b. Kansas

***1900 Census, Omaha, Douglas, Nebraska**, Robert is with wife #2 and two sons, Thomas and LeRoy. It states that he was born in Indiana, and that both of his parents were born in Ohio. Ellen was born in Illinois, Thomas in Nebraska, and LeRoy in Missouri. It says that Robert is an upholsterer. It is odd that Robert believes both of his parents were born in Ohio, (this could have been "Falls of the Ohio River" in Shelby, Kentucky as stated earlier) and it is also odd that Thomas and LeRoy's father was born in Indiana and their mother in Ohio.*

COX FAMILY ANCESTRY

Robert L. Foster's wife, SARAH SALLY ANN COX, was the daughter of JOHN COX (b. 24 Apr 1809 Beaufort, VA d. 31 Jan 1865 Frankfort, Marshall, KS) and DORCAS FOSTER, who was the daughter of Harrison Foster Sr. and Anna Margaret (Bartlett).

***The 1850 Census of Mackinaw, McLean, IL** has this family:*
John Cox age 45 b. VA
Dorcus, age 33 b. KY
Daniel age 15, b. IL
Sally Ann age 13, b. IL

Betsy age 12, b. IL
Joseph age 9 b. IL
Margaret age 5 b. IL
John is a farmer with land valued at $400. There are three Henline families on the same page (John Sr., John Jr. and Martin), and a Patterson family. On the same page are MARY L FOSTER, age 8, and AARON FOSTER, age 5, living with Isaac and Elizabeth Haines. These are the children of James T Foster and Phebee Foster. Dorcas (Foster) Cox was Phebee's aunt and James T Foster may have been related to Dorcas by other than marriage to her niece. Presumably, the reason these children are living with the Haines family would be that both James and Phebee (Foster) Foster had passed away prior to 1850.

John Cox b. 1809 was previously believe to be the son of JOHN COX Sr. (b. 1760 Fort Chiswell, Botetourt, VA d. 1840 Owen, KY) and REBECCA DUNN (b. 1762 Henry, VA d. 1840). Married 28 Jul 1780. However, current records have lead to some confusion regarding this and more research is needed.

John Cox Sr. was the son of WILLIAM COX (b. abt 1743 Lancaster, PA) and JEAN unknown b. abt 1745.

1810 Census, Botetourt, Virginia, USA, *Image 11*
John Cox 1-1-0-1-0-2-2-0-1-0-0-0

1820 US Federal Census, Botetourt, Virginia
John Cox: 2-0-0-1-0-1-1-2-0-0-1-0-2
James Cox: 0-0-0-1-0-0-0-0-1-0-0-0-1 (this is probably John's son)

William Cox was the son of Joshua Cox (b. 22 Apr 1694 Ulster, Cork, Ireland d. 1747 Lancaster, PA) and MARY RANKIN (b. 1697 Lancaster, PA d. 1747 Lancaster, PA). Married 26 Feb 1724.

Joshua Cox b. 1694 was the son of RICHARD COX (b. 25 Mar 1650 Bandon, Cork, Ireland d. 3 May 1733 Dunmanway, Cork, Ireland) and MARY BOURNE (b. 1658 Cork, Ireland d. 1 Jun 1715 Dunmanway, Cork, Ireland). Married 1673.

Richard Cox b. b. 1650 was the son of RICHARD COX Sr. (b. 1610 Kilworth, Cork, Ireland d. Jul 1651 Brandon, Cork, Ireland) and KATHERINE BIRD b. 1628 Kilworth, Cork, Ireland c. 1650 Brandon, Cork, Ireland). Married 1 Jun 1642.

Richard Cox Sr. b. 1610 was the son of MICHAEL COX (b. 1575 Wiltshire, England d. 1620 Kilworth, Cork, Ireland and unknown wife.

Michael Cox b. 1575 was the son of John Cox (b. 1550 Pitminster, , Somerset, England d. 1581 Brame, Ely, England, and unknown wife.

****

ROBERT L. FOSTER b. June 20, 1834 d. Aug. 16, 1904
SARAH ANN (COX) b. Dec. 23, 1836 d. Dec. 27,1884
Were married Aug. 20, 1856, Illinois. To this union were born:

1. MAHALA b. Nov. 20, 1858 d. in infancy
2. CLARISSA b. Mar. 1, 1860 d. Feb. 25, 1936
3. MALINDA b. Sept 23, 1862 d. Dec. 19, 1912
4. DANIEL b. June 23, 1866 d. Sept. 16, 1943
5. HARRISON b. Oct. 8, 1868 d. Nov. 2, 1872
6. DORCAS b. June 13, 1871 d. Sept 16, 1904
7. JOSEPH b. Nov. 6, 1873 d. 1942

I am continuing research on Robert Foster's 2nd family, but so far have had little luck (Note pg. 54)

ROBERT L. FOSTER b. June 20, 1834 d. Aug. 16, 1904
MARGARET ELLEN (HOWARD) b. Jan. 25, 1851 d. Sept 18, 1935
Were married Jan. 11, 1890, Iowa. To this union were born:

1. THOMAS HARRISON b. Jan. 25, 1891 d. Sept. 6, 1957 m. IDA abt 1923 and had:
   a. MAUDE b. abt 1924
   b. ELSIE b. abt 1926

   Thomas H Foster, born in Iowa, and a WWI veteran, moved to San Jose, Calif. in 1927. He married twice, but had no children by wife #2 Ruth. At present I have no further knowledge of either wife, except: --wife #1 Ida, last known address, Kelso, Wash., and Thomas had: --Maude and Elsie. Thomas is buried in Golden Gate National Cemetery, San Bruno, Calif. The 1900 Census of Omaha, Douglas, Nebraska says he was born in Nebraska.

2. WILLIAM LEROY b. Apr. 12, 1897 Greer, MO d. Mar. 13, 1957 San Jose, CA, m. OLIVE abt 1917 and had:
   a. BARBARA b. abt 1918
   b. ROBERT b. abt 1920

      William L. Foster married Olive____. She died before he did, at least there is no mentioning of her in the obituary. William was blind for several years, and died of a heart attack aboard a bus in San Jose. He is buried in Santa Clara City Cemetery. To Olive and William were born:--Barbara and Robert, whose last known address was Portland, Oregon.

      The 1900 Census of Omaha, Douglas, Nebraska confirms that he was born in Missouri.

CLARISSA, 2nd child of Robert L & SARAH ANN FOSTER, born on a farm 3 miles east of Frankfort, Kansas, was taken to Washington County. Here she grew to adulthood, met and married in Haddam, Ks. To her second generation cousin, CHARLES FRANKLIN FOSTER, pg. 150 (son of Aaron Blueford Foster and Eliza Jane (Foster, grandson of Aaron Foster b. 1804 and Sarah Royston Patton). Clarissa is buried in Bayard, Nebraska, where one of her descendants still lives. Their family and descendants are listed under Charles Franklin Foster later in this book.

Notes:
1900 Census, Adell, Sheridan, Kansas

Charles Foster age 46 b. IL
Clarissa Foster age 40 b. Kansas
Mattie M. Foster age 19 b. Missouri
Shanie B. Foster age 16 (son) b. Kansas
Guy W. Foster age 13 b. Kansas
William E. Foster age 11 b. Kansas
Bertha E. Foster age 9 b. Kansas
Carl E Foster age 6 b. Kansas
Lola B Foster age 4 b. Kansas
Alise F Foster age 1 b. Kansas

1910 Census, Kiawa, Harper, Oklahoma
Charles F Foster age 56, married 33 years, b. IL, F b. IL M b. IL
Clarice Foster age 50 (mother of 10, 10 living) b. Kansas, F b. IN, M b. IL
Bert Foster age 25 b. Kansas, father b. Illinois, mother b. Kansas
Edgar Foster age 20 b. Kansas, father b. Illinois, mother b. Kansas
Bertha Foster age 19 b. Kansas, father b. Illinois, mother b. Kansas
Carl Foster age 16 b. Kansas, father b. Illinois, mother b. Kansas
Lola Foster age 14 b. Kansas, father b. Illinois, mother b. Kansas
Alice Foster age 12 b. Kansas, father b. Illinois, mother b. Kansas
Francis Foster age 8 b. Kansas, father b. Illinois, mother b. Kansas
******

Foster families come and families go – but this history of the Fosters and allies families goes on generation after generation.

MALINDA, 3rd child of Robert L & SARAH ANN FOSTER, was born on the old homestead just east of Frankfort, Kansas. When about 7 years old, her family moved to Washington County, and settled on a farm south of Haddam, Ks. Here she grew to adulthood, met and married Marcus M. Slover.

A few years after they married, Malinda and Marcus Slover moved to the old Solomon River Settlement, where they bought a farm. Here they lived till Marcus' death, at which time Malinda settled near the now-gone town of Raymond, Oklahoma. Marcus Slover is buried in the Allison Cemetery, southeast of Jennings, Ks. Malinda is buried in a cemetery near the now-gone town of Raymond, Oklahoma.

MARCUS M. SLOVER b. Aug. 27, 1860 d. Mar. 26, 1905
MALINDA (FOSTER) b. Sept. 23, 1862 d. Dec. 19, 1912
Were married Jan. 1, 1885 Kansas. To this union was born: NELLIE GERTRUDE b. Nov. 9, 1885 d. Oct. 5 1975.

Notes:
1870 ***Census, Mill Creek, Washington, Kansas****, Pg. 5 No. 319*
Robert Foster age 36, b. Indiana, farmer, land $300
Sarah age 35 b. Illinois
Clarissa age 10 b. Kansas
Malinda age 8 b. Kansas
Daniel age 4 b. Kansas
Harrison age 2, b. Kansas

1880 Census, Independence, Nodaway, Missouri

Robert age 45 b. Indiana, farmer, mother born in Kentucky
Sarah A age 45 b. Illinois, father b. Virginia, mother b. Kentucky
Malinda age 17 b. Kansas
David age 13 b. Kansas
Dorcas age 9 b. Kansas
Joseph age 6 b. Kansas

1895 Kansas Census, Haddam, Washington, Kansas
M Slover, age 34, b. IL
Malinda Slover, age 32 b. KA
Nellie H. Slover, age 9 b. KA

NELLIE GERTRUDE (GERTIE) was born near Haddam Kansas, and came west with her parents to the old Solomon River settlement. Here, she grew to adulthood, met and married John Harvey Wilson. They married in Oberlin, Kansas and set up housekeeping on the Solomon River, near her old home. In later years, they moved to eastern Kansas, to Lenora, Oklahoma, then back to the Solomon River.

John Wilson is buried in the Jennings, Kansas Cemetery. Gertrude then moved to St. Helens, Oregon, where she resided for many years. Today, she makes her home with her youngest son, Mark Wilson, in Beaverton, a suburb of Portland, Oregon.

Social Security Death Index *<http://www.ancestry.com/*
about Nellie Wilson
Name: Nellie Wilson
SSN: 540-60-4022
Last Residence:97056 Scappoose, Columbia, Oregon, United States of America
Born: 9 Nov 1885
Died: Oct 1975
State (Year) SSN issued: Oregon (1965)

JOHN H. WILSON b. Sept 9, 1883 d. July 26, 1932
NELLIE GERTRUDE (SLOVER) b. Nov. 9,1885 d. Oct. 4, 1975
Were married Aug. 9, 1905, Kansas. To this union were born: 1. WILLIAM ARTHUR, 2. VIOLA BELLE, 3. CLAUDE HARVEY, 4. ROY WALLACE, 5. HAZEL JANE, 6. KENNETH GEORGE, 7. MARK. Details on children:

1. WILLIAM ARTHUR b. Jan. 20, 1907 Jennings, KS d. Apr. 2, 1968 Tulsa, OK. Married GLENNA HEITMAN 1929 in Norton, Kansas. Their son: CHARLES DUANE b. Feb. 11, 1933.
2. VIOLA BELLE b. Feb. 29, 1908 Jennings, KS d. Apr. 2, 1968, m. IRA KEEVER on Oct. 18, 1933 in McCook, NB. They moved to Sterling, Colorado, where she died and is buried. Her husband is still living (in 1979). Their children: a. DONNA LUCILLE, b. MARK EUGENE, c. CAROLYN JOY, d. TOLA. Details on children:
    a. DONNA LUCILLE m. CLIFFORD AHMAN in Denver, CO. Their children:
        1) BRENT
        2) MICHEAL
        3) GREGORY
        4) CHRIS.

b. MARK EUGENE, m. JO ANN EVERS in Sterling, CO. Their children:
    1) CINDA
    2) CHRISTENA
    3) DOUGLAS

c. CAROLYN JOY m. RONALD BROOKMAN in Denver, CO and lives in Torrance, CA, where their son was born: JOHN DAVID.

d. TOLA m. ROGER TRAUTMAN in Denver, CO, and now lives in Astoria, Illinois, where their children were born:
    1) PAUL ROGER
    2) LODY LYN
    3) CARA

e. BETH LOUISE m. ROBERT KREMS in Denver, CO where their children were born: PEMIE LYN. All of Viola and Ira Keever's children were born in Bird City, Kansas and went with their parents to Sterling, Colorado.

3. CLAUDE HARVEY b. May 20, 1909, born in Eskridge, Kansas, made the swing to eastern Kansas, to Oklahoma, back to Kansas, then to Oregon. In St. Helens, Ore., he married Norma Walborn, Jan. 5 1951. They have a daughter:-- Catherine Heather. Catherine H. was born in St. Helens, Ore., and married in Napa, Idaho to Paul Truesden, Oct. 15, 1970. They have a child:--Nicole Dawn.
4. ROY WALLACE b. Mar. 27, 1911 in Lenora, Oklahoma, went with his mother to St. Helens, Oregon. Here he met and married Mildred Josephson, Nov. 10, 1939. Their children: -- Janet Lorraine, Boyd Roy, Lyle Allen. Janet L. married #1 Lester Rall -- #2, John Peterson. I have no other data on either marriage. Boyd R. married Joan Horn. She was a widow with a son: -- Dicky Horn, Feb. 25, 1964. --- No other children to marriage #2.
5. HAZEL JANE b. June 4, 1914 in Lenora, OK, came to St. Helens, Oregon with her mother. Here she met and married JOHN FRANCIS HREN Mar. 8, 1941 Longview, WA.
    a. JOHN JOSEPH m. BARBARA JOHNSON Sept. 12, 1969 in Scappoose, Oregon. This town, with the odd-sounding name, probably Indian in origin, is located between St. Helens and Portland, Oregon.
    b. JANE HAZEL (This is the first time I have run into a reversal of Christian names between a mother and her daughter.)
6. KENNETH GEORGE b. July 23, 1923 d. June 16, 1937
7. MARK WAYNE b. Feb. 13, 1927 Jennings, Kansas. Went with his mother to St. Helens, Oregon and married JOSEPHINE WINANS. They had: MARCIA JOSEPHINE, who married LEO D. QUARTY.

The material on this Wilson family was given to me by Gertie Wilson.

In case you are wondering where we are, we are in the midst of the family line of Polly, Eldest daughter of Harrison & Anna Margaret (Bartlett) Foster, through Polly's son Robert to grandson, Daniel.

Now that we have had that refreshing pause you should be wide awake and ready to get jogging again. I know that this material has been lying around for some time, some

data as long as 300 years, but some has been lost for all time due to that long period, so let us get moving before more valuable data is lost.
******Chart pg. 40*******

DANIEL, 4th child of ROBERT L. & SARAH ANN (COX) FOSTER, was born in Brown Co., Kansas, where his parents resided for a short time. For some reason unknown to me Daniel went to Warwick, Pennsylvania, where he met and married ALICE CATERHINE GETZ. They lived in Osborne Co. and in Haddam, Kansas, then moved to Fresno, California. Daniel & Alice C. Getz Foster are buried in Fresno, Calif.

Arthur G Foster (son of Arthur Henry Foster) wrote: "My Dad's father and mother -- Grandma (Alice Catherine Getz) and Grandpa (Daniel Foster)-lived in Biola, California, near Fresno. They came to visit and stayed a couple of times when I was growing up at the Salt works. Grandma Foster always brought along her Bantam chickens including a very mean rooster which could fly up on the garage roof, and could peck you and scratch you with his spurs if you got too close!

Grandpa's car was a huge Overland (air-cooled engine) which had plenty of room in the back and on top for chicken cages and baggage. I once went up in the Sierras with Grandpa Foster and Dad and his brothers to get a tree trunk for firewood for their kitchen. The piece of trunk was six feet in diameter and eight feet long (sawed from the 50- foot original trunk of a giant tree). It was the only load on a trailer that they towed down a narrow mountain road from which you could look nearly straight down on the San Joaquin River thousands of feet below.

Back in Biola, they sawed up the trunk and chopped it into firewood. My cousins, Frank and Foster Curtis, came to visit at the same time. Their Mom was my Dad's sister, Aunt Myrtle. She and Grandma Foster always smiled at me and made me feel loved.

My cousins, Clyde and Cecil Foster were sons of my Dad's brothers. Frank and Foster Curtis were sons of Dad's sister, Myrtle. One Christmas in Biola, all five of us made a solemn vow to own a home, a car (and other "stuff") by a certain date in the 20th century. The amazing thing is we all actually succeeded later on in keeping that most solemn vow.

Another of Dad's sisters, Aunt Emma, had daughters. When they visited us from Kansas, we practiced being girl and boy friends, but fortunately without any hanky-panky." --Arthur Glenn Foster, grandson of Daniel Foster, son of Arthur Henry Foster)

DANIEL FOSTER, b. June 23, 1866 d. Sept. 16, 1943
ALICE CATHERINE GETZ b. Mar. 24, 1868 d. Jan. 7, 1952
Were married Mar. 19, 1888, Penn. To this union were born:

1. MINNIE VIOLA b. Mar. 15, 1889 d. 9 Sep 1974 m. CHARLES AARON WILSON
2. ELMER JACOB b. May 20, 1891 m. NORA BIGGER SMITH
3. ARTHUR HENRY b. Mar. 28, 1893 d. May 25, 1968 m. LENORA THOMAS
4. JOSEPH EDWARD b. Jan. 15, 1895 d. Oct. 2, 1954 (twin)
5. JESSIE E. b. Jan. 15, 1895 d. Jan. 24, 1895 (twin)
6. ALBERT ROBERT b. Dec. 19, 1896 d. 28 Apr 1984 m. #1 RACHEL ELIZABETH CURTIS
7. EARL CHESTER b. Apr. 9, 1899 d. Sept 18, 1968 m. WINIFRED GLADYS CASE
8. MYRTLE SYBILLA b. Mar. 5, 1902 d. 31 Oct 1981 m. #1 FRED GRATTO
9. JOHN MARTIN b. Apr. 4, 1904 d. Mar. 5, 1959 m. FAYE OLIVIA SMITH

MINNIE VIOLA (# 1 above), born in Osborne Co., Kansas, married in western Ks. to CHARLES AARON WILSON, nephew to John H. Wilson, pg. 41. After the birth of their children, Charles & Minnie Wilson moved to Fresno, California. In later years, both lived in the Masonic Home, Union City, Calif., where Charles died. Minnie V. was still living in the home in early 1972. *Note from Adrienne: John H Wilson was Charles' brother, not uncle.*

CHARLES AARON WILSON b. June 26, 1885 d. Mary 1972
MINNIE VIOLA (FOSTER) b. Mar. 15, 1889 d. 9 Sep 1974
Were married Jan. 15, 1910, Kansas. To this union were born:

1. EMMA CATHERINE b. Jan. 28, 1911 d. 11 Mar 1996 m. ALBERT HENRY ANDERSON Oct. 28, 1934 in Oberlin, Kansas, and made their home in Fresno, Calif., where their children were born. Albert H. is buried in Fresno. Children:
   a. JOLENE RUTH b. Oct. 6, 1935 m. and divorced M.S. MACY. No children
   b. GLENNA ROSE m. JOHN D. BROWN, Nov. 10, 1956. Children:
      1) DAVID JOHN
      2) JEFFREY DALE
   c. CHARLENE KAY m. CARL HUNTER FORD June 26, 1959. Their children:
      1) WALTER HENRY
      2) TINA LYNNE
      3) MICHILE CARLENE
2. DANIEL ELBRIDGE b. May 8, 1913 m. ROSALIE RONEY July 15, 1939, Calif. Rosalie b. Apr. 27, 1917. Children:
   a. MICHAEL WARREN
   b. LAWRENCE ALAN m. LAURIE GRAHAM June 1966
   c. KATHLEEN DEBORAH
   d. APRIL LENNEA
3. ERNEST EUGENE m. AVA BURROWS May 30, 1941. Ava b. Nov. 22, 1917. Children:
   a. DOUGLAS ALLYN m. JUDY CIUMAN July 21, 1966
   b. PAMELA JO
4. MYRTLE DEBORAH b. Dec. 6, 1918 m. JAMES LAWRENCE SMITH June 30, 1937. He was born Jan. 10, 1914. Children:
   a. EVALYN LORRAINE m. WENDELL DANIEL GRATH July 17, 1958. Children:
      1) STEPHEN BRUCE
      2) KENNETH BOYD b
   b. JAMES CLARENCE Jr. m. SANDRA LEE CORNELIUS b. Nov. 1, 1940. Children:
      1) DUANE KEVIN
      2) DEREK TODD
   c. KEITH AARON m. BETTY LOU JONES Oct. 30, 1964. Children:
      1) TAMMI RANAE
      2) DONALD WAYNE
5. RUTH MARJORIE b. June 19, 1923 d. Sept. 9, 1962

ELMER JACOB, 2nd child of DANIEL & ALICE CATHERINE (GETZ) FOSTER, was born near Haddam, Kansas. He married NORA BIGGER SMITH but had no children.

ARTHUR HENRY, 3rd child of DANIEL & ALICE CATHERINE (GETZ) FOSTER, was born in Bentonville, Arkansas, where the family resided for a time. During WWI he was with the 43rd Infantry Division, which took its training near Salt Lake City, Utah. He liked the country so well he decided to make it his home. After the war Arthur found employment with the Morton Salt Co. of Salt Lake City as a machinist. This factory was founded by his wife's grandfather, Thomas Coslett Thomas and was called the Royal Salt Company until it was later bought by Morton Salt. Five generations of Thomas' descendants (all Fosters) have worked at the Salt Lake Factory. Later, Arthur Henry Foster became supervisor of the salt evaporation ponds, a job he held until retirement after 40 years with the company. His grandson, John Frederick (son of Wanda Foster Frederick), is currently the Factory Director of the Morton Salt Co., SLC Division.

In Utah ARTHUR HENRY met and married LeNORA, daughter of MARY ELIZA (MAMIE) COON & JOHN PHILLIPS THOMAS. John P. Thomas was a world-class battle-ax and club juggler who performed on vaudeville until his leg was badly injured when he was pinned between two train cars at the railroad yard where he worked his day job. The leg was amputated and he used a wooden leg the rest of his life. LeNora and her sister Edrie had been trained by and performed with their father until his accident. More on the Thomas Family following this line of Fosters.

LeNora (Thomas) Foster, wife of Arthur Henry Foster, and her family and ancestors are members of the Mormon Church, and Arthur Henry joined the church while his son was serving in WWII as a navigator in the Air Force. One of the church's special services is to honor the ancestors of its members. It was through LeNora's efforts that I got most of the material on this family, especially the descendants of Robert L. Foster, youngest member of the Polly-Dennis Foster family.

AUTHUR HENRY FOSTER b. Mar. 28, 1893 Bentonville, Ark. d. May 25, 1967 Salt Lake City, Utah
LENORA (THOMAS) b. Apr. 9, 1901 Coonville, Pleasant Grove, UT d. Aug, 9, 1983 SLC, Utah
Were married Dec. 5, 1919, Utah. To this union were born:

1. COSLETT THOMAS b. Feb. 25, 1921, died same day
2. ARTHUR GLENN b. Jan. 8, 1922 Saltair, Salt Lake, UT d. Oct 1, 2001 Salt Lake City, UT
3. WANDA MARY-ALICE b. Apr. 27, Saltair, Salt Lake, UT 1924 d. 2007 Salt Lake City, UT
4. GLORIA LENORA b. July 14, Salt Lake City, UT 1928 d. 7 Dec 2011 Salt Lake, UT

ARTHUR GLENN FOSTER (#2 above – Adrienne's father) was born in Saltair, Utah, which was the community made up of employees of the Morton Salt Company, where his father worked. He met GLORIA THOMPSON in Salt Lake City, Utah at the Salt Lake Community Pool and later, while serving at an Air Base near San Marcos, Texas, he sent for Gloria to come and marry him, which she did on 13 Jun 1943. Soon after, his squadron was sent to England where he served in WWII as a B-17 navigator. He was in several of the Schweinfurt raids over Germany and his plane was shot down during one of these raids. Everyone bailed out except the pilot and Glenn, who was sent back to check on the bombardier. The plane was hit again and Dad fell out the bomb bay doors, hitting his head on one of the doors as he exited the plane. He doesn't remember pulling his parachute chord, but somehow the parachute opened and he woke up on the ground staring up into the faces of two German farmers who had been recruited as soldiers.

Dad was able to overpower them and ran across fields and hid in bushes while dogs tracked him. He walked for miles in a river to throw them off the scent, and at night walked on roads paved with asphalt, which are more difficult for dogs to track. When he saw headlights he dove into bushes and hid. At last he arrived at the border and was treated by a French doctor for a back injury sustained when he hit the ground unconscious. The French Underground, for whom my family will be forever grateful, kept Dad in hiding while he told them everything he knew of planned allied targets and trained them in weapons and combat. They eventually smuggled him into Switzerland, where he stayed with other allied pilots for nine months until he was sent back to the United States.

His family knew nothing of his whereabouts for nearly a year, but Gloria prayed and received a strong feeling that Glenn was alive and unharmed. It was during this time that his father, Arthur Henry Foster, went out to the Salt Flats where they lived and prayed that God would spare his son. A plane flew overhead, circling him and dipping its wings. He took that as a sign from heaven that Dad was okay and he decided to join the Mormon church and stayed an active member for the rest of his life.

During his many years in the Air Force, Arthur G. took his family to many posts around the globe. Most of his children were born on military posts, two in Alaska, others in the US, and one in the Tunisian Desert. Their daughter, Adrienne (child #7), is one of the few, if not only, American children to be baptized in the waters of the Mediterranean Sea on the shores of Tripoli, Libya, North Africa, while she and her parents and family were stationed there at Wheelus Air Force Base, which at that time was operated by the U.S. Air force. There is considerable contrast, and half a world between the zero degrees of Alaska and the shadeless 113 degrees of the Tunisian Desert (actually the Sahara Desert).

While living there the family members served in 19 positions in The Church of Jesus Christ of Latter Day Saints, under difficult circumstances. They were under the jurisdiction of the French Mission 1500 miles away. They were in much danger from some of the local Arabs who were very antagonistic towards Americans, but other Arabs were friendly, and some of the country's leaders were also friendly to them. Those friends had been educated in Great Britain and other places, and they tried to improve their living standards, to lift themselves and their countrymen above the poverty and life that had been theirs for hundreds of years.

The Fosters also attended Arab weddings and serves as guest teachers in the schools and helped to provide medical help and employment to some local citizens. The Fosters endured the dreadful dust storms of the hotter time of the year. However, they also enjoyed an occasional swim in the beautiful Mediterranean Sea. They visited many of the ancient and famous ruins on the northern Libya coast at Sabratha near Tunis and Leptis Magna on the Caire Highway.

Child #12, Kelvin Tanner, was born at Wheelus AFB, located in Suk el Giuna, Tagiura, Tripoli, Libya, North Africa, with his eleven brothers and sisters also living there. Arthur "Glenn" Foster was a Major in the Air Force at that base. He served as the Chief of Plans and Requirements, Communications-Electronics Directorate, HQ 17th Air Force, with responsibilities affecting 27 air bases in the Mediterranean Countries.

Arthur G. Foster worked in 1963 at Vandenberg Air Force Base, California as a Nuclear Engineer---(nuclear weapons effects on ballistic missile weapon systems, Hill Air Force Base, Utah 1965 until retirement.) He was a Consulting Engineer in relativistic power development with private industry. Registered Professional Engineer, Electrical Engineering in State of Ohio#19235 and State of Utah #2222. This family are all members of The Church of Jesus Christ of Latter Day Saints.

In 1964 Dad retired as a Lt. Colonel, after 22 years in the US Air Force, but he continued to work for a few years for the Eyring Institute in Provo Utah on the development of synthetic diamonds and then went back to work for the Air Force as the Director of the Missile Hardness Program at Hill AFB, Utah. It was here that he developed the Lithium battery in order to facilitate start-up for missile testing. He offered the formula to the Defense Department in Washington, but they weren't interested, so he gave the formula to the Israeli government, who immediately began manufacturing batteries and putting them to use in military flashlights and communication equipment. Later, Israel sold the formula back to US companies.

He personally invented the long-range communications antenna used by the military today. The immediate benefit of this antenna first became evident during the Cold War when the Soviet Union used Electromagnetic frequency (EMF) blasts to disrupt communications and electronic function in U.S. embassies. Glenn's antenna was impervious to EM interference and so the soviet plan failed.

ARTHUR GLENN FOSTER b. Jan. 8, 1922 Saltair, Salt Lake, UT d. Oct 1, 2001 Salt Lake City, UT
GLORIA (THOMPSON) b. May 19, 1923 d. Jan 18, 2007 Salt Lake City, Salt Lake, Utah
Were married June 13, 1943, San Marcos, Texas. To this union were born:

1. KATHERINE b. Mar. 12, 1944 Salt Lake City, UT d. 23 May 2009 Stansbury Park, UT

2. REBECCA JEAN
3. GLORY LYNN (GOGI)
4. ARTHUR GLEN (BUTCH) JR.
5. MARSHA
6. KENNETH STEWART
7. ADRIENNE
8. BLAINE THOMAS
9. BRIAN JOHNSON b. Nov. 14, 1955 Elmendorf AFB, Anchorage, Alaska d. Jan 31, 1983 SLC, UT
10. WARREN SCOTT
11. TRUDY
12. KELVIN TANNER b. Feb. 15, 1960 Wheelus AFB, Suk el Giuna, Tagiura, Tripoli, Libya, North Africa, d. 2001 Salt Lake City, Utah
13. MARALEE
14. CORWIN THOMPSON
15. DANA GETZ
16. LOEN STAKER

Wow! I'm glad I don't have to feed a family as large as that!

KATHERINE (Kathie) FOSTER (#1 above) married RAYMOND LEE SHEPHERD, and lived in Orem, Utah, where Raymond was an instructor in the college. They moved to Stansbury Park near Salt Lake City and bought the home that Mormon Prophet Ezra Taft Benson was born in. Kathie was a paralegal for a prominent Salt Lake attorney for many years. She held numerous callings in her ward and stake and was involved in many community events. Kathy died sooner than anyone expected one day while napping peacefully on the couch. The cause was heart failure.

RAYMOND LEE SHEPHERD Sr.
KATHERINE FOSTER b. Mar. 12, 1944 d. 23 May 2009 Stansbury Park, UT
Were married June 4, 1963, Utah. To this union were born:

1. RAYMOND "LEE" Jr. m. #1 JULIE PHILLIPS (divorced). and had 1) CLAYTON, 2) KASEY, 3) COLTEN, 4) KELSEY, and 5) CARLY. Lee married #2 KAMI GOODALL (divorced) and had 1) KANYON and 2) KALEB. Lee Married #3 DEBORAH. Lee has worked many different construction jobs, including backhoe operator, and drove semi-trucks for many years. He currently works in construction.
2. DUANE WINSTON m. KELLY. They have 7 children: 1) ETHAN KIMBALL, 2) HUNTER TAFT (who recently married MICHELLE CELESTE HUDDLESTON), 3) JACK HARRISON, 4) EMMA ELIZABETH, 5) CONNOR REID, 6) KADEN McKAY, and 7) BREVAN THOMAS. Duane works for an oil company in Utah.
3. PRESTON OWEN m. TINA (D), m. WENDY WILSON. Preston is a construction supervisor for a commercial construction company in Utah.
4. KRISTINE
5. DAVID GLENN

6. PAUL ALEXANDER m. HEATHER ELKINGTON. They have 4 children: 1) DALLIN ELKINGTON (currently serving an LDS mission in So. Korea, 2) ANDREW JOHN, 3) CELIA ISABEL, and 4) LILLIAN ABIGAIL. Paul is a very successful endodontist in Georgia and is a Mormon Bishop. His wife sings like an angel and is a professional vocalist. She sings and acts in theatre productions and has produced several CD's.
7. LILLIAN KARABETH
8. STEWART L. m. JAMIE MICHELLE PETERSON and had: 1) PORTER OWEN, and 2) SAXON LUKE.

REBECCA (Becky) JEAN FOSTER, 2nd child of ARTHUR GLENN & GLORIA (THOMPSON) FOSTER, married STEPHEN KENYON CORNWALL, who was born in Salt Lake Co., Utah. They were married in Salt Lake City, UT. Becky graduated from the University of Utah in English education and taught school and college for many years. She has published several books on Mormon Church history which are used as sources by today's historians, including the biography of Mormon Prophet Spencer W. Kimball, "The Handcart Companies," and "Audacious Women." She started her own publishing company, Uintah Springs Press, in 2000. REBECCA married #2, JOHN BARTHOLOMEW and lives in Washington State. She and her husband live on a ranch in Washington with several llamas, dogs, and cats.

STEPHEN KENYON CORNWALL
REBECCA or "BECKY" JEAN (FOSTER)
Were married Aug. 23, 1968, Utah (divorced). To this union were born:

1. NATHAN KENYON, P.A. married REBECCA CHAMBERS, and has 4 children: 1) SAMUEL, 2) NATALIE, 3) ALISON, 4) ADELAIDE. Nathan served as an Army Medic in Iraq and Afghanistan for many years and is now a Physician's Asst. at a medical clinic.
2. JOEL m. KELLY and they have a daughter, RHIANNON. Joel is a Geologist and sink hole specialist in Florida, the capitol of sink holes.
3. BABY GIRL died at birth

GLORY LYNN (GOGI), 3rd child of ARTHUR GLENN & GLORIA (THOMPSON) FOSTER, married ANTHONY OGDEN VAN DUREN, who was born in Salt Lake City, Utah. Gogi graduated from the University of Hayward in California in Music Education and taught music in the schools for many years. She started three youth symphonies in the Bay area which still function today. She is an accomplished musician, composer, and artist. Toney is a retired Accountant and is an accomplished musician as well as expert in woodworking. He has built beautiful wooden canoes, Adirondack chairs, and cabinets.

ANTHONY OGDEN VAN DUREN
GLORY LYNN "GOGI" (FOSTER)
Were married Oct. 20, 1969, Utah. To this union were born:

1. NICHOLAS ANTON, who married SHANNON KELLER (no children, but lots of dogs). He was a professional musician for many years and now breeds Show Mastiffs and paints animals and landscapes.
2. DREW, who married ROBIN DANIELSON and they have 2 children: 1) JAKOB, and 2) LINDSEY. Drew is an aeronautical engineer and Robin taught school for many years. Drew is an accomplished cellist.
3. LARA LYNN, who married JAMEY GARDNER and had 2 daughters: 1) MADELINE and 2) REESE. Jamie is an engineer and Lara has a degree in business and works at home with her computer. She is also a very accomplished violinist.

ARTHUR GLENN JR, 4th child of ARTHUR GLENN & GLORIA (THOMPSON) FOSTER, served an LDS mission in the Peru-Andes Mission and obtained his Masters Degree in Middle East Studies from the University of Utah. He married MIRIAM from Bolivia. He works as Security Manager for Burton Lumber in SLC. They have no children but have often babysat and cared for Skye Brian Sauer, their deceased brother Brian's grandchild.

MARSHA, 5th child of ARTHUR GLENN & GLORIA (THOMPSON) FOSTER, served an LDS mission in Brazil and afterwards met and married RODNEY JAY SR., who also served a mission in Brazil. Rodney worked for many years as a psychiatric assistant at the Utah Mental Hospital and is now retired. Their children:

1. JEANETTE who served an LDS mission in Korea, married COLIN BOOTH and has 8 children: 1) JULIA, 2) CALEB, 3(MEDLEY, 4) BRIGHAM, 5) GLORIA ANGEL, 6) JENSON, 7) LYDIA, and 8) BRONSEN. COLIN is a Marketing executive and Jeanette performs, teaches and composes music.
2. Dr. RODNEY Jr. who served an LDS mission in Finland, married MELISSA STRUVE, a Registered Nurse, and became an Emergency Room Doctor. They have 5 children: 1) NATHAN, 2) ANNIKKA, 3) AUBREY, 4) JOSIE, and 5) HENRY.
3. PETER who served an LDS mission in Russia, married KIRA WILKEN, and became an attorney. They have 2 children: 1) ADLEE and, 2) MASON.
4. JILL, a dietician who married STEWART CRAIG, a professional artist. They have 3 children: 1) ABIGAIL, 2) GABRIEL, and 3) PENELOPE.
5. SALLY who married SHANE TALBOT and has 4 children: 1) MAEGAN FRANCIS, 2) SPENCER SHANE, 3) JOSHUA DILLON, and 4) LEWIS GLENN.
6. JOANIE who married AARON OLSEN and has 5 children: 1) LUKE, 2) EMMETT, 3) NOAH,
4) LILY JANE, and 5) AUDRA. She sings professionally and teaches vocal lessons.
7. JESHUA who married LESLIE MARIE STAY Nov. 22, 2011 in Draper, Utah. They have a daughter, Sophie.
8. TIMOTHY MICHAEL who married ELISA ANGEL STEPHENSON Apr. 8, 2011 in St. George, Utah. They have two children: 1) JESSE and 2) OLIVIA GRACE.
9. ARIEL NATALIE who served an LDS mission in Romania and married JARED BRUTON and has a daughter, VIVIAN WYNNE.

10. THOMAS HARRISON, who served an LDS mission in Brazil and married CAMILA SOUSA. They have a son: TANNER.
11. JARED STEPHENS who served an LDS mission in Argentina and married DAIANA VERENISE INSFRAN CENTURION and has a son, NATHANIEL GLENN.
12. JEREMY, a high-school track star who served an LDS mission.
13. EMILY

KENNETH STEWART FOSTER 6th child of ARTHUR GLENN & GLORIA (THOMPSON) FOSTER served an LDS mission in Australia, and married JOANNE BELLO in 1974. He graduated from the University of Utah and started his own advertising agency. He is a consultant for the University of Utah Adult Education Department and for the NY Stock Exchange in Continuing Education. He served in a Stake Presidency for the Mormon Church for 12 years in Salt Lake City. Children:

1. MATTHEW, who married BRITTANY and has two children, ABIGAIL and _______.
2. JASON, m. WHITNEY PAINTER and has three children, a daughter named SAILOR, and two sons named LENNY, and CHIP.
3. KELSEY, who graduated from the U. of Utah with a degree in history and works for the Utah Bar Association.

ADRIENNE 7th child of ARTHUR GLENN & GLORIA (THOMPSON) FOSTER, served an LDS mission to Uruguay and married JOHN ROBERT POTTER in 1982 in Salt Lake City, Utah. John has been an IT Manager and Director, a CIO, a manager of a server department for a large hospital, and a Project Manager for the same hospital. Adrienne has spent her life as a child safety activist and founded the websites Kidsread.net and Kidsindanger.net. She also taught piano and guitar for many years. Their Children:

1. GRACE ELIZA m. JEREMY RINDLISBACHER, P.A. and they have a son, TAYVIN JEREMY, and a daughter, BROOKE ELIZA. Grace graduated with a degree in Music Education and plays various instruments and sings. Jeremy is a Physician's Asst. at an Urgent Care Clinic.
2. CHARITY ANN graduated with a degree in Bassoon performance.

BLAINE THOMAS 8th child of ARTHUR GLENN & GLORIA (THOMPSON) FOSTER was called to serve an LDS mission to Spain but had to return home from the Language Training Mission for medical reasons. Blaine is diagnosed as schizophrenic and manic depressive and currently lives in a psychiatric ward.

BRIAN JOHNSON 9th child of ARTHUR GLENN & GLORIA (THOMPSON) FOSTER, married CAROL ZIMPFER and had DANIEL. This marriage ended in divorce and Brian married LISA JOYCE JENSEN and had RACHAEL MELISSA, who has a son named SKYE BRIAN SAUER. Skye's father is MICHAEL WILLIAM SAUER. Brian loved poetry and art and was very kind-hearted. One time when he and his brother Warren were throwing snowballs at passing cars a man stopped his car and chased Warren. Just as he was about to catch Warren, Brian jumped out from behind a tree and yelled, "It was me who did it! Catch me if you can!" The man ran after Brian but couldn't catch him and gave up. Meanwhile Warren had escaped. Sadly, Brian passed away 31 Jan 1983 from an accidental drug overdose. Lisa supported Rachael and Skye for many years, working at an auto rental company and as a hotel clerk. Sadly, she passed away on 10 May 2016 from heart failure caused by damage from an episode of Rheumatic fever as a child. Skye lives with his father now.

WARREN SCOTT 10th child of ARTHUR GLENN & GLORIA (THOMPSON) FOSTER, served an LDS mission to Arizona and married KAYE JACKMAN. Warren served as an Air Traffic Controller and Supervisor in the ATC in Anchorage, Alaska and in Palmdale, CA until he retired in 2010. He served as a contract Air Traffic Controller during the war in Afghanistan for one year and now teaches his expertise in his field to others. He enjoys hiking, rock-climbing, kayaking, hunting, and fishing in Alaska, as well as playing the guitar and singing, and acting in local productions. He was the Casting Director for locally-filmed comedy, "The Moose Movie." Their children:

1. SARAH served an LDS mission in Venezuela, married TODD STICE and has three children: BRIELLE, ASHTON, LAINEY. She is a fitness coach, a vocalist and pianist.
2. SCOTT served an LDS mission to Recife, Brazil and is a rather amazing professional singer and guitarist, as well as an ocean gold-miner.
3. DEVAN served an LDS mission to Mexico City, Mexico, married MAURA ALLEN in 2010 and has a daughter, CAPRI. They have another child on the way. He sings and plays the guitar.
4. LEVI JACKMAN has a beautiful singing voice and is a professional photographer.
5. RACHELE m. JOHN ROHDE in 2011 and had MYLA. She has a beautiful voice and is a beautician.
6. MARTIN (MARTY) served an LDS mission to Caiubai, Brazil. He sings and plays the guitar.
7. APRIL also sings and is active in band and drama in her High School and very involved in Young Women's in the LDS Church.

Tragically, Warren lost his wife and these children lost their mother on July 7, 2016 due to pancreatic cancer. Their father took all of these musical children on a hike up Kaye's favorite mountain in Alaska to sing and play farewell songs to her.

TRUDY 11th child of ARTHUR GLENN & GLORIA (THOMPSON) FOSTER, married Dr. STEVEN RUSSELL, who is a retina surgeon and Director of Retina Research at Iowa State University. Trudy has a degree in English and in Interior Design, and likes to write. Their children:

1. CHRISTOPHER RUSSELL, an attorney who married JENNIFER (JEN) YOUNGBLUT (b. 1 Sep 1983 Iowa) and had three children: NATHAN CHRISTOPHER, ANDREW JONATHAN, and AMELIA ANN.
2. Dr. JONATHAN FOSTER RUSSELL, a pediatrician who married ROBIN RIBNIK. They have a son, JONATHAN FOSTER RUSSELL, Jr.
3. CAROLYN REBECCA or "DAZI," and attorney who married DANIEL JOSEPH WALLACE.

KELVIN (KELLY) TANNER, 12th child of ARTHUR GLENN & GLORIA (THOMPSON) FOSTER, married #1 BONNIE TAYLOR and had:

1. SHANE
2. SHANNA
3. STEVE

KELLY divorced Bonnie and later married TERESA LUCIE BECK who was born in Australia. When Kelly was 11 he had an accident on the family swing, which hung from a very tall tree and extended over a river. He fell into the shallow, rocky river, landed on some rocks, and broke his arm and his nose. Later he had a car accident and broke his jaw. He had an on-the-job injury while working as a carpenter and accidentally sawed off all of the fingers of his right hand. After 13 hours of microsurgery the fingers were reattached. This was when microsurgery was first being implemented. He eventually lost his little finger but all the other fingers regained much of their previous function, although the hand was often painful for the rest of his life. Later, Kelly had a motorcycle accident in which he broke both legs.

One day Kelly woke up with a terrible pain in his throat. Lucy took him to the hospital, but the doctors could not find the cause. For a week he couldn't eat, and could drink very little. Lucy took him back to the hospital and demanded a Cat scan, which was scheduled for the following day. It revealed a tumor the size of a baseball in his throat. Because of Kelly's hyperactivity, his marijuana use, and alcohol use, the painkillers the doctors administered had no effect. When the pain became unbearable Kelly checked himself out of the hospital and went to use his marijuana. Unfortunately, the combination of drugs, medication, alcohol, and the terrible pain put Kelly in a state of mind where he took his own life via a rifle shot through the chin. Because paramedics were nearby they were able to put him quickly on life support. He arrived at the hospital brain-dead but with his organs still thriving, and he became an organ donor. One man received his heart, four people received parts of his liver, and others received parts of his eyes and joints. We were shocked and saddened at his passing, but gratified to know that some good could come of it. He lives on in our hearts.

Lucie had 5 children from a previous marriage.

MARALEE 13th child of ARTHUR GLENN & GLORIA (THOMPSON) FOSTER married #1 GREG JONES and had:

1. BENJAMIN ALLEN m. STEVIEE MARIE DUNN in 2012. They divorced
2. ELYSE m. DEREK JOHNSON in 2010 and had EMMA MADELINE.

Maralee divorced Greg and had OLIVIA. She married #2 GREG TIFFIN in a beautiful ceremony in Canyonlands National Park. No children in this union, but Greg adopted Olivia. Maralee is a loan representative and Greg Tiffin is a real estate agent.

CORWIN THOMPSON 14th child of ARTHUR GLENN & GLORIA (THOMPSON) FOSTER married COLETTE KENNEDY and had:

1. MEGAN m. JUSTIN DALTON and has three children: CHASE, CARTER TODD, and CAPRI CHANLEE or "CC."
2. HALEY m. JAVIER S. PUELLO
3. COLESON

Cory managed a Burton Lumber Store for many years and was then promoted to District Manager. He later became District Sales Manager for Burton Lumber. He has served as a Bishop in the Mormon Church in Salt Lake City. Colette has been a Dental Assistant for many years.

DANA GETZ 15th child of ARTHUR GLENN & GLORIA (THOMPSON) FOSTER, served a mission for the LDS church in Texas and later married #1 LAUREL MILLIGAN and had:

1. BETHANY (Bennie)
2. DILLON

They divorced and Laura married Tadd Giles. DANA m. CHRISTINE, who had two children from a previous marriage whom Dana is raising, a daughter named HANNAH CHRISTINE and a son named RILEY. Dana owns a trucking firm in Salt Lake City, and Christine often helps manage it.

LOEN STAKER 16th child of ARTHUR GLENN & GLORIA (THOMPSON) FOSTER married Cherilyn Benson and had:

1. MORGAN, who recently graduated and was Valedictorian of her High School.
2. BRANDT, who is currently serving an LDS mission in So. Africa.
3. NICHOLAS
4. ISAAC

Loen graduated from the Univ. of Utah in Sports Therapy and works in a related field. Cherilyn is a physical education teacher.

Flavius: Pausing here I see that the grass needs mowing, plums and pears need picking, and other jobs need attention before the fall rains set in. Sept. 18, 1972 is a fine Indian Summer Day – Ho Hum!!

WANDA MARY-ALICE, 3rd child of ARTHUR & LeNORA FOSTER (their 1st child died at birth), was born in Saltair, Utah. She married In Salt Lake City to HENRY OSTELL FREDERICK.

HENRY FREDERICK b. Apr. 21, 1919 d. 9 Feb 1993 SLC, Utah
WANDA MARY-ALICE b. Apr. 27, 1924 d. 2007 SLC, Utah
Were married Dec. 3, 1943, Utah. To this union were born:

1. DANIEL ALLEN b. Apr. 20, 1947 d. 1985 of cancer
2. JOHN ANDERSON

DANIEL ALLEN married ANGELIKA WOBBE, who was German-born, Feb. 19, 1950. Their children: 1) DIANA and 2) CINDA ANN, 3) CHRISTINE, and 4) STEPHANIE.

JOHN ANDERSON married CATHEY PISTORIUS, in Salt Lake City, Utah, May 22, 1971. He is currently the Factory Director of the Morton Salt Plant in Salt Lake City and is the 5th generation of Fosters and descendants who have worked for that company. They have three sons.

GLORIA LeNORA, youngest child of ARTHUR & LeNORA (THOMAS) FOSTER, was born in Salt Lake City, Utah, and married WAYNE EBBESEN DRAPER.

WAYNE EBBESEN DRAPER b. July 5, 1925 d. 2010
GLORIA LeNORA b. July 14, 1928 d. 7 Dec 2011
Were married Sept. 11, 1946, Utah. To this union were born:

1. WAYNE MELVIN m. BEVERLY COLBERT and had
2. SARAH LEE "RUSTY" m. BRENT LEE POLL 12 Dec 1967.

WAYNE MELVIN DRAPER was born in Highland, Bingham Canyon, Utah, and is a veteran of Viet Nam. He married BEVERLY COLBERT in Salt Lake City, Utah Sept. 21, 1965 and had two children: 1) WAYNE PATRICK, who married TAMMY and had a daughter, VANESSA; and 2) SCOTT.

SARAH LEE DRAPER (#2 above) married Brent Lee Poll, Dec. 12, 1967. He is a Viet Nam veteran and they live in Salt Lake City, Utah.

****

ALBERT ROBERT, 5th child of DANIEL & ALICE CATHERINE (GETZ) FOSTER and grandson of ROBERT L. FOSTER, was born in Missouri where his family resided for a time. He married and parted from wife #1 RACHEL ELIZABETH CURTIS.

ALBERT ROBERT FOSTER b. Dec. 19, 1896 MO d. Apr. 28, 1984 Turlock, Stanislaus, CA
RACHEL ELIZABETH (CURTIS) b. Aug. 23, 1902 d. Apr. 14, 1934 McCook, NB
Were married May 24, 1919, Calif. To this union was born: CECIL WARREN.

CECIL WARREN FOSTER b. Dec. 19, 1920 Alameda, CA d. Jul 10, 1991 Josephine, Oregon
JEWELL BRAY b. Dec. 6, 1926 B. Dec. 6, 1926
Were married May 24, 1919, Calif. Their children:

1. KATHERINE ELIZABETH m. WILLIAM DILTZ
2. BARBARA JEAN b. Oct. 24, 1944 d. May 12, 1965 m. DANIEL WILSON
3. DONNA FLORINE bm. EDWARD VIDAS
4. SALLY ANN m. LESTER O'NEIL
5. JOHN ALAN
6. ROBERT WARREN b. July 8, 1955 d. July 8, 1969
7. PATRICK THOMAS
8. TINA NANETTE

Cecil W. Foster divorced Jewell, and is now married to #2 RITA JEAN KINNEY.

ALBERT ROBERT FOSTER (above) married #2 LILLIE ELVIRA AMELIA NELSON. She was a widow with a son, DONALD F. CARLSON, who was killed while serving in the U.S. Navy in WWII. Albert and Amelia now live in Phoenix, AZ.

ALBERT ROBERT FOSTER b. Dec. 19, 1896 d. Apr. 28. 1984
LILLIE ELVIRA AMELIA (NELSON) b. Feb. 25, 1899
Were married Feb. 14, 1934, Calif. To this union were born:

1. RICHARD WAYNE b. June 5, 1935 m. LAURA CODERRE in Connecticut (Laura b. 11 Mar 1937). Children:
   a. KEVIN ROBERT
   b. LYNN ANNE
2. DANIEL ELMER m. JEANNIE PEARSON.

Albert married and divorced Laura Hathway after Lilllie's death.

EARL CHESTER, 6th child of DANIEL & ALICE CATHERINE (GETZ) FOSTER, was born southeast of Dresden, Ks., in the old Solomon River Settlement. He married WINFRED GLADYS CASE, but I don't know if the marriage was in Kansas or Utah.

EARL CHESTER b. Apr. 9, 1899 KS d. 18 Sept 1968 Grass Valley, NV
WINFRED GLADYS CASE b. Apr. 27, 1901Idaho d. Jan. 21, 1985 Castro Valley, Alameda, CA
Were married Feb. 11, 1920. To this union were born:

1. CLYDE LESTER b. Mar. 4, 1921 m. BARBARA DECKER Oct. 6, 1946. She was born Nov. 2, 1927. Their children:
   a. NANCY ELANE
   b. JEFFERY EARL
   c. GREGORY CLYDE
2. JEAN BABEANETTE b. Aug. 14, 1925 d. June 23, 1971 m. #1 MERTON THOMAS LEWIS Feb. 1943. He was born Sept. 25, 1926 and is now dead, but I have no data. However they were separated at the time. Their children:
   a. CAROL JEAN m. TIMOTHY DALE ERSKIN June 26, 1965. Their children:
      1) TANARA DAWN
      2) KIMBERLY ANN
   b. THOMAS EARL m. JOCELYN JANICE ANDERSON, no data.
   c. CATHERINE MARIE
3. BETTY JANE m. DELBERT HARRIS, no data.

***** Chart pg. 45 *****

MYRTLE SYBILLA, 7th child of DANIEL & ALICE CATHERINE (GETZ) FOSTER, was born in Haddam, Kansas. She married twice, the first ending in divorce.

FRED E. GRATTO b. abt 1900

MYRTLE SYBILLA (FOSTER) b. Mar. 4, 1902 Haddam, KS d. Oct 31, 1961 Santa Cruz, CA
Were married Feb. 2, 1920. To this union were born:

1. FRANK b. Nov. 1, 1921 d. Nov 1981 San Francisco, CA m. ETHYL CARLSON and had a child:
   a. CHERIE (Cherie I)
2. FOSTER b. Oct. 5, 1923 Los Angeles, CA d. Jul 17, 2004 Audobon, Camden, NJ m. CAROL LEWIS Dec. 2, 1943 and had one child: MICHAEL.

Myrtle S. Foster married #2 WILLIAM AMOS CURTIS, Jan. 4, 1929. No children were born to marriage No. 2, but he adopted Myrtle's children, who now use the surname Curtis. To add to the confusion that could result from this name change, Frank, who was married many times (Married 8 or 10 times, divorced only 3 times, nabbed by the law), has two daughters named Cherie. I often wonder if he identifies them as Cherie I and Cherie II???

FRANK CURTIS (#1 above), son of MYRTLE & FRED GRATTO, adopted son of WILLIAM AMOS CURTIS, married #2 MERCEDES GONZALES, and had two children:

1. CHERI (II)
2. WILLIAM AMOS

****Chart pg. 45****

JOHN MARTIN, 8th child of DANIEL & ALICE CATHERINE (GETZ) FOSTER, was born in Haddam, Kansas. He went to California with his parents where he met and married FAYE OLIVE SMITH. Both are buried in the Sanger, Calif. Cemetery.

JOHN MARTIN FOSTER b. Apr. 5, 1904 Haddam, KS d. Mar. 5, 1957 Alameda, California
FAYE OLIVE (SMITH) b. Aug. 21, 1911 OK d. Aug. 9, 1964 Alameda, California
Were married Neb. 3, 1929, Calif. To this union were born: 1) GILBERT RAY, 2) RONALD E.:

1. GILBERT RAY b. Dec. 30, 1929 Fresno, CA d. Jan. 12, 1997 Alameda, CA, m. NANCY STEADMAN and lived in Oakland, CA. Children:
   a. CHERYL ANN
   b. CONSTANCE LYNN
   c. CATHLEEN LOUISE
2. RONALD EUGENE m. EMILE STEADMAN (Nancy's sister) May 3, 1954 and they lived in Oakland, CA. Children:
   a. CYNTHIA RENE
   b. GREGORY
   c. MORTON

With these words, Polly Foster's (dau. of Harrison Foster) line draws to an end.

JOSEPH, last child of ROBERT L. and SARAH "SALLY" ANN COX, married his step-sister, CLARA ADELINE "ADDIE" SMITH. Both are buried in San Francisco, Calif.

They had no children but adopted 2 children: 1) MARIE, who married M. BARNES and lives in San Francisco. MARIE had RICHARD, who died in the Navy in 1970 leaving a wife and two daughters. 2) ROBERT, who lives in Chicago, Ill, with his wife, a son and a daughter.

ROBERT L. FOSTER b. 1834 married #2, MARGARET ELLEN HOWARD, widow of THOMAS H. SMITH. To Margaret's first marriage was born: 1) LEWIS, 2) CLARENCE, 3) FLORENCE, 4) CHARLOTTE, who married a Mr. HICKS, and lived in Los Angeles, and 5) ADELINE (ADDIE) who married JOSEPH FOSTER (above). These children were all born in Hancock Co. Illinois.

As noted in the second chart, pg. 40, Robert and Margaret had 2 sons:

1. THOMAS H. FOSTER, born in Iowa and a WWI veteran, moved to San Jose, Calif. In 1927. He married twice but had no children by wife #2 RUTH. At present, I have no further knowledge of either wife except: --wife #1, IDA, last known address Kelso, Wash., and Thomas Had: MAUDE and ELSIE. Thomas is buried in Golden Gate Cemetery, San Bruno, Calif.
2. WILLIAM LEROY FOSTER married OLIVE. She died before he did, at least there is no mentioning of her in the obituary. William was blind for several years, and died of a heart attack aboard a bus in San Jose. He is buried in the Santa Clara City Cemetery. To Olive and William were born: 1) BARBARA, and 2) ROBERT, whose last known address was Portland, Oregon.

* * * * * THE THOMAS FAMILY * * * * *

The first Thomas in this line was THOMAS (Tom) THOMAS, born 1775 in Pontgwynfe, Llandebie, Llanddeusant, Car., So.Wales and died in 1856 in South Wales. His descendant and Adrienne's grandmother, LeNora Thomas Foster notes on this family group sheet that she "obtained some of this information from The Great Gen. Library at Aberystwyth. Cardigan, Wales. The dates, etc. (were) from death certificates which I was able to get from the Registrar at Carmarthen, before the price of them became so expensive. That's where I found William Thomas who was with his father when Thomas died. I'm still trying to learn if there were still more children."

She also notes that although she has listed a William Thomas, Jr. on the group sheet (born Oct 1818 in same town as John Thomas and buried 4 Nov. 1818) whom she believes he is the grandson of Thomas Thomas. She wrote, "I guess this is because of the fact that Wm. Jr. died shortly after his birth and that there was a William in attendance at Thomas' death. (So, the older William needs to be found.) William Jr., could have been another child of Thomas and Hannah's though, as it wasn't uncommon for children to have the same names as a sibling. Also, the fact that Hannah and Thomas were not married until 1800, if this Wm.Jr. was a grandson, it would have meant that his father who would have been born around 1801-ish and would have been very young to have had a child born in 1818.....so I think Wm. Jr. is probably a son of Hannah and Thomas. (Note from Adrienne: Actually at that time it was not uncommon for girls to marry at age 14 or 15) There is a huge gap in birth years from John Thomas to William, Jr. so there probably were more children in between."

From Anthony Thomas, a cousin in Wales:
THOMAS THOMAS -- John Thomas's father was named Thomas Thomas and not much is known about him other than he was born in 1775 Pontgwynfe, Llandebie, Llanddeusant Par. Carm. He then got married to Hannah Rowland in 1800 at Brecon Or Llandebie, Llanddeusant Par. Carm., So. Wales and he died in So. Wales on the 25th November 1856 aged 81 at High Street, Llandovery, Llanddeusant Par., Carm., So. Wales Pontgwynfe, Llandebie, and also buried there

Clara Davies Miller wrote, "My grandfather, my father's father, was John Thomas. He was born and died in South Wales, Great Britain. My grandmother, my father's mother, was Mary Coslet Thomas, wife of John Thomas. My father, Thomas C. Thomas being one of 21 children born out of this union. She (Mary) was born and also died in Wales, G.B. at the ripe old age of 105 years old and she was only a small little woman about 5 feet. My father T. C. Thomas (Thomas Coslett Thomas) was only one of family to come to America.

THOMAS THOMAS married HANNAH ROWLAND and not much is known about her other than she was born in 1773 in Breconshire, S Wales, She then got married to John Thomas in 1800 Brecon Or Llandebie, Llanddeusant Par. Carm., So. Wales , she also had a kid named William born in 1818 but also died that year in Pontgwynfe, Llandeusant Par., Carm., So. Wales. She then died on 23rd Aug 1865 in Parlase, Llandilio,Jamaica?, S Wales Parlase Llandilo-Talybout, aged 92 and is buried at Pontardulais, Llandilo-Talybout, So. Wales. -- from Anthony Thomas, a cousin in Wales, GB.

THOMAS THOMAS b. 1775 South Wales d. 25 Nov 1856 South Wales
HANNAH ROWLAND b. 1773 Breconshire, South Wales d. 23 Aug 1865
Married 1800 Carmarthenshire, South Wales. Children:

1. JOHN THOMAS b. 1802 South Wales
2. REESE THOMAS b. abt 1811 who m. ELIZABETH and had 1) SARAH, 2) ELIZABETH Jr.
3. WILLIAM THOMAS Jr. b. Oct 1818

Clara Davies Miller wrote, "My grandfather, my father's father, was John Thomas (#1 above). He was born and died in South Wales, Great Britain. My grandmother, my father's mother, was Mary Coslet Thomas, wife of John Thomas. My father, Thomas C. Thomas being one of 21 children born out of this union. She (Mary) was born and also died in Wales, G.B. at the ripe old age of 105 years old and she was only a small little woman about 5 feet. My father T. C. Thomas (Thomas Coslett Thomas) was only one of family to come to America.

JOHN THOMAS b. 1802 South Wales d. 1851 South Wales

MARY COSLET b. 1807 Wales d. 1912!! South Wales (yes, that's correct)
Married 18 Feb 1831, Carmarthen, South Wales. Known Children:

1. COSLET b. 26 May 1833 Carmethen, South Wales
2. DAVID b. 23 Mar 1835 Carmethen, South Wales
3. WILLIAM b. 8 Mar 1836 Carmethen, South Wales
4. ARTHUR b. 1838 Carmethen, South Wales
5. JOHN b. 1839
6. ANN b. 1840 Carmethen, South Wales
7. THOMAS COSLET b. 21 Feb 1841 Carmethen, South Wales
8. MARY b. 1842 Carmethen, South Wales
9. ENOCK b. 1845 Carmethen, South Wales m. CATHERINE HUGHES and had 1) MORGAN, 2) MARY, 3) DAVID, 4) CATHERINE.
10. JOSEPH b. 1848 Carmethen, South Wales
11. ANNE b. 1851 Carmethen, South Wales

THOMAS COSLET THOMAS (#7 above) was a poet, author, weaver, and salt miner. He built and operated the Royal Salt Plant in Salt Lake County which later became the Morton Salt Company. Thomas and Elizabeth had 7 children, four of whom were stillborn and three of whom lived to adulthood. He married #1), ALICE POWELL ROWLAND on 3 Oct 1870. She was born 18 Jul 1853 in Monmouthshire, South Wales and d. 25 Feb 1871 in Salt Lake City, Utah, along with her new baby. They had no children. Thomas and his family joined the Church of Jesus Christ of Latter Day Saints (Mormons) and immigrated to Utah, but Alis died in the Salt Lake Valley only four months after she and Thomas Coslet were married. Thomas Coslet later met Elizabeth Phillips and married her on the 19th of August 1872 in the Salt Lake LDS Temple and was sealed to his parents the same day. Elizabeth was the daughter of John Phillips and Sophia Thomas. Thomas Coslett Thomas married #2) ELIZABETH PHILLIPS.

THOMAS COSLET THOMAS b. 21 Feb 1841 South Wales d. 16 Jan 1908 Provo, UT
ELIZABETH PHILLIPS b. 4 Jan 1839 South Wales d. 15 Sep 1893 SLC, UT
Married 19 Aug 1872 in Salt Lake City, Utah. Children:

1. DANIEL PHILLIPS b. 8 Feb 1874 d. 11 Jan 1938 Provo, Utah, m. MARY ELLEN REES 20 Oct 1899.
2. JOHN PHILLIPS b. 15 May 1876 d. 12 May 1956 Salt Lake City, Utah
3. SOPHIE "EFFIE" PHILLIPS b. 15 Nov 1878 d.19 May 1942 Los Angeles, California, m. REES DAVIES 15 Feb 1899
4. COSLET PHILLIPS 7 Nov 1881 d. 24 Jan 1944 Salt Lake City, Utah, m. MATHILDA JENSON 8 Sep 1904
5. Stillborn daughter b. abt. 1883
6. Stillborn daughter b. abt. 1885
7. Stillborn daughter b. abt 1887

JOHN PHILLIPS THOMAS (#2 above), father of LeNORA THOMAS who married ARTHUR HENRY FOSTER, operated his own school of boxing and athletics in Salt

Lake City, 1891-1897. He also worked in the Salt Lake City railroad yard. In later years he developed and raised thoroughbred White and Bard Plymouth Rock chickens very successfully. He and his daughters, Edrie, Arvilla, and LeNora, juggled bowling pins and battle axes on the Vaudeville circuit for many years. He was known at one time as the world's greatest club juggler. He worked at the railroad yard and was planning to go to California to make his debut in motion pictures but before he could go he had a terrible accident—one that happened to many railroad workers in that time. In doing his rather dangerous job of hitching and unhitching train cars, two cars that were hitched together separated when the hitch broke, and one train rolled backwards and pinned John to the car behind it. His leg was crushed and had to be amputated. He had a wooden leg for the rest of his life, and never made it to Hollywood, but he continued juggling for 20 more years and trained his children in that art. He worked as a machinist, inventor and in salt milling at the Morton Salt Plant, which was founded by his grandfather. His children, grand-children, and great-grandchildren called him "Pop."

JOHN PHILLIPS THOMAS b. 15 May 1876 SLC, Utah d. 12 May 1956 SLC, Utah
MARY ELIZA "MAMIE" COON b. 7 Jan 1879 SLC, Utah d. 1 Oct 1971, SLC, Utah
Married 10 May 1899 Coonville, Utah. Children:

1. LeNORA b. 9 Apr 1901 d. 9 Aug 1983 m. ARTHUR HENRY FOSTER, father of ARTHUR GLENN FOSTER and grandfather of ADRIENNE FOSTER POTTER.
2. EDRIE b. 20 Sep 1904 d. 16 May 1898 never married.
3. ARVILLA b. 10 Aug 1910 d. 15 May 1976 and m. CALVIN YOUNG WELLS.
4. JOHN COSLET b. 23 Aug 1913 d. 23 Aug 1964 m. WANDA SCOTT.
5. Major OWEN DANIEL b. 30 May 1916 d. 16 Dec 1988 SLC, UT (U.S. Air Force, WWII), m. WINNIFRED "WINNIE" MARGARET HALL.

ARVILLA THOMAS (#3 above) married CALVIN YOUNG WELLS, a local realtor:

CALVIN YOUNG WELLS b. 5 Apr 1904 SLC d. 13 Oct 1972 SLC
ARVILLA (THOMAS)
Married 29 Apr 1935. Children:

1. JAMES THOMAS, a business realtor who married LUANNA and had 7 children.
2. QUENTIN THOMAS, former Mayor of Sandy, Utah, who married Patricia and had 3 children.
3. MARY JACQUELYN.

JOHN COSLET THOMAS (#4 above) married WANDA SCOTT in May 1936, whom he later divorced. Their son: RAOUL RAMON b. 17 Dec 1937 in Kamas, Summit, Utah and died 1 Sep 1993 in Salt Lake City, Utah. Wanda Scott was 17 Mar 1919 in Burley, Cassia, Idaho.

MAJOR OWEN DANIEL THOMAS married WINNIFRED (Aunt Winnie) MARGARET HALL. Uncle Owen served in the U.S. Air Corps (now known as Air Force) in England in WWII and afterwards became a Geologist for Phillips Petroleum. He was the Director of Exploration for Phillips for most of his life and traveled around the country and the world in that capacity, discovering many new oil fields that kept cars running and helped manufacturing of plastic in his day and up to the present time.

MAJ. OWEN DANIEL THOMAS (USAF, Ret.) b. 30 May 1916 d. Dec 1988
WINNIFRED MARGARET (HALL) b. 16 Nov 1923 d. 10 Sep 2014
Married 15 Dec 1945 Omaha, Douglas, Nebraska. Children:

1. MARY JEAN
2. KATHLEEN EDRIE
3. DAVID OWEN
4. JOHN HALL
5. PAUL MICHAEL
6. JAMES VAUGHN
7. ROBERT HALL
8. MARY ELLEN

***** HARRISON FOSTER JR. *****

HARRISON JR., 4th child of HARRISON & ANNA FOSTER, was born in Bourbon Co., KY, and was taken by his parents to Nicholas and later to Clark County. His mother died in 1815 when he was 9, and when Harrison Jr. was barely 12 years old his father, Harrison Sr., died, leaving the children orphans. In 1820, Harrison Jr. joined the other children in their hike to Switzerland Co., Indiana, where they knew other Foster relatives lived. Here, he grew to manhood and met and married Ellender Foster, pg. 74 (daughter of Robert Foster, who fought alongside Harrison Foster Sr. in the Northwest Indian War). Evidently none of her family was in Switzerland County at the time, because it was Harrison's brother, Aaron, who signed the marriage bond.

In 1830, Harrison Jr., his brother William, their families and unmarried sister, Dorcas, trekked to McLean Co., Illinois, joining their brother Aaron who had arrived two years earlier. With the arrival of Polly in 1842, all of Harrison & Anna Foster's children had migrated to Illinois, except sisters Phebe, who had died, and Lettice, who lived in Missouri.

Harrison Jr. and William took up land on the banks of the Mackinaw River opposite the old Patton Settlement, about 1 1/2 miles apart. In putting up his cabin, Harrison chose a faulty ridgepole. An early snowstorm, wet and heavy, came so deep it was the talked-of event for many years. Under the weight, the ridgepole gave way during the night, filling the cabin with snow. Bundling up his family, Harrison Jr. took them 1 1/2 miles upriver to his brother, William's place. Here, they remained till Harrison's cabin could be rebuilt.

James Adams, who married Aaron's daughter Margaret, pg. 147, once told how immune Harrison's children had become to the cold. He said that the children would often skate on the frozen surface of the Mackinaw River barefooted. According to James, Harrison's son Aaron often ran around wearing nothing but a long, homespun wool shirt, and barefooted. Once the three-year-old was missing for quite some time, and when found was fast asleep in a snowdrift, wearing nothing but his long shirt. Naturally, the family worried but the little tyke never even caught a cold.

Tough little rascal, wasn't he? And I complain when it gets below freezing and warmly dressed. But, I always did say that ice and snow were for polar bears and penguins!! Along with his farming, Harrison built a saw mill, which he ran till he sold the farm. At that time, he moved into Pleasant Hill, where he built a general store. When the town got a post office under the name Selma, he became the first and only postmaster, setting aside a corner of this store for the purpose.

In 1859, Harrison, Robert L. Foster (son of Dennis Foster and grandson of Robert Foster b. 1770), pg. 40, Aaron Foster (son of Aaron Foster and Sarah Royston Patton), pg. 149, John Cox (married Dorcas Foster – youngest dau. of Harrison Sr. and Anna Margaret Foster) pg. 117, and Isaac Smith (married Sarah Foster – dau. of Harrison and Ellender Foster) formed a wagon train bound for Kansas. They landed in Marshall County, where Harrison took up a piece of land, near "Barret's Mill," just east of present-day Frankfort, KS. Until they moved to Washington Co., Kansas, Robert L. & Sarah Ann (Cox) Foster helped Harrison Jr. run his farm. Ellender died in 1855 and on May 1, 1867, Harrison Jr. married #2, Ellen Ault, a widow with four children: 1) MARY A b. abt 1814, 2) ELIZABETH b. abt 1849, 3) JAMES b. abt 1853, and I don't have the name of the fourth child. There were no children born to Harrison and Ellen.

Ellender Foster is buried in the Pleasant Hill Cemetery, McLean Co., Ill, with a tombstone: - "Ellen, daughter of R and B Foster, age 50." Harrison Foster Jr. and his brother-in-law, John Cox, are buried in the Morrison Cemetery, three miles east of Frankfort, Kansas, but neither has a tombstone.

HARRISON FOSTER, Jr. b. 1806 d. 1869
ELLENDER (FOSTER) b. 1805 d. Dec. 29, 1855 (daughter of Robert Foster b. 1770 and Bathsheba Williams). Were married Jan. 5, 1825 Indiana. To this union were born:

1. SARAH b. Nov. 22, 1825 d. Dec. 12,1893 m. ISAAC R. SMITH
2. WILLIAM b. Feb. 16, 1827 d. Oct. 6, 1901 m. MARY ELIZABETH FOSTER, dau. of Dennis and Mary Polly Foster)
3. ROBERT b. Nov. 8, 1828 d. Sept 28, 1846
4. ELIZA JANE b. Sept. 28, 1830 d. Nov. 12, 1902 m. AARON BLUEFORD FOSTER (son of Aaron Foster and Sarah Royston Patton.)
5. AARON b. 1831 d. Apr. 13, 1886 m. Matilda Hutson (dau. of Richard Hutson & Eliz. Moore)
6. CATHERINE b. 1834 d. 1857 m. George Washington Foster (son of George Archibald Foster and Tabitha Hutson)
7. MARGARET b. June 7, 1836 d. May 25, 1853
8. FRANCIS b. 1838 d. young
9. ANDREW JACKSON. b. 1840 d. Union Army, Civil War

10. RUTH BATHSHEBA b. 1842 d. 1877 m. Benjamin Franklin Kelly

SARAH (#1 above), born in Switzerland Co., Indiana, came to McLean Co., IL with her parents. Here she grew to adulthood, met and married Isaac R. Smith. Isaac, born in Kentucky, was a cousin to William Smith, who married Malinda Foster, pg. 37. Sarah and Isaac's six eldest children were born in Illinois, the last three in Kansas, where the family arrived in 1859. They bought a farm near Barrett's Mill east of Frankfort from the government for $1.25 an acres. Isaac was killed or died in the Union Army during the last part of the Civil War, and in 1865 the widow took her family to Nemaha Co., Kansas. After son Eli married, the family moved back to the homestead, where she too, died. Both Sarah & Isaac are buried in the afore-mentioned Morrison Cemetery, Marshall Co., Kansas.

ISAAC R. SMITH b. 1824 d. Jan. 15, 1863 (died fighting in the Civil War)
SARAH (FOSTER) b. Nov. 1825 d. Dec. 12, 1893
Were married Nov. 28, 1844, Illinois. To this union were born:

1. ELIZABETH b. Sept 24, 1845 d. 1918 m. GEORGE BRAXTON MIZE
2. HARRIET W. b. 1847 m. HERMAN SHUBERT
3. SUSAN b. 1848 m. AUGUST ALBRIGHT
4. MARGARET b. 1851 m. AARON HOUTS
5. ELI b. Apr. 7, 1856 d. May 22, 1938 m. SELMA SHUBERT
6. ROBERT b. May 28, 1858 d. Jan. 27, 1893 m. RUTH NICHOLAS
7. ABRAHAM LINCOLN b. Dec. 25, 1861 m. #1 MINERVA and #2 Unknown
8. ISAAC Jr. b. 1864 m. ARZILLA HOWES
9. SARAH died in infancy

1850 Census, Mackinaw (south side), McLean, Illinois

Isaac age 25, b. Kentucky, laborer,

Sarah age 24, b. Ohio

Elizabeth age 5 b. Illinois

Harriett age 4 b. Illinois

Susan age 4 mos. b. Illinois

Next door are Sarah's cousins, William and Elizabeth Foster and Harrison and Mary Foster, also Rachel Foster.

They are in 1860 census of Vermillion, Marshall, Kansas Territory.

1870 Census, Lachnane, Brown, Kansas

Sarah age 45 (Isaac had passed away), Land at $1,200, house $270

Harriet age 21 b. Illinois

Eli age 15 b. Illinois

Abraham (Lincoln) age 9, b. Kansas

Isaac age 6 b. Kansas

ELIZABETH, daughter of ISAAC R. SMITH & SARAH (FOSTER), born in Illinois, went with her parents to the homestead in Marshall Co., Kansas, where she grew to adulthood. In May of 1865 she went with her mother to Nemaha Co., where Elizabeth met and married George Mize in Seneca. They lived in Marshall County, then in 1870, they made their final home in Brown Co., Kansas, where both are buried.

GEORGE BRAXTON MIZE b. 20 Sep 1836 Barren, KY d. 3 Oct 1912
ELIZABETH (SMITH) b. Sept 24, 1845 McLean, IL d. 1819 on a Saturday
Were married Oct. 15, 1865 Kansas. To this union were born:

1. WILLIAM H. b. 22 Jul 1866 d. 1930
2. ORADA MARGARET b. 1867 d. 1915
3. ANNA or Annie b. 3 Nov 1867 d. 14 Mar 1949 m. JOHNS
4. HARRIET OR HATTIE FLORENCE b. 23 Jul 1869 d. 1941 m. BIEN
5. GEORGE WASHINGTON b. 31 Dec 1870 d. 10 Jun 1947 d. 10 Jun 1947
6. SARAH or SADIE ELIZABETH b. 7 Jul 1872 d. 1930 m. TEMPLETON
7. ALICE DELILAH b. 7 Apr 1874 d. 28 May 1947 m. NICHOLAS
8. CHARLES HERMAN b. 19 Jan 1880 d. 11 May 1866
9. FRANK BENGMAN b. 10 Jan 1882 d. 19 Sep 1914
10. MYRTLE BESSIE 5 May 1886 d. 4 May 1964
11. HARVEY b. 27 Jun 1888

Note: Dates for this family are from www.ancestry.com from the family tree of a descendant.

HARRIET W. SMITH, second child of ISAAC R. and SARAH (FOSTER) SMITH, born in McLean Co., Illinois, was taken by her parents to Marshall County, and later, by her mother to Nemaha Co., Kansas. Here she grew and married Herman Shubert. To this union were born: 1) ARCHIE, 2) HERMAN JR, 3) EVA, 4) PEARL, 5) CLARENCE, 6) CHARLEY

SUSAN SMITH, 3rd child of ISAAC R. and SARAH (FOSTER) SMITH, born in McLean Co., IL, also made the swing to Marshall County, and later to Nemaha Co, Kansas. Here she grew to adulthood, met and married August Albright. To this union were born: 1) WILLIAM, 2) HARRIET.

MARGARET SMITH, 4TH child of ISAAC R. and SARAH (FOSTER) SMITH, born in McLean Co., Illinois, made the swing to Marshall County, then to Nemaha Co., Kansas. Here she grew to adulthood, met and married AARON HOUTS. They made their home in Marquette, Michigan. Their children: 1) CLARA, 2) MINNIE, 3) MARGARET.

No doubt Archie and Minnie are nicknames. I would prefer Christian names, but in this case, I'll have to be satisfied with nicknames.

ELI SMITH, 5TH child of ISAAC R. and SARAH (FOSTER) born in McLean Co., Illinois, made the swing to Nemaha Co., Kansas. Here he grew to manhood, met and married in Hiawatha, Kansas to Selma Shubert. Selma Shubert and Herman Shubert (above – married Harriet W. Smith) were brother and sister.

Soon after marriage, Eli moved back to Frankfort, Kansas and took over the family homestead, which he had inherited. With him went his mother, and her younger children. Here Eli and Selma lived to celebrate their 64th wedding anniversary, which was attended by all their children. Eli and Selma Smith are buried in the Morrison Cemetery three miles east of Frankfort, Kansas.

ELI SMITH b. Apr. 7, 1856 d. May 22, 1939
SELMA (SHUBERT) b. Apr. 5, 1858 d. May 5, 1948
Were married Oct. 16, 1874, Kansas. To this union were born:

1. CARL ELROY b. Jan. 1, 1881 d. Mar. 5, 1956
2. EDNA LORENA b. Mar., 18, 1886 d. Apr. 24, 1972 m. #1) WILLIAM COOPER, #2) H. R. ANDERSON
3. VERNA b. June 8, 1890
4. FLOY (FLOYD?) b. b. Feb. 11, 1894 d. Mar. 24, 1968
5. MAUDE b. b. Aug. 9, 1897 d.
6. Otis L. Smith b. 1900

EDNA LORENA SMITH (#2 above) was born on the Smith homestead east of Frankfort, Ka. On attaining adulthood, she married WILLIAM COOPER. He died during the flu epidemic of WWI. Some years later, Lorena married #2, H. R. Anderson, Oct. 21, 1937. H. R. died Apr. 12 1947, and Lorena moved to Huxton, Colorado, where her sister Verna lives. No children were born to this 2nd marriage.

WILLIAM COOPER b. d. Feb. 27, 1919
LORENA (SMITH) b. Mar. 18, 1886 d. Apr. 24, 1972 Bu. Huxton, Colo.
Were married Feb.8, 1909, Kansas. To this union were born:

1. MILTON b. Sept 21, 1911
2. AGNES b. Mar. 20, 1915
3. MARGARET b. May 12, 1918

MILTON COOPER (#1 above) married MARGARET MCKELLAR, June 18, 1933. To this union were born: 1) GRETCHEN, 2) CARMEN, 3) MICHAEL.

AGNES COOPER married FORREST REDDISH, June 24, 1944. No children.
MARGARET COOPER married LEO DOERR, Feb. 9, 1942. No children.
All three of Lorena's children live in Denver, Colorado.

ROBERT (BERT) SMITH, 6TH child of ISAAC R. and SARAH (FOSTER), was born on the old Marshall County homestead, and grew up in the Frankfort, Kansas area. He married RUTH NICHOLAS, and moved to Topeka, Kansas, where both are buried. A daughter and a niece both live in Topeka, but I have gotten no answers to my letters.

ROBERT SMITH b. May 28, 1858 d. Jan. 27, 1893
RUTH (NICHOLAS) b.
Were married in Kansas. To this union were born:

1. ROBERT Jr.

2. WALTER
3. NORA
4. LILLIAN

ABRAHAM LINCOLN SMITH, 7th child of ISAAC R. and SARAH (FOSTER) SMITH, was born in Marshall County, and grew to manhood in the Frankfort, Kansas area. He made the "run," when the Cherokee Strip was opened up for settlement, and lived on his Oklahoma homestead till his death. He is buried in the Pond Creek area of Oklahoma.

Lincoln was married three times, but I have very little on any of his families, although I have written four of his descendants. Lincoln married #1 in Kansas, and has one child. When wife number one died, this son lived with his grandmother, Sarah (Foster) Smith for many years. Their son:--Walter b. in 1884 d. Feb. 21, 1961.

Walter married Mary____, and had children, but all the information I have on the family, is that Mary was still living in 1970.

Marriage #2 begat a son:-- Harold. Again no data. Now to marriage #3 on which I have done better, but not much better.

ABRAHAM LINCOLN SMITH b. Dec. 25, 1861
MINERVA
Were married 1886 Iowa. To this union were born:

1. MARGARET b. 1888 d. 1966
2. PEARL b. Feb. 16, 1890, still living in 1970
3. SARAH b. 1892, still living in 1971
4. PLEASANT born in 1894, died as a youth

MARGARET (#1 above) married a Mr. Bowles, both buried in Oklahoma. No data.

PEARL (#2 above) married CHARLES BREWER, and lived near Jefferson, Oklahoma till the "Dirty 30s," when they moved to California. My latest information had her living in a rest home in Bell, Calif. 1970. Their children: 1) CHARLES Jr. b. 1910, 2) GEORGE b. 1913, 3) DOROTHY b. Mar. 15, 1917, who married Mr. BRADY.

ISAAC SMITH Jr., 7th child of ISAAC R. and SARAH (FOSTER) SMITH, Isaac Smith Jr., was born on the old Frankfort, Ks. homestead. While visiting relatives in Haddam, Ks., 75 miles away, he met and married Arzilla Howes.

Grandpa F. J. Foster wrote:--Isaac Smith married Arzilla Howes, a girl that grew up in our neighborhood in Washington Co., Kansas. ***Family chart pg. 56***"

ISAAC SMITH b. 1864 Frankfort, Marshall, Kansas
ARZILLA HOWES b. abt 1865 Wisconsin
Married in 1884. Children:

1. LOTTIE M b. Jun 1885 KS
2. LULA M b. Feb 1887 KS
3. HARRY B b. Nov 1889 KS
4. ORA E b. Feb 1893 KS
5. ELMER b. Mar 1895 OK
6. ANDREW b. Jun 1896 OK

1900 Census of Watonga, Blaine, Oklahoma

Isaac Smith age 35 b. Kansas, farmer, married 16 years

Arzilla age 33 b. Wisconsin, married 16 years, mother of 7 children, 7 living

Lottie age 14 b. Kansas

Lula age 13 b. Kansas

Harry age 10 b. Kansas

Ora E age 7 b. Kansas

Elmer age 5 b. Oklahoma

Andrew A age 4 b. Oklahoma

WILLIAM, 2nd child of HARRISON Jr. & ELLENDER FOSTER, was born in Switzerland Co., Indiana, and went with his parents to McLean Co., Illinois. Here, he met and married his cousin, MARY ELIZABETH FOSTER (daughter of Dennis and Mary Polly (Foster) Foster. Their family is given on pg. 33. (above with Elizabeth's parents)

ELIZA JANE, 4th child of HARRISON Jr. & ELLENDER FOSTER, was born in McLean Co., Ill. She married her cousin, AARON B. FOSTER (son of AARON FOSTER & SARAH ROYSTON PATTON). Their family is given under Aaron's family.

AARON, 5th child of HARRISON Jr. & ELLENDER FOSTER, was born and lived out his life in McLean Co., Illinois. Aaron married MATILDA HUDSON, who was born in Hancock Co., Indiana. Both are married in the Pleasant Hill Cemetery, McLean Co., Illinois.

AARON FOSTER b. 1830 d. Apr. 18, 1886
MATILDA (HUDSON) b. 1832 d. Apr. 19, 1894
Were married Apr. 10, 1853, Indiana. To this union were born:

1. ELI D b. 1854
2. ROSA BELL b. 1856 d. Sept 8, 1884 m. JOHN JOHNSON
3. MINERVA b. 1856
4. PHOEBE b. 1858
5. ISABEL b. 1859 m. MR. BROCK
6. JANE b. abt 1861 m. Rev. L. E. PAUL
7. MORTON O. b. abt 1863 m. ANNA M. STEWART
8. ANDREW JACKSON b. Aug. 14, 1867
9. AARON SHERMAN b. Aug. 14, 1867 d. Feb. 13, 1960
10. ALBERT b. 1868
11. MARY ALICE b. Aug. 30, 1870 d. Sept 17, 1955

ELI D. married ANNA PAUL and had: 1) CLARENCE, 2) OTT.

Here we are again, at the end of the page and no place to go.

MORTON O. (#4 above) married ANNA M. STEWART and had: 1) BLANCH, who married R. M. BAIRD, Jan. 14, 1914, 2) VELDA who married DONALD J. PATTERSON Feb. 12, 1916.

AARON SHERMAN (#6 above) married MABEL CARTER in 1892 and had: 1) MILDRED who married EARL DUHAM, 2) ALBERT, 3) ALLINE who married ELMER BROWN and bore: a) CHARLES, b) SARAH ESTHER, c) DONALD.

CATHERINE, 6th child of HARRISON b. 1806 & ELLENDER FOSTER, was born and grew to adulthood in McLean Co., Ill. Here, she met and married #1 JOHN BISHOP, and bore *HOWARD in 1853. After John's death Catherine married #2 GEORGE WASHINGTON FOSTER Jr. (son of George Archibald and Tabitha Hutson Foster). They moved to Kansas City, Missouri, where she died while he was away on a surveying party in Kansas Territory. They had a son: HENRY HARRISON b. Dec 1855.

After Catherine died, the two boys went to live with their grandfather, Harrison Foster, in Illinois, and went with him to Kansas. When Harrison died in Kansas the boys went back to Illinois to live with other relatives. They have yet to be traced. **New information: Howard Bishop is found in the 1865 Census in Vermillion, Marshall, Kansas, and in the 1870 census living with his Uncle William, Catherine's older brother, and his family in Martin, McLean, Illinois:*

1870 census of Martin, McLean, Illinois

William age. 43

Elizabeth age 44 b. Maryland (this must be a mistake)

Harrison age 22 b. IL

Evaline age 18 b. IL

"Jepe B" Jesse age 11 b. IL

Mary E age 8 b. IL

***Howard Bishop age** 17 (this is the son of Catherine Foster and her 1st husband, Howard Bishop, both of whom died)*

Rachel age 50 b. Ind.

Howard is in the 1880 Census in Martin, McLean, Illinois and in 1910 he is living with his niece and nephew in Wapella, DeWitt, Illinois.
Family chart pg. 56.

RUTH BATHSHEBA, last child of HARRISON & ELLENDER FOSTER, was born in McLean Co., Illinois, and went to Kansas with her father. Here she grew up, met, and married BENJAMINE KELLY, a Civil War Vet. They moved to Osborne Co., Kansas, where Ruth died. Later Benjamin moved to California, where he died. They had three children.

BENJAMIN FRANKLIN KELLY b. abt 1834 d. 9 Jul 1914 Sawtelle, Los Angeles, CA
RUTH BATHSHEBA FOSTER b. 7 Jun 1842 d. 15 Nov 1904
Children:

1. ALICE JESSIE b. 17 Dec 1868 Wisconsin d. 16 Mar 1956 San Diego, CA, m. MORDECAI DURNBAUGH (b. 23 Oct 1853 Waynesboro, Franklin, PA, d. 19 Jan 1934 Sweetwater Valley, San Diego, CA.) She is in the 1880 Census, Dist. 208, Corinth, Osborne, Kansas. *Source: Wickersheimer, Duff Family Tree, Owner: KarenDuff49 <http://www.ancestry.com/*
2. GUY EDMOND KELLY (above) b. May 30, 1875, married his cousin, IDA E. FOSTER (daughter of Harrison Foster III and Flora Osborn) on June 16, 1896 McLean, Illinois. They lived in McLean Co., Ill. Where their child was born and all are buried. Child: BLANCH L. b. June 10, 1897 d. 26 Jan 1918.
3. REX b. 1879

Here ends the families of HARRISON & ELLENDER FOSTER, but don't panic, there are many bags and boxes full of Fosters still unpacked. Surely you will find your family among those in the pages ahead.

***** PHEBEE FOSTER *****

PHEBEE, 5th child of HARRISON & ANNA MARGARET (BARTLETT) FOSTER, was born in Nicholas Co., Kentucky, and was taken by her father to Clark County. When only 10 years old her father, the last surviving parent, died. A year later she made the long hike through Daniel Boone's woodlot with her brothers and younger sister to Switzerland Co., Indiana. Here, Phebee grew to adulthood, met and married GEORGE ARCHIBALD FOSTER (son of Robert Foster and Bathsheba Williams).

Phebee's married life was short and she died during childbirth with her second child, who didn't live. It isn't known if Phebee died in Switzerland Co., Ind., or in Shelby Co., Kentucky, where George remarried. (For more on George Foster's family, see pg. 75 plus.)

GEORGE ARCHIBALD FOSTER b. 1804 Ohio d. Oct. 9, 1874 Haddam, Washington, Kansas
PHEBEE (FOSTER) b. 1808 Nicholas, KY d. 1828 Switzerland, Indiana
Were married Nov. 19, 1825, Indiana. To this union were born:

1. Unknown baby b. 1826
2. WILLIAM HARRISON b. July 28, 1827 d. Dec. 26, 1905
3. Unknown baby b. 1828

WILLIAM HARRISON married #1) TELITHA (or Talitha) HENLINE, widow of Thomas Wiley, pg. 141 and daughter of WILLIAM HENLINE b. 1792 Boone, KY d. 1870 Lawndale, McLean, IL, and #2) NANCY TAYLOR b. 1798 Madison, KY d. 1870

Lawndale, McLean, IL. Telitha had a son, WILLIAM H. WILEY, who made his home with his stepfather till they moved to Montgomery Co., Ks. His family is given on pg. 141.

William & Telitha made their home in McLean Co., Illinois till 1872, at which time they joined relatives in Montgomery Co., Kansas. In 1880 William and his son, Allan D. Foster owned adjoining farms in Rutland township. Telitha's son, W. H. Wiley owned one 7 miles away.

Most of the descendants of William & Telitha Foster still reside in southeastern Kansas and west central Missouri, not far from the place where they were born. William served in the Civil War (*see below) Both William and Telitha are buried in the Rutland cemetery, south of Elk City, Kansa, and a short way northeast of Havana, Ks.

War Record of McLean County and other papers (Transactions of the McLean County Historical Society, vol. 1, Bloomington, 1899), p. 56: 33rd Illinois Infantry, Company A. Recruits.* ***William H. Foster;* *residence Bloomington; enlisted Mch 31, 1864; discharge July 14, 1865.*

1860 Census, Martin, McLean, Illinois.

William H Foster age 35, b. KY, farmer, land $600, estate $400

Telisha Foster, age 35 b. Illinois

Anderson Wyley, age 14 b. Illinois (there are numerous Wyleys on the following page)

Allen D. Foster, age 4 b. ILL

Emma Ellis, age 1 b. IL

1870 Census, Martin, McLean, Illinois.

William age 42, b. Kentucky, His farm is worth $2500. His estate is worth $750.

Telitha age 43, b. Kentucky

Allen D age 14, b. Illinois

Tempie age 7, b. Illinois

Emily age 15, b. Illinois

There are also two different William and Elizabeth Foster families living next door to each other in this same town. One is the son of George and Phebee Foster, the other is the son of William Foster and Catherine Lineback. This proves an additional close connection between Harrison Foster (grandfather of William H Foster, and Robert Foster, grandfather of the other William Foster. Harrison and Robert fought in the Battle of Fallen Timbers together (Northwest Indian Wars). George Henline, age 49, b. KY also lives in this town with wife Margaret. He is no doubt a relative of Telitha Henline Foster, wife of William H. Foster.

WILLIAM H. FOSTER b. July 28, 1827 d. Dec. 26, 1905
TELITHA (HENLINE) b. Jan. 9, 1828 d. Dec. 20, 1905
Were married Dec.28, 1854 Illinois. To this union were born:

1. EMILY b. 1855 (note 1870 census above)
2. ALLEN DALLAS b. Apr. 1, 1856 d. June 13, 1928

3. EMMA or "Ellis" ELEANOR b. 1859 d. 1869
4. TEMPA "Tempie" b. Feb. 21, 1862 d. May 25, 1936

TEMPA FOSTER was born in McLean Co., Illinois, and came with her parents to Montgomery Co., Kansas. Here, she grew up, met and married SAMUEL PHINNY. They seem to have had no children. Tempa & Samuel are buried in the Rutland Cemetery.

ALLEN DALLAS FOSTER was born in McLean Co., Illinois and came with his parents to Montgomery Co., Kansas. Here he grew to manhood, met and married #1) AQUILLA ANN GRIFFITH. Allen and Aquilla owned a farm in Rutland Township, where their children were born. Allen D. and Aquilla Foster are buried in the Rutland Cemetery. Allen D. had a second marriage that ended in tragedy for him and his wife.

ALLEN DALLAS FOSTER b. Apr. 1, 1856 d. June 13, 1928
AQUILLA (GRIFFITH) b. Mar. 1, 1857 d. June 29, 1921
Were married Dec. 18, 1881, Kansas. To this union were born:

1. FRANK LEONARD b. Aug. 9, 1882 d. Feb. 10,1950
2. BERT B. b. Sept 2, 1885 d. Aug. 25, 1967

FRANK LEONARD was born and grew to manhood in Montgomery Co., Kansas, where he met and married JESSIE MAUDE CAVENAR, in Elk City. They lived on a farm till retirement, and both are buried in Elk City.

FRANK LEONARD b. Aug. 9, 1882 d. Feb. 10,1950
JESSIE MAUDE (CAVENAR) B. Nov. 9, 1886
Were married Jan. 2, 1906, Kansas. To this union were born:

1. LEONARD ALLEN b. Feb. 28, 1907 m. Edna Ann McCarty
2. WILBER JOHN b. Oct. 12, 1908
3. FERN AQUILLA b. Jan. 1, 1911
4. MARGARET AMELIA b. Dec. 18, 1912
5. JACK FRANK b. Sept. 7, 1915
6. WILMA GRACE b. Apr. 19, 1920
7. FRANK EARL b. June 3, 1922
8. CHESTER CLARENCE b. June 22, 1924
9. MARY LOUISE b. Apr. 4, 1927

LEONARD ALLEN (#1 above), born in Montgomery Co., Kansas, where he grew to manhood, met and married EDNA MAE McCARTY, in Cherryville, Ks. Their children, all living with families of their own, are: 1) AQUILLA ANN, 2) BILLIE KEITH m. CAROL DEAN PARKS and had a son – GEORGE ALLEN FOSTER, 3) GARRY GLENN, 4) BETTY JO, 5(FRANK DELANO.

WILBER JOHN FOSTER (#2 above), born and raised in Cherryville, Kansas, married VIRGINIA GRETCHEN RINCK. Wilber J. is a veteran of WWII and served in Europe. In 1946 the family moved to Seattle, Washington, where Wilber went to work for Boeing

Aircraft Co. He has now retired, and expects to travel, fish and hunt as long as life will let him. (These three hobbies seem to interest most of those with the Foster name.)

WILBER JOHN FOSTER b. Oct. 12, 1908
VIRGINIA (RINCK) b. May 12, 1913
Were married Aug. 10, 1941, Kansas. To this union were born:

1. JOHN STANLEY m. Madeline Hudson 13 Jul 1968
2. ROBERT HUGH

JOHN STANLEY was born in Seattle, Washington, where he finished High School, met and married MADELINE HUDSON. July 13, 1968, Washington. To this union was born: SEAN.

FERN AQUILLA FOSTER (dau. of FRANK LEONARD and JESSIE (CAVENAR) FOSTER) married DOYLE TRAYLOR. They had two sons, 1) HAROLD, 2) GENE, who were killed in an auto accident in 1944; and a daughter, 3) CHARLOTTE.

MARGARET AMELIA, 4th child of FRANK LEONARD and JESSIE (CAVENAR) FOSTER, married REX LEE or Bub ROBERTS. Their children, three of whom are married: 1) REX LEE JR, who had a daughter – MARGARET M who married Mr. QUIDACHAY, 2) PATTY, 3) SHARON, 4) BRENDA.

JACK FRANK FOSTER, 5th child of FRANK LEONARD and JESSIE (CAVENAR) FOSTER, married and divorced. I have no wife's name but it makes little difference because no children were born to this union.

WILMA GRACE FOSTER, 6th child of FRANK LEONARD and JESSIE (CAVENAR) FOSTER, married CECIL REED. They had a child who is married: COYLENE.

FRANK EARL FOSTER married NORMA JAMES, in Texas where he was working at the time. For Norma, this was the second marriage-go-round and she had three children named PRICE. Frank and Norma now live in Elk City, Kansas.

FRANK EARL FOSTER b. June 3, 1922
NORMA JAMES b. Jan. 7, 1929
Were married May 26, 1959, Texas. To this union were born:

1. MICHAEL (PRICE)
2. GREGORY (PRICE)
3. JAMES (FOSTER)
4. CHARLES (FOSTER)
5. MICHELLE (FOSTER)

Frank Earl's wife Norma is involved with her James family genealogy and also gave me much help with her Foster family. Her brother-in-law, Wilber Foster of Seattle, Washington, was also helpful with the families of Frank & Jessie Foster. However neither have come up with the promised old family pictures for my photo chapter.

Chart pg. 64.

BERT B., second child of ALLEN D. & AQUILLA FOSTER, was born on the old farm in Rutland Twp. of Montgomery County, 10 miles south of Elk City, Kansas. Here he grew to manhood, met and married DORA AMELIA MICHELL. She was born on a farm north of Elk City. Bert & Dora Foster spent their lives on a Montgomery County farm, where they raised beef cattle. Both are buried in the Oak Hill Cemetery in Elk City, Kansas.

BERT B b. Sept 2, 1885 d. Aug. 25, 1967
DORA AMELIA MICHELL b. Sept 5, 1888 d. June 5, 1961
Were married Jan. 8, 1913, Kansas. To this union were born:

1. FRED EARL b. Oct. 22, 1914
2. PAULINE JULIA b. Dec. 17, 1915
3. EMMET L. b. Mar. 19, 1917
4. WANDA AMERICA b. Apr 17, 1918
5. WAYNE H. Oct. 19, 1919
6. LAVELLE LAURA July 20, 1925
7. BERT B. Jr. Oct. 19, 1926 d. Nov. 3, 1969
8. JAUNITA MAXINE b. Jan. 12, 1929
9. TREVA MAE b. Aug. 7, 1930

Three children died in infancy, one a twin to Lavelle Laura, above.

FRED EARL FOSTER (#1 above) was born on the Rutland Twp. Farm. In El Dorado, Kansas, he met and married IRYS PAINTER. For several years, Fred was an auto mechanic, working in several towns in Montgomery County. Their children were born in three of these towns. In later years, they moved to a farm, where they still live, farming and raising beef cattle.

FRED EARL FOSTER b. Oct. 22, 1914
IRYS PAINTER b. Jan. 18, 1923
Were married Feb. 25, 1939, Kansas. To this union were born:

1. FRED EARL Jr.
2. BELVA RUTH
3. DORA LORAINE
4. JIMMIE LEON
5. HARRIET BERTIE
6. AGATHA AGNES
7. ELEANOR DENE
8. GLEN ELDON
9. FRED EARL FOSTER Jr. (#1 above) married HELEN LEWIS Aug, 16, 1969.

BELVA RUTH FOSTER (#2 above) married JOHN CALVIN McKENZIE July 1, 1961. John was born Mar. 26, 1931. They live in Sherman, Texas, and had two children: 1) died in infancy, 2) DELMA CHARLENE b. Aug. 2, 1963.

DORA LORAINE was married three times, and divorced twice. Marriage #1, ORVILLE L. COLE Mar. 15, 1961, had one child: BETTY MAXINE b. Dec. 21, 1961.

#2 LESTER F. COOK, July 24, 1963. Their children: 1) FREDERICK LEE, 2) VESTA STARR.

#3 RONALD LOWELL NELSON in 1867. Their children: 1) DAVID BRUCE, 2) MICHAEL WAYNE.

JIMMY LEON, 4th child of FRED EARL and IRIS (PAINTER) FOSTER, also married twice and divorced one. #1 CAROLYN JEAN HARVEY, Nov. 24, 1961. They had a child: MISTI DIANE.

#2 LOIS DANIELLE ______, a divorcee with two children, Feb. 11, 1967. Her children: 1) DEBORAH JANE BATTERSON, 2) DAYLA DANIELLE BATTERSON.

Jimmie Leon and Lois Danielle Foster's child: VALORIE DAWN.

HARRIET BERTIE FOSTER, 5th child of FRED EARL and IRIS (PAINTER) FOSTER, lived with two different men, and had children by one of them: GEORGE HAYS. Children of Harriet and George: 1) HARRIET LaMAY, 2) DIRK SHAWN.

AGATHA AGNES FOSTER, 6th child of FRED EARL and IRIS (PAINTER) FOSTER, married DONALD EUGENE EDWARDS Nov. 14, 1970. They have a child: DONALD WAYNE Jr.

ELEANOR DENE FOSTER, 7th child of FRED EARL and IRIS (PAINTER) FOSTER, married CHARLES EDWARD NORTH, May 4, 1968. They had a child: CHARLES ALLEN Jr.

GLEN ELDON 8th child of FRED EARL and IRIS (PAINTER) FOSTER, married SUSAN ANN JONES Dec. 26, 1970. They have a child: ROBERT EUGENE.

PAULINE J. FOSTER, 2nd child of BERT & DORA (MITCHELL) FOSTER, was born south of Elk City, Kansas. For several years, she and her sister, Wanda A. had their own hair styling shop in Fredonia, Wilson Co., Kansas. Pauline married DANIEL EVERETT BRONSON in Fredonia, where they still live. Daniel retired in 1970 after many years with the Union Gas Co.

DANIEL E. BRONSON b. Feb. 5, 1906
PAULINE JULIA FOSTER b. Dec. 23, 1915
Were married Nov. 27, 1940, Kansas. To this union were born:

1. WAYNE DANIEL
2. KAREN KAYE

WAYNE DANIEL BRONSON married ROBERTA LYNN McPURDY, Apr. 9, 1965. They divorced. They have two children: 1) TINA ANN, 2) PATRICIA KAY.
Chart pg. 67

EMMET L. FOSTER, 3rd child of BERT B. & DORA FOSTER, was born on the farm south of Elk City, and spent some years farming in Montgomery Co. He is a Navy veteran of WWII. (A big salute to him from all of us) After the war, he moved to Springfield, Missouri, where he took up the brick mason trade and is now a contractor in the building trade in that city. Much of the material on Bert B. & Dora Foster's families was furnished by him. He married FAYE HASHAGEN in Ozark, Missouri. She too was born in Montgomery Co., Kansas, near Elk City.

EMMET L. FOSTER b. Mar. 19, 1917
FAYE (HASHAGEN) b. Apr. 15, 1921
Were married Sept 19, 1940, Missouri. To this union were born:

1. LARRY GLENN
2. RONALD LEE
3. CONNIE SUE
4. DARRELL RAY b. May 9, 1948 d. May 8, 1964. Buried White Chapel Memorial Gardens, Springfield, Missouri.

LARRY GLENN FOSTER (#1 above), born in Elk City, Kansas, went with his parents to Springfield, Missouri, where he grew up, met and married DEBRA ANN MEESE. She was born in Springfield, and they married May 19, 1967. Their children were born in Springfield, Mo: 1) GARRY EMMET, 2) TOBY GLENN.
***
RONALD LEE FOSTER, 2nd son of EMMET L. FOSTER and FAYE (HASHAGEN) FOSTER was born in Nixa Missouri and married LESLIE LYNN MORTON June 21, 1963. She was born in Springfield, Mo. Their children: 1) TERRY LYNN, 2) JEFFERY LEE.
***
CONNIE SUE FOSTER, 3rd child of EMMET L. FOSTER and FAYE (HASHAGEN) FOSTER, was born in Nixa, Missouri, married RONALD EUGENE GILL Dec. 16, 1966.. Ronald was born in Springfield, Mo. Their child: ANGELA SUE.
*** Chart pg. 67 *****

WANDA AMERICA, 4th child of BERT B. & DORA (MITCHELL) FOSTER, was born, married, and bore her children in Elk City, Kansas. For years, she was pardner with her sister in the hair-styling business. Wanda L. married in Fredonia, Wilson, Kansas, to JOHN DELBERT McELWAIN, where she still lives.

JOHN DELBERT McELWAIN b. July 8, 1818 d. Sept 11, 1971
WANDA AMERICA (FOSTER) b. Apr. 17, 1918
Were married Nov. 14, 1940, Kansas. To this union were born:

1. GLENDA JEAN
2. JANET DEE
3. GENNETH ELLEN
4. JUDY SUE
5. JAMIE LYNN

6. JOHN LEE

GLENDA JEAN, (#1 above) born in Elk City, Kansas, married DARREL WAYNE McLAUGHLIN Oct. 29, 1965. They have two children: 1) SHERRIE DAWN, 2) JAY BLAIN.

JANET D. #2 above) was born in Elk City, Kansas and married KENNETH DELBERT IMLER Dec. 14, 1963. Their children: 1) MATTHEW DENNIS, 2) MARK WILLIAM, 3) KENDRA LEA b.
GENNETH ELLEN, (#3 above) born in Elk City, Ka., married JAMES MOON Dec. 10, 1966. Their children: 1) LEESE DAWN, 2) JAMIE LYNE.

JUDY SUE, (#4 above) born in Elk City, Kansas, married BENJAMIN SKIPPER Oct. 14, 1967. No children.

JAMIE LYNN, son of GENNETH ELLEN & JAMES MOON, born in Elk City, Kansas, married ELEANOR ELAINE _____. They have no children but Eleanor has a child from a previous marriage: TRACY DAWN BAUMGASTEL.
Chart pg. 67

WAYNE H. FOSTER, 5th child of BERT B. & DORA FOSTER, was born in Elk City, Kansas. Wayne H. was in the Air Force during WWII, during which time he met and married in Lansing, Michigan to BARBARA LOUISE HOWELL. After the war, Wayne H. tried Farming, but gave it up to be a building contractor.

WAYNE H. FOSTER b. Oct. 19, 1919
BARBARA LOUISE (HOWELL) b. Aug. 16, 1926
Were married Feb. 28, 1946, Michigan. To this union were born:

1. TROY DUANE
2. LINDA KAY
3. KENNETH WAYNE
4. BARBARA LEE

TROY DUANE (#1 above), born in Elk City, Ks., married SHARON CRABTREE Dec. 10, 1966. Their children: 1) KENNETH DUANE, 2) BETTY JO, 3) PAUL ALLEN. All were born in Sault St. Marie, Michigan.

LINDA KAY, 2nd child of WAYNE H. & BARBARA LOUISE (HOWELL) FOSTER, born in Elk City, Kansas, married DOUGLAS A. LEWIS, Dec. of 1967. Their children: 1) RUSSELL ALLEN b. in Charlotte, Mich., 2) TRACY LYNN b. in Vicksburg, Mich.

KENNETH WAYNE, 3rd child of WAYNE H. & BARBARA LOUISE (HOWELL) FOSTER, born in Elk City, Kansas, was married twice, but the 1st one did not take. #2 MARSHA ____, and they have one child: AMY MARIE.

****

LAVELLE LAURA, 6th child of BERT B. & DORA FOSTER, was born in Elk City, Kansas. After attaining adulthood, she met and married JIM T. GROUNDWATER. He is a superintendent for the Santa Fe Railroad.

JIM T. GROUNDWATER b. May 17, 1919
LAVELLE LAURA (FOSTER) b. July 20, 1925
Were married Sept. 28, 1947, Kansas. To this union were born:

1. PEGI ANN
2. JOANNE
3. RAYMOND
4. DONALD
5. PAUL

PEGI ANN married ROBERT STOSICK and has a child: HEATHER
JOANNE married JOE DOWNUM
***Chart pg. 67 ***

BERT B., Jr. 7th child of BERT B. & DORA FOSTER, was born in Elk City, Kansas. Bert B. Jr. is a veteran of WWII and the Korean Conflict. Returning home, he worked in an airplane factory, then as a carpenter. He died in Arkansas City, Kansas and is buried in the Oak Hill Cemetery, Elk City, Kansas.

Bert B Foster Jr. married JUNE HARDIN. She had been married previously to a man named KELSO and had a son whom Bert Jr. adopted.

BERT B. FOSTER Jr. b. 19 Oct 1926 d. Nov. 3, 1969
JUNE (HARDIN) b. Apr. 12, 1928
Were married July 25, 1949, Kansas. To this union were born:

1. TERRY MICHELLE
2. SHEILA RAE
3. SHARON KAY

DANNY GENE (KELSO - child of June Hardin and #1 Mr. Kelso), married REBECCA CARSWELL, Sept 29, 1967. They had a child, who died.

WAUNITA MAXINE, 8th child of BERT B. & DORA FOSTER, was born in Elk City, Kansas. She is married to MERVIN VERN DAVIDSON, who works for the Santa Fe Railroad. Waunita is a cosmetologist, like her sisters, and has won several awards for hair styling. The Davidson children were all born in Emporia, Kansas.

MERVIN VERN DAVIDSON b. Sept 14, 1926
WAUNITA MAXINE (FOSTER) b. Jan. 12, 1929
Were married Aug. 13, 1949, Kansas. To this union were born:

1. DIANA JANE
2. BETTY JEAN
3. JOHN ALLEN

DIANE JANE (#1 above) married RALPH MARTIN MALONEY Sept 18, 1967. They divorced after the birth of their child: ANTHONY MARTIN b. May 10, 1968 in Emporia, Kansas.
Chart pg. 67

TREVA MAE, 9th child of BERT B. & DORA FOSTER, was born in Elk City, Kansas. She married WILFORD FEHR, and they live in Emporia, Kansas, where their children were born.

WILFORD FEHR b. July 27, 1924
TREVA MAE (FOSTER) b. Aug. 7, 1931
Were married Sept 29, 1950, Kansas. To this union were born:

1. STEPHEN
2. DAVID

Allen Dallas Foster (son of William Harrison Foster and Telitha Henline) married #2, a Mrs. Jones, a widow with four children, and during a family argument he killed both her and himself.

This ends the families of PHEBEE & GEORGE ARCHIBALD FOSTER b. 1804.

***** **A SECOND FAMILY OF FOSTERS** *****

In his history Grandpa F. J. Foster gave me in 1938 he listed this family as given here, noting that there were two marriages. Since he had known George A. Foster through ages 10 to 19 it is assumed that his family division is correct.

ROBERT FOSTER, (DNA - Paternal Haplogroup R1b1b2a1a2f*), father of most of this family, first appeared on the screen in 1793, when he was on the Nicholas Co. Kentucky tax list. He is in adjacent Bourbon Co., KY in 1794 when he is found in the same company with William Foster's son Harrison, serving in Capt. Joseph Colvin's Company of Kentucky Mounted Volunteers in the Northwest Indian War. Shortly after returning from a victorious engagement known as The Battle of Fallen Timbers, which took place near Maumee, Ohio, Robert returned to Bourbon County and married his first wife, Elizabeth Leary on Nov. 13, 1794, daughter of Dennis Leary and sister of Dennis Leary Jr. Elizabeth Leary was the mother of: 1) SAMPSON, 2) DENNIS, pg. 31; 2nd wife Bathsheba Williams was the mother of: 1) GEORGE A. 2) ELLENDER, pg. 55, 3) JAMES T. pg.31, 4) RUTH, 5) SILVIN (Sullivan), who married and had RICHARD & ROBERT. It is now believed but not yet proved that Bathsheba and Robert are also the parents of William Foster born around either 1802 or 1809, who married Elizabeth Raines 17 Aug 1829 in Switzerland Co., Indiana. Elizabeth Raines was the daughter of Mary Ann (Moore) Raines Hutson and her first husband, Thomas Raines, who died rather young. Mary Ann's daughter by her 2nd husband, Jacob Hutson, Tabitha, married George Foster, son of Robert Foster b. 1770.

Robert was gone from the 1804 tax list, and I (Flavius) have failed to find positive trace of him since (more has been learned since Flavius' passing, below). However, Elizabeth, daughter of Robert's son, Dennis, once told Gr. Grandfather S. J. Foster that Robert and wife #2 died in Indiana.

DENNIS FOSTER lived in Shelby Co., Kentucky till 1831, at which he moved to Hancock Co., Indiana. The family resided in Hancock County till 1842, during Elizabeth's age 6 to 17, so she was old enough to have remembered. Therefore, Robert Foster and wife #2 MAY have died in Hancock Co., Indiana.

Grandpa F. J. Foster thought that this second line of Fosters were blood-related to our line, but 18 years of steady research has only turned up this much. Robert Foster married wife #1 in Kentucky where some of his children were born. At least two children, GEORGE in 1804, and ELLENDER in 1805 were born to wife #2 in Ohio. Identity of wife #2 is only the letter B. on Ellender's tombstone. *(Note from Adrienne: We now have much more data on this family thanks to the internet, sharing of data, genealogy publications, and much prayer. We now know that wife #2 was Bathsheba Williams, sister of Rawleigh Williams with whom Robert served in the Northwest Indian Wars, and daughter of John and Sarah (Sullivan) Williams.) John Williams was a Revolutionary soldier who died either during the war or shortly after, probably from battle wounds or sickness.*

ROBERT FOSTER b. 1770 Virginia (DNA - Paternal Haplogroup R1b1b2a1a2f*), his death date and place are not yet proven, but the location is believed to be Marion or Hancock Co., Indiana. Married #1 **ELIZABETH LEARY** 13 Nov 1794 Bourbon Co., KY. Elizabeth b. 1780 Hampshire, VA, d. 1799 in Nicholas or Bourbon Co., Kentucky. Two of his gggg-grandsons had their DNA tested and were found to be in the Haplogroup above.
Children:

1. SAMUEL OR SAMPSON b. 1795 Nicholas, KY, m. Anna Jones 15 Sep 1818 Clark Co., KY
2. DENNIS b. 1799 Nicholas, KY, d. 6 Sep 1846 McLean, Illinois, m. Mary Polly Foster 4 Jan 1819 Clark Co., KY. Mary Polly is the daughter of Harrison Foster and Anna Margaret Bartlett. Harrison is the son of Revolutionary Soldier William Foster and Sallie Slade. Their children are listed previously with Mary Polly Foster's family.

Sadly, I have been unable to locate more information on Samuel/Sampson other than the following, which reveals that Sampson was probably a nickname, and Samuel was the given name:

GUARDIANSHIP: *John LEARY is appointed guardian to* ***Sam'l FOSTER****. Surety: Henry CURTRIGHT. 1 June 1812 (Note: this was necessary because their father was away fighting in the War of 1812) . Source: BOURBON COUNTY LOOSE PAPERS,*
1811-1813 (LDS Microfilm #183080) –Note: Henry Curtright is the brother of Sarah Curtright, who married Dennis Leary Jr., uncle of Dennis and Samuel Foster.
GUARDIANSHIP: *John LARY (who signs LEARY) is appointed guardian of* ***Dennis FOSTER****.*

Surety: Henry CURTRIGHT. 1 June 1812. Source: BOURBON COUNTY LOOSE PAPERS, 1811-1813 (LDS Microfilm #183080)

MARRIAGE:

Samuel Foster to Anna Jones 15 Sep 1818, Clark County, witnessed by Jacob Hutson (Note: Jacob Hutson's daughter Tabitha married George Foster, half-brother to Samuel through Robert's 2nd wife Bathsheba Williams)
Dennis Foster to Polly Foster 14 Jan 1819, Clark County
Source: Kentucky Marriages 1802 to 1850 - www.ancestry.com

Flavius Foster , author of "Seedlings of William Foster," collaborated with my mother (Gloria T. Foster), grandmother (LeNora T. Foster), and sister (Kathie Foster Shepherd) on Foster genealogy. He wrote a letter to my sister around 1978, signed with his own hand. In it he wrote:

"Anthony and Mary A. Moore came to Virginia in time for the Rev. War, but he deserted us after 4 months, and moved to Kentucky, settling near Lexington, Fayette County. They had 8 children, but I'm going to use only three (3) of them. Sara b. Va. - Elizabeth b. Va. - Mary Ann b. Va.
#2 - Andrew Hutson had 3 children:--SAMUEL - JACOB (Ky.) - RICHARD (Va.) They too lived in Fayette and Clark Co., Ky.
#3 - Mary Ann Moore m. #1 Thomas RAINS, and had two children. She married #2, Jacob HUTSON, and had TABITHIA, who married GEORGE FOSTER, Dennis' (our 3ggfather) brother.
#4 - Elizabeth MOORE married Richard HUTSON, lived in Hancock Co., Ind.
#5 - Sarah MOORE married JOHN LEARY, lived in Hancock Co., Ind.
***Now here is more news**; 1850 US Census of Hancock Co., Ind. In the family of John & Sarah (Moore) Leary's son, THOMAS is listed:--PERRY J. HUTSON, aged 7 years. ***In Richard & Elizabeth (Moore) Hutson's family is listed a ROBERT J (L) FOSTER and a JONES FOSTER. On Sept. 11, 1818, Jacob Hutson witnesses a marriage between a SAMUEL FOSTER & ANNA JONES. ***Now, what does all the above add up to????? Could Grandpa have been wrong when he wrote that Dennis Foster's full-brother's name was Sampson, and it was really, Samuel?"*
The above is an exact transcription of Flavius' letter , however, copies are available from Adrienne Foster Potter at apnewz@yahoo.com

Robert Foster married:
#2 BATHSHEBA WILLIAMS 28 May 1800 Nelson Co., KY. Bathsheba b. 1773 Virginia They were married May 28, 1800 Nelson County, Kentucky. She was a sister of Rawleigh Williams of Nelson County, KY, who was in the same company with Robert and Harrison Foster during the Northwest Indian War and the Battle of Fallen Timbers.

"Know all men by these presents that Msrs. Robert Foster and James Hughes (Note: James is the husband of Bathsheba's sister Cynthia) are held and firmly bound unto his Excellency James Garrard the Governor of Kentucky in the full and just sum of fifty Pounds current Money to the payment of which will and truly to be made to his Excellency Aforesaid and his successors, we bind ourselves our heirs executors and

administrators jointly and severally firmly by these presents sealed with our seals and dated this 27th day of May 1800 ----
The condition of the above Obligation is such that if there should be no lawful cause to obstruct a Marriage Shortly intended between the above bound Robert Foster and Baersheba William both above the age of twenty-one years --- for which a license has issued then the Above Obligation to be Void else to remain in full power and virtue. Signed: Robert G(?) or S(?) Foster and James Hughes. Witness: Ben Grayson (clerk)" -- Record obtained directly from Clerk of Nelson Co. KY

Children of Robert Foster and #2 Bathsheba Williams:

1. WILLIAM b. about 1802 d. 1840 m. ELIZABETH RAINES (dau. of MARY ANN MOORE – mother-in-law of #2 George Archibald below -- and #1 THOMAS RAINES) more below
2. GEORGE ARCHIBALD b. 1804 d. 9 Oct 1874 m. TABITHA HUTSON (dau. of JACOB HUTSON & MARY ANN MOORE)
3. ELLENDER b. 1805 d. 29 Dec 1855 m. HARRISON FOSTER Jr.
4. JAMES T. b. 1807 d. before 1867 m. PHOEBE FOSTER (dau. of WILLIAM FOSTER & CATHERINE LINEBACK)
5. RUTH b. 1809
6. SULLIVAN b. 1811 d. bef. 1847 m. SARAH SALLY HUTSON—sister of Tabitha Hutson above (he is named for his grandmother's maiden name of Sullivan.)

NEW DATA ON ROBERT FOSTER b. 1770 OF BOURBON, KENTUCKY

The reason Flavius Foster and LeNora, Gloria, and Kathie Foster had such a hard time finding data on Robert Foster has come to light now that they are all gone. There was a fire at the National Archives that burned the records of an entire department, including those of gggg-grandfather, Robert Foster b. 1770. Thankfully, a few historians had transcribed parts of these records and published them in books before the fire occurred. One of these is "*AMERICAN MILITIA IN THE FRONTIER WARS, 1790-1796*," by Murtie June Clark, published by Clearfield. Though rich in data, this book had at one time become obscure, but after many years of prayer I found it in a tiny LDS Genealogy library in Orange County, California. It is also found now on ancestry.com. Robert Foster is found on pg. 46 next to Harrison Foster and Michael Hornback. Four of Robert's children eventually married four of Harrison's children or grandchildren.

Murtie June Clark revealed that Robert and Harrison Foster had fought as comrades in the Battle of Fallen Timbers on Aug. 20, 1794. Michael Hornback (witness to estate sale of James Foster d. 1790 of Bourbon, KY) was originally in their company but was transferred to Baker's spies, also under Maj. Gen. Charles Scott's command. This battle--a major part of the Northwest Indian War--was a decisive victory for the Americans and resulted in the treaty that granted them the right to inhabit the Northwest Territory. Robert and Harrison were listed in a Company of Mounted Volunteers, July 10 to Oct 23, 1794, in Capt. Joseph Colvin's Company, Major Notley Conn 's Battalion, under Major General Charles Scott, and served from July 10 to Oct 23, 1794. By their dates of service and the company in which they served we know that they fought in the

Battle of Fallen Timbers on Aug. 20, 1794 in Maumee, Ohio (near Toledo, OH) under Capt. Joseph Colvin, who later served as a State Representative from Bourbon County. Harrison and Robert Foster both lost their horses on Sept 3, along with several other men. This was a frequent occurrence, as horses were often stolen by Indians or spooked by wolves.

General Charles Scott commanded the Kentucky Mounted Volunteers in the Wayne Campaign (General "Mad Anthony" Wayne) 1793-94 in the Northwest Indian War. A warrior named Tecumseh was also in the Battle of Fallen Timbers, who would later become the Indian Chief who would unite five tribes with the British and French against the Americans in the War of 1812 in Ontario, Canada. One of General Wayne's officers was 21-year-old William Henry Harrison, who would command troops as a General in the War of 1812 and later become the 9th President of the United States. A treaty was finally signed by the Indians and the Americans, in which the Indians agreed to withdraw to northern Ohio, but not all the Indians approved the treaty and there was fighting between Indians and settlers for the next 20 years in this region.

I discovered more “genealogy gold” a year later when I found the estate sale of James Foster who died in Bourbon, Kentucky in 1790, at the Salt Lake City Genealogy Library. At first I was unable to link the sale in any way to Robert Foster b. 1770, but when I investigated the three witnesses, one of whom was Michael Hornback, I realized the connection. Besides serving in the Northwest Indian War with Robert Foster, Michael Hornback is a distant cousin by marriage of Elizabeth Leary, Robert's first wife who died so young. The relationship is that Elizabeth Leary's grandfather, Thomas Leary, married #2 Margaret Hornback around 1755. Margaret and Michael Hornback both descend from Warnarr Hornback b. 1645, whose genealogy has been published and is available from various sources. The Hornback, Curtright, and Leary families migrated together from Hampshire Co., Virginia to Bourbon Co., Kentucky and are found in the censi of both locations. Since Hornback and Curtright are unusual “tracer” names it is evident that these are the same families.

Did Robert Foster and Harrison Foster know each other before they enlisted in the same company in 1794? It seems likely that they did, in accordance with the belief of Flavius Foster's grandfather that they were blood relatives, but more research is needed. It is likely that James Foster who died in Bourbon Co. around 1790 is either the father or uncle of Robert Foster b. 1770. The question remains, is James Foster: 1) the long-lost son of George Foster and Margaret Grigsby who was born about 1745 and is found with his brothers in the census below? or 2) James b. 30 Sep 1733 Abingdon Parish, the son of John Foster of Abingdon Parish, Prince William, VA, who married Jane? or 3) one of the members of the large family that immigrated from Ireland around 1750 and included Robert Foster and Margaret McCord--who settled in Adams Co., Ohio. Robert and Margaret Foster had numerous children and named none of them Robert, but it is highly interesting that there are two Robert Fosters in the Adams, OH census in 1820 (one in Wayne Co., one in Meigs Co.). Are these Irish Fosters related to the Prince William Co. Fosters? Again, more research is needed, but one of the most telling clues is that several of the Fosters of Prince William Co., Virginia all ended up near each other in Bourbon and Clark Counties, namely:

1. Rev. Soldier William P. Foster, son of George & Margaret (Grigsby) Foster
2. Jeremiah Foster, son of William II—George Foster's brother
3. John Foster, brother of No. 2, Jeremiah.

George and Margaret Foster had a son named James who disappeared from Prince William Co, about whom very little is known. Is he the James Foster who died in Bourbon Co., KY in 1790? Maybe if enough of us compile our data the truth will come to light.

1783-1786 VA Tax Lists-Greenbrier County (adjacent to Monroe Co., WV)
Fosster, John (spelling from original document retained)
Fosster, James
Foster, Robt.

Details of children of Robert Foster and #2 Bathsheba Williams:

WILLIAM FOSTER, 1st child of ROBERT FOSTER & BATHSHEBA (WILLIAMS) a. abt 1803 d. bef. 1853, married ELIZABETH RAINES 17 Aug 1829 in Switzerland Co., Indiana. Elizabeth was the daughter of Mary Ann Moore and #1, Thomas Raines. Their children:

1. MARY ANN b. abt 1830 m. HENRY LANKFORD 23 Jan 1853 (Henry Loyal below was the bondsman for this marriage)
2. LUCINDA b. abt 1831 m. HENRY LOYAL 23 Mar 1847
3. WILLIAM Jr. b. abt 1833

William Foster died and Elizabeth Raines Foster married a Mr. Riche, as noted in the marriage bond of her daughter Mary Ann:

Shelby Co. KY Marriages 1834-1869 *by Ella Richardson Hasskurl:*
*Henry Lankford and Mary Ann Foster, dau. of Elizabeth (Raines) Riche (late Foster) 23 Jan 1853, bondsman *Henry Loyal. Note: *Henry Loyal m. Lucinda Foster, dau. of Wm. Foster and Eliz. Raines, on 23 Mar 1847.*

Carolyn "Wiggi" Dietz, a descendant of Jacob Foster and Mary Ann Moore wrote to me that their family tradition was that this William Foster was the son of Robert Foster. The record below proves that there were TWO William Fosters in Switzerland County, Indiana in 1829—one who got married and one who performed the marriage.

Indiana Marriage Collection, 1800-1941
Name: ***William Foster***

Spouse Name:	*Elizabeth Raines*
Marriage Date:	*17 Aug 1829*
Marriage County:	*Switzerland*
Performed By:	***Foster, William*** *(Note: this is the son of Harrison Foster)*

Elizabeth Raines (wife of William Foster), was the daughter of Mary Ann Moore (mother-in-law of George Archie Foster b. 1804) and her 1st husband Thomas Raines. When I learned the following facts I decided to place William, husband of Elizabeth Raines, into Robert's (b. 1770)

family. I had always suspected that Robert had more children but more research is needed on this line :
1. George Archie's known brother Sullivan named a son William;
2. William son of Robert married Elizabeth Raines in Switzerland, IN, where many of our Fosters lived for a time;
3. William, husband of Elizabeth Raines lived in Shelby, KY at the same time that Mary Ann Moore (his mother-in-law) and Dennis Foster lived there,
I decided to place William, husband of Elizabeth Raines, into Robert's (b. 1770) family, but remain open to the fact that William could be a nephew of Robert rather than a son. I had always suspected that Robert had more children but more research is needed on this line because there were so many Fosters in Bourbon Co., Kentucky. (Adrienne Potter)

NEW DATA ON BATHSHEBA WILLIAMS AND HER ANCESTORS

Thanks to the research of Julie Richards and the DAR we now know the parents of Robert Foster's second wife, Bathsheba Williams:

DAR Patriot Index *- Centennial Edition, Bk. III: "John Williams b. 1740 Virginia, d. D 1782 Virginia, married Sarah Sullivan. He was a Lt. in the Virginia troops."*

John Williams died either during or shortly after the Revolutionary War, and his will – which names Bathsheba as Barshelea--follows the family data below. Keep in mind that with their Scotch-Irish accent Bathsheba and Barshelea would be pronounced nearly the same way, and they spelled names as they heard them. Barshelea could have been a loving father's nick-name for the biblical name of Bathsheba, or it could have been derived from the Gaelic word "barrag" which means daughter or girl-child, and Sheila, a common Irish name.

WILL OF JOHN WILLIAMS (b. 1740) – Note: Will was located in Jefferson Co., KY, near Nelson County where John William's children ended up, and where John Williams died.
I John Williams do make this my last will & is as followeth vis:
It is my desire that my friend Morias Hansbrough take my too small sons William & Rawleigh & one bed-2'd. That my Daughter Sarah have the bed I now ly on, My cow & calf, and to have the care of my little Daughter, **Barshelea**. 3'd that Robert Akin have my son John , & my Daughter Santha. 4th I leave my son George Sullivan Williams the residue of my estate after my just debts are paid-Lastly: I leave my friend Morias Hansbrough, Executor to this my last will & testament
Seal '& deliver 'd In presence of) his Henry Floyd &
Benja Pope) Jno x Williams (seal
mark
At a court held for Jefferson County on the 8th January, 1783
The above will proved & admitted to record
Test Mer 'th Price Clk. Jeff Cur
This will is on record at the Jefferson County courthouse in Kentucky
A copy was made Aug. 1979

Note from Dot Smithson, a Williams descendant:
I believe John's father is Roger Williams. Ancestry (.com) has John- Roger-Shadrack-Roger-Shadrack. Roger Williams, (but no sources). Founder of RI was the brother of the last Shadrack. James Williams was the father of Shadrack & Roger. I haven't tried to prove any of this, but the family did come from Wales. If I can help with more information, let me know. descendant Dot Smithson dot1927@roadrunner.com

John Williams was with George Rogers Clark during the building of Fort Nelson in Louisville, Ky. His will is the third will on record in Louisville, Ky. –from descendant Rita Marsh

Noble Nash, husband of Sarah Williams, is in the US Federal Census for 1810, 1820, and 1830 in Shelby County, Kentucky. In the 1830 Census, he is listed as "North of the road from Louisville, to Frankfort, Shelby, Kentucky." This is the same location given in the 1830 Census for Dennis and George Foster, sons or Robert Foster and Bathsheba Williams. Sarah (Williams) Nash--sister of Bathsheba--and her husband Noble raised Bathsheba from the time she was a small child since the Williams children were orphans, having lost their mother (Sarah Sullivan Williams) in 1780 and their father (John Williams) in 1782. (see will of John Williams b. 1740).

It may have been this sad little fact that endeared Robert Foster to Bathsheba when he showed up in Nelson Kentucky with two small, motherless boys, perhaps visiting her brothers Rawleigh and William, with whom he served in the Frontier Wars (Battle of Fallen Timbers)--or he may have been visiting his Foster cousins in Nelson County (John and William Foster) who were the children and grandchildren of Anthony Samuel Foster b. 1691 Essex, VA. Having been an orphan herself since about age 2 or 3, Bathsheba must have been drawn to this lonely and brave young man as he struggled to keep his babies fed and clothed. In the remainder of Bathsheba's life we know that she had at least five children with Robert and that they left Kentucky and probably wound up in Indiana, but more research is needed. Because she raise my ancestor, Dennis Foster, from the time he was an infant, I feel as much kinship to her as I do my blood-ancestor, Robert Foster's first wife Elizabeth Leary.

It is possible that Bathsheba was married before Robert: Source -
US and International Marriage Records:
Thomas Millsap b. 1762 VA m. Barsheba Williams b. 1777

JOHN WILLIAMS b. 7 Jun 1740 Loudoun, Virginia d. Dec 1782 Nelson, Kentucky
SARAH SULLIVAN b. 1744 Virginia d. abt 1780 Nelson, Kentucky or Jefferson, Virginia.
They were married in 1764, probably in Virginia.
Children:

1. GEORGE SULLIVAN WILLIAMS b. 1765 Virginia
2. SARAH WILLIAMS b. 1767 VA m. NOBLE NASH (B. 1765 PA)
    a. THOMAS b. 1800
    b. HARMON b. 13 Dec 1803
    c. CYNTHIANA b. abt 1805 m. WILLIAM O'NAN (b. abt 1803 Franklin, KY

3. JOHN b. 1769
4. CYNTHIA or SANTHA b. 1772 m. JAMES HUGHES 3 Jan 1786 (b. abt 1775) and had:
   a. MARGARET b. 1790
   b. WILLIAM b. 1803
5. **BATHSHEBA (or Barshelea)** b. 1773 m. ROBERT FOSTER 28 May 1800 (b. 1770). Children listed under Robert Foster.
6. RAWLEIGH or RALEIGH b. 5 Oct 1777 d. 16 Oct 1843 Daviess, KY m. ROSANNA or ROSY DUNCAN 9 Sep 1802. Children listed below.
7. WILLIAM b. 1775 d. 9 Apr 1829 Pike, Missouri, m. NANCY HUGHES (sister of JAMES HUGHES) 26 Sep 1791 Nelson Co., KY.

Children of RAWLEIGH (#6 above) and ROSANNA (DUNCAN) WILLIAMS:

1. MARY DUNCAN b. 2 Jul 1803 d. 1870 m. THOMAS DANIEL 10 Jan 1821 (b. 14 Feb 1790 d. 20 Dec 1856). They had: 1) RALEIGH, 2) ROSA A, 3) JOHN W, 4) SARAH E.
2. JOHN b. 1805
3. GEORGE SULLIVAN b. 1 Apr 1807 d. 9 Oct 1896 m. ELIZA S. BECKLEY 24 Mar 1831. (Eliza b. 4 Oct 1810 d. 15 Apr 1844). George m. #2 LUCY SWOPE 18 Sep 1845. (Lucy b. 24 Jan 1823 KY d. 5 Aug 1893. Children below.
4. MISENA ANN WILLIAMS b. 27 Jun 1810 d. 27 Apr 1817 Daviess, KY
5. HENRY HARRISON b. 14 Feb 1813 d. 10 Apr 1817 Daviess, KY
6. J J b. Abt 1815 d. 3 Dec 1829 Daviess, KY
7. ROBERT DUNCAN b. 1 May 1817 Daviess, KY d. 6 Dec 1842 Daviess, KY m. SARAH ANN JOHNSON 21 Dec 1838 (b. abt 1819) and had: 1) ROBERTA ANN who married JOHN T. HARRISON and had KITTY and GUY; 2) MARY CLEOPATRA.
8. MADISON b. 15 Nov 1818 d. 24 Nov 1846 Daviess, KY, m. ANNA MARIE CAMERON 14 Jan 1841 and had: 1) CAMDEN who married HAL MOSELEY, 2) VIOLA who married JUDGE WILLIAMSON, 3) HAMILTON who married ? GARNER.
9. JAMES HENRY HARRISON b. 3 Sep 1820 d. 17 Feb 1911 m. SARAH JANE BRYANT 28 Jan 1845 (b. 18 Feb 1824 d. 22 Dec 1915). Children listed below.
10. JOHN DUNCAN b. 14 Feb 1824 Nelson, KY d. 15 Mar 1897 Daviess, KY m. #1 NANCY DUNCAN JONES, m. #2 SARAH ELLEN JOHNSON. Children listed below.

GEORGE SULLIVAN WILLIAMS b. 1 Apr 1807 d. 9 Oct 1896 (son of Rawleigh and Rosanna (Duncan) Williams)
ELIZA S. BECKLEY Eliza b. 4 Oct 1810 d. 15 Apr 1844. They were married 24 Mar 1831
Their children:

1. WILLIAM MOORE b. 28 Dec 1831,

2. JAMES MADISON b. 26 Jan 1834 d. 15 Apr 1904 m. REBECCA JONES and had Albert and Lucy Moore;
3. JOHN WESLEY b. 10 Feb 1836,
4. WILLIAM b. 6 Feb 1838,
5. REBECCA ANN b. 23 Mar 1840,
6. BENJAMIN FRANKLIN b. 21 Jan 1842,
7. Baby WILLIAMS b. 10 Mar 1844.

GEORGE SULLIVAN WILLIAMS married #2 LUCY SWOPE 18 Sep 1845. (Lucy b. 24 Jan 1823 KY d. 5 Aug 1893. Children:

1. ELIZA JANE b. 13 Jul 1846 d. 19 Apr 1914, m. CHARLES FRANKLIN GILLIM,
2. NANCY ELLEN b. 14 Jan 1848 d. 9 Aug 1890,
3. CHRISTOPHER RALEIGH b. 21 Nov 1849 d. 2 May 1893 m. ALICE COFFMAN 26 Nov 1879. Child: CLAUDE YANDALL b. 25 Mar 1881 who married #1 GEORGIA LANDIS MUNDAY and #2 NELL LONG, who had RALEIGH;
4. RUTH ANN b. 25 Oct 1851 d. 13 Dec 1940 m. ABRAHAM V. MORRIS 29 Oct 1868. Children listed below.
5. MARY ARABELLA b. 8 Dec 1853 d. 5 Mar 1826, m. NICHOLAS HOPE 15 Sep 1887
6. ROSA MALINDA b. 11 Feb 1856 d. 11 Feb 1933 m. CASSIUS MERRITT FORD 28 Sep 1875
7. GEORGE WASHINGTON b. 5 Aug 1858 d. 7 Sep 1896 m. EMMA McINTYRE 5 Dec 1884
8. IDA BELL b. 22 Feb 1862 d. 7 Dec 1930 m. REV. ISAAC NEWTON STROTHER 10 Oct 1883.
9. LORENA EMMA b. 22 Sep 1864 d. 12 Aug 1943 m. REV. NORRIS LASHBROOK 15 Mar 1892 (he died 27 Nov 1935). Child: LAWRENCE CARLIN LASHBROOK who married #1 PATTY THOMAS 1919 and #2 BEULAH LASHBROOK aft 1930.
10. SALLY DELL b. 16 Feb 1867 d. 25 Jan 1895 m. HERMAN DALE JONES 25 Dec 1889. Children below.

CHILDREN OF ROBERT FOSTER b. 1770 and BATHSHEBA WILLIAMS:

WILLIAM FOSTER, probable first child of ROBERT FOSTER & BATHSHEBA (WILLIAMS) b. abt 1803 d. bef. 1853, married ELIZABETH RAINES 17 Aug 1829 in Switzerland Co., Indiana. Elizabeth was the daughter of Mary Ann Moore and #1, Thomas Raines. Their children:

1. MARY ANN b. abt 1830 m. HENRY LANKFORD 23 Jan 1853 (Henry Loyal below was the bondsman for this marriage)
2. LUCINDA b. abt 1831 m. HENRY LOYAL 23 Mar 1847 (some trees think it is Lloyd rather than Loyal)
3. WILLIAM Jr. b. abt 1833

William Foster died and his widow, Elizabeth Raines Foster, married a Mr. Riche, as noted in the marriage bond of her daughter Mary Ann. *Shelby Co. KY Marriages 1834-1869 by Ella Richardson Hasskurl:*

Henry Lankford and Mary Ann Foster, dau. Of Elizabeth Riche (late Foster) 23 Jan 1853, bondsman Henry Loyal

GEORGE A. FOSTER (2nd son of ROBERT and BATHSHEBA FOSTER) b. 1804 Ohio d. 9 Oct 1874 Haddam, Washington, Kansas.
PHEBEE FOSTER b. 1808 Nicholas, KY d. 1828 Switzerland, Indiana
Married 19 Nov 1825 Switzerland Co., Indiana. Children:

1. Unknown baby b. 1826
2. William Harrison b. 28 Jul 1827 KY d. 26 Dec 1905 Montgomery, Kansas
3. Unknown baby b. 1828

p. 63
PHEBEE FOSTER, 5th child of HARRISON & ANNA MARGARET (BARTLETT) FOSTER, was born in Nicholas Co., Kentucky, and was taken by her father to Clark County. When only 10 years old her father, the last surviving parent, died. A year later she made the long hike through Daniel Boone's woodlot with her brothers and younger sister for Switzerland Co., Indiana. Here, Phebee grew to adulthood, met and married GEORGE ARCHIBALD FOSTER (son of Robert Foster and Bathsheba Williams).

Phebee's married life was short and she died during childbirth with her third child, who didn't live. It isn't known if Phebee died in Switzerland Co., Ind., or in Shelby Co., Kentucky, where George remarried. (For more on George Foster's family, see pg. 75 plus.)

Phebee's husband, George A. Foster, son of Robert, was born in Ohio and went with his parents to Shelby, Kentucky, where he met and married #2 Tabitha Hutson, and their children were born. In the 1850's "Gone to Kansas" was the slogan of the day. George was in Hancock Co., Indiana at the time, but urged on by relatives who had gone to Kansas earlier, he hit the trail for Kansas in 1859. In Washington Co., Ks. George bought government land near Haddam (Mill Creek), where he and Tabitha lived out their lives, and are buried.

Sullivan and George A. Foster, brothers, married Sarah and Tabitha Hutson, who were sisters. George is in the 1830 census of Shelby, Kentucky, with 2 sons under age 5, a daughter age 5-10, his wife, and a female slave age 24-36. This means he had two sons and a daughter before he married Tabitha Hutson in 1830, who are probably his children with his first wife Phebee. In the census of his son Thomas, in 1880, Mill Creek, Washington, Kansas, it states that George was born in Ohio.

Dennis, George, James, and John Foster are all found in the 1830 census of Shelby County, KY living on the same road (address: North of the Road From Louisville to Frankfort, Shelby). I think it's safe to assume that Dennis, George, and James, are the three sons of Robert Foster that Flavius lists in "Seedlings of William Foster," and John could be an uncle. (There was a John Foster in Nicholas or Bourbon, KY, who was the son of John Foster Sr., and grandson of Anthony Samuel Foster, who lived in Nelson, KY for a few years.) Also found in Shelby in 1830 are Alex Foster, Stephen M Foster, and William Foster.

George A. Foster is in the 1870 census of Mill Creek, Washington, Kansas, but calls himself Robert (after his father) instead of George. He is with Tabitha and son Thomas.

GEORGE A. FOSTER b. 1804 OH d. Oct, 9, 1874 Kansas
TABITHA (HUTSON) b. 1809 d. 1883
Marriage bond Dec. 5, 1830, Shelby Co., Kentucky. To this union were born:

1. JAMES b. 1831 Shelby, KY d. 17 Jul 1910 Kansas City, KS m. ELIZABETH HUTSON
2. GEORGE WASHINGTON b. 6 Oct 1833 Shelby, KY d. July 17, 1910 Kansas m. #1 CATHERINE FOSTER, and #2 ANNA MARIA MYERS
3. MARTHA b. 1835 Shelby, KY
4. JONAS b. abt 1836 Indiana
5. MARY ANN b. 1837 m. AARON S McCARTER 20 May 1855 Hancock, IN
6. DENNIS b. 1838 Shelby, KY
7. RACHEL b. 1839 Shelby, KY
8. JOHN WESLEY b. 1840 Indiana d. 1819 m. #1 LIZA MELINDA CRUMP 1856 McLean, IL, #2 ELLIE FLETCHER, #3 PERNINIE PATTERSON
9. SARAH ELIZABETH b. 31 Oct 1842 Shelby, KY d. 9 Feb 1920 m. #1 ALBERT BRUNSON 1859 in Kansas (D), and #2 SAMUEL THOMPSON 1878 in Kansas.
10. SAMPSON L b. 24 Nov 1845 Shelby, KY d. May 1917 Topeka, Shawnee, KS m. JEANETTE TURNIPSEED Feb 1866 Kansas.
11. ROBERT ARCHIE b. 9 Aug 1847 Shelby, KY d. 22 Sep 1923, m. HENRIETTA TURNIPSEED 12 Apr 1872 Kansas (sister of Jeanette above).
12. THOMAS JEFFERSON b. 1 Jan 1859 Shelby, KY d. 9 Feb 1940 Haddam, Washington, KS, m. ELIZABERTH M. OLIVER 1880
13. SUSAN b. 1852 Indiana
14. DONAHUE b. abt 1854

JAMES, (#1 above) born and grew to adulthood in Shelby Co., Ky., went to Hancock, Indiana, where he met and married ELIZABETH, daughter of William & Julia A. Hutson. As noted earlier, William and James' mother were double cousins. In 1859, James and Elizabeth Foster joined his parents in the trek to Kansas. Here, in Washington County, James took up land, and their children were born. In the 1800s James & Julia moved to Argentine, a suburb of Kansas City, Kansas, where they died and are buried in the Maple Hill Cemetery.

I have two marriage dates for James, one taken from WPA records in Hancock Co., Ind., and one from James' family records, Nov. 16, 1858. None of the family contacted knows of a daughter born earlier than those in the list, yet there is an unaccounted-for grandson in the 1880 census. But indications are that he was Julia Irene's love child, as she wasn't married at that time. (Hints, etc.).

Note from Adrienne: I believe the above is incorrect due to the age given for James in the 1880 census below. I believe that the first wife of James' father, George, who was Phebee, had more children than previously believed, and that children credited to Elizabeth were actually Phebee's.

In the 1880 Census of Mill Creek, Washington, Kansas James and Elizabeth are shown with most of their children. Popejoy Foster is listed as a grandson, not a son. James is 54 in this census, meaning he would have been born about 1826. This would mean he is the son of George Archie's first wife Phebee Foster, rather than his second wife Tabitha.

JAMES FOSTER b. 1831
ELIZABETH (HUTSON) b. 1838 d. Sept 25,1890
Were married July 30, 1856 ??, Indiana. To this union were born:

1. SOPHRONIA JANE b. July 15, 1859 d. Sept 6, 1896
2. JULIA IRENE b. 1861 m. Mr. EVANS
3. WILLIAM ARCHIE b. 1864
4. JONATHAN WEST b. 1866
5. ADA C. b. 1868
6. MARGARET b. 1873
7. LILLY b. June 10, 1875
8. JOSEPH (POPEJOY) b. May 13, 1880 grandson

SOPHRONIA J (#1 above) was born and grew to adulthood in Washington Co., Ka. Here, too she met and married #1 RAYMOND NORTON. They moved to Lincoln, Nebraska, where their children were born. They divorced, after the birth of: 1) Fred Leonard, 2) Clarence.

For that day and age, there were a lot of divorces in George Foster lines. *Sophronia and Albert are in the 1880 census of Guide Rock Precinct, Webster, Nebraska, Pg. 4, Supv Dist No. 79, Enum. Dist. No. 76. They have been married 1 year, and he was a farmer.*

CLARENCE, 2nd son of Sophronia and Raymond Norton, married and divorced ANNIE CROMILLER, one of three sisters who married into Sophronia's families. Clarence and Annie had RAYMOND b. May 4, 1910 d. 1948. He married and had RAYMOND Jr.

FRED LEONARD, 1st son of Sophronia and Raymond Norton, born in Lincoln, Neb., married #1 MARY AMMEL, who gave him six children before dying in childbirth.

FRED LEONARD NORTON b. abt 1876
MARY AMMEL b. abt 1878
Married in Kansas. Children:

1. JOHN LESLIE b, 22 May 1904
2. FLOYD
3. HAROLD FAYE b. 25 Jul 1912

4. JULIE J
5. Baby Norton #1 died young
6. Baby Norton #2 died young

Fred L married #2, ANNIE CROMILLER, his ex-sister-in-law. They had a child who died young.

JOHN LESLIE (#1 above) married IRENE and had two children: PATRICIA IRENE and LLOYD LESLIE.

FLOYD (#2 above) married MARY RICE and had FLOYD Jr.

HAROLD F. NORTON (#3 above) married #1, ALEENA BODLEY. She died and Harold remarried, but had no other children. Harold and Aleena's children: 1) HAROLD FAYE Jr. 2) ARTHUR LEONARD, 3) MARY ANN.
HAROLD NORTON Jr. married SHARON McDANIEL and had: 1) VINITA MARIE, 2) BRIAN WAYNE.

ARTHUR L. married #1 DARLENE COONS and had: 1) CRYSTAL LYNN, 2) LAURA MARIE, 3) MICHAEL DEAN. ARTHUR L. married #2 BEVERLY CROMWELL and had MARLENA JEAN.

MARY A. NORTON married RAYMOND L. WOOD and had RAYMOND LEWIS Jr. and PATRICK KYLE.

Some of the Norton family still reside in the Kansas City area, but I have failed to locate any of them.

SOPHRONIA J. FOSTER, daughter of JAMES FOSTER and ELIZABETH HUTSON, married #2, ALBERT PRINCE TROWBRIDGE, and lived in the Kansas City, Kansas area, where their children were born. Sophronia divorced him also. Later Albert died and is buried somewhere in Kansas City, Ks., but I don't know if Sophronia married a 3rd time or where she is buried.

ALBERT PRINCE TROWBRIDGE b. 23 Feb 1861 d. 6 Feb 1933
SOPHRONIA J. FOSTER b. 15 Jul 1859 d. 6 Sep 1896
Were married 8 Jun 1879 in Kansas. Children:

1. DILLARD b. 18 Aug 1882
2. MARY A. b. 21 Jan 1885
3. JAMES LLOYD b. 22 Jan 1886
4. INA b. Sep 26 1895
5. BABY #1 died in infancy
6. BABY #2 died in infancy

See you tomorrow morning on top of pg. 79

DILLARD (#1 above), born in St. Joe, Missouri, married KATHERINE CRONMILLER, who was born in Paola, Kansas.

INA, born in Kansas City, Missouri, married ARLIE TRIGG. They had a son: ARCHIE PRINCE, who married DELLHIA ? and had two sons: 1) ROBERT, 2) KENNETH.

JAMES L. TROWBRIDGE (#3 above) married VIOLA ISABEL CRONMILLER, sister to Katherine two paragraphs above. James was born in Gaylord, Kansas and Viola (Ola) in nearby Paola. Later they moved to California where both died and where Viola is buried. James is buried in Kansas City, Kansas.

JAMES LLOYD TROWBRIDGE b. 22 Jan 1886 d. 13 May 1934
VIOLA (CRONMILLER) b. 16 Mar 1887 d. 31 Mar 1963
Were married Apr. 16, 1907. Children:

1. JAMES LAWRENCE b. 22 Feb 1909 m. MARGARET TREVARTON
2. JUANITA WYNONA b. 22 Dec 1914 m. EDGAR SIMMONS
3. NAOMA RUTH B. 31 Oct 1918 m. CHARLES MOORE
4. GEORGIA MARIE b. 1 Aug. 1921 m. EUGENE HAGAN
5. INFANT (died in infancy)

JAMES LAWRENCE (#1 above) was born in Stockton, Kansas, and his wife and children in Kansas City. He married MARGARET TREVARTON.

JAMES L. TROWBRIDGE B. 22 Feb 1909
MARGARET TREVARTON b. 14 Jun 1912 d. 1 Jul 1797
Were married 1930 Kansas. Children:

1. LAWRENCE LYLE b. 10 Nov 1930 d. 6 Jan 1958 m. DOROTHY JEAN ROSLER
2. ALBERTA JEAN m. FLOYD MILLER
3. PHILLIP LLOYD m. BETTY JEAN
4. KATHRYN MAY m. GLEN FALL
5. MARVIN KEITH m. ANN SUTERA
6. ENID LAVERNE m., CLYDE HINDS
7. NADINE LOUISE m. JERRY PITTMAN

LAWRENCE L. (#! above) was a policeman who married DOROTHY JEAN ROSLER and had a son: - LYLE EDWARD b. 18 Feb 1958.

ALBERTA JEAN (#2 above), born in Kansas City, married FLOYD MILLER and had: -- 1) JAMES FRANKLIN, 2) LARRY ALBERT, 3) JAMES F who married PATTY BARNHARD ON 10 Jul 1970.

PHILLIP L. (#3 above) married BETTY JEAN but had no children. However, she had two children by a former marriage: -- 1) KELLY and 2) DEANA JEAN. And they adopted 3) DAVID LLOYD.

KATHYRN M. TROWBRIDGE (#4 above) married GLEN FALL and had: --- 1) SHARON LYNN, 2) DONNA LOUISE, 3) GLENN EUGENE, 4) LAURA ANN. SHARON LYNN married MICHAEL SINCLAIR and had MICHAEL Jr.

MARVIN F. TROWBRIDGE (#5 above) married ANN SUTERA and had: 1) BRENDA.

ENID L. TROWBRIDGE (#6 above) married CLYDE HINDS and had: 1) JEFFERY KENT, 2) DAVID LEE.

NADINE L. TROWBRIDGE (#6 above) married JERRY PITTMAN and had BRIAN JAY

JAUNITA W., daughter of JAMES & VIOLA TROWBRIDGE, married EDGAR SIMMONS and had: 1) GARY, 2) DONNA, 3) CAROL ANN.

GEORGIA M., daughter of JAMES & VIOLA TROWBRIDGE, married EUGENE HAGAN and had: 1) LLOYD EUGENE, 2) KATHY MARLENE, 3) MELODY DAWN, 4) PAUL RICHARD.

NAOMA R. daughter of JAMES & VIOLA TROWBRIDGE, married CHARLES H. MOORE. He was born 21 Sep 1916 and d. 12 Dec 1966. They had: 1) CHARLES WILLIAM who married NANCY JANE BARNABOVI on 25 Oct 1941 and had: 1) ELIZABETH ANN, 2) DAVID LOUIS, 3) BRIAN CHARLES.

WILLIAM A. 3rd child of JAMES & ELIZABETH FOSTER, married EVA AMMEL and lived out his life in the Kansas City, Kansas area. Here too, his children were born and his only son, Harvey,still lives at Bonner Springs, a few miles west of KCK. At present I don't know where William and Eve are buried (1971).

WILLIAM A. FOSTER b. 1864
EVA (AMMEL)
Were married in Kansas. Children:

1. ALPHIA b. Jan 1891
2. CLARA b. 10 Mar 1895
3. HARVEY GEORGE b. 20 Aug 1896
4. ADA ELIZABETH b. May 1898
5. MARGARET MAE b. Apr 1900
6. DELIA b. 26 Jul 1902
7. CHRISTINE b. 1904
8. TENIA b. 1904

CLARA (# 2 above) married #1, AUSTIN STEWART; #2 EARL KERWICK, #3 BILL SULLIVAN. No children were born to marriages 1 & 3. CLARA & EARL KERWICK had a daughter, JUNE, who married LOUIS PATTERSON, and had a son JAMES LEWIS.

HARVEY G. (#3 above) married #2 HELEN TIMMONS SEDGWICK, and now lives in Bonner Springs, Kansas. By a former marriage Helen had 3 children: 1) BARBARA

JEANNE, who married FRANK DOBBE, 2) HELEN JOANNE, who married A. GEARY, 3) CHARLES WILLIAM, who married SUZANNE STOFSKOPF.

ADA E. FOSTER (#4 above) married twice, and had no children to marriage #2, DILLARD TROWBRIDGE. To ADA E. and #1 LEE RICE were born 5 children: 1) MARY, 2) RUTH, 3) HENRY, 4) ROY, 5) PAUL.

RUTH, daughter of ADA E., married #1 MR. SHOEMAKER, and had a son. She then married #2 ROBERT (BOB) VISCOSKY, and had a daughter, but I have no names.

p. 82 – SECOND FAMILY OF FOSTERS; JAMES' FAMILY continued:

MARY, 2nd daughter of ADA E. FOSTER married three times. #1 WARD THOMPSON, no data. I don't have a name for husband #2, for the son born to this union. #3 was to her cousin, FLOYD NORTON, pg. 78. They had a son: FLOYD Jr.

MARGARET MAE FOSTER, 5th child of WILLIAM FOSTER & EVA AMMEL, married HARRY HEZIKAH (Hezekiah?) HOPPER, and had: 1) HARRY Jr., 2) MARGARET.

HARRY FOSTER Jr. married #1 MARY MANSFIELD, and had three children. He married @2 JEAN, and had another child. I have no other data.

MARGARET FOSTER, daughter of MARGARET MAE FOSTER and HARRY HOPPER, married KENNETH CHILDERS. Their children: 1) LARRY, 2) PHILLIP, 3) DAVID, 4) MARILYN, 5) CAROLYN.

DELIA FOSTER, daughter of WILLIAM ARCHIE FOSTER & EVA AMMEL, married JESSE PORTER ATHERTON. To this union were born: 1) HELEN LOUISE, b. 10 Jun 1921, 2) KENNETH MELVIN b. 4 Mar 1923, 3) BERNICE NADINE b. 10 Oct 1924, 4) ALICE MARIE b. 8 Aug 1926.

KENNETH MELVIN ATHERTON (#2 above) married BETTY KUHLMAN. Their children: 1) MICHAEL LEE, 2) DANNY LOUIS, 3) DONNA JEAN, 4) KENNETH ROBERT.

DONNA JEAN ATHERTON (#3 above) married WAYNE MORRIS.

KENNETH ROBERT ATHERSON (#4 above) married CANDACE BUMM 8 May 1971.

BERNICE NADINE ATHERTON, dau. of DELIA FOSTER and JESSE PORTER ATHERTON, married HERBERT McKENLEY JONES on !5 Feb 1942 and had: 1) HERBERT DEAN, and 2) JOYCE.

HERBERT DEAN ATHERTON (son of BERNICE ATHERTON and JESSE PORTER) married SANDY and had JEFFREY DEAN.

ALICE MARIE ATHERTON, daughter of DELIA FOSTER AND JESSE PORTER ATHERTON, married #1 ARTHUR MODRELL, and had: 1) ARTHUR HAROLD, 2) EDWARD LEROY, 3) CHERYL LOUISE.

ARTHUR HAROLD ATHERTON married and divorced MARGARET ANDERSON and had JAMES ARTHUR ATHERTON.

ALICE MARIE ATHERSON married #2, WILLIAM C. BUTLER, who adopted the children of marriage #1 and they had LILLIE MARIE.

"GEORGE WASHINGTON, 2nd child of GEORGE and TABITHA (Hutson) FOSTER, was born and grew to manhood in Shelby Co., Kentucky. In 1854, he went to McLean Co., Illinois with his parents. Here he met and married his cousin, CATHERINE FOSTER, widow of JOHN BISHOP, by whom she had a child. Soon after their marriage, George and Catherine Foster moved to Wyandotte, now Kansas City, Kansas.

In the spring of 1856, George left his family behind, and went further west as a lineman for a government survey party. He drove the first stake on the 6th principal meridian west of Washington D.C., where is crosses the 40th parallel; Kansas-Nebraska line. He helped survey over some fine farm land, and took advantage of his job to pick out a fine farm in what is now Washington Co., Kansas.

During the summer of 1856 George and some surveyor friends crossed over into Indian land, now Jewel County, on a buffalo hunt. While they were out, an Indian War Party passed in behind them and attacked settlements along the Kansas-Nebraska line. They killed many whites and took two women prisoners in the area of Beatrice, Neb. At Butt Oak, Kansas, they killed many people, and when George's hunting party returned, they found a young girl crucified to a fence gate, with large nails driven through her hands and feet. But she lived to tell her grandchildren of the experience. In 1926, when we moved back from eastern Kansas, I was with my father when he talked with one of the ex-captives, then over 86 years old.

After Catherine died, George Foster returned to McLean County, Illinois for a time (with his sons). When George returned to Kansas, Catherine's sons, Howard Bishop and Henry Harrison Foster remained with relatives till old enough to care for themselves....Catherine...is buried in Kansas City...NEW INFORMATION: Howard is in the 1870 and 1880 US Federal Census of Martin, McLean, IL, living with William Foster, brother of Catherine Foster. In the 1910 US Federal Census he is living with Grace and William Luster in Dist. 85, Wapella, DeWitt, Illinois.

GEORGE WASHINGTON FOSTER b.6 Oct 1833, Shelby, Kentucky d.17 Jul 1910 Kansas CATHERINE FOSTER (dau. of HARRISON & ELLENDER FOSTER) b.1834 McLean, Illinois d.1857 Kansas City, Missouri. They were married 24 Feb 1855 in

Illinois. To this union was born: HENRY HARRISON FOSTER b. Dec 1855 McLean, Illinois.

> She is on pg. 63 and 83 of Seedlings of William Foster
>
> CATHERINE, 6th child of HARRISON b. 1806 & ELLENDER FOSTER, was born and grew to adulthood in McLean Co., Ill. Here, she met and married #1 JOHN BISHOP, and bore HOWARD in 1853. After John's death Catherine married #2 GEORGE WASHINGTON FOSTER Jr. (son of George Archibald and Tabitha Hutson Foster). They moved to Kansas City, Missouri, where she died while he was away on a surveying party in Kansas Territory. They had a son: HENRY.

Again George Jr. returned to Kansas, where he met and married #2, Ann Mariah Myers. They tried farming, but it was during a period of years that were very dry, and swarming with grasshoppers that ate every green thing that tried to grow. For ages grasshoppers had been the scourge of the plains states, and were only brought under control by modern insecticides. The same insecticides some of the "wonder boys" are trying to abolish.

The hard times of 1860--61 proved too much for George Jr., so he and Anna removed to Iowa. As we all know, the Civil War was in progress at that time, and George decided to enlist in the Union Army. Not wishing to sit at home twiddling her thumbs while her man was fighting for his country, Anna decided to go along. On Aug. 12, 1862, George Jr. enlisted in I Company, 39th, Iowa Infantry Volunteers, and his wife, Ann, enlisted in the same regiment as a nurse.

On December 30,1862, while on his first campaign, George Jr. was taken prisoner, at a place known as Parker's Crossroads, Tennessee. Nine days later, George Jr. and some other prisoners tunneled under their stockade and escaped from the Rebels. George returned to his unit, where he remained till May 12, 1863, at which time he was discharged due to ill health, brought on by dysentery.

After the war, George Jr. again went to Kansas, this time to remain till his death. Again he tried farming, this time in the Haddam, KS area, where his children were born. In later years, he and Anna retired to Argentine, a suburb of Kansas City, Kansas. George Jr. was the first Civil War veteran to be buried in "Soldier's Mound," in the Maple Hill Cemetery, Argentine, and Anna Mariah, as an Army nurse, was buried at his side." "Seedlings of William Foster" by Flavius Foster, Bk II, pgs. 83,84.

His Civil War report says that his residence at the time of enlistment was Bloomington, McLean, Illinois and he was a private in Company H. It states that he was 32, with dark hair, hazel eyes, and dark complexion. His occupation is farmer and he joined the army 5 Feb 1862. He was discharged for disability 1 Jul 1862. Source: http://www.ilsos.gov/genealogy/CivilWarController

George Washington Foster married #2 ANNA MARIA MYERS daughter of MR. MYERS OR MAYERS on 2 Jul 1860 in Kansas. Anna was born in 1844 in Ohio and died 10 Jan 1922.

George and Anna had the following children:

1. MATILDA ANN was born on 6 Mar 1860.
2. MARY CAROLINE was born on 6 May 1866.
3. MARION LEONARD was born on 2 Feb 1869. He died on 29 Jul 1954.

1900 US Federal Census
G W Foster, head, age 66 b. Oct 1833 KY, age 66, father b. OH, mother b. Louisiana
Anna M Foster, wife, age 56 b. Nov 1843 OH, father b. VA, mother b. OH
Malissa J Meyer, boarder b. Jun 1854 OH age 45, father b. VA, mother b. OH

MARY CAROLINE, 2nd child of George Foster, Jr. and Anna Myers, married WILLIAM JORDON and had a daughter: LULA, who married ARTHUR BELL. To this union were born: 1) VIRGINIA, 2) MARK, 3) PAUL, 4) RACHEL.

MATILDA ANN FOSTER, 1st child. of GEORGE WASHINGTON FOSTER, was born on 6 Mar 1860 in Haddam, Washington, Kansas. She went with her parents to Kansas City, where she grew to adulthood. In Missouri she met and married JOHN FRANKLIN WAGONER. Their children later changed the family name by dropping the O, and the new spelling is used here for all of John& Matilda's children. For many years the family lived in Denver, Colorado, where both she and John are buried.

JOHN FRANKLIN WAGONER b. 18 Aug 1848 d. 1 Feb 1921.
MATILDA ANN FOSTER, b. 6 Mar 1860 in Haddam, Washington, Kansas.
They were married 4 Jul 1875 in Missouri and had the following children:

1. MINNIE A was born on 5 Sep 1878.
2. LEVILA PINKNEY was born on 3 Jun 1882. She died on 11 Jul 1951.
3. EVA DELIAH was born on 19 Apr 1885. She died on 5 Mar 1922.
4. JESSE WARREN was born on 14 Jul 1882. He died on 14 Jul 1964.
5. LOUIS WYMAN was born on 15 Oct 1895.
6. CLAUDE RAYMOND was born on 27 Nov 1902.
7. EDNA IONA was born on 31 Mar 1905.

MINNIE A. (#1 above) married #1 ELWOOD LEE LYONS and had 2 children. Elwood died and Minnie married #2 GEORGE DEAN and divorced him, then #3 GENE KLABER and divorced him. She then married #4 CLIFFORD COX on 12 Jun 1943. There were no children born to the last three marriages. I have no other data on this family.

ELWOOD LEE LYONS

MINNIE A. (WAGNER) b. 5 Sep 1878
Married 7 Sep 1907 in Kansas. Children:

1) LESTER ELWOOD b. 21 Jul 1909
2) EARL EDMUND b. 13 Aug 1911

LESTER ELWOOD was married twice and had children by both marriages. Number 1 was to MAGGIE WOOD 10 Sep 1930. Their children: 1) ELWOOD LEE, 2) LANNY EARL, 3) ELEANOR FAY. Maggie died and he married #2 ARDITH ALICE and had: 1) DONNA MARIE, and 2) LESTER GLENN.

EARL E. LYONS (#2 above) married and divorced JOANNE DUGGINS 1 Nov 1935. They had a child: BEVERLY JO.

LEVILA PINKNEY WAGNER, dau. of JOHN FRANKLIN WAGONER and MATILDA ANN FOSTER, married GEORGE DESPAIN. Their children: 1) ROSCOE b. 1901, who married HELEN FERRELL, 2) PANSEY b. 1903, who married ROBERT NEELEY, 3) HENRY b. 1914, who married HELEN CONNELL and has children, but I have no data.

JESSE WARREN WAGNER, (son of JOHN FRANKLIN WAGONER and MATILDA ANN FOSTER) b. 14 Jul 1892 d. 14 Jul 1964
BESSIE MAE (TYSON) b. 4 Nov 1895
Were married 21 Jul 1912 in Kansas. Children:

1. THOMAS BEDFORD b. Aug. 1, 1915
2. WARREN LeROY b. 9 Oct 1917
3. VERA BERNICE b. 14 Feb 1919
4. Infant - died in infancy

THOMAS BEDFORD (#1 above) married MILDRED M> VAN LIEW on 2 Sep 1936 and had: 1) DONALD WARREN, 2) TEDDY WAYNE b. 19 Feb 1942 d. 22 Mar 1963.

DONALD WARREN married GLORIA JEAN MARKHAM 12 Jun 1959 and had 1) CHERYL ANN, 2) TEDDY WAYNE, 3) RICHARD ALLEN.

WARREN LeROY married DONNA M> COOK and had: 1) KENNETH WARREN, 2) RAYMOND LLOYD, 3) MOLLY MELINDA.

KENNETH WARREN, son of WARREN LeROY WAGNER and BESSIE MAE (TYSON), married KAREN JUSTICE and had JENNIFER.

VERA BERNICE, daughter of WARREN LeROY WAGNER and BESSIE MAE (TYSON), married FRANCIS J. SCHMITT and has a son: DALE JOSEPH who married ROBIN O'NEIL. Their children: 1) ANDREW ALLISON, 2) DWAYNE PHILLIP, 3)

CHRISOTOPHER ETHAN. DWAYNE PHILLIP married KATHLEEN ANN WHEELER but had no children.

*****

LOUIS WARREN WAGNER, son of JOHN FRANKLIN WAGONER/WAGNER and MATILDA ANN DORCUS FOSTER, married CECILE BEATRICE BEASLEY 15 Jun 1918. Their children: 1) DORIS RUTH b. 4 Apr 1920, who married ROBERT WELCH, 2) DONALD DWANE b. 17 Jul 1928, who married VIRGINIA and had two children: BILLY JO, who married JIM PRESTON 20 Dec 1969; and SHERRY LYNN.

CLAUDE RAYMOND. WAGNER, son of JOHN FRANKLIN WAGONER and MATILDA ANN DORCUS FOSTER, married JESSIE ETHEL HAYS 11 Mar. 1920 and had a child: LAWRENCE RAYMOND b. 9 Apr 1923 who married MARTHA LOU CABLE on 26 Jul 1947 and had two children: 1) NANCY ELLEN, 3) DAVID LAWRENCE. (chart p. 85 of "Seedlings")

EDNA IONA WAGNER married her former brother-in-law, GOLDIE JAMES SCHRADER. Goldie was married to her sister, EVA DELIAH, who had died, and there were no children born to the 1st marriage. EDNA & GOLDIE'S children: 1) BONNIE JUNE b. Aug.26,1924, who married ALLEN ALT; 2) LOIS JEAN b. 15 Feb. 1929, who married Allen Alt's brother, MAYNARD ALT; 3) JAMES GOLDIE b. 13 Jul 1933, who married RUBY IRENE JACKSON in 1958.

MARION LEONARD FOSTER, last child of GEORGE & ANNA MARIAH (MEYERS) FOSTER, was born on the old homestead south of Haddam, Kansas, where he grew to manhood. Later, he moved to Kansas City, Kansas, where he ran a ferry on the Kaw River. After tiring of this job, Marion Leonard, or LEN took up the trade of millwright, a job he held till retirement, at which time he moved to Edwardsville, Kansas, where he opened up a blacksmith and cabinet shop.

While employed on the ferry run, Marion Leonard met and married MARY MELINDA TROWBRIDGE. All their children were born in the Kansas City area, and both Marion and Mary Foster are buried in the Edwardsville Cemetery.

MARION LEONARD FOSTER b. Feb. 2, 1869 d. 29 Jul 1954
MARY MELINDA (TROWBRIDGE) b. 8 Aug. 1876 d. 27 Jan. 1944
Were married 3 Jul 1893 in Kansas. To this union were born:
No pets or children below this line: ---

1. LEO ELLSWORTH B. 9 Sep 1896 d. Nov 1962
2. WALTER b. 13 Mar 1899 d. 17 Apr 1962
3. GLADYS VIOLA b. 29 Jul 1902

4. LEONA DOROTHY b. 6 May 1917 (Adopted)

LEO ELLSWORTH, a WWI veteran, served his time on the old battlewagon USS Idaho. After the war be became a weigh master in large grain transfer elevators in the Edwardsville-Kansas City area. Leo E. was married three times, but had no children,. He is buried in the Kansas City, Mo.

Leo E's last wife, who is still living in the Kansas City area was ETHEL SPADER b. 6 Feb. 6, 1895 and had an adopted child at time of marriage: ROBERT GRIFFIN.

WALTER (#2 above), too, was a grain master in the Kansas City area, and spent his life at the trade except for a four-year period during WWII, when he was Deputy Sheriff of Wyandotte Co., KS. Many of Walter's descendants, and his wife, still live in Kansas City. He married LALA VIOLA CARPENTER. Walter is buried in Kansas City, KS.

WALTER FOSTER b. 13 Mar 1899 d. 17 Apr 1962
LALA (CARPENTER) b. 1 Jul 1895
Were married 1918 Kansas.
Children:

1. LEONARD ARTHUR b. 30 Aug. 1919
2. WALTER JR. b. 24 Oct 1924
3. LALA JUNE b. 29 Oct 1927

LEONARD ARTHUR FOSTER is an Army Veteran of WWII and spent his time in Panama, France and Germany. Before and since WWII, Leonard A. has been a fireman in Kansas City, Kansas. Now as fire Captain he has over 30 years of service in the fire department. He married #1, HAZEL EARLINE BIDWELL, by whom he has three children. Hazel is buried in Chapel Hill Cemetery, Kansas City, Kansas.

LEONARD & HAZEL FOSTER'S children: 1) SONNEE MAE, m. JIM BREEZE; 2) LYNN RAE m. RICKY MARTIN SMILEY.

After his first wife's death Leonard A. married a childhood friend, HELEN RUTH McGONIGAL. She has a son, LARRY PETERSON, by a prior marriage. No children were born to marriage number two.

WALTER FOSTER JR., son of WALTER FOSTER SR. AND LALA CARPENTER, was born in the Kansas City area. During WWII he served on the old Battlewagon USS California. This ship of the "Old Navy" was known as the "Prune Barge," the meaning of the name depended on the tone of the speaker. For 18 years until his job was terminated Walter Jr. was a weigh master. Since 1965 he has been with the Kansas Turnpike Authority, working in a toll house.

Soon after his discharge from the Navy Walter Jr. met and married MARJORIE ELLEN SIMS. She was born in Missouri, raised in South Dakota, then returned to Kansas where they were married. Today the Sims and Foster families live on the same block in Kansas City, Kansas. With her husband working shift duty and her son on his own, Marjorie works days for a doctor. She still finds time to do family genealogy and it was through her that I got my material on the families of George b. 1833 & Anne Maria (Meyers) Foster.

WALTER FOSTER JR. b. 24 Oct 1924
MARJORIE SIMS b. 20 Jan 1928
Were married 10 Jan 1947, Kansas.
Child:
RICHARD LEE

LALA JUNE, dau. of WALTER SR. AND LALA (CARPENTER) FOSTER, born in Kansas City, Kansas, married #1 R. REEVES and they divorced with issue. In 1955 she married #2 HUGH LOUIS KENT. He was a widower with children: 1) BARBARA ANN; 2) JAMES LOUIS; 3) BRUCE ALAN; 4) CAMILE GAY.

LALA JUNE (FOSTER) and HUGH KENT b. 28 Jul 1916, have the following children: 1) ALAN LEE; 2) DENISE RENEE.

My eyes and both fingers are getting tired, and this chair harder and harder, yet the Fosters go on and on. See you tomorrow.

GLADYS V., last child of LEONARD AND MARY MELINDA (TROWBRIDGE) FOSTER, married twice, but no children were born to #2, TRISCLE ROBERT ANDERSON, who was born 27 Apr 1887 and d. 13 Nov 1970. GLADYS married and divorced #1 EDWARD WOLFF. She then spend 15 years working for the Holliday Sand Co. of Kansas City, KS. Their children: 1) BETTY JANE b. 28 Sep, 1920; 2) RONALD DONALD b. 18 Sep 1922.

BETTY JANE (above para.) also married twice, with no children born to #2, JOE PAT BALLARD, b. 11 Aug. 1925. Marriage number one was to JAMES LEAKE. Their children: 1) JAMES JOSEPH and ROBERT ARTHUR (twins). Robert married KATHERINE RUMFIELD.
JAMES JOSEPH (#1 para. above) married MARY RUBY. Their children: 1) MARIE ANNETTE, 2) ANN LORRAINE, 3) ROBERT ALLEN; 4) MARY LOUISE.

ROBERT D. WOLFF, son of EDWARD and GLADYS VIOLA (FOSTER) WOLFF, married AUDREY MARIE GALLAGHER, who was born 17 Dec 1921. Their children: 1) DENNIS MICHAEL; 2) KIRK ALLEN; 3) DARREL DEAN.

DENNIS MICHAEL WOLFF (#1 above) married BARBARA WRIGHT.

KURK ALLEN WOLFF married DARLENE ESPY. Their children: 1) ROSS ALLEN; 2) JOEL MICHAEL;

LEONA DOROTHY FOSTER, the adopted daughter of LEONARD & MARY (Trowbridge) FOSTER, married ELDON CULP b. 12 Jul 1911. I have no data on this family.

This ends my material on the families of George Washington and Anna Maria (Myers) Foster. It also brings us back to the other families of George W. Sr. and Tabitha (Hutson) Foster. (**Note from Adrienne: I've never seen George's name written as George W. Sr. I've yet to see evidence of his correct middle name, although I've seen him in the census as George Foster and as Robert Foster (both b. 1804 Ohio).

MARY, 4th child of GEORGE & TABITHA (HUTSON) FOSTER, was born in Kentucky and went with her parents to Illinois. In McLean county she met and married AARON S. McCARTER, (b. 1804 OH according the 1880 Census of Mill Creek, Washington, KS) a veteran of the Mexican War. After the birth of their 1st child they moved to Washington Co., KS. After their children were born, Aaron moved out because of Mary's flirting with other men. Aaron had a great deal to do with this, due to his meanness to the family.

This meanness rubbed off on their eldest child, GEORGE, who married an Oliver girl. She couldn't stand his meanness and left him. George then remarried, and died suddenly, it being thought by neighbors his death was due to his 2nd wife's "cooking," seasoned with rat poison. Another child of this marriage, a daughter, was horribly burned and suffered for three days before dying.

The children of Mary and Aaron S. McCarter were: 1) GEORGE; 2) MARTHA b. 1862; 3) HANNAH; 4) ALICE; 5) THOMAS b. 1873; and 6) the child who died of burns. Chart pg. 76 of "Seedlings..."

"Seedlings of William Foster," by Flavius Foster, p. 91
JOHN WESLEY, 7th child of GEORGE AND TABITHA (HUTSON) FOSTER, was born in Kentucky and made the swing with his parents through Indiana, to McLean County, Illinois. He too was on the 'wild' side, being forced at the age of 16 to marry #1 LIZA

MELINDA CRUMP. They had a daughter, MARIE in 1856 who lived with her Crump grandparents.

The Crump family was well-to-do, and this marriage not to their liking, so it failed. John W. joined his father's family in Washington Co., KS, with whom he was living in 1860. Here again, John read the warning light in a parent's eyes and decided to marry his daughter, ELLIE FLETCHER. To this union was born an unnamed daughter, whom I have been unable to locate.

By the time he was 25 JOHN W. seemed to have settled down and married #3, PERNINIE PATTERSONA (Note: Some records show her name as Paulina). The Patterson family of Washington Co., Kansas was a large one, and many of them married into different Foster families, but for some reason most of these marriages never lasted. This family lived a mile southeast of Haddam, and had their own cemetery, one half mile south of town, and is mentioned in other parts of this history.

HEY! There if goes again, 10 pm, and another day's work done.

JOHN WESLEY FOSTER b. 1840 Indiana d. 1918
PERNINIE (PATTERSON) b. 1852 Indiana
Were married in 1868, Kansas. To this union were born:

1. WILLIAM H. b. May 1870; m. Alice 1891
2. CHARLES b. 1873
3. MARY
4. FRED
5. BARBARA b. 1879
6. CLINT
7. LEONARD b. 24 Dec 1882 d. 4 Aug. 1942

New data: WILLIAM H (#1 above) married twice, first to Alice in 1891 and had: 1) EARL C b. May 1892; 2) EDGAR R b. Jul 1894; 3) ELENA or EDNA M b. Jul 1894 (twin); 4) WILLIAM C b. Jun 1896; 5) ARLIE L b. 1899. Alice died between 1899 and 1905 and William H. married ORPHA in 1905. Orpha was born 1872 in Indiana. Wife #1 Alice was born June 1872 in Indiana.

CHARLES (#2 above) married twice, but no children born to number one. #2 MARTHA AWENS. Their children: 1) GENE; 2) DELPHIA; 3) ALTA; 4) CLARA.

BARBARA FOSTER (#5 above) married a cousin, EDWARD BRUNSON, pg. 93. Their children: 1) BLANCH; 2) MARY; 3) JESSIE; 4) OTTO; 5) MABLE; 6) WILLIAM. Mable and one other daughter died in a home fire.

LEONARD (#7 above) married his cousin, DIXIE LAVADA FOSTER, pg. 103, daughter of THOMAS JEFFERSON FOSTER and ELIZABETH M. OLIVER. Thomas Jefferson Foster was another son of George Archibald Foster and Tabitha Hutson.

JOHN WESLEY FOSTER married #4 HATTIE MAE SPINKS.

JOHN WESLEY FOSTER b. 1840 d. 1918
HATTIE MAE (SPINKS) b. 1880 d. 1951
Were married 1894 Kansas. To this union was born:

1. ELSIE MAE b. 1 Jan 1895 – married three times, but since there were no children born to the last two marriages I'll not give them here. Husband #1 WALTER (DUTCH) BROWN (b. 1888 KS) m. 1910. Children: 1) WILLIS (GOLDIE) b. 30 Sep 1912 in Kansas; 2) CASINA MISSOURI RUBY b. 1919 KS; 3) MICKEY MARYLAND b. abt 1916; 4) MARYLYNN b. 1922 KS.

WILLIS (GOLDIE) BROWN (#1 in para. above) was born in Armourdale, Kansas. He married PANSY LARRBY in 1940. Their children: 1) WALTER LEWIS; 2) JOHN WILFORD; 3) PATRICIA EILEEN; 4) DARRELL RAYMOND.

WALTER LEWIS (#1 in above para.) married MARY TIGER. JOHN WILFORD married MARIE MUSSMAN; PATRICIA EILEEN married JOHN WHELLER; DARRELL RAYMOND married CRSTAL DETHRIDGE.

CASINA MISSOURI RUBY BROWN, (dau. of ELSIE MAE FOSTER and WALTER "DUTCH" BROWN) born 23 Jun 1919, married RICHARD NEIL and bore: 1) LORETTA ALBERTA; who married RONALD HARVEY. Their children: 1) CINDA; 2) JEFFERY; 3) PATRICIA; 4) STEPHEN; 5) GREGORY.

In looking over the families of GEORGE & TABITHA FOSTER I have arrived at the conclusion that they marry and divorce their mates "by the numbers" – 1-2-3-Hike!

***Chart pg. 76 of "Seedlings"

SARAH ELIZABETH, 8th (or 9th) child of GEORGE & TABITHA FOSTER, was born in Kentucky, made the swing through Indiana, and Illinois to Kansas. She grew to adulthood south of Haddam, in Washington County. Here, too, she met and married ALBERT BRUNSON. This was the first marriage in the newly formed county, but like so many weddings in her family, this one ended in divorce. SARAH E. remarried #2, will be given later.

Sometime during their married life Sarah and Albert moved to Almena Norton County, Kansas, Here they separated, but Albert remained here until his death and is buried in the Norton, Ks. Cemetery.

ALBERT BRUNSON b. 1846 d. 1925
SARAH ELIZABETH FOSTER b. 31 Oct 1842 d. 9 Feb 1920
Were married June 1859, Kansas. To this union were born:

1. CHARLES ALBERT b. 20 Nov 1866 d. 7 Sep 1928
2. JOSEPH b. abt 1868
3. EDWARD b. abt 1870 m. BARBARA FOSTER
4. AMY b. abt 1872
5. DAISY b, abt 1874 m. LEE McDONALD
6. RICHARD WESLEY b. 27 Jun 1867 m. SADIE

JOSEPH (#2 above) married and had a son, but I have no names. DAISY married LEE McDONALD and had a son, CECIL, who married and had 3 children.

CHARLES ALBERT BRUNSON was born in Haddam, Kansas, was married in Kansas City, KS, died and is buried in Norton, KS. After he married he moved to Norton County, Kansas, where his children were born, and where some of his descendants still live. In his notes Grandpa F. J. wrote that one of his sisters married a man named NOAH ALKIRE, but I have yet to find this family.

New data:
NOAH ALKIRE b. Oct 1853 IL (son of ISAAC H AND LUCINDA BESSETT ALKIRE)
AMY (BRUNSON) Oct 1861 KS
Married in 1877, to this union were born:

1. CORA A. B. 1879 KS
2. MAY A. B. 1880 KS
3. THOMAS J B. 1882
4. NELLIE L B. 1883
5. ARTHUR RAY 1885
6. PETER B. 1889
7. JOSEPH B. MAY 1890
8. EVA LOUISE B. JUN 1894
9. LUEVA B. 1895
10. GERTRUDE B. JUL 1897

CHARLES ALBERT BRUNSON b. 20 Nov 1866 d. 7 Sep 1928
IDA LUSADA (GADBERRY) b. 11 Oct 1867 d. 31 Oct 1961
Were married Feb. 28, 1888 Kansas. To this union were born:

1. ALBERT ARTHUR b. 28 Dec 1890 d. 6 Feb 1963
2. MARY ELIZABETH b. 15 Jan 1894 d. Jan 1946
3. RILEY WILLIAM B. 2 Nov 1896 d. 3 Mar 1961

4. RAYMOND CHARLES b. 8 Jan 1899
5. MYRTLE ELIZABETH b. 22 Nov 1900
6. BERTA IRENE b. 2 Mar 1908

ALBERT ARTHUR, born in Argentine, Kansas, married ANNIE AMNDA WHITLOCK in Grand Island, Nebraska. All their children were born in Nebraska. After Annie's death Albert A. did a bit of running around and married #2 NELLIE MARRIATT in Idaho. Annie is buried in Forest Hill Cemetery, Kansas City, MO. Albert A. died in Lumpkin, Georgia and is buried in Mount Hope Cemetery, Dahlonega, Georgia.

ALBERT ARTHUR BRUNSON b. 28 Dec 1890 d. 6 Feb 1963
ANNIE AMANDA (WHITLOCK) b. 29 Jul 1895 d. 17 Feb 1953
Were married Aug. 1913, Kansas (don't know why this differs from above).
Children:

1. MAXINE MARGARET b. 14 Jul 1914
2. FRANCELIA MAE b. 16 Jul 1922
3. LAMOYNE ARTHUR b. 11 Jun 1928
4. DARRO DEAN

MAXINE MARGARET BRUNSON, born in Grand Island, Nebraska, married in Olathe, Kansas to AARON THOMAS O'DALL. Their children: 1) JUDITH ANN; 2) PATRICIA KAY.

MAXINE"S daughter, JUDITH ANN was born in Independence, Missouri and married GARY WALTER JOHNSON 24 Jun 1960. He was born 2 Apr 1937. Their children: 1) KIMBERLEY RENA; 2) TIMOTHY CRAIG.

PATRICIA KAY, DAU. OF MAXINE MARGARET BRUNSON and AARON THOMAS O'DALL, married EVERETT LeROY MARTIN on 29 Aug. 1929. He was born 17 Jul 1944. Their children, born in Independence, MO: 1) TRECIA LeDEAN; 2) MARTIN LeROY.

FRANCELIA MAE, 2nd child of ALBERT A. and ANNIE (WHITLOCK) BRUNSON, was born in Bloomington, Nebraska and married HAROLD IRVING PEEBLES. He was born 27 Mar 1918. Their children: 1) RICHARD L.; 2) GARY DEAN; 3) STANLEY CRAIG, who married PAULETTE JOAN SPRING and had a child: KIMBERLEY ANNE.

DARRO DEAN BRUNSON, 4th child of ALBERT A. and ANNIE (WHITLOCK) BRUNSON, was born in Orleans, Nebraska and married in Miami, Oklahoma to BETTY FRANCENE CRAMER on 5 Aug. 1963. She was born in jasper, Missouri 20 Dec 1941. Their children: 1) AARON A.; 2) DARRO DEAN Jr.

MARY ELIZABETH BRUNSON, 2nd daughter of CHARLES ALBERT and IDA LUSADA (GADBERRY) BRUNSON, born in Norton, Kansas, married in Grand Island, Nebraska to SCOTT FRANKLIN THOMAS. Both are buried in Kansas City, Kansas.

SCOTT FRANKLIN THOMAS b. 2 Dec 1891 d. May 1941
MARY ELIZABETH (BRUNSON) b. 15 Jan 1894 d. Jan 1946
Were married in 1919 in Nebraska. Children:

1. BERNICE b. 26 Dec 1915
2. CHARLES LeVERNE b. 29 Nov 1916
3. OLIVER b. 1918
4. LUSADA JEAN b. 9 Jun 1920
5. LUCILLE JANE b. 9 Jun 1920 (twin) d. 1929

BERNICE, born in Almena, Kansas, married CLIFFORD EVERETT ADAMS, who was born Jan. 10, 1915. There were married and all their children born in Kansas City, Kansas. Their children: 1) MARILYN SUE, 2) JOHN SCOTT.

MARILYN SUE married in Kansas City to ARTHUR N. PAOVOLA 10 Aug. 1957. He was born Dec. 1, 1937. Their children: 1) CHERYL ANN, 2) PAMELA SUE, 3) MICHAEL SCOTT.

JOHN SCOTT (son of Bernice Thomas and Clifford Adams), married SUE ANN JOHNSTON 29 Jan 1966.

CHARLES L. (son of Scott Thomas and Mary Brunson), married Alice and had: MARY ALICE.

LUSADA JEAN. (dau. of Scott Thomas and Mary Brunson) married RAYMOND GOODE and had a child: DARLENE.

RILEY WILLIAM BRUNSON (son of Charles Albert Brunson and Ida Lusasa Gadberry Brunson) was born, raided and died in Norton Co., Kansas. He married MARY MILDRED CONARTY 27 Feb 1929. She was born 28 Oct 1905 d. 12 Jan 1968. Riley, Mary and their child are all buried in the Norton, Kansas Cemetery. They had a child that died shortly after birth: LARETA DARLENE 7 Jun 1943.

RAYMOND CHARLES. BRUNSON (son of Charles Albert Brunson and Ida Lusasa Gadberry Brunson) was born in Almena, Norton Co., Kansas, where he spent much of his life. Here, too he met and married EDNA SNOW OLSON, and their children were born. Raymond and Edna now live in La Cygne (in 1979), about 80 miles south of Kansas City, Kansas.

RAYMOND BRUNSON b. 8 Jan 1899

EDNA S. (OLSON) b. 28 Sep 1898
Were married August 26, 1918 Kansas. To this union were born:

1. WAYNE DUANE b. 27 Mar 1920
2. GLENN DALE b. 18 Sep 1921

WAYNE DUANE (above) married and divorced #1, PAULINE SCHMITT in Denver, Colo. He married #2 ELIZABETH LEE HIERONYMUS, Apr. 21, 1946 (It's up to you to pronounce her name.) Elizabeth L. was born Mar. 8, 1920 and was Wayne's ex-sister-in-law. No children were born to either marriage.

GLENN DALE (.2 above) retired from the Army as a Master-sergeant in the late 1960's and is now farming near Norton, Kansas, and doing bookwork for the Chrysler garage in town. He married #1, Elizabeth L. above, and they divorced. On Jan. 22, 1946 he married #2, ESTHER IRENE BERRY, in Kansas City, Ks. She was born in Nebraska Feb. 7, 1918, and their youngest child was born in Frankfort-on-the-Main, Germany. Their children: 1) LINDA SUE, 2) DAVID LEON, 3) JAMES GEORGE.

MYRTLE E. BRUNSON (5th child of Charles Albert Brunson and Ida Lusasa Gadberry Brunson) was born in Norton, Kansas and went with her parents to Argentine, Kansas. Here she met and married HUGH ARLIE MOFFITT, and their children were born. They now live in California. Their children: 1) JOHN ALLEN, 2) RICHARD LEE.

Like meteors in the sky here we come, here we are, there we go!

P. 97

JOHN ALLEN (above) was born in Kansas City, MO and married in Woodland, California to ELIZABETH GAYLE CROWIS Dec. 30, 1951. She was born in Thomas, Oklahoma Oct. 31, 1932. To this union were born: 1) DEBORAH ANN, 2) DENICE ALLENE, 3) DARLI ELIZABETH.

RICHARD LEE (son of Myrtle Brunson and Hugh Arlie Moffitt) was born in Kansas City, Missouri, and married GRACE KLINE Dec. 4, 1952. Their children: 2) SUSAN KAY, 2) ROSALE ANN.

BERTHA IRENE, last child of CHARLES & IDA BRUNSON, was born in Almena, Kansas, and went with her parents to Argentine, Ks. In nearby Kansas City, Missouri, she met and married ROBERT DOONE SINEY, Dec. 28, 1931. He was born in Kansas City, Mo., Sept. 10,1900. After the birth of their only child, Bertha and Robert moved to El Monte, Calif. Their child: BETTYJEANE.

BETTY JEANE (paragraph above) was born in Kansas City, Ks., and went with her parents to Pasadena, California, where she met and married R. C. STROHMEIER, Aug.

11, 1961. He was born in California Mar. 10, 1927. They how live in Colorado, where their children were born. Their children: 1) SCOTT ALLEN, 2) GREGG ROBERT, 3) KRISTA LEE. –All born in Alamosa, Colorado.

Now that we have polished off that family, let's start on the 2nd family of SARAH ELIZABETH FOSTER (8th child of George and Tabitha Foster). After divorcing Albert Brunson, Sarah E. married #2, SAMUEL THOMPSON, who died and is buried in Kansas City, Kansas. SARAH E. is buried in Arroyo, Colo.

SAMUEL THOMPSON b. Jan. 16 1838 d. Dec. 3, 1914
SARAH E. (FOSTER) b. Oct. 31, 1842 d. Feb. 9, 1920
Were married 1878 Kansas. To this union were born:

1. CLARA S. b. Feb. 18, 1880 d. Mar. 3, 1902
2. AUSTINE P. b. Sept 16, 1883 d. Dec. 6, 197-

CLARA S. (No. 1 above) married TOBE FEEMAN and had a son: SILVA.

AUSTIN P. (No. 2 above) was born in Argentine, KS and spent his life in the Kansas City area. Here he married PEARL BARRETT) and their children were born. Both parents are buried in Memorial Park Cemetery, Kansas City, Kansas.

AUSTIN THOMPSON b. Sept. 16, 1883 d. Dec. 6, 1970
PEARL (BARRETT) b. Mar. 3, 1889 d. Aug. 28, 1968
Were married in Kansas. To this union were born:

1. MARIEL (or Muriel) GERTRUDE b. Oct. 14, 1908
2. CLAUDE HAROLD b. Feb. 25, 1913
3. OREN ELEANOR b. May 2, 1916
4. DARREL LOUIS b. May 16, 1920 d. Jan. 24, 1943 WWII

MARIEL/MURIEL G. was born in Argentine, Kansas and married HARRY MARKLEY Jan. 8, 1911. Their children: 1) KARLA ANN, 2) KAREN LYN.

KARLA A. married JIM BRENNER and had a child: KRISTA RAE

KAREN L. married DAVID ENNES Apr. 3, 1971.

CLAUDE H. (#2 above) married DOROTHY BRENNERMAN and had: 1) JOYCE ELLEN, 2) GAIL.

OREN E. (#2 above) married NELSON ROBINETT, who was born Apr. 18, 1915. Their children: 1) HAROLD WARREN, 2) ROGER MICHAEL, 3) NELCYNE DARREL DEAN, 4) JAMES LEE.

HAROLD W. (para. above) married #1 LAWANNA and had a child: TANYA JEAN. HAROLD W. married #2 BRENDA PORTER and had: 1) DARREL WAYNE, 2) KIRK NELSON, 3) BRYANT.

ROGER MICHAEL (son of Claude and Dorothy Thompson) married and divorced JANET FITZPATRICK and had one child: AUDRIA.

NELCYNE D. ROBINETTE (dau. of OREN ELEANOR THOMPSON & NELSON ROBINETTE and granddaughter of AUSTIN THOMPSON) married JOE DILL, b. Mar. 6, 1938. Their children: LORNA KAY and MARK JOE.

R.I.P. SARAH ELIZABETH (FOSTER), your family, as many of them as I have found, are now bound within the pages of this family history. (Chart pg. 76 of original book)

* * * * *

SAMPSON, 9th child of GEORGE & TABITHA FOSTER, also made the big swing from his birthplace in Kentucky, through Indiana and Illinois to Washington County, Kansas. Here he grew to manhood, met and married JEANETTE C. TURNIPSEED. John Cox married #1, my Dorcas Foster (Flavius still speaking) and #2, the mother of Jeanette above, and if you will read John Cox's 2nd family, pg. 126, you will see that Turnipseed-Cox-Foster-Patterson is a much-intermarried clan, when combined with the data in this chapter.

Sampson and Jeanette spent their married life in Haddam, Kansas and their children grew up in this area. When Jeanette died, Grandfather Silas J. Foster preached her funeral. She is buried in the "Foster Cemetery" 2 ½ miles south of Haddam. Sampson died in the mental hospital in Topeka, Kansas. (Jeanette and Henrietta next page were twins.)

SAMPSON FOSTER b. Nov 14, 1851 d. May 8, 1917
JEANETTA (TURNIPSEED) b. July 25, 1851 d. 1894
Were married Feb. 1866 in Kansas. To this union were born:--

1. WILLIAM HARRISON b. 1872 d. Sept 21, 1949
2. JESSIE b. 1875
3. LuELLEN or Luella b. Nov 11, 1877 d. in Sacramento, CA
4. STELLA b. abt 1879
5. ARTHUR b. 1881 d. during WWI (Veteran)
6. HARVEY abt 1883

One son died in infancy.

Jessie married William T Hudgins around 1895 (b. 16 Feb 1869 KS d. 8 May 1966 Roseville, Placer, CA) and bore triplet girls who died soon after birth, and a son, Archie Faye b. 7 Mar 1896 d. 21 Apr 1960 Sutter, CA. Seedlings, pg. 99 original book.

Ancestry.com also lists the following children:
Hallie Harold Hudgins (f) b. 18 Jan 1905 OK d. 8 Sep 1961 Co Ca, Lan Song, Vietnam
Oral Kester Hudgins (m) b. 9 Feb 1909 Butler, Custer, OK d. 26 Dec 1975 Sutter, CA
Claude Orval Hudgins b. 5 Jan 1910 OK

LuELLEN married SHANNIE BURT FOSTER (p. 154), a distant Foster cousin (son of CHARLES FRANKLIN FOSTER and CLARISSA FOSTER—also a cousin). Charles Franklin Foster was the son of Aaron Blueford Foster and Eliza Jane Foster (dau. of Harrison Foster Jr. and Ellender Foster. Clarissa was the daughter of Robert L. Foster and Sarah (Sally) Ann Cox. which continues to reveal the tradition in those days of cousins marrying cousins.

SHANNIE BURT FOSTER b. 10 Sep 1883 Solomon Riv. Settlement, KS d. 27 May 1955 Placer, CA.
LuELLEN FOSTER b. 11 Nov 1877 Haddam, Washington, KS d. in Sacramento, CA.
They were married about 1903. Their child:
LESLEY FRANKLIN FOSTER b. Dec 18, 1913 d. 27 Dec 1931 Placer, CA.

Shannie Burt and Lesley Franklin Foster are both buried in Sylvan Cemetery, Citrus Heights, Sacramento, California, USA.

LuEllen's grandfather Foster and Shannie B's great-grandmother Foster were brother and sister, pgs. 76 & 56. Shannie B's maternal grandmother was John Cox's daughter by his 1st marriage, and the mother of LuEllen was his step-daughter by marriage #2. (pg. 126)\

Flavius wrote that Shannie B. died in Nebraska and LuEllen in Van Nuys, CA; however this differs from records we have available today.

ROBERT A., 10th child of GEORGE & TABITHA FOSTER, was born in Kentucky and made the long swing through Indiana, Illinois, and to Washington Co., Kansas. Here he grew to manhood, met and married HENRIETTA TURNIPSEED, twin to his brother Sampson's wife. For many years they farmed southeast of Haddam, KS, then they retired to California and are buried in Roseville, CA.

ROBERT ARCHIE FOSTER b. Aug. 9 1847 Shelby Co., KY d. Sept 22, 1928
HENRIETTA (TURNIPSEED) b. July 25, 1851 McLean, IL d. Oct. 10, 1942 Los Angeles, CA
Were married 12 Apr 1872 in Kansas. To this union were born:--

1. MARGARET B b. Apr 2, 1873 d. 1919
2. CHRISTOPHER b. Apr 23, 1877 d. Nov 23, 1897
3. WALTER b. Apr 10, 1880 d. Feb 9 1968

4. INA DELL b. Aug 5, 1883 d. Aug 3, 1960
5. BESSIE b. Jan, 28, 1890
6. NORA CECILE b. Sept 5, 1892

MARGARET B. married but I have no material on her.

WALTER was born and grew to manhood near Haddam, Kansas. According to stories I have heard from his daughters, Walter had the knack of getting into hot water with his parents. Like all youngsters, Walter often became so engrossed in childhood games, and put off bringing the cows in till the last minute, but once he got caught. Night had fallen and a heavy fog rolled in while he was tracking the cows across the unfenced prairie. Hopeless lost, Walter finally found the cows lying down chewing their cud. Luckily, the cows knew the way home, but Walter was quite late getting back and his father quite torqued.

Another time his father showed Walter a litter of baby pigs. His father pointed out the female pigs he planned to keep for breeding, the pigs he planned for market, and a pig he planned to butcher for meat.

In his boyish mind Walter thought he would help things along, so the next morning he took the designated pig down to Mill Creek, where he butchered it. Walter's mother was very put out by the too-early demise of the pig, and showed her displeasure. The pig was baked but Walter found it less painful to eat his share while standing.

One of Walter's favorite stories was of the time two grown men swore that had seen a ghost in the local cemetery. According to them, they were walking past the cemetery just after dark when the ghost had risen from a grave. It then had spread its sheeted arms and called to them. When the story was repeated by others a few days later an investigation of the cemetery was made. A big goose had made her nest behind a tombstone, and when disturbed she would rise, spread her wings, and hiss at the intruders.

Walter married twice but the one made in Kansas didn't last. There were no children born to this marriage. Walter then went to Shamrock, Texas, where he met and married #2, MAUDE LEE HIATT. Maude L. had three children from a previous marriage:-- LENNIS LEROY ALLEN, VERNON RAY ALLEN, and VERNELL ALLEN, who married Miss Miller.

Walter and Maude L. Foster's first child was born in Shamrock, Texas, and then they moved to Oklahoma, where the other child was born. Later the family moved to Southern California, then last to Wofford Heights, California, on the shores of Lake Isabella. Walter is buried in the Wofford Heights Cemetery. Maude L. lives with her two daughters in Wofford Heights (in 1979).

WALTER FOSTER b. Apr 10, 1880 d. Feb 9, 1968
MAUDE (HIATT) b. Sept 19, 1896

Were married Jul 9, 1930 in Texas. To this union were born:--

1. BETTY JEAN b. Nov 26, 1931
2. CECIL JEANETTE b. Sep 26, 1934

BETTY JEAN, born in Shamrock, Texas, went with her parents to Oklahoma, then to California. In the Los Angeles, Calif. area Betty Jean met and married WALTER PAUL FLEMING. Their children were born near Los Angeles. They then moved to Wofford Heights, Calif. Here, they own a building in pardnership with the Rogers family below, in which Paul runs a bakery and the Rogers's run a sporting goods store. Betty & Paul own a fine house overlooking Lake Isabella.

W. PAUL FLEMING b. Mar 27, 1929
BETTY JEAN (FOSTER) b. Nov. 26, 1931
Were married Jan 21, 1949 in California. To this union were born:--

1. LYNDIA JEANETTE
2. JIMMY PAUL
3. RANDALL FOSTER

CECILE JEANETTE, born in Oklahoma, went with her parents to California. Here she grew to adulthood and met and married FAY HARRY ROGERS. Their two eldest children were born in Van Nuys, California and the other two in Bakersfield. They now live in Wofford Heights, where they run a sporting goods store.

F. HARRY ROGERS b. 15 Dec 1928
CECILE JEANETTE FOSTER b. 26 Sep 1934
Were married Jul 31, 1954 in California. To this union were born:--

1. CINDE LYNETTE
2. SANDY FAY
3. CHRISTOPHER b. June 7 1965 d. July 18, 1966
4. ANDREW HARRY

INA DELL, 4th child of ROBERT & HENRIETTA FOSTER, born in Kansas, married FRED BYFIELD Mar 4, 1903 and had: 1) ELMER LOUIS b. 28 Dec 1903, 2) LLOYD DELMAR b. 2 Jan 1906, 3) CALVIN KENNETH b. 10 Oct 1909, 4) ALMA HENRIETTA b. 2 Jun 1917.

BESSIE, 5th child of ROBERT & HENRIETTA (TURNIPSEED) FOSTER, born in Kansas, went with her parents to California. Here she grew to adulthood and met and married GEORGE FLETCHER Nov. 12, 1917. George died April 13, 1945 and BESSIE lives with her daughter in Van Nuys. They had: LOIS MOZELLE b. 6 Feb 1921, who married LENNIS LEROY ALLEN May 23, 1941. He was born Jan. 11, 1921. (Note pg. 101, para. #4) Children:--1) LORIE JEAN, 2) STEVEN LENNIS, who married MARGARET ANN CRAIG April 30 1977.

ADDITIONAL INFO ON BETTY (FOSTER) FLEMING family (dau. of Walter Foster and granddaughter of Robert and Henrietta Foster.

LINDA JEANETTE married ROY LOU McKINNEY Jan. 13, 1973. He is an auto mechanic. Linda works in a hospital in Lake Isabella, California, where they live. Children: 1) VALERIE BROOKE, 2) LAURIE JEANETTE & TROY PAUL, twins.

JIMMIE PAUL married MARILYN SARGENT Aug. 19, 1972. They live in El Cajon, California, where he is employed in heavy construction. Children: 1) TAMMIE MARIE, 2) JESSE DANIEL, 3) JOHN ALAN & JOSEPH ANDREW, twins.

RANDALL F. FLEMMING married ESTHER SUSANNA ARIAS Sept. 21, 1974. They live in Orange Cove, California, where they own and operate a bakery. Children: 1) RANDALL FOSTER, 2) BRANDEE NICOLE, 3) CANDEE SUZETTE.

INA DELL (FOSTER) & FRED BYFIELD family continued (Ina Dell is the dau. of Robert and Henrietta Foster). Children: 1) ELMER LOUIS b. 28 Dec 1903, 2) LLOYD DELMAR b. 2 Jan 1906, 3) CALVIN KENNETH b. 10 Oct 1909, 4) ALMA HENRIETTA b. 2 Jun 1917.

ALMA HENRIETTA married #1, ALFRED OTTO THOMAS Dec. 24, 1938. Children: 1) DONALD GENE, 2) BILLY WAYNE, 3) NOLAND HENRY.

ALMA HENRIETTA married #2, JOHN HENRY MILLER (deceased). Children: 1) PATRICIA ANN, 2) JOHN HENRY Jr., who never married.

ALMA HENRIETTA married #3 EDWARD A. RITTER May 13, 1955, no children.

DONALD GENE married MARILYN N. and had 1) GEOFFERY O., 2) JENNIFFER C.

BILLY WAYNE married ANITA ZORN and had BILLY WADE.

NOLAND HENRY married KATHLEEN KIRN and had: 1) SHANE LEON, 2) MELISSA KAY.

PATRICIA A. MILLER (Alma's daughter from her second marriage) married RICK PAINTER and had: 1) WILLIAM EDWARD, 2) DIANA.

* * * * *

NORA CECILE, 6th child of ROBERT & HENRIETTA (TURNIPSEED) FOSTER, born in Kansas, came with her parents to California. Here she grew to adulthood and met and married #1 LYNN MaGEE. After he died she married #2, LOUIS JOHNSON, and today lives in Wofford Heights, California. She has no children. Chart p. 76.

* * * * *

THOMAS JEFFERSON, 11th child of GEORGE and TABITHA FOSTER, was born near Frankfort, Kentucky, and came to Washington Co., and settled near Haddam, Kansas. Here he grew to adulthood, tried farming, then took up the blacksmith trade, running his own shop until his death. Here too, he married 4 times. #1, EVA REED, ended in divorce. #2 MARY ELLEN FOSTER, widow of Taylor Pickett, (p. 149 – dau. of Aaron Blueford and Eliza Jane Foster) lasted only a few months when she died. #3 ELIZABETH OLIVER, a widow with a child:--MARY MORLEY.

To this last marriage were born:--1) ROLLO, Mar. 16, 1880; 2) LEONA, 3) DELBERT, 4) DIXIE LAVADA.

ROLLO (Ollie) was a barber in Linn, Kansas, who retired to Washington, Ks., where his is buried. I have no other data on him.

DIXIE LAVADA married her cousin, LEONARD FOSTER, p. 92 (son of JOHN WESLEY and PERNINA FOSTER and grandson of GEORGE ARCHIE FOSTER. Their children:--1) GLENN, 2) AMMIEL b. 1913, 3) LLOYD, 4) FRANCIS DALE b. 24 Aug 1920 Havelock, KS, 5) MARGIE, 6) LOUIS. When last heard of many of these children lived around Topeka, KS.
New data from Bonnie Johnson, granddaughter of Dixie Lavada. FRANCIS DALE (#3 above) married MAY BLEVINS in 1941. Francis died suddenly in 1953. They had four children: 1) JOHNNY DALE, 2) DONNA MAY, 3) RAYMOND LEWIS, 4) FRANCES KAY.

Bonnie Johnson wrote: "Glenn changed his name and kinda' disowned his family. Ammiel married Fern and they lived in Topeka. I last saw them in 1969. Lloyd married Irene--they were both in a fatal train wreck in the 40's. He was killed and she became disabled. They had three kids: 1) Gary Ray, 2) Ruby Lynn, and 3) Penny Sue. Aunt Irene just died in 2009. Louis married Jean and they had four kids: 1) Butch, 2) Cheryl, 3) Leonard and 4) Margie. I heard both Louis and Jean have died in the past five years. Dixie's sister, Leona Bradley lived two streets away in Paxico Ks from the 1940's through the 1960's when she died. My email is floridafauna@gmail.com."

In subsequent emails Bonnie wrote: "There is an awful lot of colorful history to Grandma, she would really have fit into today's society but was way before her time. To me she was absolutely wonderful, so full of love and lots of hugs. Boy did she ever love to laugh. She had one Gold Front Tooth that always made her look so pretty when she smiled. She was the only Grandma I ever knew. My other grandparents were all dead. Tracey's email is tlscatt@hotmail.com

My niece, Tracey, has most of the information on the Fosters. She has been researching and compiling documentation since about 1996.... Dixie's name was Lavada Dixie Foster b. 1892 in Haddam KS d. 1982. Many times she would switch it (her name) around, sometimes Dixie and sometimes Lavada. She is the same Lavada Dixie Allen that died in 1982 in CA. She has a daughter, Dorsaline, that lives in Carson city CA. Dorsaline was the reason Grandma was moved from Paxico KS to CA in the early 70's. Dorsaline and Marvine (Kansas City) are the daughters of Herman Officer, and half sisters to the Fosters. All of the Foster kids are dead and all of their spouses. The last one, Irene, was married to Lloyd and died about nine months ago. All of Dixie's grandkids are still alive I believe. We kind of lost track of each other since my Mom, May, who was married to Francis, died in 1982. Bonnie

Dixie died 30 Jan 1982 in Carson, Los Angeles Co., California.

THOMAS JEFFERSON FOSTER (11th child of George and Tabitha Foster) married #4, SARAH JANE GINGERY in Haddam, Washington, Kansas. Till his death Thomas J. ran his blacksmith shop and is buried in Haddam, Kansas Cemetery.

After the death of his wife Dixie Lavada Foster, Leonard Foster moved in with his father-in-law. When Thomas J. also died, Leonard took over support of the family, moving them to nearby Mahaska, Ks. Here, Leonard died and is buried. Sarah J. Foster continued to live in Mahaska until the fall of 1971, although her remaining son had married and left home. At that time, Sarah J. fell and broke her hip. After a long stay in a hospital, Sarah J joined her son, James S. Foster in Fairbury, Nebraska, where she still lived in 1972. (Note: this information conflicts with what Bonnie Johnson wrote above regarding Dixie's death date. Perhaps we have two separate Dixies to sort out.).

THOMAS FOSTER b. Jan 18, 1850 d. Feb 9, 1930
SARAH GINGERY b. Sep 23, 1891
Were married Nov. 6, 1923, Kansas. To this union were born:--

1. HOWARD ERNEST B. June 23, 1924 d. Sept 23, 1944 KIA WWII
2. JAMES SAMUEL b. July 19, 1926

JAMES SAMUEL married #1 WILMA J. ASTHEMAN, in Haddam, Kansas. In 1969 they separated and Wilma moved to California, where she died. The eldest son lived in Ft. Riley, Ks., in 1972, and the second son was farming near Washington, Ks. The other children were not married.

JAMES SAMUEL and wife #2, ANNA EGBARTS, whom he married Dec. 17,1971, live in Fairbury, Nebraska. James S. is a house painter. In 1972 they had no children.

JAMES S. FOSTER b. July 10, 1926
WILMA ASTHEMAN
Were married Dec. 24, 1948, Kansas. To this union were born:--

1. SAMUEL STEPHEN
2. JERRY LEE
3. ROBERT EUGENE b. July 15, 1954 d. same day
4. RAYMOND LeROY
5. SUSAN

JAMES T. FOSTER, 4th child of ROBERT and BATHSHEBA (WILLIAMS) FOSTER, was born in 1807 in Kentucky and ended up in McLean Co., Illinois, where he married PHOEBE FOSTER 20 Dec 1840. Phoebe was born around 1822 in Switzerland Co., Indiana to WILLIAM and CATHERINE (LINEBACK) FOSTER. William was the eldest son of HARRISON & ANNA MARGARET (BARTLETT) FOSTER. Phoebe Foster died before 1850.

John and Dorcas (Foster) Cox are shown in the census below:

1850 US Federal Census, Mackinaw, McLean, IL:
John Cox age 45 b. VA
Dorcus Cox, age 33 b. KY (this is Dorcas Foster, daughter of Harrison & Anna Margaret (Bartlett) Foster)
Daniel Cox age 15, b. IL
Sally Ann Cox age 13, b. IL
Betsy Cox age 12, b. IL
Joseph Cox age 9 b. IL
Margaret Cox age 5 b. IL

John Cox is a farmer with land valued at $400. There are three Henline families on the same page (John Sr., John Jr. and Martin), and a Patterson family—both are families who intermarried with the Fosters. On the same page is **MARY S or L FOSTER**, age 8, and **AARON FOSTER**, age 5, living with Isaac (b. 1824 OH) and Elizabeth A. Haines (b. 1829 IN). I believe these are probably the children of James T Foster and Phebee Foster. Dorcas was Phebee's aunt and James T Foster may have been related to Dorcas by other than marriage to her niece. Phebee (Foster) Foster died in 1850 and James was either dead by then or serving in the military.

I found George HUTSON (husband of Ruth Foster) and James Foster enlisted together at New Albany, Indiana as Privates in Company K on 18 Jun 1846 in Col. Churchill's Regiment in the Mexican American War. They were mustered out in New Orleans. *Source: U.S., Adjutant General Military Records, 1631-1976 for George Hudson, Indiana 1908, Indiana in the Mexican War.*

I found James living next to George Archie Foster, son of Robert, in the Census below:

1859 Kansas State Census Collection, Washington, Washington
George Foster May 1859 (date of settlement) -- This is George Archie Foster
James Foster May 1859

MARY LUCINDA FOSTER, probably daughter of JAMES T and PHOEBE FOSTER, was born in 1842 in McLean Co., Illinois and later died in 1880 in Missouri. She married WILLIAM BRANSON 12 Jun 1859 in Grundy, Missouri, where her grandmother CATHERINE LINEBACK lived after her husband, WILLIAM FOSTER died. William was born about 1835 in Virginia. Children of Mary Lucinda and William Branson: 1) JAMES WILLIAM BRANSON b. 26 Jun 1861 in Grundy, MO and d. 21 Nov 1920 in Memphis,

Shelby, TN. He married Fannie Dodson, who was born in 1882 in Mississippi. Their children: 1) THOMAS W. b. 1903, 2) JAMES F b. 1905., 3) CHARLES J. b. 1908.

The following proves that Aaron B Foster is a child of James and Phoebe Foster:

Jas. Foster in the Iowa, Select Marriages, 1809-1992
Name: Jas. Foster
Gender: Male
Spouse: Phebe Foster
Child: Aaron B. Foster

AARON B. FOSTER was born in March 1845 in McLean Co., Illinois and later died 25 Apr 1910 at Leavenworth, Kansas. He married Lucy Smith 17 Sep 1877 but they later divorced. Lucy was born 14 Aug 1852 in McLean Co., Illinois and later died 27 Feb 1907 in Leon, Iowa. Their daughter: NELLIE G. FOSTER.

Aaron enlisted in the army 19 Mar 1872, at age 24 yrs. Source: "U.S. Army, Register of Enlistments, 1798-1914 Record for Aaron B Foster, U.S. Army, Register of Enlistments, 1798-1914" ancestry.com. He enlisted in Trenton Missouri, and lived in Leon, Iowa at the time of his discharge. His reason for disability was deafness and rheumatism which began at McMinnville, TN, probably in the battle that was fought there. He is buried in Section 27, Row 6, Grave No. 3896. His daughter, NELLIE BENNETT, who lived at 714 Washington, Kansas City, Missouri, was notified of his death.

Military Records, US National Home for Disabled Volunteer Soldiers 1866-1938
Aaron Foster
Place of Enlistment: 25 Jul 1862, Trenton, MO
Rank: Prvt
Company: B - 23rd MO Infantry
Discharge: 23 Jun 1865, Fairfax, Norfolk, VA
Cause: Expiration of service
Disability: Deafness, Rhuematism
Born: Illinois, Age: 46, Height: 5'6", Complexion: Fair, Eyes: Blue, Hair: Dark
Occupation: Laborer
Residence subsequent to discharge: Leon, Iowa
Marital Status: Married
Wife: Mrs. Maggie Foster, Leon, Iowa
Religion: Protestant
Dates of Readmission: 17 Jul 1891 to 4 Nov 1891; 14 Jan 1898 to 3 Oct 1900; 28 Aug 1901
Date of death: 25 Apr 1910
Cause of death: Pulmonary tuberculosis
Remarks: Died at hospital 10:55 pm, location of grave: Sec 27, Row 6, Grave No. 3896, ***Mrs. Nellie Bennett, dau.*** *714 Washington, Funeral 2:30 pm Apr 27, 1910, Rev. James M. Payne, Chaplain, Pension $42, personal effects appraised at: $14.*

U.S. Veterans Gravesites, ca.1775-2006 *<http://www.ancestry.com/ about Aaron Foster*
Name: Aaron Foster
Death Date: 25 Apr 1910
Cemetery: Leavenworth National Cemetery

Cemetery Address: P. O. Box 1694 4101 S. 4th St, Traffic Way Leavenworth , KS 66048
Buried At: Section 27 Row 6 Site 7

U.S. Army, Register of Enlistments, 1798-1914 *<http://www.ancestry.com/ about Aaron B Foster*
b. 1848 IL
age at enlistment: 24

NELLIE G FOSTER, daughter of AARON B. FOSTER, was born in June 1872 in Missouri and later died 12 Dec 1952 in Macon, Missouri. She married WILLIAM E BENNETT 15 Nov 1892 in Macon, Missouri. William was born Feb. 1870 in Missouri and later died before 1930.

WILLIAM E. BENNETT b. Feb 1870 d. Bef 1930
NELLIE G. FOSTER b. Jun 1872 d. 12 Dec 1952
Married 15 Nov 1892. Children:

1. WILLIAM MILLER b. 31 Aug 1893 d. 3 Mar 1974 Altamonte Springs, Seminole, FL
2. CLINTON F b. Jul 1895 Missouri
3. HELEN ELIZABETH b. 18 Feb 1900 d. 19 Oct 1995 Albuquerque, Nernalillo, NM
4. ROBERT E b. 1906 Iowa
5. KATHERINE b. 1912 Iowa d. San Jose, Puerto Rico, married MR. FOSSETT.

WILLIAM MILLER BENNETT (#1 above) married ESTHER AMELIA PETERSON, who was born 31 Jul 1892 in Boone, Boone Co., Iowa and later died 25 Mar 1971 in Spirit Lake, Dickinson, Iowa. their children:

1. BETTY MAE BENNETT b. 12 Oct 1915 d. 30 Sep 1971 Minneapolis, Hennepin, Minnesota who married WILLIAM REED CRAWFORD b. 22 May 1915 Memphis, Hennepin, MN d. 11 Aug 1992 St. Paul, Ramsey, MN,
2. JANE M. BENNETT b. 1917, who married GAYLORD MATZ,
3. WILLIAM B. BENNETT b. 1924 Iowa.

HELEN ELIZABETH BENNETT, 3rd child of WILLIAM and NELLIE (FOSTER) BENNETT, was born 18 Feb 1900 in Missouri and married LINTON HOFFMAN in 1920. He was born in 1896 in Missouri. Their child: CHARLES D. HOFFMAN b. 1922 Missouri.

KATHERINE BENNETT, 3rd child of WILLIAM and NELLIE (FOSTER) BENNETT, was born in 1912 in Iowa and later died in San Jose, Puerto Rico, although I don't know how she ended up there. She married MR. FOSSETT. Sadly, I have not yet found other information on these children of William and Nellie Bennett.

* * * * *

SULLIVAN FOSTER, 5th child of ROBERT and BATHSHEBA (WILLIAMS) FOSTER, was born in 1811 in Kentucky and married 18 Nov 1831 to SARAH/SALLY HUTSON, the twin of MARY ANN/POLLY HUTSON who married John J. Fawkes. The twins are daughters of JACOB & MARY ANN (MOORE) HUTSON, who are also the parents of Tabitha Hutson, wife of George Archie Foster, who is Sullivan's brother. So again, twin sisters married brothers in the Foster family. His name is sometimes spelled "Silvan" but he is no doubt named after his grandmother's surname of Sullivan. There is a marriage record for him and Sarah in Indiana Marriages 1802-1892.

Sullivan Foster served in the First Regiment of Indiana Volunteers in Company H, commanded by Capt. John McDougal in the Mexican American War -- Marion County, IN. Capt. McDougall later became Lt. Gov. of California and also served one two-year term as the state's governor. Sullivan was mustered in 20 Jun 1846, at New Albany, Indiana, by Colonel Samuel Churchill. New Albany was the location for rendezvous for all of the Indiana volunteer soldiers which had been determined by Indiana Governor James Whitcomb on May 22, 1846. Sullivan was discharged 24 Aug 1846 in New Orleans, Louisiana, also by Col. Churchill. Source:"Indiana in the Mexican War," by Oran Perry, Adjutant General, Indianapolis, 1 Aug 1908. This Company consisted mostly of soldiers from Marion County, Indiana, called the Marion Volunteers. His service record states that he was in Company 'H' of the 1st Indiana Infantry. Sullivan's Company lost a well-loved fellow soldier named Luther M. Beck when he drowned in the Rio Grande while trying assist a party of soldiers that had gone hunting.

*Source for these records is **"Indiana in the Mexican War,"** by Oran Perry, Adjutant General, Indianapolis, 1 Aug 1908. This Company consisted mostly of soldiers from Marion County, Indiana, called the Marion Volunteers. Captain: James P. Drake, Captain, Colonel, 1st Regiment, Company H, Marion County. Mustered in 20 Jun 1846, at New Albany, Indiana, by Colonel Samuel Churchill, transferred 25 Jun 1846, elected Colonel, mustered out 16 Jun 1847 at New Orleans, Louisiana, by Colonel Samuel Churchill. He emigrated to Georgia, after the war and eventually died there.*
***Sullivan Foster**, Private, Marion County. Mustered in 20 Jun 1846, at New Albany, Indiana, by Colonel Samuel*
Churchill, discharged 24 Aug 1846.

I also found Sullivan in the book, "Marion County Indiana Records, Miscellaneous," by June E. Darlington, on pages 38C and 90F. On pg. 38C he is in Wayne Township, Marion County, along with Stephen, George, and Robert Foster, listed as residents. On pg. 90F Robert Foster purchased land in Twp 17 Range SE on 27 Jun 1834 in Marion County. It is interesting to note that Bedford Addison Foster b.1770 is in the 1840 census of Wayne, Marion, IN. Bedford is the son of a different Robert Foster who married Sarah, who was the son of George Foster and Margaret Grigsby. He is a cousin of our maternal Fosters. The Stephen Foster mentioned above is found in Shelby, KY in 1830 along with Alex Foster, Dennis Foster, and George Foster. I have a copy of a land transaction between Sullivan Foster and Alexander Foster in Indiana. Alexander was the assignee of Sullivan Foster, who filed Bounty Land Warrant No. 18,223. The sale took place at Crawfordsville, Montgomery Co., Indiana. I don't yet know the relationship of Stephen and Alexander Foster to these other Fosters, other than the fact that they lived next to each other in Shelby Co., KY and seem to have immigrated together to Marion Co., Indiana.

It is highly likely that Sullivan had a son named Sullivan who married Lucinda Brizendine. The Brizendines were in Union Hancock, Indiana in the 1850 Census. Hancock is adjacent to Marion County.
Other Foster/Brizendine marriages:
1. Richard Brizendine married Mary Foster 30 Oct 1852 in Marion, IN.
2. Sarah Brizendine m. William Foster 13 Oct 1853 Marion, IN.
3. Sullivan Foster m. Lucinda Brizendine 1855
4. Patsy Foster m. Leroy Brizendine 1847 (he is in the 1850 Census in Indiana with a wife Martha and 6 children. Ann Foster and Mary J. Foster are living with him.
Also, Sullivan Foster m. Phebe Hanthorn 18 Nov 1852 Marion, IN. There were some Learys and Hutsons in Marion, IN in 1860 also. Sullivan's father Robert Foster was first married to Elizabeth Leary. The Hutsons were in-laws of Robert's son George Archibald (Sullivan's brother) as well as Sullivan himself. The Brizendines who married into the Foster family are either siblings or cousins.
Source: 1850 to 1860 Marriages Of Marion County, Indiana

Note that many Brizendines are found with the Learys, Reeves, and Hutsons in the 1840 Census of Hancock, Indiana. Elijah Leary below is the son of John Leary, son of Dennis Leary Sr. (Elizabeth Leary's father—she was Robert Foster b. 1770's first wife:

1840 US Federal Census, Union, Hancock, Indiana
Isaac Brizendine
Burke or Brook Brizendine
Edmund Brizendine
Young Brizendine
LeRoy Brizendine
James Reeves
Garland Reeves
George Reeves
ELIJAH LEARY
Richard Hutson
William Hutson
Eli Reeves
James K. Leary
Sarah Leary

Indiana Marriages to 1850 *<http://www.ancestry.com/search/*
about Foster, Sullivan
Spouse 1: Foster, Sullivan
Spouse 2: Hutson, Sarah
Marriage Date: 18 Nov 1831
Marriage Location: Indiana Clark County

Some of the Indiana marriage records say the marriage occurred in Clark Co, others say it occurred in nearby Orange Co. Speculation might reveal that one of them came from each county, or they lived in the part of one county that later became the other county since these counties were close by.

Indiana Marriage Collection, 1800-1941 *<http://www.ancestry.com/search/*
about Sullivan Foster
Name: Sullivan Foster
Spouse Name: Lucinda Brizendine
Marriage Date: 17 Jul 1855
Marriage County: Hancock
Source Title 1: Hancock County, Indiana
Source Title 2: Index to Marriage Records 1828-1920 Inclusive Volu
Source Title 3: W. P. A. Original Record Located County Clerk's Of
Book: C- 3
OS Page: 291

Following are the possible children of Sullivan Foster and Sarah/Sally Hutson—but more research is needed:

1. MARTHA PATSY b. 1828 m. LeROY BRIZENDINE 16 Jan 1847 Hancock Co., IN (b. abt 1810 Charlotte, VA d. 1870 Indiana. Their child: JOHN BRIZENDINE b. 1859
2. ROBERT b. abt 1833
3. RICHARD b. abt 1833
4. WILLIAM b. abt 1834 m. SARAH BRIZENDINE 13 Oct 1853 Hancock Co., IN (b. abt 1833 IN). Their child: William Foster b. 1855 Center, Hancock, Indiana
5. SULLIVAN Jr. b. abt 1835 m. LUCINDA BRIZENDINE 17 Jul 1855, Hancock Co., IN. Lucinda b. 11 Jul 1831 VA d. 1888 Indiana
6. MARY b. abt 1837 m. RICHARD BRIZENDINE 30 Oct 1852 Marion Co., IN. Richard b. abt 1831 Indiana.

* * * * *

* * * NEW DATA: RUTH FOSTER * * *

RUTH FOSTER, 7th child of ROBERT and #2 BATHSHEBA (WILLIAMS) FOSTER was lost for 200 years and assumed to have died young until I found her in the Salt Lake Family History Center in 2015. I was perusing the index of a book about Marion County, Indiana because I had found earlier a listing that showed that her brothers, George and Dennis Foster, sons of Robert, owned land there. I marked every Foster listing and made Xerox copies to study later. When I returned home I was stunned to find that I was looking at copies of two important legal documents that revealed the mystery of Ruth's life:

"Complete Probate Records, Marion County, Indiana," *p. 248, Family History Library, books, 3rd floor*
"26 Mar 1849 - R.L. Walpole, attorney, says RUTH HUDSON (Ruth Hoover married George Hudson (probably Hutson) 2 May 1846, Marriage Book 4:293; Jonas Hoover married RUTH FOSTER 2 March 1837, Marriage Book 2:152) was formerly the wife and widow of Jonas Hoover, deceased, who owned # 1/2 NE 1/4 Section 21, Township 16, Range 3 of 786 acres and E 1/2 SW 1/4 Section 29, Township 16, Range 3 of 80 acres...deceased has 4 minor

children, Mary Margaret Hoover age 10 years, John Hoover age 9 years, Andrew Hoover age 7 years, and Susan Hoover age 5 years...30 May land appraised by William McCaw, Percy Hosbrook, and James A. McIlvaine; John G. Weeks guardian of minors 22 August settled."

Note: Tabitha Hutson who married George Archie Foster had brothers named George and William. The Hutson name was frequently spelled as Hudson rather than Hutson. It is likely but not proven that the George Hudson named in the first line above and the William Hudson named in the paragraph below were Tabitha's brothers or cousins. Note that Sara Sally Hutson, another sibling of Tabitha, married Sullivan Foster, brother of Ruth Foster on 18 Nov 1831 in Clark Co, Indiana.

***"Complete Probate Records, Marion County, Indiana,"** p. 268*
"February 1850 Term - Estate of Jonas Hoover, deceased.
30 March 1846 George Hoover filed relinquishment of Ruth Hoover (Jonas Hoover married Ruth Foster 2 March 1837, Marriage Book 2:152; Ruth Hoover married George Hutson 2 May 1846, Marriage Book 4:293), widow, of her right to administer, in favor of himself, who says Jonas Hoover died 10 March 1846 and left $900 personal estate. George Hoover (married Sarah Jane Glover 12 December 1833, Marriage Book 1:219) granted administration and he files $1800 bond secured by Andrew Hoover...15 April filed inventory appraised by Daniel Landrey and William Cossell, including notes of William Cossell (married Hannah Hoover 15 October 1835, Marriage Book 2:70), John Long (married Polly Cossell 15 Jan 1837, Marriage Book 2:142), and William Hudson (Hutson).
...sale notice proved by Daniel Landrey and Perry Hoover, who saw notices put up at Daniel Hoover's grocery on the National Road, one at Thomas Railsback cross roads, and one at the cross roads 4 miles NW of Indianapolis on the Lafayette Road, all in Hancock County..."

1840 US Federal Census, Wayne, Marion, Indiana
p. 10
George Foster age 30-40 (this is George Archie Foster and Tabitha Hutson)
Jonas Hoover age 30-40 (this is Jonas and Ruth (Foster) Hoover)
Bedford Foster age 60-70 (a grandson of George and Margaret Grigsby Foster)
Jeremiah Nesbit age 50-60
pg. 22
William Cox(probable relative of John Cox Jr. who married Dorcas Foster, daughter of Harrison)
Nancy Cox
Bedford Foster age 60-70 (he is probably listed twice because he owned several tracts of land)
William Royston (related to Sarah Royston Patton who married Aaron Foster, son of Harrison)
Peter Royston
p. 20
Robert Foster age 20-30 (son of Bedford Foster above)
Stephen Foster age 50-60 (likely son of Bedford Foster above)
also:
Andrew Hoover
George Hoover

1850 US Federal Census, Wayne, Marion, Indiana
Geo M Huston (Hutson) age 35 b. KY
Ruth Huston age 32 b. IN
Jn W Huston age 14 b. IN (son of Ruth and #1 Jonas Hoover)
Jan W Huston age 12 b. IN (dau. of Ruth and #1 Jonas Hoover)
Harriett Huston age 5 b. IN

Joseph Huston age 1 b. IN
Apparently Ruth's two eldest children from her first marriage have joined her even though they were taken away from Ruth when she first married George. Perhaps their names were changed to hide their identity from relatives who took them when Ruth's 1st husband died.

1860 US Federal Census, Center, Hancock, Indiana
George Hudson age 43 b. KY, farm laborer
Ruth Hudson age 41 b. Ohio
Harriet E Hudson age 13 b. IN
Joseph S Hudson age 11 b. IN
Sarah E Hudson age 9 b. IN
Ira M Hudson age 7 b. IN
Juliette A Hudson age 5 b. IN
George J Hudson age 3 b. IN
same page:
Richard Hudson age 74 b. VA Farmer
Elizabeth Hudson age 73 b. VA
Matilda Hudson age 27 b. KY
Aaron Foster age 28 b. IL farm laborer (son of Ellender and Harrison Foster- Matilda above is his wife)
Phoebe Foster age 1 b. IN

1870 US Federal Census, Eden, Decatur, Iowa
George W Hutson age 62, farmer, b. KY
Ruth age 56 b. Ohio
Sarah J age 18 b. IN
Julia A age 16 b. IN
Ira M age 14 (male) b. IN
George F age 13 b. IL
Thomas L age 11 b. IL
Next door:
Joseph Hutson age 21 b. IN
Polly Hutson age 30 b. Michigan

***1880 US Federal Census** 062, Eden Decatur, Iowa*
George W Hutson age 64, farmer, father b. VA, mother b. TN
Ruth Hutson age 61, wife, b. IN, father b., VA, mother b. KY
George K Hutson age 27, son b. IN
Thomas L. Hutson, age 17, son b. IL
Maggie E Hutson age 12, granddaughter b. IL, father b. IN, mother b. IN

living next door:
JC LaForge age 46, b. NY Millwright
Mary S LaForge age 39 b. Michigan
Nellie C LaForge age 16, dau. b. IA
Earl C LaForge age 10, son b. IA
Elsie Moore age 19, Servant b. OH
Lenore Wells age 22, niece b. WI
***Addie Hutson** age 24 b. IN (relationship not stated)*
***Pauline Hutson** age 43, sister of JC LaForge, b. OH*
Jennie McCarter, age 4, niece, of JC LaForge b. WI

Iowa State Census 1885 Eden, Decatur, Iowa
George W Hutson age 70 b. KY farmer
Ruth Hutson age 65 b. IN keeping house
Thomas Hutson age 22 b. IL farmer
Maggie Hutson age 17 b. IL
New family, same house:
George T Hutson age 26 b. IN farmer
Minerva Hutson age 19 b. Decatur, Iowa keeping house
John W Hutson age 1 yr b. Decatur, Iowa
William H Hutson age 6 mos. b. Decatur, Iowa

From all of this data we can now list Ruth's two families:

JONAS HOOVER b. 1791 North Carolina d. 10 Mar 1846 Marion Co., Indiana
RUTH FOSTER b. 1819 Ohio d. after 1885 probably in Eden, Decatur, Iowa
Married 2 Mar 1837 in Marion Co., Indiana. Children:

1. MARY MARGARET b. 1839 d. 1895 California, married JOHN SINKS
2. JOHN W b. 1840 m. MARY ANN SYLVESTER
3. ANDREW b. Dec 1842 m. SARAH E ADAMS
4. SUSAN b. 1844

MARY MARGARET HOOVER (#1 above) married JOHN SINKS 9 Oct 1856 in Marion County, Indiana and had:

1. HENRY A SINKS b. Aug 1857 Decatur, Marion, Indiana d. 2 Jun 1936 in Spangle, Spokane, Washington, married NANCY CATHERINE ORR who was born Sep 1858 in Prairieville, Tipton, Indiana and died 9 Nov 1928 in Spokane, Washington.
2. ASHER OTTO SINKS b. Nov 1859 Indiana d. 24 Sep 1938 Portland, Multnomah, Oregon, married Maud Viccie Hammons in about 1898. She was b. 29 Feb 1868 PA d. 1955. Children: 1) LENORE DELL b. 1899 who married GLEN ALFRED WOLFE, 2) GROVER PAUL 8 Feb 1891, 3) VICTOR HAMMOND 14 Jan 1893.
3. LENORE E. b. abt 1863.

Regrettably, I haven't had time to locate information on the descendants of the Sinks children.

JOHN W. HOOVER, 2nd son of JONAS and RUTH (FOSTER) HOOVER was born in 1840 in Indiana and married MARY ANN SYLVESTER 20 Dec 1864 in Marion Co., Indiana.

ANDREW HOOVER, 3rd son of JONAS and RUTH (FOSTER) HOOVER, was born Dec 1842 in Marion Co., Indiana and married SARAH E. ADAMS 2 Apr 1862 in Miami, Indiana. Their children:

1. CORA HOOVER b. 1863 Indiana, married LON GLAZE b. abt 1861 Indiana. Their son: FRANK GLAZE b. 1880.
2. ROBERT HOOVER b. 1867
3. CALVIN "Callie" C HOOVER b. 2 Jan 1872 Fulton, Indiana d. 21 Dec 1931 Fulton, Indiana, married FLORA ETTA RANNELS 20 Nov 1893 in Rochester, Fulton, Indiana. Their child: HAROLD HOOVER b. 2 Sep 1894 d. 19 Sep 1980 Tecumseh, Lenawee, Michigan. HAROLD married ESTHER LEILA GROVE 3 Jul 1915 Fulton, Indiana. She was born 26 Feb 1895 in Rochester, Fulton, Indiana and died 31 May 1944 in Dundee, Monroe, Michigan. They had two children: 1) ALICE or ALEE b. 1920, 2) ISABELLE E. b. 1922.

RUTH FOSTER HOOVER's husband JONAS was married before his marriage to Ruth. His first wife was NANCY MARY DEAL (abt 1785 to abt 1836), by whom he had two known children: 1) CATHERINE b. abt 1827, and 2) JANE M. b. abt 1829. Ruth married #2 GEORGE HUTSON, after the death of Jonas. For some unknown reason Jonas' family took Ruth's children away at the time of his death and they lived with relatives for a few years. Did they try to take her land too? Was Jonas' land shared with someone in the family who felt "obligated" to take control? Two of the children are later found back with Ruth – another mystery to solve.

GEORGE HUTSON b. abt 1816 KY d. after 1885
RUTH FOSTER b. 1819 Ohio d. after 1885
Married 2 May 1846 in Wayne, Marion, Indiana. Children:

1. HARRIETT E. HUTSON b. 1847 Indiana
2. JOSEPH S. HUTSON b. 1849 Indiana, m. POLLY b. 1840 Michigan
3. SARAH E. HUTSON b. 1851 Indiana
4. IRA MILTON HUTSON b. 1853 Indiana m. SARAH M. TIFT
5. GEORGE FRANKLIN HUTSON b. 1858 Hancock Co., Indiana d. 1939, m. ELLA SLY
6. THOMAS L. HUTSON b. 1863 Illinois, m. MARTHA COOPER 1 Jul 1888 Page, Iowa. (she was born about 1865)

IRA MILTON HUTSON (#4 above) married SARAH M. TIFT 4 Mar 1878 in Decatur, Iowa, where his family had moved earlier. Sarah was born in 1843 in Will, Illinois and later died in 1888 in Van Wert, Decatur, Iowa. Their children: 1) ARMAND D HUTSON b. 25 Feb 1880 Van Wert, Decatur, Iowa, d. 13 Aug 1967 in Iowa; 2) OREN LESTER HUTSON b. 31 Jan 1881 Franklin, Decatur, Iowa.

GEORGE FRANKLIN HUTSON, 5th child of GEORGE and RUTH (FOSTER) HUTSON was born in 1858 in Hancock Co., Indiana and married ELLA MINERVA SLY 25 Feb 1880 in Eden, Decatur, Iowa, where his parents lived at the time. Ella was born 1866 in Decatur, Iowa and died in 1917 in Iowa. Their children: 1) JOHN WASHINGTON, b. 18 Dec 1881 in Hancock Co., IN, 2) CHARLIE b. Apr 1883 in Decatur Co., Iowa; 3) WILLIAM HENRY b. 7 Oct 1884 in Decatur Co., Iowa, d. Nov 1929 in Econtuchka, Seminole, Oklahoma; 4) PEARL HUTSON b. Mar 1896 in Kansas.

WILLIAM HENRY HUTSON, 3rd child of GEORGE FRANKLIN and ELLA MINERVA (SLY) HUTSON, was born in Decatur, Iowa and married GENNETTE or NETTIE MAE HARDWICK around 1908. she was born in 1893 in Byrdstown, Pickett, Tennessee and later died in 1939 and Greenridge, Scott, Arkansas. Their children:

1. THOMAS MALAND or MALIN b. Apr 1910
2. HENRY ALLEN b. 28 Jun 1914
3. LILLIE MAE b. 3 Sep 1918 m. JOHN THOMAS WALKER
4. DOVIE LUCEAIL b. 17 Sep 1921
5. WILLIAM EUGENE b. 21 Jul 1924
6. BETTIE JANE b. 12 Oct 1927

JOHN THOMAS WALKER b. 17 Aug 1898 Yell, Arkansas d. 3 Feb 1973 Porterville, Tulare, CA
LILLIE MAE HUTSON (#3 above) b. 3 Sep 1918 Waldron, Scott, Arkansas d. 19 Oct 1995 Porum, Muskogee, Oregon. Married about 1933. Children:

1. GEORGIA ANN
2. LUECRECCIA
3. JOHN THOMAS, Jr.

GEORGIA ANN WALKER (# 1 above) married LUTHER MORTELL GOFF around 1944. Luther was the son of Rev. ELDRIDGE LAFAYETTE GOFF (1894 – 1979) and WILLIE ARMADIE SWAFFORD (1893 – 1972) Luther and Georgia Ann had 13 children:

1. CRECCIA LEE
2. DOUGLAS MONROE
3. DAVID DWAIN
4. CHARLESS LEE
5. DALE
6. RAY
7. ROY
8. ALFORD
9. MARLIN
10. SHEILA
11. SHIRLEY
12. LELA

CRECCIA LEE (#1 above) married CHARLES FREDERICK HURST 25 Nov 1968 and had: 1) BRENDA, who married BILL HOOD, 2) LINDA, who married PHILLIP MICHAEL and had Althea, Pamela, Leannia, Remington, and Thomas; 3) SUSAN who married another MR. HURST and had THOMAS; 4) CLARISSA, who married DAVID WAGNER and DAVID Jr.

LUECRECCIA WALKER, 3rd child of JOHN THOMAS and LILLIE MAE (HUTSON) WALKER, was born 22 Jul 1939 in Booneville, Logan Arkansas and later died 23 May 1995 in Porum, Muskogee, Oklahoma. She married MR. SMITH. John Thomas Walker's mother is listed in the census as Genevieve, age 71, born in Arkansas.

DOVIE LUCEAIL HUTSON, 4th child of WILLIAM HENRY and GENNETTE (HARDWICK) HUTSON, was born 17 Sep 1921 in Arkansas and later died 25 Nov 1995 in Tulsa, Tulsa, Oklahoma. She married #1 MR. CHANCE who either died or divorced her. She married #2 GUSTUS MARSHALL SMITH 25 Oct 1891 in Boonville, Logan, Arkansas. Gustus was born about 1919 in the same place and later died 10 Feb 1985 at Fort Smith, Sebastian, Arkansas. Apparently she divorced Gustus and married #3 HUGH G. BARNETT 2 Mar 1940 in Logan Co., Arkansas. Hugh was born in 1875 in Tennessee. I didn't find any children by these marriages, but that doesn't mean there aren't any.

WILLIAM EUGENE HUTSON, 5th child of WILLIAM HENRY and GENNETTE (HARDWICK) HUTSON was born 21 Jul 1924 in Arkansas and later died 3 Jun 1992 in Dewar, Okmulgee, Oklahoma. He married IVADALE JOHNSON 1 Apr 1946 in Mexico. Ivadale was born 23 Mar 1925 in Arkansas and later died 31 Aug 1991 at Ft. Smith, Sebastian, Arkansas. Their children: 1) DONALD LEE, 2) BILLIE EUGENE, 3) JAMES THOMAS, 4) Unknown.

BETTIE JANE HUTSON, 6th child of WILLIAM HENRY and GENNETTE (HARDWICK) HUTSON, was born 12 Oct 1927 BRANSDALL, OSAGE, OKLAHOMA and later died 7 Dec 2003 at Greenwood, Sebastian, Arkansas. She married ISAAC ELIJAH "Lige" SCANTLING 15 Sep 1884 Waldron, Scott, Arkansas, who died 19 Dec 1978 in Bowman, Cleveland, Arkansas. I was unable to locate their children.
* * * * *

This ends my material on our 2nd Foster Family. Let's hope we can learn more about earlier families before the tides of time erase their footprints from the sands.

THE LEARY, HORNBACK, AND FOSTER CONNECTION

In 2009 a distant Leary cousin (Charles Leary) contacted me (Adrienne) through ancestry.com and shared data that he had gathered on the Leary family. It had been his dream to learn the father of Dennis Leary before he died. Around the same time another Leary cousin contacted me with news of a Leary Bible record that was now online. We three shared our data by email and examined what we had. Amazingly, we each seemed to have a piece of the big puzzle and when it was put together it was evident that we now knew Dennis' father, brother, and more.

Charles Leary had found "Early Records of Hampshire Co. (VA), Synopsis of Wills: Hornback, Daniel 3 Mar 1778, Wife: Magdalene, 3 children: 1. Abraham, 2. James, 3. Solomon. To Abraham Coffman; Elizabeth Anderson, wife of John, and their daughter; to *Thomas Leary's children: Daniel, Dennis and one daughter,* (Note: meaning Dennis' daughter) to John Anderson's three children: Mary, Thomas, and Margaret; Exec. Wife and William Hornback. Witnesses: Simon Hornback, Charles Meyers, Sam C. Curtright."
Charles realized his dream of finding Dennis' father when he located the book "Hornbeck Hunting II," by Shirley Hornback. On p. 71 (last paragraph) it states that Daniel and Dennis Leary are believed to be the sons of Thomas Leary, who is believed to be the husband of Susannah or Susan Hornbeck, the daughter of Daniel Hornbeck of Hampshire, VA.

Shirley Hornbeck explains it further on page 30: "Daniel (Hornback) had six grown children when he made his will Mar 3, 1778. Daniel's will mentions wife Magdalena and sons Abraham, James, Solomon and his unborn child as Magdalena was pregnant. He mentions children of John and Elizabeth Anderson; ***sons of Thomas Leary***; and Abraham, Catherine and Susannah Coffman whose relationship was not stated. Daniel willed to Magdalene one third of a tract of land where they lived containing 43 acres as long as she remains a widow but if she married she obtained no part... ***He gave to Thomas Leary's sons Daniel and Dennis one daughter's part***, ...Daniel's property was located on the banks of the South Branch of the Potomac River in Hampshire Co, VA.

Dennis Leary is found in the US Census of 1782 in Hampshire County, Virginia, along with Samuel Curtright (a.k.a. Cartright, Cutright, Curtwright), Samuel Hornback, Abram Hornback, James Hornback Sr., James Hornback Jr., and Simon Hornback. In 1800 he is found in Bourbon, Kentucky with some of the same Hornbacks and Curtrights. Dennis' father had married Margaret Hornback, although it is believed she was the second wife, and not Dennis' mother. Hornback and Curtright are unusual "tracer" names. There is practically zero probability that the Learys, Hornbacks, and Curtrights of Hampshire, VA are NOT the same as the Learys/Hornbacks/Curtrights found later in Bourbon, Kentucky. Dennis Leary's son Dennis Jr. later married Sarah Curtright in Bourbon Co., Kentucky and the names of their children are listed in the Leary/Lary Bible.

Daniel Lary, Dennis Lary Sr., and Dennis Lary Jr. are all together in Bourbon, KY in the "Second Census of Kentucky 1800" on ancestry.com pg.168. John Lary is in the regular 1800 Census of Stoner, Bourbon, KY. We concluded that Dennis Sr. and Daniel are the brothers mentioned in the Hornbeck will. Note the consistency in the spelling of the names in each census, which is more evidence that they are related. So I think that Elizabeth Leary is the daughter of Dennis Sr., and the Lary/Leary Bible names the children of Dennis Jr. This would explain why Dennis witnessed Elizabeth's marriage and why she named her second son Dennis.

We also found the following Revolutionary Record for Dennis Leary/Lary:
"Daughters of the Revolution Patriot Index" pg. 1600: "Dennis Lary b. 1753 VA d. 1811 KY."
LARY, DENNIS

Dennis Leary (pg. 545), enlisted 18 May 1778 in same company as John Williams for the duration of the war, recruited by Sgt. Ben Todd. (John Williams is the father of Bathsheba Williams--after Dennis Leary's daughter Elizabeth died, her husband Robert Foster b. 1770 married #2 Bathsheba Williams.) Source: "Muster Rolls and Other Records of Service of Maryland Troops in the American Revolution, 1775-1783," publ. by Clearfield, Publ . by the authority of the state of Maryland under the direction of the Maryland Historical Society and Maryland State Archives, repository: www.ancestry.com.

"Hornback Hunting" reveals that Thomas Leary died in or about 1775 when his estate was administered by the then living Daniel Hornbeck. The wife of that Thomas Leary was already deceased thus validating Daniel Hornbeck claiming Daniel Leary and Dennis Leary as his grandchildren in the Will. One source I saw on ancestry.com showed the wife of Thomas Leary as Margaret. I am preferring to believe that "female Hornbeck" who married Thomas Leary and died prior to 1778--at which time Magdalene was pregnant with a baby, who shortly thereafter was born and named Margaret. Families habitually name a child born later in life after an earlier child who died. That's my theory: "female Hornbeck" was Margaret Hornbeck who married Thomas Leary about 1755-1760 and died before 1778. Her memory was carried on in the baby born post Daniel Hornbeck's death and named Margaret. The younger Margaret Hornbeck married Benjamin Van Vactor in KY on 24 or 25 Mar 1793.

Leary cousin Denise Dunn wrote that William H Rice and Archives Office in Charleston provided documents of appraisement of the estate of Thomas Leary, which was assigned to Daniel Hornbeck in Hampshire Co on March 24, 1775, which would suggest he likely died early in 1775.

THOMAS LEARY b. 1733 Ireland d. 1775 Hampshire, Virginia (now WV)
Married unknown. Known children:

1. DANIEL b. 1750 Hampshire, Virginia
2. DENNIS b. 1753 Hampshire or Hardy, Virginia

Thomas married #2 MARGARET HORNBACK abt 1755 (Margaret b. 1746 d. 1777)

DANIEL LEARY (#1 above) served in the 2nd Pennsylvania Regiment of Foot from Jan. 1777 to Sept. 1778 under Major William Williams and Col. Henry Bicker, and later under Capt. Joseph Howell. He was at Valley Forge in February 1778. Daniel Lary married Elizabeth Scott Jan. 29, 1798 Bourbon Co. *Source: Early Kentucky Settlers,*

1700s-1800s, Kentucky Marriage Records, Bourbon County, 1786-1800 pg. 69. She was most likely not his first wife.

DENNIS LEARY (#2 above) married Unknown wife and had at least:

1. DENNIS Jr. b. 18 Mar 1773 Hardy, West Virginia d. 1824 Bourbon, Kentucky, m. SARAH CURTRIGHT
2. ELIZABETH b. 1780 d. 1799 Nicholas, Kentucky m. ROBERT FOSTER
3. JOHN 6 Oct 1786 d. 11 Aug 1834 Hancock Co., Indiana m. SARAH MOORE

Dennis LEARY Jr. was born on 18 Mar 1773 in Hardy Co, VA. In about 1783 he moved, with wife-to-be Sarah Curtwright, and father Dennis Sr., to live in Clintonville, Bourbon Co, KY. He was father of 13 children with first spouse Sarah between 1795 and 1818 in Kentucky. He is listed as Dennys Lary, 5 males under 10, one 26-44; 4 females 10-15, one 26-44, in the US Census in 1810 in Stoner, Bourbon Co, KY. In 1810 Dennis Lary & spouse under 44 are of age consistent with Dennis Lairy Jr. & Sarah in 1780 VA records in Hampshire Co, VA. About 1820 a schoolhouse was built on his farm east of Clintonville which unfortunately was burned about 1825. Dennis Jr. died in 1824 in Bourbon Co, KY. He was a farmer. His family is shown in the Lary Bible below:

LARY/LEARY BIBLE RECORDS: Leary cousin Denise Dunn found online a Leary family bible that named Dennis Leary Jr., son of Dennis b. 1753, along with his wife and children.

Dennis b. 1773 d. 1824 Bourbon, KY, USA, m. abt 1793 to Sarah Curtright (b. 13 Sep 1777 Hardy, VA d. 1839 Bourbon, KY).
Children:
Rachel Leary b. 1795
Sam Leary
Thomas Leary b. 1798
Elizabeth Leary b. 1799 (this is a niece of my Elizabeth Leary, probably named after her since she was born the year Elizabeth died)
Dorothy Leary b. Oct 1803
Daniel Buell Leary b. 13 Jan 1806
Henry Leary b. Jan 1808
John Curtright Leary b. 2 Jul 1810
Malinda Leary b. Oct 1812
Washington DC Leary b. Jul 1815
Cornelius Leary b. 19 Aug 1816
Eliza Leary b. 16 Oct 1817
Cyrus Leary b. 12 Sep 1818

The above is an exact transcription of the Bible record. Following is more data on this family:

DENNIS LEARY Jr. b. 18 Mar 1773 Hardy, WV d. 1824 Bourbon, KY

SARAH CURTRIGHT b. 18 Sep 1777 Hardy, Virginia d. 1839 Bourbon, KY.
Married in 1795. Children:

1. RACHEL b. 23 Feb 1796 Shelby, KY d. 3 Apr 1877 Hancock, IN, m. ISAAC WINN
2. SAM (no dates for him, indicating that he may have died at birth
3. THOMAS b. 1798 d. abt 1846, m. SUSANNAH HORNBECK
4. ELIZABETH b. 1799 (the year that her aunt died) d. 1811
5. DOROTHY b. Oct 1803 d. 1826
6. DANIEL BUELL b. 13 Jan 1806 Bourbon, KY D. 29 Mar 1886 m. SARAH A. THOMAS
7. HENRY b. Jan 1808 m. HARRIETT BOOTE
8. JOHN CURTRIGHT b. 2 Jul 1810 d. 8 Oct 1875 Bourbon, KY, m. MARY ALLEN PENDLETON
9. MALINDA b. 1812 d. 1815
10. WASHINGTON D C b. Jul 1815 d. 1831
11. CORNELIUS b. 19 Aug 1816 d. 12 Jan 1858 Bourbon, KY m. CLARISSA PARVIN
12. ELIZA b. 16 Oct 1817 d. 1824
13. CYRUS b. 12 Sep 1818 d. 1824

RACHEL LEARY (#1 above) was born in Shelby Co., KY and went with her parents to Switzerland Co., Indiana where she grew up and married ISAAC WINN. They are in the 1850 US Census in Harrison, Hancock, Indiana.

ISAAC WINN B. 1 Nov 1799 KY d. 20 Aug 1858 Greenfield, Hancock, IN
RACHEL LEARY b. 23 Feb 1796 Shelby, KY d. 3 Apr 1877 Hancock, IN
Were married 24 Oct 1821 Switzerland Co., Indiana. Children:

1. JAMES H b. abt 1822
2. MARGARET b. 20 Jun 1824 m. WILLIAM EDGELL
3. MILTON b. 1828
4. IRA b. 1830 d. 6 Mar 1908 Burlington, Coffey, Kansas
5. MONROE b. 7 Aug 1834 d. 7 Jul 1909 Bridgewater, Adair, Iowa
6. JOHN b. abt 1836
7. MARY J b. 1838 m. Henry Sante and had 1) FANNY 1865, 2) PALMER 1868

THOMAS, 3rd child of DENNIS LEARY Jr. and SARAH (CURTRIGHT) married SUSANNAH HORNBECK (aka HORNBACK) on 2 Sep 1813 in Clark Co, KY. In 1760 and in 1770 she was living with her son-in-law Zephaniah Hornbeck and Susan in the census in Campbell Co, KY. Susannah aka "Susan" HORNBECK (daughter of James HORNBECK and Kiziah) was born about 1796. She died between 1870 and 1880 in KY. She was also known as "Aunt Sukie".

THOMAS b. 1798 d. abt 1846
SUSANNAH HORNBECK b. abt 1796 d. Bet 1870 and 1880 in Kentucky
Children:

1. HENRY J b. 1815 m. MATILDA COOK

2. THOMAS Jr. b. abt 1825 m. MARY JANE HARRIS and had:
   a) JOHN b) CLAY c) LULIA d) ELIZABETH e) MEEK OR MERID
3. SUSAN b. 1821 d. 1877 m. ZEPHANIAH HORNBECK
4. MARY b. 1834

The Learys are found in: **"History of Bourbon, Scott, Clark, and Nelson Counties, Kentucky:"**
"Daniel Lary, Farmer; P.O. Newtown; was born in Bourbon County, Jan. 13, 1806; his father was Dennis Lary, who was born in Hardy County, Va., in 1773, and was by occupation a farmer, and died in Bourbon County in 1824; the maiden name of his mother was Sarah Curtwright, who was born in Hardy County, Va., in 1777; came to Kentucky in 1783; died in 1839. His parents had 13 children; he was educated in Bourbon County, and began life as a farmer; was married in Hancock County, Ga., June 1835; maiden name of his wife was Sarah A. Thomas, born in 1815; his wife's father was Frederick G. Thomas, born in Edgecomb County, N.C. her mother being Rebecca Eskridge, born in Edgefield District, S.L. He has been engaged in the business of farming and trading; had two children, both of whom are dead, named as follows: Theresa and Sophia. Politics, Democratic; member of Granger's Mutual Benefit Association. Mr. Lary is a man of fine intellectual attainments, an enterprising citizen, and has been quite an active man in politics, having filled the position of Representative, from his county, in the Legislature with considerable credit to himself and constituency, in 1876 and 1876."

HENRY LEARY, 7th child of DENNIS LEARY Jr. and SARAH (CURTRIGHT), married HARRIETT BOOTE. Harriett was b. 1817 in Louisiana. Their child, ELIZA was born 1841 and married M. H. Kendall 10 Mar 1859 Bourbon, KY. Children of Eliza (Leary) and M. H. Kendall: 1) RUSSELL B, 2) WILLIAM S, 3) GEORGE H, 4) JOHN MILTON, 5) AMOS J, 6) L Q LAMAR, 7) H D L, 8) CHARLES T, 9) MARY.

JOHN CURTRIGHT LEARY, 8th child of DENNIS LEARY Jr. and SARAH (CURTRIGHT), married MARY ALICE PENDLETON, daughter of General E. PENDLETON. She was born 12 Sep 1819 and d. 27 Nov 1905. Their children: 1) A P LEARY b. 17 Aug 1856, married JENNIE H HENDERSON 27 Apr 1881 in Kentucky, 2) AMELIA P b. 19 Jun 1851 d. 20 Jan 1854 Clintonville, Bourbon, Kentucky.

"AP Lary, farmer, P.O. Clintonville; is a son of J. C. Lary, and a grandson of Dennis Lary, who emigrated from the Old Dominion at an early day. J. C. Lary married Mary A., the daughter of Gen. E. Pendleton of Clark County, who served in the war of 1812, under Gov. Isaac Shelby. Capt. V. M. Pendleton, of Company D, 8th KY Cavalry, who was killed at Mt. Sterling, was an uncle of our subject. A. P. Lary was born Aug 17, 1836 in Bourbon County. He was married April 27th, 1881 to Miss Jennie H. Henderson. Mrs. Lary is a member of the Christian Church. Mr. Lary owns 175 acres of land near Clintonville, where he engages in farming and raising short-horn cattle; his home is known as "Glencoe," where he lives in the enjoyment of the confidences and esteem of his neighbors." **Source: " History of Bourbon, Scott, Harrison and Nicholas Counties, Kentucky pg. 558"**

MALINDA LEARY, 9th child of DENNIS LEARY Jr. and SARAH (CURTRIGHT), died when only three years old.

WASHINGTON D C LEARY, 10th child of DENNIS LEARY Jr. and SARAH (CURTRIGHT), died in 1831 at age 16.

CORNELIUS LEARY, 11th child of DENNIS LEARY Jr. and SARAH (CURTRIGHT), married CLARISSA PARVIN 12 Jan 1858 in Bourbon, KY There is another Cornelius Leary who served under Gen. Charles Scott in the Northwest Indian War in 1794, who is probably an uncle of this Cornelius.

ELIZA LEARY 12th child of DENNIS LEARY Jr. and SARAH (CURTRIGHT) died in 1824 at age 7.

CYRUS LEARY 13th child of DENNIS LEARY Jr. and SARAH (CURTRIGHT) died in 1824 at age 6.
****

ELIZABETH LEARY, 2nd child of DENNIS LEARY Sr. and unknown wife, was born in 1780 and married ROBERT FOSTER 13 Nov 1794 in Bourbon, Kentucky. Children:

1. SAMPSON or Samuel b. 1795 believed to have married Anna Jones 16 Dec 1818 Clark, KY
2. DENNIS b. 1799 d. 6 Sep 1846 McLean, IL, m. Mary Polly Foster (dau. of Harrison Foster and Anna Margaret Bartlett).

Elizabeth died in 1799, probably in childbirth with son Dennis, and Robert Foster married #2 BATHSHEBA WILLIAMS in Nelson, Kentucky in 1800.

JOHN LEARY, 3rd child of DENNIS LEARY Sr. b. 1753 and unknown wife, was born in Kentucky, grew up and married SARAH MOORE 19 Mar 1812 in Clark County, KY. Source: *Kentucky Marriages, 1802-1850,* which mistakenly spells Leary as "Leacy." Sarah Moore is the daughter of Joseph Anthony Moore (b. 8 Jan 1780 Hardy, WV d. 21 Feb 1853 Shelby, Kentucky) and Mary Ann ______ (b. abt 1770 Hardy, WV.) Sarah's sister Mary Ann Moore is the mother of Tabitha Hutson who married George Archibald Foster (son of Robert Foster b. 1770).

1840 Census, Union, Hancock, Indiana *(all are Heads of households)*

James H. Leary

Levi Leary (Leakey)

Sarah Leary

Elijah Leary (pg. 1)

Eli Reeves

Richard Hutson

William Hutson

1850 Census, Union, Hancock, Indiana

Sarah Leary, age 65 b. KY

Same census, next door:

James H. Leary age 57, land value $2,500, b. KY

Neoma Leary age 29, b. No. Carolina

Sarah E Leary age 12 b. IN

Esther A Leary age 9 b. IN

Martha L. Leary age 7 b. IN

Maria L. Leary age 5 b. IN

Margaret E Leary age 3 b. IN

John L. Leary age 1 b. IN

Same census, next page:

Levi Leary age 40 b. KY

Edith Leary age 32 b. NC

James W Leary age 16 b. IN

Eliza J. Leary age 11 b. IN

Sarah E. Leary age 9 b. IN

Harvey J. Leary age 6 b. IN

JOHN LEARY b. 6 Oct 1785 Kentucky d. 11 Aug 1834 Hancock Co., Indiana
SARAH MOORE b. 3 Mar 1788 Kentucky d. 22 Dec 1853 Hancock Co., Indiana
Children:

1. ELIJAH b. 15 Feb 1806 KY d. 27 Feb 1848 Union, Hancock, IN, m. ELIZABETH MARTINDALE
2. LEVI b. 10 Feb 1810 KY d. 10 Mar 1865 Center, Hancock, IN, m. EDITH REEVES
3. JAMES H. LEARY b. 16 Jan 1812 KY d. 4 Sep 1891 Center, Hancock, IN, m. NAOMI or NEOMA REEVES.
4. THOMAS J. LEARY b. 4 Feb 1816 d. 25 Mar 1889 Center, Hancock, IN, m. #1 REBECCA PRICE and #2 MARGERIE JOHNSON
5. RACHEL LEARY b. abt 1815

ELIJAH LEARY (#1 above) b. 15 Feb 1806 KY d. 27 Feb 1848 Union, Hancock, Indiana married
ELIZABETH MARTINDALE (b. abt 1808) on 13 Feb 1826 in Switzerland Co., IN. Their child: Anna b. 12 Aug 1838.

LEVI (#2 above) married EDITH REEVES 17 Dec 1833 in Hancock, Indiana. She was the daughter of James Reeves (1780-1849) and Elizabeth Madden (1784-1856). Their children:

1. JAMES W b. 1834 IN m. EVALINE ROBERTS 17 Dec 1862 Hancock, IN
2. ELIZA L b. 1839 IN

3. SARAH E b. 1841 IN
4. HARVEY J b. 1844 IN
5. MARTHA S b. 1854 IN m. THOMAS WALKER abt 1878 and had ELMER b. abt 1879

JAMES H LEARY, 3rd child of JOHN LEARY and SARAH (MOORE) married NAOMI REEVES, sister of Edith Reeves above, 14 Dec 1835 in Hancock, Indiana. Their children:

1. SARAH E b. abt 1838 d. Beg 1876 m. WILLIAM RILEY COX 17 Feb 1856 Hancock, IN and had 1) HATTIE b. 1859, 2) ANGIE b. 1862, 3) FANNIE b. 1864, 4) STELLA b. 1867. After Sarah's death William Cox married her sister Maria below.
2. ESTHER A b. 1841 Indiana
3. MARTHA J b. 1843 IN m. THOMAS WALKER 13 Apr 1869 Hancock, IN
4. MARIA L b. 1845 IN m. WILLIAM R COX 17 Feb 1876 Hancock, IN (after Sarah #1 died). Children: 1) WILLIAM O b. 1881, 2) EDDIE M b. 1887, 3) ROSCOE N b. 1889, 4) LUNA LEE b. 1892. After Maria died William m. #3 HANNAH D in 1894 and had THOMAS JEFFERSON b. 1894.
5. MARGARET E b. 1847 IN m. JAMES FULLER 2 Feb 1876 Hancock, IN
6. JOHN L b. 1849 Indiana
7. ELLEN b. 1850 Indiana married Unknown and had Alice.
8. MARY b. 1852 IN m. ADAM BANKS 19 Apr 1885
9. ALICE b. 1854 IN m. JAMES HAGANS 27 Oct 1877 Hancock, IN
10. MINERVA b. 1856 IN
11. LAURA b. 1859 IN
12. OLE SCOTTON b. 1868 (adopted)

THOMAS J LEARY, 4th child of JOHN LEARY and SARAH (MOORE), married REBECCA PRICE Jan 5, 1837 in Franklin Co., Indiana. She was born abt 1817 in Delaware. Their children:

1. ELIZA J b. 1839 Indiana
2. JOHN M b. 1841 m. MARY E. REEVES (b. abt 1846 IN) on 30 Sep 1866 and had: 1) ELAM M b. 1868, and 2) VIOLA E b. 1869.
3. PERRY J b. abt 1844 IN m. ELIZABETH A McCRUDER 9 Apr 1865 in Hancock, IN and had: 1) ARTHUR b. 1866, 2) MARSHALL b. 1869, 3) GEORGE C b. 1871, 4) CHARLES C b. 1879, 5) HOWARD b. 1894
4. WILLIS J b. 1847 IN m. MARGARET ___ abt 1868 and had OLIVER in 1869.
5. DAVID M b. 1850 Indiana
6. JOSEPHINE b. 1857 Indiana

THE MOORE, HUTSON (or Hudson), AND FOSTER CONNECTION

Due to the many intermarriages of this Foster clan with that of the Moore/Hutson/Leary families I'll give them a little rundown here. Joseph Anthony (b. 1780) & Mary Ann MOORE had 8 children, three given here:

1) SARAH married JOHN LEARY, brother or cousin to Elizabeth Leary above.
2) ELIZABETH MOORE, married RICHARD HUTSON. Both families lived out their lives in Hancock Co., Indiana.
3) MARY ANN MOORE (mother-in-law of William Foster b. abt 1802 who is the son of Robert Foster and Bathsheba Williams) married #1 THOMAS RAINES (abt 1778 – abt 1811) and #2 JACOB HUTSON, brother of Richard Hutson.

Richard & Elizabeth Hutson/ Hudson were the parents of Matilda who married Aaron Foster, pg. 61(son of Harrison Jr. and Ellender Foster), and grandparents of Elizabeth Hutson who married James Foster p. 76 (son of George A Foster and Tabitha Hutson). The father of Richard and Jacob Hutson was ANDREW HUTSON of Virginia, where his sons, RICHARD and SAMUEL were born. Andrew's son JACOB was born in Fayette Co., Kentucky.

ANDREW HUTSON b. abt 1770 Virginia
ANN CHENEY b. abt 1771
Children:

1. RICHARD b. 3 Dec 1785 VA or TN d. 31 Aug 1873 Hancock IN m. ELIZABETH MOORE
2. JACOB b. 11 Nov 1791 KY d. 8 Jul 1859 Otter Village, Ripley, IN m. MARY ANN MOORE (sister of Elizabeth above)
3. SAMUEL b. abt 1895

RICHARD HUTSON (#1 above) b. 3 Dec 1785 in Virginia or Tenn. d. 31 Aug 1873 Hancock Co., Indiana
ELIZABETH (MOORE) b. 1787 Virginia
Known children:

1. WILLIAM b. abt 1813 Kentucky m. Julia A.
2. ELIZABETH b. 1827 Fayette, KY m. Henry Dunn
3. PHEBEE b. 1830 Kentucky
4. MATILDA b. 1832 Kentucky m. Aaron Foster (son of Harrison Foster and Ellender (Foster))
5. unnamed daughter who married a *JONES and had: 1) JAMES B., 2) MARGARET E., 3) SOPHRONIA J., 4) CLARISSA.*(Note: George A and Tabitha Foster had a son *JONAS. It is possible that this is who married the unnamed Hutson daughter)*

**Note Aaron Foster, pg. 61.

WILLIAM HUTSON was born abt 1813 in Kentucky and married JULIA A. _____, who was born abt 1811 in Kentucky. They lived in Hancock Co. Ind. Their known children:

1) ELIZABETH,
2) * * THOMAS,
3) JAMES.

Note James Foster pgs. 76-77

MARY ANN, daughter of ANTHONY & MARY ANN MOORE, was born in Virginia Jan. 8, 1780 and went to Fayette Co., Ky., with her parents. Here she met and married #1 THOMAS RAINES and their two children were born: 1) ANTHONY, and 2) ELIZABETH, who married a WILLIAM FOSTER (family stories say that he was a brother of George Archie Foster but it is not yet proved.)

In 1807 (after Thomas Raines' death) Mary A. married #2 JACOB HUTSON. Jacob was born in 1790 and was 17 when married. Mary Ann was 27. Most of their children were born near Lexington, KY, but at least one, Tabitha, was born near New Orleans, Louisiana, as shown in the census. Jacob, a veteran of the battle of New Orleans, took his family back to Kentucky, and soon began "looking" for land in Indiana.

In the late 1820s, after making at least seven trips to Indiana, Mary A. got the electrifying news that Jacob had a second wife and seven children. A divorce followed and Jacob joined his Indiana family in Jennings County, where he is buried. Mary Ann and both her parents are buried in Shelby Co., Kentucky.

From descendant Carolyn Dietz: "Mary Ann was a midwife and local doctor. She is on the member list for the Coffee Creek Baptist Church with her children Tabitha, Wm, Sally, Polly and James, but no Jacob. This is in Jennings Co, IN, the same county where Jacob moved after they split. It is said he had a farm there, as well as the one in KY, and that's why he had to be gone for long stretches at a time.....to take care of business at the other property. Maybe more family legend but it rather makes sense. Jacob petitioned and received Bounty Land for his service in the War of 1812, in 1853 and 1855. Said he served twice, once for himself and once as a substitute for someone else. The govt. only accepted his claim for his own service as they couldn't prove that he subbed for anyone. ... He is later mentioned on the Rolls of the US Supreme Court as he sold his Bounty Land to 2 separate people, yet neither knew of the other transaction. It wasn't until one of the men tried to sell the land that it was discovered what he did. "

Descendant Julie Richards disputes some of Flavius research: "Mary Ann and Jacob were not married until after mid-1810 at the very earliest, probably not until after the war ended - her first husband, Thomas Raines, was still alive in 1810. Mary Ann and Jacob only had three children together- Tabitha, William and Ambrose - I should say, there were only two children of Jacob and Mary Ann living in 1821. Ambrose was their last born around 1822. William and Ambrose were both born in Clark Co. KY. Mary Ann's father Anthony Moore is buried in Clark Co., KY. I don't know where her mother died.
Yes, Mary Ann divorced Jacob. Yes, he married Anna Griggs, but that took place just before the divorce from Mary Ann was final - 1824/25. Jacob and Anna Griggs did not have seven kids together while Jacob was still married to Mary Ann. Yes, he settled in Jennings IN, where Anna was from. After leaving Mary Ann, he came back once (just long enough to get her pregnant with Ambrose), and left shortly thereafter and never returned. He did not go back and forth between Mary Ann and Indiana/Anna seven times.
I believe Mary Ann was older than Jacob, but I don't think the age difference was as significant as stated in the book, and they didn't marry as early as stated in the book."

Mary Ann Hudson's Divorce
October 7, 2013

By Neil E. Mellen (with a few revisions in parentheses by Adrienne Foster Potter)

Mary Ann (Moore) Rains (a.k.a. Raines) married Jacob Hudson (a.k.a. Hutson) on 21 November 1818 in Clark County, Kentucky.[1] Almost exactly five years later, on 24 November 1823, Mary Ann filed for a divorce in the Clark County circuit court. She alleged that, "during the two years last past and upwards," Jacob had abandoned her and failed to provide any support for her or for their children.[2]

Mary Ann had another, more pressing, reason for seeking a divorce. Her father, Anthony Moore, died in 1822, and Mary Ann inherited a third of his "considerable" estate.[3] A few months after Anthony Moore's death, Jacob Hudson returned to Clark County and tried to sell his (i.e., Mary Ann's) share of her father's estate. Mary Ann asked the circuit court to enjoin Jacob from selling the property. For good measure, she added her father's executor as a defendant and asked the court to enjoin him from paying any of the estate's proceeds to Jacob.[4]

In June 1824, Mary Ann filed an amended petition, adding yet another ground for the divorce: Jacob had entered into an adulterous second marriage with "a certain Anna Griggs of Switzerland County in the State of Indiana." Jacob, who was living in Indiana with his new wife, did not respond to the suit. The circuit court granted Mary Ann a divorce on 14 April 1825.[5]

The divorce file contains several useful bits of genealogical information. First, Mary Ann's amended petition confirms that her husband is the same Jacob Hudson who married Anna Griggs - a question that has long puzzled both women's descendants. Second, witness statements taken in the divorce case provide a few clues about Jacob that may be helpful to other researchers trying to track down this elusive character. Finally, the court papers suggest that Jacob was not the father of some children who were previously assumed to be his.

Mary Ann

Mary Ann was the eldest of three daughters of Anthony and Mary (Ann) Polly Moore. The 1850 census says that she was born around 1784. Anthony Moore first purchased land in Clark County in 1799, but the deed implies that he was already living in the county by that time. The family lived on the waters of Johnson Creek, in the northwest corner of Clark County.[6]

Mary Ann married Thomas "Rayns" on 6 September 1805 in Clark County. The 1810 census lists Thomas with a wife and one child. He is found in the Clark County tax lists through at least 1811. He apparently died before Mary Ann married Jacob Hudson in 1818, but his date of death is not known.[7]

Mary Ann and her extended family left Clark County by the time her divorce suit was decided: a deed selling the family property on Johnson Creek, signed 19 April 1825, describes Mary Ann, her mother, and her two sisters as Shelby County residents. The 1830 Shelby County census lists Mary Ann as head of her household.[8]

In December 1832, Mary Ann filed a lawsuit seeking $1,000 from her brother-in-law, John Leary, for assault and battery. She alleged that Leary "did beat wound bruise & ill treat" her and that he took $1,000 that was her rightful property. The jury ultimately awarded Mary Ann $85 in damages. No transcript of the trial survives to clarify what happened.[9]

Mary Ann joined Burks Branch Baptist Church in June 1834. She married a third time, to Peter M. Matthews, on 25 February 1840 in Shelby County. He was a native of Dutchess County, New York.[10]

Mary Ann died in February 1853. Peter Matthews remarried in 1856 in Anderson County and died in 1859 in Shelby County.[11]

JACOB HUTSON b. 11 Nov 1791 Lexington, Fayette, Kentucky d. 8 Jul 1859
MARY ANN MOORE b. 6 Jan 1780 Virginia d. 21 Feb 1833 Shelbyville, Shelby, KY
They were married 21 Nov 1818 in Clark Co., Kentucky (Source: Kentucky Marriage Bonds). Children:

1. TABITHA b. 1814 d. 1883 m. GEORGE ARCHIBALD FOSTER (son of Robert Foster & Bathsheba (Williams)
2. MARY ANN or Polly b. 25 Dec 1852 m. JOHN J. FAWKES
3. SARAH or Sally (twins) d. Bef 1855 m. SULLIVAN FOSTER (son of Robert Foster & Bathsheba (Williams)
4. SAMUEL b. abt 1818 d. Bef 1847
5. JAMES b. abt 1820 d. abt 1833
6. GEORGE b. 28 Mar 1828 d. 22 Dec 1888
7. AMBROSE ALLEN b. 1822 d. 20 Dec 1893 m. EUNICE ANN ADAMS
8. SUSAN b. 1825 d. 25 Feb 1901 m. GEORGE W. FAWKES (brother of John Fawkes above)

Due to the divorce, it was Mary Ann Hutson who signed the marriage bond between daughter Tabitha and George A. Foster, son or Robert Foster of Bourbon, KY.

Jacob Hutson was Mary Ann Moore's second husband. Her first husband was Thomas Raines.

THOMAS RAINES b. at 1778 d. 1811
MARY ANN MOORE b. 6 Jan 1780 Virginia d. 21 Feb 1833 Shelbyville, Shelby, KY .
They were married 5 Sep 1805 in Clark Co., Kentucky. Children:

1. ANTHONY b. abt 1805
2. ELIZABETH b. abt 1808 m. WILLIAM FOSTER, son of ROBERT FOSTER b. 1770. William was born in 1802 and died in 1840. William and Elizabeth were married 17 Aug 1829 in Switzerland County, Indiana. Note that Elizabeth's half-sister SARAH married William and George Foster's younger brother Sullivan.

MOORE FAMILY

The Moore family has been traced to Jacob Moore b. abt 1750 and Elizabeth _____ b. abt 1751, who are the parents of JOSEPH ANTHONY MOORE who married MARY ANN ______. Descendant Carolyn "Wiggi" Dietz believes Joseph Anthony's father was Phillip Jr. who died in 1778, however there is no source data yet.

1820 US Federal Census, Clarke, Kentucky

Jacob Hudson

Anthony Moore (living next door)

JOSEPH ANTHONY MOORE b. 8 Jan 1780 Hardy, Virginia d. 21 Feb 1853 Shelbyville, Shelby, KY
MARY ANN _____ b. abt 1770 Hardy, Virginia
Their children:

1. ELIZABETH b. 1787 VA m. Richard Hutson abt. 1810 (children listed above with Richard Hutson)
2. SARAH b. 3 Mar 1788 KY d. 22 Dec 1853 Hancock, IN m. JOHN LEARY (brother of Elizabeth Leary)
3. MARY ANN b. 8 Jan 1780 d. 21 Feb 1833 Shelbyville, Shelby, KY m. #1 THOMAS RAINES, #2 JACOB HUTSON, #3 PETER MATTHEWS. Her children are listed above with Jacob Hutson.

1820 US Federal Census, Clarke, Kentucky

Jacob Hudson (Hutson)

Anthony Moore (living next door)

Joseph Anthony Moore was from Hampshire, VA, as were the Learys, according to cousin Julie Richards. Dennis Leary is found in the US Census of 1782 in Hampshire County, Virginia. John Leary, who married Sarah Moore, Mary Ann Moore's sister, was the executor of Joseph Anthony' Moore's estate.

Jacob Moore, father of Joseph Anthony Moore, is listed in "American Militia In The Frontier Wars" p. 73 in the same company as Cornelius Leary. They were in Capt. Jeremiah Briscoe's Company in Major John Caldwell's Battalion commanded by Major General Charles Scott. Date: July 8, 1794. Simon Hart and Pryer Payton are in the same company. The Hart and Payton families figure prominently with the Foster Family since William Foster, The Revolutionary Soldier, migrated to Kentucky with Timothy Peyton and his second wife was Sarah Hart.

As noted on pg. 63 George A. Foster married wife #1, Phebee Foster, dau. of Harrison and Anna Margaret (Bartlett) Foster, of Flavius' line of Fosters in Indiana where their son was born. It isn't known where Phebee died but probably in Shelby Co., Kentucky.

LETTICE FOSTER

LETTICE, 6th child of HARRISON & ANNA M. FOSTER, pg. 29, was born in Nicholas Co., KY and went with her father to Clark Co. It is not known when or where her mother died (Note: Anna Margaret Bartlett d. 1815 Bourbon or Clark Co., KY), but it was before Harrison's passing. At the latter event, Lettice became the ward of Abraham & May Davenport, and was taken to Missouri. As noted in the headings of the Harrison Sr. and Aaron Foster chapters, the rest of the Foster children migrated to Indiana, then to Illinois. Thus Lettice became "lost" to the rest of the family.

Years passed and all 3 of Lettice's sister and a brother died. Only Harrison Jr. and Aaron Foster were left by the time Lettice was found again. I don't know if Harrison Jr. ever saw this sister again, but it was Aaron who found Lettice in California in 1857. Of this meeting, the only one know to have taken place, F. J. Foster, Aaron's grandson, later wrote:--"They finally located her (Lettice) through a Foster who ran the river a lot—a salesman who traveled the Mississippi by boat. After the lapse of 37 years, Father S. J. Foster saw her and Grandfather Aaron Foster meet."

From Kentucky, Lettice was taken to Boone Co., Missouri, where she grew to adulthood, met and married CALEB FENTON III. Caleb was born in Princess Ann Co., MD, married in KY and had 4 children. Before going on, I'll list this first family.

CALEB FENTON III b. 12 Sep 1796 d. 3 Apr 1867
ACHSAH (LEE)
Were married 15 May 1817, Kentucky. To this union were born:

1. MARIAH b. 21 Apr 1818 m. JACOB MARCH
2. JAMES J. b. 5 Jun 1820 d. 5 Feb 1869 m. SARAH DRANE
3. ANN AMANDA b. 22 Nov 1821 m. JOHN PURCELL
4. JOHN C. b. 1827 d. 24 Mar 1897 m. SARAH HOFFMAN
5. MASSIEX died in infancy

Anna A. (#3 above) married #2 PETER KEMPER, a farmer and local Baptist Minister, Rocky Fork Church, Hinton, Missouri, who married most of the local couples during his lifetime.

LETTICE FOSTER and CALEB FENTON were married in Boone County, Missouri. They lived out their lives farming hear Hinton, Mo. After Caleb died, Lettice spent the rest of her life with her daughter Martha J. Caleb, Lettice, and her guardians, Abraham & Mary Davenport are all buried in the Rocky Fork Cemetery, Hinton, MO. The children and some other descendants are also buried in that area, such as the Searcy Cemetery mentioned later.
CALEB FENTON III b. 12 Sep 1796 d. 3 Apr 1867
LETTICE FOSTER b. 20 Jun 1811 d. 12 May 1893
Were married 8 Jan. 1832, Missouri. To this union were born:

1. WILLIAM HENRY HARRISON b. 5 Jun 1835 d. 21 Apr 1900
2. SARAH ANN b. 1 Aug 1839 d. 17 Jul 1886
3. MARTHA JANE b. 16 Dec 1844 d. 3 Jul 1909

WILLIAM H. H. married #1 LUCINDA STICE, and made their home on a farm on Silver's Fork of Lerche Creek. William is buried in the Rocky Fork Cemetery and Lucinda in the Searcy Family Cemetery.

WILLIAM H. FENTON b. 5 Jun 1835 d. 21 Apr 1900
LUCINDA (STICE) b. 15 Nov 1838 d. 8 Sep 1876
Were married 27 Mar 1856 in Missouri. Children:

1. ADA REVES b. 10 Feb 1857 d. 29 Mar 1885

2. JAMES THOMAS b. 3 Jun 1858 d. 22 Feb 1902
3. ANDREW BLUFORD b. 19 Sep 1862 d. 26 Mar 1932
4. ANNA ELIZA b. 30 Mar 1865 d. 22 Dec 1888
5. WILLIAM EMMETT b. 29 Sep 1874 d. 25 Apr 1967

ADA REVES married WASHINGTON MORDICIA 16 Nov. 1871.
JAMES T. married CORA PHILLIPPI 9 Feb 1882
ANDREW B. married MECIE DRANE, 6 Nov 1884

ANNA ELIZA, 4th child of WILLIAM H. & LUCINDA (STICE) FENTON, was born, and grew to adulthood near Hinton, Mo., where she met and married WILLIAM ARSTUS POLLOCK. She is buried in the Dripping Springs Cemetery, near Hinton, Missouri.

After Anna's death William A. Pollock married #2 SALLIE JANE GRIGGS, 27 Aug. 1891. This 2nd marriage lead to an interesting situation, note pg. 123. William A. and Sallie J. Pollock are buried in Memorial Cemetery, Columbia, Mo. To this union were born: 1) JOHN LEE 4 Jul 1892; 2) SAMUEL WILLIAM 6 Mar 1894; 3) HERMAN ORVITTE 4 Jan. 1896; 4) GEORGE CLESS b. 26 May ? d. 1924; 5) CHARLES EVERETT 7 Feb. 1902 d. 16 May 1953; 6) ARCHIE ALONZO 22 Nov 1904.

Now back to Anna Eliza Fenton's family.

WILLIAM POLLOCK b. 10 Jan 1854 d. 29 Jul 1941
ANNA E. (FENTON) b. 30 Mar 1865 d. 22 Dec 1888
Were married 30 Dec 1880, Missouri. Their child: MARGARET ANN b. 5 Nov 1882 d. 6 May 1960.

MARGARET ANN was born in Boone Co., Missouri, where she grew to adulthood, met and married DANIEL ERNESTON FOLEY. Their children were born in this county, and many of them still reside there.

DANIEL E. FOLEY b.3 Oct 1872 d. 3 Nov 1939
MARGARET (POLLOCK) b. 5 Nov 1882 d. 6 May 1960
Were married 18 Mar 1897, Missouri. Children:

1. WILLIAM HENRY HARRISON b. 14 Mar 1898 m. RUTH MELLOWAY 29 Apr 1924.
2. NANCY LEOTA LaRUE b. 12 Sep 1899 d. 13 Mar 1922 m. PHILLIP LARGENT 2 Jan. 1919
3. MARVIN EDWARD b. 16 Sep 1901 d. 16 Nov 1953 m. EVA RICE 24 Dec 1923
4. ROBERT LEE b. 15 Mar 1903 m. #1 CARRIE R. LOYDE 26 Apr 1927; #2 ARTELL DORCEY 28 Oct. 1950.
5. OSCAR ERNESTON b. 2 Nov 1905 m. married ALITA MAE ANDERTON 26 Jun 1926
6. LILLIAN MAE b. 2 Dec 1907 m. ANDERSON FORSEE 21 Apr 1924.
7. EDNA TRIMBLE b. 23 Oct 1909 m. CECIL NELSON STULL 9 Mar 1931.

CECIL NELSON STULL b. 8 Aug 1907
EDNA TRIMBLE (FOLEY) b. 23 Oct 1909
Were married 9 Mar 1931 Missouri. Children:

1. NELSON ERNESTON
2. THURMAN LOUIS
3. MARGARET LOU
4. JENELLE BERNICE
5. RICHARD DeLANO
6. RALPH SYLVAN

NELSON E. married EDITH M. FORD 23 Dec 1954. Their children: 1) DAVID, 2) DeLORIS, 3) JERRY DEAN, 4) MARTIN, 5) EDNA MAE, 6) CURTIS, 7) HOLLY.

MARGARET E. married EDWARD A. MACY, 3 Jun 1958 and had: 1) SHELLY, 2) CHARLES CHASE, 3) WILLIAM, 4) SAMUEL, 5) PATRICK & MICHAEL (twins).

THURMAN L. married NANCY LOUISIA GRABE, 11 May 1956, who furnished me the material on the Foley-Pollock family. Thurman L. is a member of the Columbia Police Force, and he belongs to the Mormon Church, which has a large genealogy library in that city. Their children: 1) ROBERT, 2) TIMOTHY, 3) KENNETH

WILLIAM EMMETT, last child of WILLIAM H.H. and LUCINDA FENTON, married CARRIE LEE BOOTHE.
WILLIAM EMMETT b. 29 Sep 1874 d. 25 Apr 1967
CARRIE LEE BOOTHE b. abt 1876 d. 6 Oct 1917
Married 12 Apr 1896, Missouri. Children:

1. LETTIE GERTRUDE b. 1 Feb 1898 d. 29 Apr 1972
2. JOHN WILKERSON b. 19 Jun 1899 d. 20 May 1934
3. EMUEL EUGENE b. 27 Sep 1900 d. 7 Sep 1944
4. ELSIE MAE b. 20 Mar 1902
5. WALLACE ATLEE b. 23 Nov 1903
6. HOLLIS LEE b. 27 Jun1906
7. ERNEST b. 27 Jun 1906
8. ETHEL BOOTHE b. 17 Jan 1908
9. CHARLES HAROLD b. 3 Mar 1909
10. HENRY DELL b. 22 Nov 1911 d. 2 Jun 1966
11. WILLIAM CECIL b. 26 Jun 1914

LETTIE G. (#1 above) married SHIRLEY LITTRELL and had a son who died young.
JOHN W. married NADINE LONG 5 Aug. 1922. No children.
EMUEL E. married MILDRED GOSLIN 16 Aug. 1935. No children.
WALLACE A. married MARY BROWN 25 Oct 1931 and had: 1) KENNETH WAYNE and 2) JERRY DALE.

HOLLIS L. married GRANCES GROOMS 19 Apr 1932. No children.
ETHEL BOOTHE married JOHN SNELL 25 Dec 1933 and lives in Columbia, MO. It was Ethel who gave me the material on the William Emmett Fenton family. Their child: RICHARD LEE.

CHARLES H. FENTON married MARGARET GRIGGS 22 Sep 1934 and had: 1) JANETTE, 2) CHARLES, 3) BETTY.
HENRY D. (#10 above) m. GRACE HUTCHINSON 28 Nov 1931 and had: PHILLIP.
WILLIAM C. married KATHRYN SANKER 9 Aug 1936 and had: 1) BEVERLY, 2) KATHY.

WILLIAM HENRY HARRISON FENTON b. 1835 (son of CALEB FENTON III and LETTICE FOSTER) married #2, ISABELLA POLLOCK, and herein lies the story. When William H.H.'s daughter ANNA E. married, William Pollock became his father-in-law. When William Pollock remarried, William H. H. performed the ceremony. When William H.H. married Isabella, W. Pollock became his brother-in-law. That made William H.H. uncle to his own grandchildren. (Wooppee!)

WILLIAM H. H. FENTON b. 5 Jun 1835 d. 21 Apr 1900
ISABELLA (POLLOCK) B. 3 Nov 1856 d. 11 Nov 1945.
Married 3 May 1877, MO. Children:

1. HINTON b. 31 May 1878 d. 16 Nov 1909
2. TURNER GARTH b. 30 May 1881 d. 7 Apr 1950
3. ELSTON BRUTON b. 5 Sep 1885 d. 27 Dec 1951
4. JOHN D.VINCEL b. 26 Oct 1889 d. 6 Jan 1960
5. JOSHUA D. b. 29 Oct 1890 d. 10 Nov 1921 m. LULU PETTY
6. ARCHIE, who died in infancy
7. LETTIE, who died in infancy

HINTON (#1 above) MARRIED ROSELLA JONES 17 Apr 1901 and had 1) LILLIAN ; 2) HARRISON b. 1903; 3) GEORGE RAY 17 Nov 1908.

TURNER G. MARRIED BERTHA BROWN 24 Mar 1901 and had 1) EDITH; 2) ROY; 3) C.H.

ELSTON BRUTON (#3 above) married BERTHA PETTY and had 1) DOROTHY; 2) WILLIAM; 3) RODGER; 4) HUBERT; 5) LEON.

JOHN D. VINCEL, #4, married EVA J. LYNES 29 May 1910 and had 1) JOEL 12 Apr 1917 d. 17 Sep 1968; 2) NANNIE MAE b. abt 1919. Nannie Mae married Waldo Palmer, a painting contractor They lived in Columbia, MO, where they were very active in the Fenton-Drane Family Association.

WALDO PALMER b. 30 Jan 1912
NANIE (FENTON) b. 8 Apr 1911

Were married 22 Jul 1934 in Missouri. Children: 1) BETTIE RUTH, 2) EVA SUE, 3) WALDO Jr., 4) JOEL ALDUS, 5) DONALD ROBERT, 6) MARTHA NAN, 7) CHARLES WESLEY.

SARAH ANN, 2nd child of LETTICE (Foster) & CALEB FENTON III, was born near Hinton, Missouri. Here, too, she grew to adulthood, met and married GEORGE THOMAS DRANE. They lived out their lives in Boone County where many of their descendants still live. Both are buried in Bethlehem Cemetery, Harrisburg, Missouri.

GEORGE THOMAS DRANE was a member of Anthony Drane's family which married to both families of Caleb Fenton III, and form the Drane portion of the Fenton-Drane family association. After the death of Sarah Ann, George T. married #2, MARY WRIGHT.

GEORGE THOMAS DRANE B. 4 Oct 1835 d. 29 Jan 1919
SARAH A. (FENTON) b. 1 Aug. 1839 d. 17 Jul 1886
Married 12 Mar 1857, Missouri. Children:

1. JAMES WILLIAM b. 8 Nov 1858 d. 20 Feb 1923
2. LETTIE MARGARET b. 12 Oct 1860 d. 22 Jul 1934
3. SELINA DORSEY b. 13 Jul 1863 d. 21 Feb 1932

JAMES WILLIAM DRANE (#1 above) married JULIA PURCELL, and they lived out their lives in Boone Co., Missouri. He is buried in the Harrisburg Cemetery and Julia in a Columbia, Missouri Cemetery.

JAMES WILLIAM DRANE b. 8 Nov. 1858 d. 20 Feb 1923
JULIE (PURCELL) B. 2 Sep 1852 d. 22 Feb 1929
Were married 20 Jan 1879, Missouri. Children:

1. MATTIE TEMPLE B. 1 Nov 1886 d. 27 Jul 1932
2. MAMIE ELIZABETH b. 20 Nov 1889 d. 28 Dec 1969

MATTIE T. married CLIFF KETCHUM 15 Nov. 1908. Cliff was born 23 Aug. 1884 d. 14 Feb 1961. They had: 1) LALA MAE 8 Jun 1910, who married HALL McLAUGHLIN 14 Dec 1930. Hall was b. 29 Apr 1907. Lala Mae had GERALD GENE 6 Dec 1931, who married SHARON LEE WARD 16 Dec 1956. GERALD GENE had 1) CYNTHIA LYNN 6 Nov 1961; 2) LISA LARAINE 6 Mar 1964.

MAMIE ELIZABETH married DEEK LONG 25 Dec 1909. He was b. 27 Dec 1885 and d. 28 Dec 1955. Both are buried in Fayette, MO. Their children: 1) LOIS NAOMI b. 27 Apr 1911; 2) NORMA DELL b. 4 Jul 1919.

LOIS NAOMI LONG (#1 above para.) married LEO BROWN 28 Jan 1934. He was b. 28 Jan 1911. Today Lois & William, who gave this data, live in Texas. Their children: 1) ELAINE SUE b. 5 Jun 1938; 2) HAROLD WAYNE b. 30 Jun 1941.

ELAIN SUE BROWN (dau. of William Leo and Lois Long Brown) married HERBERT HUGH BREWARD 7 Sep 1957. He was b. 2 May 1932. Their children: 1) BRENT LAYNE, 2) ERIC LORNE, 3) STEPHANIE LYNNE.

HAROLD WAYNE BROWN (son of William Leo and Lois Long Brown) married MARY GAYLE GRIFFIN 20 Jul 1962, and bore: JEFFERY DWAYNE.

NORMA DELL LONG (dau. of DEEK and MAMIE ELIZABETH DRANE LONG) married COLLINS FRANKLIN DYER. He was b. 19 Oct 1921. Their child, KARRON KAY, married HOWARD WILLIAM PURINTON 5 Feb 1966 and bore: STACEY NICOLE.

LETTICE or LETTIE MARGARET DRANE (dau. of George Thomas and Sarah Ann (Fenton) Drane), met and married ANDREW JACKSON WATSON in Boone Co., Missouri. Both are buried in a Harrisburg, Missouri, cemetery. Jerry Watson, grandson, gave me the material on this family.

ANDREW JACK WATSON b. 31 Jan 1856 d. 10 Dec 1940
LETTIE (DRANE) b. 12 Oct 1860 d. 22 Jul 1934
Married 10 Oct 1876, Missouri. Children:

1. DORA LINA
2. NELLIE GERTRUDE
3. MARY LEE
4. TRESSIE MARIE
5. JAMES THOMAS
6. MARIVA ETHEL
7. NETTIE EDITH
8. GOLDIE THELMA
9. ERNEST SILVIE b. 11 Aug 1887

ERNEST SILVIE (#9 above) b. 11 Aug 1887, married ICY IRENE COCHRAN 14 Nov 1906. She was b. 28 Jul 1887 d. 26 Feb 1972, and had one child: TRAVIS P. b. 25 Jun 1908 d. 7 Jul 1947. TRAVIS P. married OMA GERTRUDE SWARD 25 Dec 1926 and had: 1) JERRY WAYNE, 2) TRAVIS DUANE.

JERRY WAYNE, son of ERNEST SILVIE, married RUTH MARIE WILMSMEYER 3 Jun 1962. They live in Jefferson City, Missouri, and have: 1) JANET MARIE, 2) MICHAEL WAYNE.

TRAVIS DUANE, son of ERNEST SILVIE, married MARY SIMS 21 Aug. 1962 and have: 1) JOHN WESLEY, 2) ROBERT DUANE.

SELINA DORSEY DRANE (dau. of GEORGE THOMAS DRANE and SARAH ANN FENTON), grew to adulthood and married in Boone Co., Missouri to GEORGE WASHINGTON DEHAM 12 Oct 1882. He was b. 11 Nov 1849 d. 21 Jan 1929. Their children: 1) MADDIE, 2) GEORGE Jr., 3) SALLIE who married O.F. HAWKINS, 4) MAE, who married CHARLES WILHITE, 5) THOMAS, who married EMMA PADE, 6) STELLA, who married PORTER STRAWN, 7) RHODA LUCILLE, who married WILLIAM BRASERTON, 8) JOHN, who married his cousin ETHEL DURHAM, 9) GRACE, who married GROVER OWEN. Chart p. 106

MARTHA JANE, last child of LETTICE (FOSTER) and CALEB FENTON III, was born in Boone Co., Missouri. Here she grew to adulthood, met and married LEVI S. WOLFE. After the death of Caleb, her mother, Lettice, lived with Martha till her death. Martha J. and Levi S. are buried in the Rocky Fork Cemetery, Hinton, Missouri.

Many of Martha Jane Fenton's descendants still live in Boone Co., especially in the Columbia, Missouri area. Other members of Lettice and Caleb's families reside in Iowa, Kansas, and Texas, as well as in other parts of Missouri.

LEVI SWAYZE WOLF Sr. b. 4 Jun 1834 d. 6 Dec 1911
MARTHA (FENTON) b. 16 Dec 1844 d. 3 Jul 1909
Married 23 Feb 1867, Missouri. Children:

1. CALEB b. 1868
2. SARAH ADA b. 20 Jun 1869 d. 13 Dec 1934
3. WILLIAM SAMUEL b. 6 Feb 1871 e. 25 Aug 1951
4. LEVI S. Jr. b. 4 Oct 1875 d. 6 Dec 1959
5. CARRIE b. 13 Sep 1876 d. 3 Jul 1968
6. MINNIE b. 15 Feb 1879 d. 26 Feb 1950

CALEB (#1 above) married and had JOHN and RUTH.

SARAH ADA (#2 above) married WILLIAM ANDREW McCALPIN 26 Dec 1888. He was b. 2 Feb 1871 d. 6 Mar 1949. Children:

1. MARY ELIZABETH b. 29 Jul 1891
2. LETTIE MAE b. 11 Sep 1896
3. GEORGE WESLEY b. 2 Jun 1900 d. 6 Jun 1954
4. WILLIAM LEVI b. 12 Oct 1905 d. 28 Sep 1964

MARY ELIZABETH (#1 above) married HAROLD R. GILPIN 1 Aug 1907 and had LAWRENCE 7 Dec. 1912.

LETTIE MAE CALPIN (#2 above) married JAMES GILPIN, Harold's (above) brother, and had: 1) HELEN, 2) MILDRED, 3) THURSTON.

WILLIAM LEVI (#4 above) married LeDANE SHORT and had LEVINA.

WILLIAM SAMUEL WOLF, son of LEVI SWAYZE WOLF and MARTHA JANE FENTON, married CLARA ELLEN SANDKER and lived out his life in Boone Co., Missouri, where he was a farmer.

WILLIAM SAMUEL WOLF b. 6 Feb 1871 d. 25 Aug 1951
CLARA ELLEN (SANDKER) b. 29 Nov 1875 d. 23 May 1970
Married 23 Nov 1892, Missouri. Children:

1. MATTIE ALVA b. 29 Sep 1896

2. VIRGIL DEWEY b. 28 May 1898
3. JANE MARIE b. 21 Nov 1900
4. SAMUEL EDWARD – died in infancy

MATTIE ALVA was born and grew to adulthood in Boone Co., Missouri. Here, too, she met and married CLYDE CLAYTON CROSSWHITE. For many years they farmed near Colombia, Mo. till they retired, and moved into that city. They have no children.

It was Mattie Alva who gave me the family material on the Wolfe Clan.

VIRGIL DEWEY (#2 above) married EXIE IRENE WILHITE 27 Mar 1917. She died 1 Jan. 1956. Their children: 1) WALTER EUGENE, 2) RAYMOND, 3) MAXINE, 4) PAUL, 5) DORIS—all dead. 6) NELSON, 7) LEO, 8) NORMA, 9) VIRGIL, 10) DONALD, 11) PHYLLIS.

JANE MARIE (#3 above) married #1 ERNEST LONG, 27 Jul 1917. He died and Jane M. is now married to #2 JAMES STEVENS.

LEVI S. WOLFE Jr., son of LEVI SWAYZE WOLF Sr. and MARTHA JANE FENTON, married BEULAH NICHOLAS and had son who died young.

Levi Jr's sister CARRIE married WILLIAM WHITWORTH and had ARCHIE. All three are buried in the Rocky Fork Cemetery, Hinton, Mo.

Let's move to page 115 where we will polish off the Wolfe pack.

MINNIE WOLFE married JAMES McCOWAN 19 May 1897. They had:

1. LESLIE b. 20 Sep 1898
2. WILLIAM T. b. 18 Feb 1902 d. 17 Mar 1939
3. MARTHA JANE b. 8 Aug 1904
4. ETHEL L. b. 12 Oct 1907 d. 8 Aug 1931
5. CHARLES b. 15 May 1910 d. 12 Jul 1914
6. VIRGIL b. 10 Oct 1914 d. 8 Oct 1936

This brings to an end the families of CALEB III & LETTICE (FOSTER) FENTON. Perhaps descendants of this line will enlarge on this data.

*** * * * * * * *DORCAS FOSTER* * * * * ***

Dorcas, last child of HARRISON & ANNA MARGARET (BARTLETT) FOSTER, was born in Nicholas Co., Kentucky and was taken by her father to Clark County. Dorcas' mother died before this move and when her father died in 1819 she became the ward of her brothers, the oldest being 17 years. In 1820, all of Harrison's children except Polly, who had married, and Lettice, who was the ward of the Davenports, decided to migrate to Indiana. They landed in Switzerland County, with Dorcas being carried piggy-back much of the way.

Dorcas grew to adulthood in Indiana. In 1830 she joined her brothers Harrison Jr. and William in a move to McLean Co., Illinois, where they joined their brother, Aaron Foster.

Here, Dorcas met and married JOHN COX, and all their children were born in the old Patton settlement (Note pgs. 131-132)

Dorcas and all the children married ** are buried in the Pleasant Hill Cemetery near Lexington, Illinois. After her death, John Cox remarried and moved to Marshall Co., Kansas, and is buried in the old Morrison Cemetery three miles east of Frankfort, Kansas. (John Cox's second family is given at the end of this chapter.)

JOHN COX b. 24 Apr 1809 d. 31 Jan. 1865
DORCAS (FOSTER) b. 7 Jul 1813 d. 31 May 1853
Married 1 May 1832, Illinois. Children:

1. LETTICE b. 31 Oct 1833 d. 13 Aug 1837
2. MARY b. 31 Oct 1933 d. 26 Apr 1839
3. DANIEL b. 1834 d. Oct 1864
4. SARAH ANN b. 23 Dec 1836 d. 27 Dec 1884
5. ELIZABETH b. 22 Feb 1841 d. 3 Nov 1923
6. JOSEPH b. 1843
7. MARGARET b. 1845
8. ELLEN died in infancy
9. CHARLES died in infancy

Note: The census shows other children living with John Cox and wife #2, Rebecca Higgs, but they are Rebecca's children from two previous marriages and are listed later in this chapter.

Daniel and Joseph Cox remained in Illinois when their father moved to Kansas in 1859. Both boys joined their father later after they had served an enlistment with an Illinois regiment in the Civil War. In Marshall Co., Kansas, both men joined a militia unit. During the fighting near Independence, Missouri, Daniel was killed while on picket duty. Joseph survived the war and was last heard on in Worth Co., Missouri. He married and had three children, but we have no names.

SARAH-ANN COX married her cousin, ROBERT L. FOSTER, pg. 40. *Note: Sarah's mother Dorcas was the sister of Harrison Foster Jr., who married Ellender Foster, daughter of Robert Foster b. 1770 and Bathsheba Williams. Ellender's half-brother, Dennis, was the father of Robert L. Foster who married Sarah Ann Cox.*

ELIZABETH, 5th child of JOHN & DORCAS (FOSTER) COX, was born and grew to adulthood in McLean Co., Illinois. Here, too, she met and married her cousin, WILLIAM LEONARD FOSTER, p. 30. *Note: William Leonard was the son of William Foster and Catherine Lineback, and the grandson of Harrison and Anna Margeret (Bartlett) Foster.* In 1872 Elizabeth and William Leonard Foster moved to Montgomery Co., KS, and took up land near their cousin William Harrison Foster, pg. 63, who married Talitha Henline. *Note: William Harrison Foster was the only surviving son of George Archie Foster and Phebee Foster. Phebee died and George Archie married again to Tabitha Hutson. George Archie was another son of Robert Foster b. 1770 and Phebee was the daughter of Harrison and Anna Margeret (Bartlett) Foster. There were four marriages between these two Foster families but the relationship other than by marriage has not yet been proven.*

William Leonard and Elizabeth (Cox) Foster's farm was a few miles south of Elk City, KS, and many of their descendant still live in that area. William & Elizabeth Foster are buried in the Rutland Cemetery, south of Elk City, KS.

With the arrival of William & Elizabeth Foster, the children of Harrison & Anna M. Foster now had the eastern third of Kansas well-covered. On the north side, the children of Harrison Jr. and Dorcas. In the middle counties, it was Aaron and his family, and in the south, it was children of Dorcas and her sister, Pheebe. And mingled with the families of the other Foster children, was their sister, Polly's children, and children of the 2nd Foster family (Robert Foster b. 1770).

Homesteading in a raw, new land was never easy, but William H. chose rich, well-watered land and prospered.

WILLIAM LEONARD FOSTER b. 25 Feb 1825 d. 13 Dec 1894
ELIZABETH (COX) B. 22 Feb 1841 d. 2 Nov 1923
Married 24 Jun 1858, Illinois. Children:

1. ELIZA JANE or LOUISA b. 1859
2. DORCAS CATHERINE b. 11 Mar 1861 d. 6 Apr 1938
3. JOHN WILLIAM b. 1862 d. 1938
4. MARGARET b. 1864
5. JOSEPH b. 1864
6. MARY ANNA b. 16 Oct 1869 d. McLean, IL
7. AARON b. 1872 d. Montgomery, KS
8. NATHAN E. b. 4 Nov 1875
9. FRANCIS b. 11 Nov 1879

JOHN WILLIAM FOSTER (#3) married BECKY WILSON. No known children.

MARY ANNA FOSTER (#6) married WESLEY HALL, and lived in Eastland, TX. Their children: 1) ELIZABETH, 2) JESSIE, 3) BERTA.

NATHAN E. FOSTER (#8 above) married wife #1 EMMA OWENS. They lived in Siloam Springs, Arkansas, where Emma is buried, in 1900. They had a child, LOLA, who married a man named JOHNSON.

Nathan E. married wife #1) EMMA OWENS and had LOLA, who married MR. JOHNSON, Nathan married #2, HANNAH RATZLOOF. I have no other data on Nathan E's families, except these children, who were born to Hannah: 1) SYLVIA, 2) PAULINE, 3) an unnamed son.

FRANCIS FOSTER (#9 above) married ALLIE OWENS. She was a sister to Emma, above, and George, pg. 120. Francis & Allie lived in Montgomery Co., KS, where their children were born. Their children: 1) GUY b. abt 1901, 2) MYRTLE b. abt 1903.

DORCAS CATHERINE, 2nd child of WILLIAM LEONARD and ELIZABETH (COX) FOSTER, was born in McLean Co., IL and came to Montgomery Co., KS with her parents. Here she grew to adulthood, met and married ARTHUR W. SIRCOULOMB. Arthur was born in Millsboro, Ohio. This couple spent their lives in Montgomery County, where many of their descendants still live. Arthur & Dorcas are buried in the Rutland Cemetery.

ARTHUR SIRCOULOMB b. 22 Dec 1858 d. 13 Dec 1928
DORCAS CATHERINE (FOSTER) b. 11 Mar 1861 d. 6 Apr 1938
Married 5 May 1877, Kansas. Children:

1. RALPH b. 13 Mar 1878 d. 31 Oct 1946
2. ELIZABETH b. 14 Aug 1880 d. 15 Oct 1970
3. ANNA JANE b. 10 Apr 1883 d. 18 Aug 1958
4. IDA MAY b. 31 Dec 1884 d. 29 Jul 1958
5. FLORA ELVA b. 28 Apr 1888 d. 10 Dec 1918
6. EDWARD b. 2 Dec 1889 d. 21 Aug 1971
7. LESTER b. 18 Sep 1984
8. BESSIE b. 6 May 1898 d. 17 Oct 1971

RALPH SIRCOULOMB (#1 above) b. 13 Mar 1878 d. 30 Oct 1946
ZELPHA (BAKER) b. 13 Sep 1882 d. 25 Nov. 1968
Married 21 Jun 1905, Kansas. Children:

1. WILLIAM VAUGHN b. 10 Nov 1908
2. AVA LaRUE b. 16 Apr 1912

WILLIAM VAUGHN SIRCOULOMB married LOIS SARAH ADAMS, who was born 16 Sep 1910. Children: 1) JOE WILLIAM, who married SHARI JEAN CUTLER in Dec. of 1969.

ELIZABETH, 2nd child of ARTHUR & DORCAS SIRCOULOMB, was born and lived out her life in Montgomery, KS. On attaining adulthood she married GEORGE OWENS. He was a brother of the sisters mentioned earlier.

GEORGE OWENS B. 23 Nov 1872 d. 24 Mar 1928
ELIZABETH (SIRCOULOMB) b. 14 Aug 1880 d. 15 Oct 1970
Married 21 Dec 1908 Kansas. Children:

1. LOUIS b. abt 1909
2. GLENN
3. ALVIN
4. LOREN
5. FLORENCE abt 1919

ANNA JANE, 3rd child of ARTHUR & DORCAS SIRCOULOMB, was born and lived out her life in Montgomery, KS. She married #1 TONY MOSS; #2 JACK PHILLIPS; and either a brother or a cousin, #3 HENRY PHILLIPS, whom she divorced and remarried. (Kind'a flighty??). Anna J. had no children.

IDA MARY, 4th child of ARTHUR & DORCAS SIRCOULOMB, was born and lived out her life in Montgomery Co., KS. Here she met and married HOMER AIKEN. Both are buried in Havana, Kansas.

Don't go away. This is just a 7th page stretch. There are more of the Sir-what's-their-faces on the pages ahead.

HOMER AIKEN b. 3 Dec 1879 d. 30 Apr 1964
IDA (SIRCOULOMB) b. 31 Dec 1884 d. 30 Jul 1938
Married 6 Apr 1904, Kansas. Children:

1. LELAND b. 5 Jun 1905
2. VERLIN E. b. 25 Apr 1907
3. HAROLD b. 21 Oct 1909
4. FLORIS A. b. 22 Aug 1914
5. BERTHA E. b. 2 Sep 1920

LELAND AIKEN was born, and still lives in Montgomery Co., Kansas. He and his wife are retired from jobs with the local school district, but he still does odd jobs to keep busy. Leland married AUDREY FOWLER, and they still live in Elk City, Kansas, near the line with Chautauqua Co., where some of the Aiken children were born.

Audrey was born in Benton Co., Arkansas, where her mother's folks settled in 1830. Her mother was a PHIBBS whose people were Cherokee and made the trek from Tennessee over the "Trail of Tears," mentioned in the Wiley chapter. Many of Audrey's folks are buried near the old Cherokee Indian Mission, which bears the inscription, "Old Baptist Mission Church, moved from Georgia over the 'Trail of Tears' in 1835."

LELAND AIKEN b. 5 Jun 1905
AUDREY (FOWLER) b. 9 Jun 1918
Married 19 Feb 1937, Kansas.
Child: Mary Ann b. 4 Feb 1939

VERLIN E AIKEN (son of HOMER AIKEN and IDA SIRCOULUMB), was born in Chautauqua Co., KS. He married GLADYS BOWMAN, and now lives in Fontana, California.

VERLIN E. AIKEN b. 25 Apr 1907
GLADYS (BOWMAN) b. 26 Jul 1902
Married 27 Dec 1929, Kansas
Children: 1) DUANE, 2) OGLANN, 3) DONNIE, 4) BUDDY
No doubt the last two are nick-names, but they are all I have.

Oh! My Aiken back! Also my tired eyes and all two fingers. I'm going to stop huntin-peckin', and call it a day.

HAROLD AIKEN, (son of HOMER AIKEN and IDA SIRCOULUMB) was born in Montgomery Co., KS and still lives in or near Elk City.

HAROLD AIKEN b. 21 Oct 1909
JOSEPHINE (KEY) b. 12 Sep 1915
Married 18 Jul 1936, KS.

Children: 1. DOROTHY, 2. DELORA A., 3. MELVIN, 4. HAROLD Jr., 5. GENEVA, 6. GEORGE LEE, 7. JULIA.

FLORIS AIKEN (dau. of HOMER AIKEN and IDA SIRCOULUMB) married ERNEST B. SMITH, who was born 2 Jun 1912 d. 16 Dec 1969. Until Ernest's death, they ran a motor court in San Diego, California, where Floris still lives. They had no children.

BERTHA E. AIKEN married #1 B.J. BERRY, who died in Australia during WWII. They had no children. Bertha married #2 JACK C. NELSON.

JACK C. NELSON b. 29 May 1921
BERTHA E. AIKEN b. 2 Sep 1920
Married 23 Feb 1946, Kansas. Children: 1. BILLIE JO, 2. LINDA KAY

FLORA, 5th child of ARTHUR & DORCAS SIRCOULOMB, was born in Montgomery Co., Kansas. She married ROCKWELL GREENLEAF, 5 May 1908. He was b. 21 Feb 1887 d. 14 Jul 1945. They had no children.

EDWARD, 6th child of ARTHUR & DORCAS SIRCOULOMB, was born, raised and died in Montgomery Co., Ks.

EDWARD SIRCOULOMB b. 2 Dec 1889 d. 21 Aug 1971
GERTRUDE (SMITH) b. 11 May 1891
Were married 12 Oct 1912 in Kansas. Children:

1. CATHERINE b. 7 Jul 1914 d. 8 Feb 1971
2. WAYNE b. 5 Mar 1916 d. 23 May 1944
   Chart p. 119

LESTER, 7th child of ARTHUR & DORCAS SIRCOULOMB, was born in and still lives in Montgomery Co., KS. Here too, he met and married BLOOMA BAKER, sister to ZELPHA, p. 124. They live in Kaney, KS.

LESTER SIRCOULOMB b. 18 Sep 1894
BLOOMA (BAKER) b. 24 Oct 1895
Married 29 Jun 1913, Kansas. Children:

1. EARLINE b. 12 Mar 1915, who married GEORGE MILLER, 2 Oct 1937 and has a son: GARY LESTER.
2. CLYRENE EASTER, b. 30 Oct 1918, who married WILEY PHILLIPS, 20 Mar 1937 and has a child: DOLLIE CLYRENE.

3. LESTER CLAIR b. 30 Oct 1918 (twin), who married WAUNITA McDERMOTT, 27 Apr 1940.
   Their children: 1) JANET JUNE, 2) CLAIR WAYNE.

Clyrene E., #2 and Lester C. #3 are twins. Chart pg. 119 (in original book)

BESSIE, last child of ARTHUR & DORCAS SIRCOULOMB, was born, married, and lived out her life in Montgomery Co., KS. Although Bessie is usually considered a nickname for Elizabeth, in this case it is a Christian name, and Elizabeth was nicknamed Lizzy (?). Bessie married THOMAS WININGER, and lived in Independence, Kansas.

THOMAS WININGER b. 10 Feb 1896 d. 11 Jan 1971
BESSIE (SIRCOULOMB) b. 6 May 1898 d. 17 Oct 1971
Married 4 Jul 1916, KS. Children: 1) PHYLLIS, 2) GERALD, 3) DARRELL. Chart p. 117

MARGARET, 7th child of JOHN & DORCAS (FOSTER) COX, born in McLean Co., IL, came with her parents to Marshall Co., KS. Here she met and married LESTER CARPENTER. Later they joined her family in the move to Washington County, where their sons were born. Between the years of 1878 and 1883 they moved to Weatherby, Davies Co., Missouri, where Lester is buried. Margaret died at the home of her son John near Valley Falls, Kansas.

Their children: 1) BELLE, 2) JOHN M. b. 12 Jul 1868, 3) WILLIAM S. b. 14 Apr 1870 d. 26 Oct 1924. WILLIAM S. married in Kansas to DORA TIPTON, a widow with three children. They moved to Texas, where William died and is buried in Valley Falls, KS. He had no children.

JOHN M., son of LESTER AND MARGARET (FOSTER) CARPENTER), went with his parents to Missouri where he met and married #1, NANCY BELLE STEWART. In 1904, they moved to Valley Falls, Kansas. Two years later, John had just arrived in town with a load of hay, when he was informed that Nancy had had a stroke while he was en route. Nancy passed away three days later and is buried in Valley Falls, KS.

JOHN M. married #2 MARY HIGGINS. They had no children. In later years John and Mary moved to Fullerton, California, where John died. He is buried in Valley Falls, KS. I don't have any more on Mary.

JOHN MARCUS CARPENTER b. 12 Jul 1868 d. 29 Aug 1950
NANCY or NANNIE BELLE (STEWART) b. 12 May 1866 d. 16 Dec 1906
Married 1895 Missouri. Children:

1. CLARENCE AUDREY b. 1897 d. 1961
2. BEAULAH ADNER b. 26 Apr 1898 d. 1976 (I found this date on ancestry.com)
3. GERTRUDE or GERTIE VELMA b. 16 May 1903 d. 26 Feb 1912

CLARENCE A. (#1 above) was born near Weatherby, Missouri, and came with his parents to Valley Falls, Jefferson Co., Kansas. Here he grew to adulthood, met and married ZELLA H. They lived in Kansas City, where Clarence died. Zella H. was still living in 1973. They had no children that I have heard of.

BEULAH, who gave me this material, doesn't know her birth date. Her mother died when Beulah was young and her father didn't remember. (Her children learned it and put it in their family history and in their Family Tree on ancestry.com). Beaulah was born near Weatherby, Missouri, and came to Valley Falls, KS with her parents. Here she grew to adulthood, met and married RALPH ROBERTSON. Their first three and last five children were born in eastern Kansas, and the other four in Colorado. In 1973 Beulah lived in Baldwin City, southeast of Topeka, KS, near one of her sons. Ralph was in a rest home at the time.

RALPH ROBERTSON
BEULAH (CARPENTER) b. about 1899
Married 1915 Kansas. Children:

1. LEOLA IRENE b. 18 Sep 1916 d. 2006
2. EDITH LUCILE b. 7 Mar 1919 d. 1994
3. GERTRUDE or GERTIE M. b. 19 Aug 1922 d. 2000
4. LOUISE MARIE b. 17 Apr 1924 d. 2001
5. FORREST RALPH b. 25 Apr 1926 d. 2002
6. DALE A.b. 8 Nov 1927 d. 11 May 1942 d. 1942
7. GRACE M. b. 26 Aug 1930 d. 5 Aug 1954
8. CLETA FAYE b. 19 Oct 1932 d. 2007
9. JOHN DEAL b. 25 Jul 1935 d. 2001
10. ALTA L. b. 30 Oct 1938 d. 2000
11. E. JANE b. 25 Nov 1940
12. DOROTHY J. b. 12 Mar 1945

This brings to the end of the JOHN & DORCAS (FOSTER) COS line. And except for my line of AARON FOSTER, it ends HARRISON & ANNA MARGARET (BARTLETT) FOSTER'S lines.

JOHN COX' s Second Family

JOHN COX married #2, Rebecca Higgs. This was Rebecca's third marriage and she had children by all three husbands. One oddity is the fact she had two sons named JOHN. However, Rebecca outlived all her husbands and many of her children.

REBECCA HIGGS married #1 JOHNSON THOMPSON 13 Dec 1838. They had three children: 1) LEVI, killed during the Civil War by a tree torn from its roots by a cannon ball. 2) JOHN 1st, who fell mortally wounded at Missionary Ridge. Both of these sons served in the 13th Kansas Regiment. 3) MARY CATHERINE, who married _____PATTERSON in Washington Co., KS. They had 10 children and lived southeast of HADDAM, KS.

Rebecca Higgs Thompson married #2, CHRISTOPHER TURNIPSEED is McLean Co., Illinois, where their three children were born and he is buried. Their children: 1) RACHEL, who never married, 2) JEANETTE, who married SAMPSON FOSTER, p. 99 (son of GEORGE ARCHIE FOSTER and TABITHA HUTSON), 3) HENRIETTA, who married ROBERT A. FOSTER, pg. 100, (another son of GEORGE & TABITHA FOSTER above). Jeanette and Henrietta were twin girls who married brothers.

In 1859 John & Rebecca (Higgs) Cox and most of her children joined his ex-brother-in-law, Harrison Foster (this is Harrison Jr. b. 1806 who married Ellender Foster, sister of George A. and Robert A. above) and their nephew, Robert Foster, in a wagon train bound for Kansas territory. All three families settled in Marshall Co., KS, a few miles east of present-day Frankfort. Here, John Cox and Harrison Foster farmed till death claimed them. John Cox is buried in the Morrison Cemetery three miles east of Frankfort, KS. Rebecca is buried in Haddam, Washington Co., KS.

JOHN COX b. 24 Apr 1809 d. 31 Jan 1865
REBECCA (HIGGS) b. 1812 d. Nov 1909
Married 1855 Illinois. Children:

1. MADISON b. 2 May 1856 d. 22 Jul 1906
2. MATILDA b. 31 May 1860 d. 14 Mar 1947
3. EMILY b. 11 Feb 1862 d. 4 Mar 1954
4. JOHN Jr. b. 1865 d. 28 Nov 1932

In 1869 Rebecca sold the Marshal County land and took her family to Washington Co., KS, where she purchased more land. With the aid of her small children she ran a farm till death claimed her.

MADISON COX, born in McLean Co., Illinois, came to Marshal Co. KS. In 1869 his mother took him to a farm she purchased in Washington County. Later, he inherited this last farm. Here, too, he grew to manhood, met and married MARGARET ANN BROWN, and both are buried.

Margaret was one of three Brown sisters: Sarah, who married a man named Davis (see pg. 155), and MARY JANE, who married MILTON S. FOSTER (p. 188). For some time Madison and half-cousin Foster were courting Margaret, but in the end Madison won her hand.

MADISON COX b. 2 May 1856 d. 22 Jul 1906
MARGARET ANN (BROWN) b. 24 Jun 1848 d. 16 Feb 1942
Married 6 Jun 1874, Kansas. Children:

1. JOSEPH WILLIAM b. 15 Jun 1876 d. 3 Jul 1889
2. MAUDE ESTHER b. 5 Feb 1879 d. 29 Aug 1958
3. ALICE HAZEL b. 13 Dec 1893

MAUDE E. married FRANCIS GRISWOLD in Washington Co., KS, where both are buried. They had a farm a few miles west of Haddam, KS.

FRANCIS GRISWOLD b. 15 May 1879 d. 2 Nov 1958
MAUDE E. (COX) b. 5 Feb 1879 d. 29 Aug 1958
Married 25 Mar 1903, Kansas. Children:

1. CHESTER b. 6 Jan 1904 d. 19 Apr 1922
2. ELVIN C. b. 2 Apr 1905 m. MILDRED HENNINGSEN
3. ESTHER b. 11 Feb 1907 never married
4. EARL b. 26 Jun 1908 never married

ALICE HAZEL COX (dau. of MADISON and MARGARET COX), married ROLAND HANSEN, a barber, and lived in Spencer Iowa, where their son was born. Later, they moved to Newell, So. Dakota, where both are buried. Their son, DARREL WAYNE, married FLORENCE TAYLOR, in Seattle, Washington 15 Apr 1944. They have: 1) TAYLOR WAYNE, 2) CHARMIAN (pronounced Charmi-ann).

Both these grandchildren are married, but Alice passed away before she could fill me in on their families.

MATILDA, 2nd child of JOHN & REBECCA (HIGGS) COX, was born in Marshall Co., Kansas, and went with her mother to the Haddam KS farm. Here, she grew to adulthood, met and married NELS STROUD. They lived in South Dakota, where both are buried.

NELS STROUD b. 28 Apr 1860 d. 14 May 1926
MATILDA (COX) b. 31 May 1860 d. 14 Mar 1947
Married 13 Feb 1886, KS. Children: 1) EDNA, 2) FAYE, 3) RAY, 4) CARL, who married HATTIE BELLINGER and had DAVID and JOYCE.

EMILY, 3rd child of JOHN & REBECCA (HIGGS) COX, was born in Marshall Co., Kansas, and went with her mother to the Washington County farm. Here, she grew to adulthood, met and married CHARLES STROUD. Charles and Nels Stroud, above, were twins, and were married in a double wedding. Charles & Emily Stroud lived and died in the Bayard, Nebraska area, where their children still live.

CHARLES STROUD b. 27 Apr 1860 d. 14 May 1926
EMILY (COX) b. 11 Feb 1862 d. 4 Mar 1954
Married 13 Feb 1886, Kansas. Children:

1. GRACE b. 6 Dec 1887 d. 21 Feb 1965
2. ALMA b. 21 Mar 1889
3. JESSIE b. 7 Aug 1893 d. 3 Jan 1968
4. LAURA b. 26 Jun 1897
5. ARTHUR b. 14 Sep 1902

GRACE married ROY MUHR and lived in Redington, Nebraska, where both are buried.

ROY MUHR b. in 1886 d. 12 May 1947, and Grace Stroud were married in Nebraska in 1909 and had: 1) VIVIAN b. 18 Mar 1910, 2) ARNOLD b. 7 Mar 1912, 3) VERNON b. 17 Jun 1914.

In Douglas Wyoming, JESSIE STROUD (#3 above) met and married:

ENCE HENDERSON b. 4 Aug 1892 d. 11 Jan 1969
JESSIE (STROUD) b. 7 Aug 1993 d. 3 Jan 1968
Married 1911 Wyoming.

1. IONE B. 25 Sep 1912 d. 30 Nov 1968
2. CURTICE b. 31 Aug 1914
3. JACK b. 9 Oct 1916
4. BOB b. 17 May 1927
5. BILL b. 14 Oct 1929
6. TED b. 7 Oct 1932
7. AMY b. 26 Feb 1934

I wish I had more than nicknames for this family. However, I ran into a snag on John Cox's 2nd family. After learning what I had on his two families, a cousin decided to write a Cox family history, and suddenly memories of my Cox cousins "dried up."

LAURA STROUD married twice and had a son by husband #1. She then married #2, CHESTER BARDEN. They had no children, but he adopted Laura's son: DWELDON, 14 May 1915. (Note: It isn't clear whether this is Dweldon's adoption date or birth date.)

ARTHUR STROUD married HARLENE, in Bayard, Nebraska. They had a daughter: PAULETTE, who married DICK HUXHOUSEN. Dick was born in Nebraska.

JOHN COX Jr., son of John Cox Sr. and Rebecca Higgs, was born east of Frankfort, Kansas, and went with his mother to Washington County. Here, on a farm, he grew to manhood, met and married ELIZA ELLEN CRAMER. Both are buried in the Haddam, KS Cemetery.

JOHN COX Jr. and ELIZA TATMAN, b. 23 Feb 1870 d. 31 Aug. 1953, had a son, ROY 16 Nov 1899.

ROY COX (previous sentence) married HALLIE TATMAN 6 Aug 1919. She was born 26 May 1902. They live in Haddam, KS, and one of their sons farms a few miles west of there. Their children: 1) ROBERT NEIL b. 4 May 1920, 2) ARLIE RAY b. 3 Oct 1925, 3) AUDREY MAE 3 Oct 1925 (twins).

Except for my Grandsire, AARON FOSTER, this ends my material on the families of HARRISON & ANNA MARGARET (BARTLETT) FOSTER.

THE PATTONS & THE WILEYS

ROBERT PATTON and his wife, whose maiden name was ESPY, left Ireland in the early 1700s, and landed in North Carolina. There were three known children born to this union:

1. An unknown son, who lived in Missouri, and three known children: a) WILLIAM, b) THOMAS, c) GEORGE.

2. MARY OR MOLLY (ROBERT'S daughter), who married a man named JOHNSON, and settled "eastward of St. Louis, Missouri, near the old lead mines." The only known child was ALEXANDER, who, when jilted by his girl, moved to McLean County, Illinois. He lived out his life with his Uncle John Patton. He was a cooper by trade. He never married nor visited his old home.
3. JOHN PATTON, son of GEORGE and grandson of No. 1 Unknown Patton, was born in North Carolina, and moved to Garrard County, Kentucky. Here he acquired land, and built his first home. Here too, he met and married MARGARET WILEY, p. 136, and their first seven children were born. TheY were the parents of SARAH ROYSTON PATTON who married AARON FOSTER (son of HARRISON & ANNA M. "BARTLETT" FOSTER).

In the fall of 1817, John and Margaret Patton (No. 3 above) moved to Switzerland Co., Indiana, where they built their second home. Eleven years later, news of wild, rich land in Illinois, just waiting for a plow, could be had for a song. John could not resist such a siren call. He sold all his unmovable goods and loaded the rest, including his family, into two wagons. The lead wagon was pulled by a 4-horse team, the second, the heavier loaded, was pulled by two yoke of oxen. A band of sheep and cattle were driven by the older children. (Note Aaron Foster chapter)

After a wet miserable drive, the Patton convoy arrived in McLean Co., Illinois, November of 1828. With John was his son-in-law, Aaron Foster, who was lucky enough to get food and shelter for his family by doing chores for a settler. The Pattons were not so lucky. The wintered in a pole cabin with their small children. There was no fireplace or chinking between the logs. They did their cooking out-of-doors, and their living quarters were little better than living outside.

The next spring, John Patton was all set to erect a cabin on the prairie when two hunters stopped for a bit. They told John of a fine stand of timber, with a river flowing through that would make a nice home site. John's inspection of the site proved to be just what he had always dreamed of owning. In later years, this fine stand of oak, maple and walnut trees and river came to known as "The Patton Settlement."

The Pattons and Aaron Foster moved into some apparently abandoned Indian teepees, and began cutting logs for a cabin. The first trees felled were of walnut, due to its resistance to ground contact and termites. While they were thus employed, the Indians put in an appearance. They had not abandoned their town, as John Patton had thought, but had been in their winter camp, hunting throughout the winter.

At first the Indians, of the Kickapoo tribe, insisted that the white men leave. But after some bargaining, during which John made them some furniture, repaired some broken guns, and agreed to fence off their ancient burial grounds, the Indians gave him the land. Some of the Indians, with some white men who had wintered nearby, helped John to erect his cabin. Soon after, these Indians joined another group of their tribesmen, who had a town about 50 miles away.

Note from Adrienne: The Kickapoo Indians had earlier kicked out other white families, such as John Hendrix, the Dawson family, Thomas Orendorff, and the Rhodes family.

The Kickapoo chief, Machina, told them, "too much come back, white man, t'other side Sangamon." These things appeared a little threatening, but the settlers refused to leave and were not molested. It is the almost unanimous expression of the settlers that the Indians were the best of neighbors. They were polite and friendly, and old Machina was quite popular among the whites, especially with the women, . He was particularly fond of children and this touched their motherly hearts." McLean County was plagued with green-headed flies that bit in the summer time, so severely that the people had to stay indoors. Wolves were a problem, as they attacked the sheep and hogs, and bounties were put on their heads. The prairie grass was very tough and took a team of oxen to plow it under. From "The Good Old Times In McLean County Illinois," McLean Chapter, pg. 3.

Back to Flavius' account: The cabin was erected on June 10, 1829. During the so-called Black Hawk War, John built a blockhouse near the end of this cabin. Later the two buildings were roofed over into one house, and a lean-to was added. The original cabin stood on the same site for 136 years, and was used as living quarters for over 100 years.

During June of 1970, my wife, Marie, and I visited the site of the old Patton Settlement. It is located on the banks of the Mackinaw River, 5 miles southeast of Lexington, Illinois. All that remains of this settlement is the beautiful Pleasant Hill Cemetery, where the town of Pleasant Hill - Selma once stood. It is a beautiful land of pleasant woodlots and rich farmlands, a fitting monument to those old settlers who lived and are buried there. John and Margaret Patton, and all their children, including Aaron Foster's wife, Sarah R. (Patton) are buried in the Pleasant Hill Cemetery.

John Patton was a man of many talents. He built his own homes down to and including the hinges on the doors, he was a gunsmith, and built and ran his own sawmill. He was very religious, holding services in his home for many years, till a Methodist church was built on land he donated, and sawed the lumber for. It was John who did so much to form Aaron Foster's life, and guide it into the ways of the Lord, and passed on through two generations of preachers in the local Methodist church."

JOHN PATTON b. 1777 d. Dec 1854
MARGARET (WILEY) b. 1782 d. 20 Jan 1850
Married 18 Aug 1803 in Garrard, Kentucky. Children:

1. SARAH ROYSTON b. 11 Oct 1804 d. 1 Oct 1845
2. CASSANDRA WILEY b. 19 Jun 1806 d. 22 Mar 1839
3. SUSANNA ESPY b. 18 Jan 1808 d. 5 Sep 1880
4. JOHN ROYSTON b. 2 Feb 1810 d. 10 Oct 1846
5. WILLIAM WILEY b. 17 Mar 1812 d.16 Oct 1852
6. MARGARET b. 18 Feb 1814 d. 28 Sep 1862
7. BENJAMIN WILEY b. 18 Jun 1817 d. 16 Feb 1892
8. JAMIMA ROYSTON b. 3 Jul 1818
9. AARON SINCLAIR b. 20 Apr 1820 d. 25 Nov 1912

10. MOSES ROYSTON b. 20 Apr 1820 d. 22 May 1854
11. CONSTANTINE b. 16 Jun 1827

(John and Margaret Patton surely overworked the surnames Wiley and Royston in their family's middle names.)

SARAH ROYSTON PATTON (#1 above) married AARON FOSTER. See next chapter.

CASSANDRA W. PATTON (#2 above) married her cousin, WILLIAM WILEY, pg. 138.

SUSANNA ESPY PATTON (#3 above) married JOHN BOYD MESSER. He was a cavalryman, a veteran of the Battle of Fallen Timbers (Northwest Indiana Wars), who arrived in McLean Co., Illinois in the fall of 1829. Note: Aaron's father, Harrison, was a veteran of the same battle.

JOHN BOYD MESSER b. 4 Aug 1807 d. 10 Nov 1876
SUSANNA ESPY PATTON b. 18 Jan 1808 d. 5 Sep 1880
Married 5 Jul 1832, Illinois. Children:

Since this is such a large family, and I just got a supper call, let's sign off here, and start later on pg. 134.

1. MARIAH JANE b. 4 Apr 1833 m. THOMAS BOUNDS
2. SIDNEY ANN b. 27 Sep 1834 M. AARON MISNER
3. JOHN PATTON b. 11 Mar 1836 d. 30 Jul 1897
4. MARGARET ESPY b. 3 Dec 1837 M. DeLONG STEWART
5. ISAAC b. 30 Nov 1839
6. MARY JANE b. 8 Oct 1841 m. JASPER LOVING
7. JAMES T. b. 16 Jul 1843 d. cholera in 1854
8. ELIZABETH ELLEN b. 24 Mar 1848 m. WILL STAGNER
9. REBECCA ADELINE b. 30 Jun 1851 m. JOHN DRAKE

JOHN PATTON MESSER (#3 above) married #1 MARY S. (last name unknown), b. 2 Feb 1842 d. 27 Dec 1867. Their children: 1) HENRY d. in infancy, 2) JOHN B. who died 7 Aug 1865, 3) IRA d. 9 Aug. 1862.
JOHN PATTON MESSER married #2 ELIZABETH JANE (no last name) b. 7 Nov 1838 d. 2 Feb 1928.

JOHN ROYSTON PATTON (son of JOHN ROBERT & MARGARET WILEY PATTON) married SARAH ANN HOPKINS, 14 Sep 1834. They had children, but all were dead by 1916. I have no other data.

WILLIAM WILEY PATTON (son of JOHN ROBERT & MARGARET WILEY PATTON) married CATHERINE SHARP, who was born in 1823 d. 30 Sep 1868 Their only child, WILLIAM SHARP PATTON lived in Missouri.

MARGARET PATTON (sibling of John and William in above paragraphs) married GEORGE HENLINE, who is no doubt related to the other Henlines who married into the Foster clan or the families of the in-laws, friends, and neighbors.

BENJAMIN PATTON (another sibling of the above) married MARY ANN CONOVER 13 Oct 1839. Mary was born 31 Dec 1815 d. 21 Oct 1907. They had no children of their own, but raised Mary Ann's younger sisters, SUSAN A. and REBECCA.

JEMIMA R. PATTON married CALVIN ADAMS, 24 Dec 1839. Calvin was born 12 Jun 1815 d. 12 May 1850. They had one child: ALMEDA.

AARON S. PATTON, one of the twin sons, married ELIZABETH McCULLOCK. They moved to Baxter Springs, Kansas, where both are buried, Their children: 1) WILLIAM, 2) BENJAMIN, 3) JOHN, 4) MOSES, 5) MARTHA, 6) ANNA, who married LON GOODNER and had 3 children.

MOSES R. PATTON, Aaron's twin brother, married Aaron's sister-in-law, MARY ANN McCULLOCK. They had a son, JACOB ALONZO.

JOSEPH PATTON married PERMELIA BURNS, but had no children.

CONSTANTINE PATTON married MARGARET BILLS. And here-in lies a story. Margaret was a sister to Rachel Bills, who married my Great-Grandfather Silas J. Foster (p. 210). All the Fosters and Pattons, except Constantine, were strong anti-slavery people. He followed the path of the Bills family, which were pro-slavery. This caused a lot of hard feelings for many years between the families of the Bills sisters.

CONSTANTINE PATTON b. 16 Jul 1827
MARGARET (BILLS) b. 3 Jul 1833
Were married 26 Feb 1849 Illinois. Children:

1. JOHN FRANKLIN b. 5 Sep 1850
2. WILLIAM FRANKLIN b. 28 Jul 1854
3. MOSES ALONZO b. 25 Jan 1858
4. JOSEPH ALBERT b. 5 Mar 1860
5. ROBERT E. LEE b. 30 Mar 1864
6. JEFFERSON DAVIS b. 26 Jan 1862 d. in infancy

WILLIAM WILEY

WILLIAM WILEY, born in Wales in the mid-1700's, immigrated to Anne Arundel County, Maryland. Here he met and married SARAH ROYSTON. In 1810 William and his brother-in-law WILLIAM ROYSTON, lived in Garrard Co., Kentucky, where they owned much land and many slaves. It was here that the Wiley and Patton families became acquainted. After the death of the elder Wileys their children immigrated to Switzerland

Co., Indiana, and later to the PATTON Settlement in McLean Co., Illinois. (Except noted) The elder Wileys are buried in Garrard Co., KY.

WILLIAM BENJAMIN WILEY b. abt 1759 (in Baltimore according to some Family Trees) d. 1817
SARAH (ROYSTON) b. abt 1759 Baltimore, MD d. 1828 Switzerland Co., Indiana
Married 1779 in Maryland. Children:

1. MARGARET b. 1781 d. 20 Jan 1850
2. THOMAS
3. CASANDRA
4. WILLIAM
5. BENJAMIN d. Feb 1815
6. JOHN ROYSTON b. 1791

MARGARET WILEY married JOHN PATTON, and her family was given earlier.

THOMAS WILEY married RHODA, and had at least one child: SARAH ROYSTON WILEY, who married her cousin, LYTLE ROYSTON WILEY (p. 140). Thomas and his brother William remained in Indiana when the other children moved to Illinois.

CASSANDRA WILEY married JOHN SMITH in Kentucky, where their two oldest children were born. The rest of the children were born in Switzerland Co., Indiana.

JOHN SMITH b. 1791 d. 1865
CASSANDRA (WILEY) b. 1796
Married 1811 Kentucky. Children:

1. AQUILLAR b. 1812 d. 1872
2. THOMAS
3. SALLY d. 12 Feb 1883
4. MARGARET
5. JOHN ROYSTON
6. WILLIAM b. 9 Sep 1819 d. 2 Aug 1865
7. SARAH FRANCES
8. SHELTON b. 1825 d. 1900

The elder sons returned to Kentucky for brides. AQUILLAR married SUSAN LOGAN, and THOMAS married NANCY HUGHES.

The rest of this family went that-a-way, but we'll head them off.

SALLY SMITH (# 3 above) married JAMES J. HENLINE (b. 1818-1905—there's that Henline name again). There were 11 children born to this marriage, but I have no names.

SARAH FRANCES SMITH (#7 above) married JOHN BURDETT.

WILLIAM SMITH (#6 above) married MALINDA FOSTER, p. 32 (dau. of DENNIS & MARY POLLY FOSTER).

SHELTON SMITH, (#8 above) married MARY POWELL.

SHELTON SMITH b. 27 Feb 1825 d. 1900
MALINDA (POWELL) b. 1834 d. 1879
Were married 16 Nov 1851 Illinois. Children:

1. EMMA
2. LUVINDA
3. CHARLOTTE
4. SHELTON Jr.
5. ALBERT
6.

SHELTON Sr. married MARY M., who died in 1886. All three are buried in the Evergreen Cemetery, McLean Co., Illinois.

BENJAMIN WILEY

BENJAMIN WILEY was born in Maryland and grew to manhood in Kentucky. Ben did a lot of exploring, during which he traveled to Tennessee. Here he met and married MARGARET HERD RODGERS.

Margaret's father, WILLIAM RODGERS, was a half-white sub-chief of the Cherokee Indian Nation. It was his sad task to lead his clan of Cherokee Indians over the "Trail of Tears," to Oklahoma, when the greedy white men wanted their homes. It was there that Margaret's sister, TIANA RODGERS married SAM HOUSTON of Texas fame.

Benjamin Wiley was with Gen. Jackson at the battle of New Orleans, Jan. 8, 1815. During the fighting Ben's musket burst. Ben found another, which also failed. Undaunted, he sprang to the top of the cotton-bale breastworks, flapped his arms and crowed like a rooster. A few days after the battle, Ben contracted measles, and foolishly went swimming in the cold river and caught cold. He died in February of 1815.

BENJAMIN WILEY and MARGARET RODGERS were married in Kentucky and had two children: 1) ANDREW JACKSON WILEY, who married SARAH BRUMHEAD in Illinois. They had a daughter, MARGARET, who married THOMAS BOTTS. Andrew J. Wiley was born 3 Jul 1842 d. 5 Jan 1862. Killed while serving in the Union Army during the Civil War.

3) WILLIAM, who married his cousin, CASSANDRA W. PATTON (p. 133). They were married in Switzerland Co., Indiana, and in 1834 they immigrated to McLean Co., Illinois. Four years later, William was on his way to the mill with grain to grind, when he was taken by colic and soon died. Six months later,

Cassandra contracted lung fever while working in a maple sugar camp, and also died. Their children were raised by relatives.

WILLIAM WILEY b. abt 1804 d. 7 Sep 1838
CASSANDRA (PATTON) b. 19 Jun 1806 d. 22 Mar 1839
Were married 16 Nov 1827, Indiana. Children:

1. MARGARET b. 1828
2. CASSANDRA b. 21 Nov 1836 d. 30 Oct 1855
3. SARAH SINCLAIR b. 22 Feb 1839 d. 3 Dec 1930
4. MALINDA died as a youth, no dates

CASSANDRA WILEY (Jr.), much to her sorrow, married David Henline. In his family notes Grandpa F. J. Foster wrote, "Angered because she became pregnant, the brutish husband kicked her in the stomach, causing her death."

He was never punished by the law, due to the family's position in the community, but no other woman would have him. In 1875, 20 years later, a history of McLean County describes him as, "Good natured and kind hearted, and loves fun and humor." (Note: Uh, did he change? –or is the History of McLean County not to be trusted?)

SARAH SINCLAIR WILEY married JEFFERSON BISHOP, in Illinois. Later, they parted and Sarah moved to Washington State, where she is buried in the Farmington Cemetery. In later years the eldest son returned to McLean Co., Illinois where married, lived, and died.

JEFFERSON BISHOP
SARAH SINCLAIR (WILEY) b. 22 Feb 1839 d. 3 Dec 1930
Were married in 1860 Illinois. Children:

1. EDGAR EDWARD b. 28 Nov 1861 d. 12 Jul 1959
2. GEORGE WILLIAM b. 11 Oct 1865 d. 29 Jul 1937

This isn't chess, but we're going to move our bishop to pg. 139.

GEORGE WILLIAM BISHOP married ELIZABETH STORKEY 10 Nov 1886.

JOHN ROYSTON, youngest child of WILLIAM & SARAH WILEY, was born in Anne Arundel Co., Maryland. He was taken by his parents to Garrard Co., Kentucky, where he grew to manhood, met and married HANNAH SAMPSON. In 1817, John & Hannah moved to Switzerland Co., Indiana, where they remained till the fall of 1835. At that time, they joined relatives in McLean Co., Illinois. Of this last move Grandpa F. J. Foster noted, "John Wiley came to Illinois and settled 'in file' just six miles from Grandfather Aaron Foster's place."

"In file" meant settling on government land at $1.25 an acre, payable over a period of time.

The fall move to Illinois by John Wiley's family was one of rain, mired wagons, and fording rain-swollen streams. To make the rain-soaked days more miserable, they were trailing a flock of sheep. After a few water crossings, the sheep would become water-soaked and tired, and would have to be manhandled over many of the crossings. In Illinois, the sheep more than paid for this discomfort with their meat, and especially their wool.

JOHN ROYSTON WILEY b. 5 Jun 1791 d. 8 Oct 1851
HANNAH (SAMPSON) b. 26 Feb 1790 d. 22 Jun 1841
Were married 10 Sep 1810, Kentucky. Children:

1. MARGARET b. 8 Jul 1811
2. WILLIAM b. 24 Aug 1812 d. 31 Mar 1891
3. LYTLE b. 7 Nov 1815 d. 10 Nov 1887
4. ELIZABETH b. 7 Apr 1819 d. 3 Dec 1894 m. HENRY HENLINE
5. JAMES ROYSTON b. 21 Nov 1820 d. 12 Dec 1882
6. THOMAS ROYSTON b. 26 Jan 1823 d. 26 Apr 1849
7. LUCINDA b. 6 Feb 1825 d. 16 Jan 1890
8. SILAS b. 20 Apr 1827 d. 10 May 1892 m. NANCY
9. MALINDA b. 9 Dec 1832 d. 16 May 1868
10. HANNAH b. 1836

WILLIAM WILEY b. 24 Aug 1812 d. 31 Mar 1891
NANCY (HOPKINS) b. 12 Apr 1824 d. 5 Jun 1914
Married 30 Sep 1841 Illinois. Children:

1. JOHN SAMPSON b. 1842 d. 10 Jun 1874
2. ROBERT HOPKINS b. 1845 d. 2 Apr 1864
3. JOSEPH S.
4. WILLIAM ROYSTON b. 26 Aug 1850 d. 7 Oct 1928
5. JAMES S. b. 17 Dec 1854 d. Sep 1913
6. AMELIA d. 1929
7. NANCY E. b. Apr 1858 d. Jan 1954

JOHN SAMPSON WILEY married MISSOURI ARNOLD. During the 1920's this family lived in Bayard, Nebraska. Their children: 1) ARNOLD, 2) NANCY, 3) LILLIAN b. 1866 d. 28 Apr 1908.

JOSEPH S. WILEY married MALISSA HENLINE in Illinois. Their children: 1) ROBERT, 2) EVERETT, 3) VIRGIL, 4) MERCER, 5) ROY.

WILLIAM ROYSTON WILEY married GERTRUDE GLENN 18 Jun 1880. Their children: 1) HAMILTON, 2) EARL, 3) ROBERT, 4) LILLIAN, 5) MILDRED, 6) RUTH.

AMELIA WILEY married STEPHEN SMITH and had: 1) PEARL, 2) HOMER, 3) JOHN, 4) ORVILLE, 5) MARK, 6) STEPHEN Jr., 7) ELIZABETH, 8) WILLIAM GEORGE.

NANCY E. WILEY married LEMUEL S. FINCHAM in 1885. He died in Feb. of 1940. Their children: 1) LAWRENCE S., 2) JAMES F., 3) EARL, 4) LEMUEL C. Jr., 1887 to 21 May 1966, who married PAULINE, 5) JAMES PALMER b. 16 Nov 1891 d. Feb 1954, who married ETHEL SUTTON, 6) GERTRUDE, who married ROY WETHERS.

* * * *

LYTLE WILEY, 3rd child of JOHN & HANNAH (SAMPSON) WILEY, was born in Garrard Co., KY and came with his parents through Indiana to McLean Co., Illinois. Her, he met and married his cousin, SARAH, daughter of THOMAS WILEY (p. 136) and RHODA. With a name like LYTLE, it was bound to end up, "Little Wiley."

LYTLE WILEY b. 7 Nov 1815 d. 10 Nov 1887
SARAH (WILEY) b. 1826
Married 13 Jun 1843, Illinois. To this union were born:

1. THOMAS ROYSTON b. 1844 d. 30 Jun 1896
2. RHONDA MARGARET b. 30 Apr 1846 d. Mar 1940 m. ALEX GILLON
3. JOHN JAMES b. 3 Dec 1847 d. 3 Nov 1944 m. SARAH HARPOLE
4. HANNAH ELIZABETH m. A. L. HUTSON
5. WILLIAM SAMPSON
6. SARAH LUCINDA m. HARVE HENLINE
7. LYTLE RICHARD d. Feb 1937 m. EMMA HARPOLE
8. MARY CASSANDRA

* * * * *

JAMES R., 5th child of JOHN & HANNAH (SAMPSON) WILEY, born in Illinois, came with his parents to McLean Co., Illinois. Here, he grew to manhood, met and married TELITHA HENLINE (dau. of William Henline of Boone, Kentucky, and Nancy Taylor). After Thomas died, Telitha married #2, WILLIAM H. FOSTER, p. 63 (Wm. is son of George Archie Foster and Phebee Foster—George Archie was the son of Robert Foster and Bathsheba Williams and Phebee was the daughter of Harrison Foster and Anna Margaret Bartlett). Telitha is buried in Montgomery Co., Kansas, Thomas R. is buried in McLean Co., Illinois. Their children: 1) WILLIAM HARRISON b. 12 Jul 1843, 2) ANDERSON b. 1846.

WILLIAM HARRISON WILEY was born in McLean Co., Illinois. Here he grew to manhood, met and married SARAH FOSTER. So far there seems to be no connection of Sarah with our Fosters (Note: It is possible that Sarah is the daughter of George W. Foster, son of Col. Peyton Foster, and Lucile Short). In 1872, William & Sarah joined his parents in the trek to Montgomery Co., Kansas, and settled in Rutland Township. Many of their descendants still live in southeast Kansas. William H. & Sarah Wiley are buried in Montgomery Co., Kansas.

WILLIAM HARRISON WILEY b. 12 Jul 1843 d. 17 Mar 1909
SARAH FOSTER b. 19 Oct 1847 d. 17 Apr 1912
Married 14 Dec 1863, Illinois. Children:

1. THOMAS b. 3 Feb 1865 d. infancy
2. CORA D. b. 15 May 1867
3. ADELINE 15 Oct 1869 d. 1927
4. WILLIAM b. 19 Jan 1872 d. 1952
5. MONTE ECK b. 3 Jan 1875 d. 1930
6. FANNIE C. b. 18 Nov 1878
7. ELIZABETH J. b. 18 Oct 1881 d. 29 Jul 1954
8. JESSIE E. b. 4 Dec 1884 d. 18 Apr 1952
9. GEORGE T. b. 4 Dec 1884 d. 1955

ADELINE (#3 above) married CHARLES PAPSON (who died 1946) and had: 1) FRANK, 2) ORVILLE b. 1891 d. 1907, 3) flora B. 19 Nov 1893 d. 10 Mar 1956, who married FRANK MAIN, 4) VADA b. 5 Sep 1898 d. 6 Jun 1964, who married RALPH JONES.

MONTE E. (#5) married ADELLA TALLEY and had: 1) LOLA, 2) BLANCH, 3) CLARENCE, 4) CLAY, 5) CARL, 6) RALPH, 7) EARL, 8) FRED b. 18 Aug 1913 d. 16 Feb 1969.

FANNIE C. (#6) married WALTER BOWERSOCK and had: 1) CHARLES, 2) BERNICE, 3) LUCAS who died Feb 1964.

ELIZABETH J. (#7) married ERNEST MENDENHALL who d. 27 Jan 1905 and had: 1) JESSIE, 2) LINNING, 3) ERNEST T. Jr., b. 24 Mar 1905 d. 12 Jan 1945.

JESSIE E. WILEY (#8) married MABLE DIXON 22 May 1909. She was born 23 Jul 1892 d. 14 Feb 1942. They had two children in Montgomery Co., K: 1) BERNICE MARJORY b. 28 Sep 1915, who married GEORGE T. MAYNOR 16 Oct 1937, and had DIANA LYNN; 2) WILLIS LEON b. 26 Feb 1923, who married NELLIE BELLE WENNIHAN 20 May 1943. Both were born in southeastern Kansas and now live in Sunnyside, Washington. Children: 1) JACALYN JOYCE, 2) CONNIE LOUISA.

JACALYN JOYCE WILEY, dau. of JESSIE & MABLE WILEY, married HENRY LUKE FARTHING 12 Feb 1966, divorced, and had KIMBERLY RENEE.

CONNIE LOUISA WILEY, dau. of JESSIE & MABLE WILEY, married MONTE JAMES CURRIER, 1 Jan 1969, and had SHAUN PATRICK 4 Jun 1969.

Thus ends the Patton-Wiley Chapter, with a big fat "."

AARON FOSTER

Aaron, 3rd child of Harrison & Anna Margaret Foster, was born in Bourbon Co., Kentucky. In 1807, the family moved to Nicholas Co., Ky., and in 1817, to Clark Co., Kentucky. Harrison's father, William had moved there some years before. It is not known, at this time, when the mother died, but it was between Oct. 22, 1813, when her youngest child was born, and June 20, 1819, when Harrison made his Will.

The children of Harrison and Anna M. Foster were William; Polly; Aaron; Harrison Jr.; Phebee; Lettice and Dorcas. The families of all these were given in earlier chapters, except Gr. Gr. Grandfather Aaron Foster. However, it is not known for sure, by me, if William or Polly was the oldest child, nor do I know where the mother was buried. Harrison Foster was buried somewhere in Clark Co., Kentucky.

Around 6 months before Harrison Foster died, Polly had married, and after his death, Lettice was taken by the Davenport family as a ward. It was during their stay in Clark County that a man tried to get two of Aaron's playmates into a fight. Instead of fighting one another, one of the boys picked up a stick and threw it at the man, but his aim was off. The stick hit Aaron in the left eye, putting it out.

In the summer of 1820, William and Aaron took the other children, less Polly and Lettice, through Daniel Boone's woodlot to Switzerland Co., Indiana. The Foster children had no horses or oxen, so they loaded their belongings onto the back of some milk cows, and Dorcas was so young, she had to be carried piggy-back much of the way. It must have been a rough trip in some ways, but they had youth and the thought of greener pastures ahead to lure them on.
In Indiana, the Foster children became acquainted with many of the families that were to be their neighbors throughout their lives. Here, too, Aaron, William, Harrison Jr., and Phebee Foster met their mates, and Phebee's death marred their happiness.

Aaron Foster became acquainted with the Patton-Wiley family in Switzerland Co., Indiana, and married SARAH ROYSTON PATTON. JOHN PATTON, her father, also became Aaron's "father image", a guiding light, he followed throughout the remainder of his life. In fact, the children's memory of their parents, Harrison and Anna M. Foster, grew so dim, Aaron's son did not even know his grandmother's name. I had a very difficult time locating her.

Aaron and Sarah Patton were married in 1824, and all was going well with them, when news of rich, unplowed land in Illinois reached them. John Patton was the first to take fire at this news, and passed it on to his son-in-law, who also got a bad case of foot itch. Sarah was much attached to her lot in Indiana, but reluctantly agreed to go to this new, untamed wilderness, giving up a comfortable home for the doubtful betterment of a frontier land. Her decision was sparked partially be the fact that her father, and his family were leading the immigration.

In the fall of 1828, the Patton-Foster convoy hit the road westward. Their lead wagon was pulled by two yoke of oxen, the other two by double teams of horses, and they trailed a herd of cattle and sheep. At first they had little trouble from the loose stock, but as the miles piled up, and numerous rain-swollen streams had to be crossed, the sheep became more and more reluctant to cross these watercourses, and had to be manhandled over many of them. In later years these sheep paid off in meat and wool. In fact, Grandmother Sarah became so proficient with her spinning of the wool, the strands so slender, they were much in demand by her neighbors for sewing thread.

Aaron and John Patton landed in McLean Co., Illinois in November of 1828. While the Pattons lived in the unchanged cabin, described in the heading of the Patton chapter, Aaron Foster was much luckier. An old settler, about the only one in that section of Illinois at that time, named John Dawson, gave Aaron a winter's job. Payment for this work was room and board for Aaron and his family. (Coming into a new land, with so few settlers, how lucky can one get?)

The past winter had been a hard one, on the new arrivals, and Aaron was all for returning to their old Indiana home, but Grandmother Sarah would not hear of such a thing. She had reluctantly given up her old home, on Aaron's insistence, and wasn't just about to return now. Finding that he was out-voted, Aaron told his wife to pick out a plot of land for their new home. She chose a plot adjoining that of her father's; section 21, Lexington Twp, McLean Co., Illinois. Later, a second plot was taken up in Section 16. Four hundred acres of land was paid off, mostly by Aaron splitting fence rails at .25 per hundred. The cost of the land, by the government, was $1.26 per acre. Section 21 was paid off August 17, 1835, and section 16, January 28, 1837.

The first logs for a school were cut in 1830, in Patton Settlement, also known as Old Town Timber. The logs were waiting for a snow so they could be sledded into position, but when the snow did come it lasted so long, and was so deep the logs could not be moved. In fact, the winter of 1829-30 was long known as "the winter of the big snow". Then came the big scare of the so-called Black Hawk war, and it was 1832 before the school was ready for its first students. The first teacher was one of Sarah's sisters, and most of the children were from the Foster, Wiley and Patton families.
In 1838, Mr. Isaac Smalley, seeking land, arrived on the banks of the Vermillion River, about 40 miles from Aaron's claim on the Mackinaw River. The Vermillion was back-full, and while seeking logs for a raft, Mr. Smalley noticed a pile of building material nearby. On arriving at the home of Aaron Foster, he was surprised to learn that he had just passed the future site of Pontiac, Illinois.

Mr. Smalley fell in love with a gently rolling hill on Aaron Foster's land, and bought 160 acres of the northeast quarter of Section 21. The plot he chose included the old Indian town and burial grounds, mentioned in the heading of the Patton chapter. In 1840, Mr. Smalley laid out a town site on this land, expecting a railroad to build through it. Two railroads did build in that direction, but both bypassed the town site.

Mrs. Smalley called a meeting of the neighbors to find a suitable name for the new town site. Among the gathering was Lydia, wife of Milton Smith, the godfather to one of Aaron's children. The Milton part of his name still exists today in my middle name. Mrs.

Smith made the following suggestion. "We call our place 'Poverty Hill.' And since this is a fairer one to look upon, if I was you, I'd call it 'Pleasant Hill.'"

A request for a post office hit a minor snag, when it was learned that there was already a Pleasant Hill post office in the state. The post office department suggested that the name be changed to Selma, Illinois, so Pleasant Hill - Selma, post office was born. The first post master was Harrison Foster Jr., who set aside a portion of his store for the purpose. Methodist Church services had long been held in John Patton's house, and now a building was built for the services, with Aaron Foster as class leader.

In 1840, Mr. Absolom Enock arrived with a load of notions, and set up shop in the home of Mr. Smalley. Later, he and Aaron built a building on Aaron's land, and they went into partnership, a union all that any man could ask for. He was class leader in his church, a respected merchant with unlimited credit, which he used sparingly, and held some elected positions in Pleasant Hill, at different times. Then disaster struck. Sarah, his wife of many years, sickened and died. She is buried in the beautiful Pleasant Hill Cemetery, overlooking the bountiful land she helped to conquer.

Aaron Foster remarried, but all was no so good as it has been. For many years the question of slavery had disrupted the well-being of our nation, and was growing steadily worse. The flames of disruption rose nearly to their peak, when Congress decided to let Kansas join the Union, by a vote of its people. Both members of the anti-slavery and pro-slavery parties rushed men into the territory—the "anti's" to settle and vote, the pros, only to vote.

(Aaron's 2nd marriage will be given later in this chapter.)

In 1901, Aaron's son, Silas J. Foster, wrote the newspaper article placed in the back of this book. There are some mistakes in his account of Aaron's early life that I discovered in my research. The Foster family never lived in Hancock County, Kentucky, although they may have lived in such a community by that name. However, I'm inclined to think, from listening to tales of the Foster's past history that my relatives were hipped on the sound of "Hancock County and also on Skiller (Schuyler) County."

Additional info on Aaron Foster from his descendants:

ACCOUNT OF AN EARLY SETTLER OF THE MACKINAW, as given by his son, Silas Jackson Foster – obtained from Laura Frey.
A short account of the life and times of an old settler on the Mackinaw, which is not given in the history of McLean County:
Aaron Foster was born in the month of May, 1804, Kentucky being his native state. His father, whose name was Harrison Foster, was born in the state of Virginia, and his grandfather, Peyton Foster, was a soldier of the Revolution from that state. I have a lock of his hair and from its appearance it was clipped from his head when he was yet a young man. My conjecture is that his mother clipped it when her son left home for the seat of war. Of course this is only conjecture, but it was a fitting occasion for doing so

when we consider that her boy was about to start on a perilous expedition from which he might never return, and so she wished to have a lock of his hair as a memento. It is needless to add that my great-grandfather fought through the war and returned home in safety, otherwise there would have been no sketch to write and I would not have been here to write it.

ACCOUNT OF AN EARLY SETTLER OF THE MACKINAW, as given by his son, Silas Jackson Foster -

A short account of the life and times of an old settler on the Mackinaw, which is not given in the history of McLean County:

Aaron Foster was born in the month of May, 1804, Kentucky being his native state. His father, whose name was Harrison Foster, was born in the state of Virginia, and his grandfather, Peyton Foster, was a soldier of the Revolution from that state. I have a lock of his hair and from its appearance it was clipped from his head when he was yet a young man. My conjecture is that his mother clipped it when her son left home for the seat of war. Of course this is only conjecture, but it was a fitting occasion for doing so when we consider that her boy was about to start on a perilous expedition from which he might never return, and so she wished to have a lock of his hair as a memento. It is needless to add that my great-grandfather fought through the war and returned home in safety, otherwise there would have been no sketch to write and I would not have been here to write it.

When Aaron was quite a small boy his father left Kentucky and settled in Hancock County, Indiana, where he died, leaving a family of seven children-three boys and four girls. When Aaron was about 13 years of age a man was trying to make his little brother and another boy fight, but instead of the boy fighting his playmate the plucky little fellow grabbed a stick and threw it at the offender, who dodged it and it struck Aaron endways in the eye, ruining it and leaving him forever sightless in that eye. After he grew to manhood the loss of the eye caused him many a hard fight, for in those days men settled their disputes in that way. It did not matter whether their grievances were real or imaginary, it was all the same and had to be settled with a fight, and whenever a fellow got crosswise with Aaron about the first thing heard was a threat to take the other eye; and you know that such threats coming from men would class them among the gorilla and crocodile of India were only calculated to arouse all the lion blood that coursed through the veins of an unfortunate man. The results were that all his antagonists met more than their match and he carried that single eye, though somewhat dimmed by age, with him to the grave.

Mr. Foster grew up to manhood in Hancock county and like many other young men of his day secured only about three months schooling, his studies consisting of a single book and that one the old Webster speller. He used to give out a favorite word from the book to puzzle us children. It was "caydayroscomusgee." I never knew the definition of the word, not having advanced much farther along the educational line than had my father. Mr. Foster knew but little about figures until he was nearly forty years of age, nevertheless he was good in mental arithmetic.

When about twenty, having become acquainted with the Patton's who lived in Switzerland County, he married Sarah R., daughter of John and Margaret Patton. I think he resided in Switzerland County until the fall of 1827, when he and the Patton's loaded their household goods and pulled out for Illinois. They all came to Old Town timber, where they spent their first winter. Mr. Foster was fortunate for old Johnny Dawson took him and his family into his house and boarded the family and team in lieu of Mr. Foster doing the chores. Early in the spring of 1825 they left Old Town and settled at and in the suburbs of what is now called Selma. They were all well pleased with the country except Mr.

Foster, who was so disgusted with it that he tried to get his wife to go back to Indiana. But she told him nay, saying to him "You were bound for Illinois, and to Illinois you brought me, and now Aaron I am here to stay." He said "Well, Sally, if that is your mind, you just select a quarter section of land and I will stay until I make money enough to enter it, and then I will pull for Indiana." She said all right and made choice of the quarter section that takes in what is now known as the Bradford homestead at Selma. I do not know as I could at this time point out the original quarter, for by the time father had made the money to enter the land (a goodly part of which he made by cutting and splitting rails at 25 cents a hundred) he had become reconciled to the country, and kept adding more land until he had accumulated over 400 acres. The first cabin he built on the place stood a few paces from the northeast corner of the Selma cemetery, near an old Indian apple tree. I think it may be that a sprout taken from that tree about the year 1836 is still standing just north of the Bradford porch, and perhaps is still bearing fruit.

Mr. Foster was well fixed the winter of the deep snow, which occurred I think the winter of 1830-31. He had but one cow in the way of stock that had not been provided with shelter, but, as luck would have it, a few days previous to the coming of the storm he had built a square rail pen about six feet high and covered it with rails; he then built it higher and stowed a few loads of "jerked" corn. So when the storm came upon him he opened a way into the pen and let the cow in. The snow being so deep it was but little work to bank with it the rest of the way so that he had a good warm place with plenty of provender for the cow. He said it was very little trouble to attend her.

As for bread, when it disappeared he followed the custom of the country- that was to prepare lye hominy or pound corn into a course meal, and many bowls of milk and hominy were eaten by the first settlers of the Mackinaw. For clothing father always kept plenty of sheep to furnish the winter's wear, and he raised flax for summer use also, also for socks, towels, table-cloths and bed-ticks. In those days people used sewing thread and Mrs. Foster was an expert in spinning the thread, and spun for many families in the neighborhood. Those were primitive times, but people seemed contented with their lot.

In politics Mr. Foster was a Whig until 1856, but ever after that he was a strong Republican. He was elected and served as constable for eight years, and also served as justice of the peace for several terms. He seemed to have been somewhat of a favorite with such men as Dr. Wakefield Magoon, Bill Allen, Judge Davis, Abraham Lincoln and Col. Gridley. The latter often called him "God-father of the people of Lexington precinct."

Mr. Foster once sent by a merchant from Selma to Philadelphia, it being customary in those days to buy goods on a year's time, and the merchant, A. Enoch by name, endorsed for him. A short time after he had made the purchase William Allen of Bloomington went to Philadelphia and bought goods of the same firm. While there he was asked if he knew one Aaron Foster living at Selma and answered in the affirmative. Then they asked "What kind of a man is he?" Mr. Allen replies, "The best man God ever made." After that his credit was fully established with the Philadelphia firm and he was urged by them to send in orders for any amount of goods, but he was cautious and did not let his Allen-given name get away with his better judgment. He often wished that Mr. Allen had not so highly lauded him, for he said, "I fell too small to fill the bill."

Mr. Foster was considered a man of good judgment and of sterling worth, and his counsel was often sought by those in trouble, as many people were more ready to trust his judgment than their own.; and some even went so far as to say that what Aaron Foster did not know was not worth knowing. But notwithstanding this he was like all other men-liable to mistakes. When he was calm and in a tranquil mood his council was number one, but he was naturally of a high temperament and when he suffered himself to become angry, then, like others, he lost all sense and reason.

Mr. Foster despised low tricks in any man and the guilty who fell under his ire generally received a lecture not soon to be forgotten. When a man was guilty of some dishonest trick against his neighbor Mr. Foster could "skin him from long taw," as we used to say, and so vividly would he picture the meanness of the offense that very few ever resented it with angry words, and on all such occasions he would talk himself out of his earnest mood, begin to laugh and all would pass of peacefully as an ocean calm after a mighty storm had shaken its waters. No one could doubt Mr. Foster's honesty and integrity, and begin honest himself, it was hard for him to believe others dishonest, and hence such belief became a source of much loss in the way of becoming surety for others.

Mr. Foster never engaged very much in the sports and pastimes which prevailed in the early days. He was no hunter, but could be induced sometimes to join in the wolf chase, though he always considered it dangerous sport. He was like the rest of the old settlers in that he loved good timber for a joke and generally made use of it.

He was a rigid disciplinarian in bringing up his children and having laid down his rules they had to be respected. The children thought him too hard on them at the time, but I now believe that parents of the present day would profit by following his example. In those days parents knew more than their children, but now the children are far in advance of the parents, the tables are completely turned- and the children are the losers. They have forgotten that commandment with the promise: "Honor thy parents that thy days may be long upon the earth." Mr. Foster's first wife died Oct. 1, 1845, and in the latter part of 1847 he was married to Helen Taylor. To his first wife were born twelve children and to his last wife were born five, making a total of seventeen. All are now dead but two of the first wife's children and two of the last. I live at Dresden, Decatur Co., Kans., N. J. Foster lives at Holton, Jackson Co., Kans., James M. lives at Silver Lake, Kans., and Martha J. lives in Tacoma, Wash. Mr. Foster was an old-time Methodist and officiated as class leader as long as he lives.

In the spring of 1856 he sold his stock of goods in Pleasant Hill and went to Leavenworth County, Kansas, just in time to be in the Kansas trouble. He lost but one horse by the borderers, but he said those were awful hot times. In 1858 or '59 he moved sixty miles northwest and settled in Jackson County, where he spent the remainder of his days. He was a strong Union man and an advocate of Lincoln's war policy. Four of his sons helped to put down the rebellion and the other one was too small to go. He was not permitted to live to the end of the war, though that was his desire. And so on the 6th day of August, 1864, another old settler of the Mackinaw crossed the stormy Jordan (but he said it was calm as he went down into the water) to join the ones that had gone before. -- Silas Jackson Foster (Aaron's son)

AARON FOSTER b. 31 Mar 1804 d. 6 Aug 1864
SARAH ROYSTON (PATTON) b. 11 Oct 1804 d. 1 Oct 1845
Married 20 June 1824, Switzerland Co., Indiana. Children:

1. JOHN B. 10 Apr 1825 d. 16 Sep 1843
2. MARGARET b. 26 Oct 1826 d. 16 Aug 1855

3. WILLIAM HARRISON b. 6 May 1828 d. 12 Oct 1846
4. AARON BLUFORD b. 13 Jun 1832 d. 16 Dec 1878
5. SILAS JACKSON b. 14 Jan 1834 d. 27 Dec 1916
6. SARAH ANN b. 22 Sep 1835 d. 1857
7. NEWTON JASPER b. 25 Jul 1837 d. 16 Jan 1921
8. AUSTIN b. 1838
9. MARY CASSANDRA b. 14 Jan 1841 d. 11 Mar 1871
10. MILTON SMITH b. 20 Jun 1843 d. 10 Dec 1872

JOHN, eldest child of AARON & SARAH R. FOSTER, was born in Switzerland Co., Indiana, and taken by his parents to McLean Co., Illinois. Here he met and married his cousin, RACHEL FOSTER, pg. 32, daughter of Dennis and Mary Polly Foster. In the 5th month of their marriage John died of milk fever (Note: today known as Undulant fever, transmitted by milk from infected cows). Their only child, SARAH, better known as Sally, was born after his death and lived only a little while after she was 5 years old. Rachel lived many years after both her husband and child passed on. Her life is given on the page above.

JOHN FOSTER b. 10 Apr 1825 d. 16 Sep 1843
RACHEL (FOSTER) B. 23 Apr 1820 d. 3 Oct 1898
Married 15 Jun 1843, Illinois. Their child, SARAH b. 8 Apr 1844 d. 3 Oct 1849.

MARGARET, 2nd child of AARON &SARAH R. FOSTER, was born in Switzerland Co., Indiana, and taken by her parents to McLean Co., Illinois. Here she met and married JAMES ADAMS. After her death, James remarried, but I have no data on the second marriage, as I have failed to locate any descendents of James' family. However, both James and Margaret Adams are buried on the old Adams homestead, on what is now know as the Ranson Farm.

In later years, James Adams described some of the difficulties encountered in his courtship day. The families of Aaron Foster and Matthew Adams lived on opposite side both the Mackinaw River. The land, now owned by the Adams family, had been the homestead of Harrison Foster Jr. See more of James Adam' description of life in old McLean County. Pg. 61.

One cold January day in 1846, James arrived at the river's edge, only to discover that the river was up, and the ice broken up, and floating downstream. He realized that he would have to hurry, if he were to do any visiting that day - but how. Then he had an idea. If he could find ice-blocks large enough to support his weight, he could pole one such block to the next, till he was across. The plan worked but James was wet to the waist, from near disastrous moments during the crossing. Late that night, or rather, early the next morning, James returned to the river, where he made and even slower crossing. But the ice blocks left behind were heavier, though fewer, and more stable. He got home just in time to start the morning chores.

(End of pg. 151.) Later in the year, James tried to ride a horse across the river, to do his courting, but he horse refused to enter the water. These two incidents convinced James that if he wanted to continue seeing his light-o-love, he would have to find a suitable way of crossing the river. He decide to build a strong raft, which proved to be a good idea, because he not only got to visit his light-o-love dry-footed, but he made a few coins ferrying passengers.

Margaret and James spent their entire lives in McLean Co., Illinois where their children were born. However, I have very little on the children. James and Margaret are buried in the Adams Cemetery in McLean Co., IL. (James Adams had a second marriage.)

JAMES ADAMS b. 3 Feb 1826
MARGARET (FOSTER) b. 26 Oct 1826 d. 16 Aug 1855
Married 9 Feb 1847, Illinois. Children:

1. BENJAMIN LEONIDES b. abt 1848 m. ELIZABETH
2. THOMAS BENTON b. 20 Jul 1850 m. EMONA CATHERINE FERGISON (b. 1 Oct 1848 IL)
3. WILLIAM WALTER b. abt 1852 m. MARGARET EDNA ERWIN

BENJAMIN L. married ELIZABETH and lived in Lexington, Illinois. Their children: HARRY, ORIE, MABLE, ROY.

THOMAS B. married EMONA CATHERINE FERGUSIN 4 Jul 1875. She was born in Illinois 1 Oct 1848. Children: BERNICE ANTONETTE b. 1 Sep 1876 and HOWARD BENTON b. 1 Aug 1882.

WILLIAM W. married MARGARET EDNA ERWIN, in Kankakee, Illinois. They had three children: 1) ELLA MAE who married SETH MILSON BUTTON and died giving birth to THYRA VIRGINIA; 2) JAMES BERGUS who married IVA G. WALLSAR; 3) and EDWARD CARMON, who married #1, EDITH MAE MAWER and had: 1) HOWARD, 2) DOROTHY. Edith died and Edward C. married #2, HESTER BENNETT, and had: 1) EDNA, 2) MARIE, 3) JAMES.
Family chart p. 146

AARON BLUEFORD, 4th child of AARON & SARAH FOSTER, was born in McLean Co. IL. Here he grew to manhood, met and married his cousin ELIZA JANE FOSTER, daughter of Harrison Foster Jr. (son of Harrison Sr. and Anna Margaret Bartlett Foster) and Ellender Foster (dau. of Robert Foster and Bathsheba Williams). Note: Eliza Jane's family was in McLean Co. by 1828 and Aaron's family moved there before 1834 so it is likely that these two cousins grew up knowing each other. All their children, but Andrew Jackson, were born in Illinois. (End of pg. 152)
In 1859, Aaron Blueford joined his father-in-law, Harrison Foster Jr., his cousin, Robert Foster, and his uncle, John Cox in a wagon train bound for Kansas. The others settled in Marshall County, but Aaron Blueford joined his father near Circleville, Jackson Co., Kansas.

While living in Circleville, Kansas, Aaron Blueford joined the local Militia, serving in Company G, 13th Kansas Infantry. Along with several cousins and three brothers Aaron B. was in the battle of "Little Blue" near Independence, Missouri.

In the year 1869, he joined his brother, Silas Jackson, and moved to Washington Co., and settled near a now extinct sulfur springs 3 miles southeast of Haddam, Kansas, paying the government $1.25 an acre for a farm.

During the fall of 1878 Aaron B. loaded his family in a covered wagon and set out to visit a cousin in Cedar Co., Missouri. They had hardly started on the return trip when Aaron B. fell sick. They returned to the cousin's home, where Aaron Blueford died, and is buried in the El Dorado, Missouri Cemetery. Eliza Jane is buried in a cemetery 2 miles south of Haddam, KS, on the west side of the highway.

Aaron Blueford donated money and time for a cemetery 2 ½ miles south of present-day Haddam, Kansas. Here his wife, Eliza Jane is buried. For some reason, unknown to me, Aaron Blueford Foster is buried in Missouri.

AARON B. FOSTER b. 13 Jun 1832 d. 16 Dec 1787
ELIZA J. (FOSTER) b. 28 Sep 1830 d. 12 Nov 1902
Married 23 Jun 1850, Illinois. Children:

1. MARY ELLEN b. 1851
2. CHARLES FRANKLIN b. 14 Nov 1853 d. 12 Sep 1942
3. MALISSA JANE b. 18 Sep 1856 d. 27 Mar 1929
4. ANDREW JACKSON b. 19 Jan 1862 d. 12 Jan 1936

MARY ELLEN FOSTER married #1, TAYLER PICKET, and divorced him after the birth of their children. She married #2 THOMAS J. FOSTER, and soon died, no children. Mary E. is buried in the Haddam, Kansas, Cemetery.

ZACHARY TAYLOR PICKET b. 25 Oct 1848 Indiana d. 25 Oct 1902 Boone, Nebraska
MARY ELLEN (FOSTER) b. 1851 McLean, Illionis d. abt 1877 Haddam, Washington, Kansas
Married in 1869, Kansas. Children:

1. GEORGE b. 26 Sep 1870
2. ELIZA JANE b. 26 Sep 1870
3. AARON BLUFORD b. 29 Feb 1872

AARON BLUEFORD PICKET married and lived in Hutchinson, Kansas. He worked for the railroad, and during a blinding snowstorm was killed by a train.

ELIZA JANE PICKET married LUE HOCKET, and divorced him after the birth of a son and a daughter. Lue Hocket is buried in the Adell, Kansas, Cemetery, but I don't know where Eliza J. is buried.

* * * *

CHARLES FRANKLIN FOSTER, 2nd child of AARON BLUEFORD and ELIZA JANE FOSTER, was born in McLean Co., Illinois, and came to Kansas with his parents. Here he grew to manhood and in Washington County met and married his second-generation cousin, CLARISSA FOSTER, pg. 40, daughter of Robert L. Foster (b. 1832) and Sarah Ann (or Sally) Cox. They moved to Bayard, Nebraska, where seven children were born, and some of their descendants still live. Clarissa is buried in the Bayard, Neb. Cemetery and Charles F. is buried in Fresno, California.

CHARLES FRANKLIN FOSTER b. 14 Nov 1853 d. 12 Sep 1942
CLARISSA (FOSTER) b. 1 Mar 1860 d. 25 Feb 1936
Married 15 Aug. 1877, Kansas. Children:

1. SARAH JANE b. 8 Nov 1878 d. 3 Feb 1954
2. MATTIE MAE b. 20 Feb 1881 d. 9 Mar 1913
3. SHANNIE BURT b. 10 Aug 1883
4. GUY WILBER b. 10 Jul 1886 d. 29 Aug 1941
5. WILLIAM EDGAR b. 14 Jul 1888 d. 20 Nov 1920
6. BERTHA ELLEN b. 12 Nov 1890
7. CARL EVERETT b. 26 Jan 1893 m. HAZEL RAYBORN
8. LOLA BELLE b. 25 Dec 1895 d. 20 Jun 1920
9. ALICE FLORENCE b. 26 Jul 1900 d. 1 Jun 1964
10. FRANCIS MARION b. 11 Oct 1901 d. 1943

SARAH JANE FOSTER married #1 WILLIAM HENRY KARNES, and later #2 JOSEPH PHELPS. No children were born to marriage #2. The Karnes children were all born in Studley, Kansas, near where Sarah J. was born. Both William H. and Sarah J. (Foster) Karnes are buried in the cemetery at Bayard, Nebraska.

WILLIAM H. KARNES b. 16 Feb 1867 d. 23 Sep 1921
SARAH JANE (FOSTER) b. 8 Nov 1878 d. 3 Feb 1954
Married 15 Feb 1897, Kansas. Children:

1. FREDDIE EVERETT b. 8 Dec 1897 d. 26 Jan 1964
2. STEPHEN EDWARD b. 26 May 1899
3. BESSIE EVA-MAE b. 26 Jan 1902 m. CRIS JEFFERS
4. NELLIE LUCINDA b. 11 Oct 1904 m. #1 CLIVE KROUGH, #2 JOHN LOWENBURG

FREDDIE EVERETT KARNES married #1, ALTA WALDEN, who died. They had a daughter, WILDA EILEEN 31 Aug. 1930. FREDDIE married #2, HELEN. All three are buried in Hoxie, Kansas. WILDA EILEEN married #1, LESLIE CRESSLER and had

KATHY KAYE. Married #2, DALE HUNTER and had: 1) LINDA DIANE, 2) WILLIAM, 3) GERALDINE EILEEN. Wilda Eileen married #3, TED VAUGHN. They have no children and live in South Lake Tahoe, California.

STEPHEN EDWARD KARNES, (#2 above) married #1, MARY RICHTER. After the children were grown they divorced and Stephen E. married #2 MAY WALLESEN on 20 Oct 1953. They have no children and live in Bayard, Nebraska. Stephen had a stroke a few months ago and has difficulty getting around.

STEPHEN EDWARD KARNES b. 26 May 1899
MARY (RICHTER) b. 6 Mar 1902
Married 23 May 1921, Nebraska. Children:

1. ROBERT WILLIAM b. 6 Feb 1922
2. RUTH ELLEN b. 6 Aug 1923
3. JAYNE ANN b. 1 Oct 1924
4. MARY LOUISE b. 12 Sep 1926
5. DeLOMA MAE b. 1 Apr 1932

ROBERT WILLIAM KARNES married #1 ELEANOR STEFGAN in 1943 and had ROBERT WILLIAM Jr.
ROBERT WILLIAM KARNES married #2, FRANCES SEIPOLA in June of 1947. In 1970 they lived in Las Cruces, New Mexico, where Robert is in the real estate business. To this union were born: 1) PHILLIP STEPHEN, 2) RODERICK OLEN.

RUTH ELLEN KARNES was born in Bayard, Nebraska, where she grew to adulthood, met and married CARL HAFFNER. They live in Goodland, Kansas, where Carl is employed by the Great Western Sugar Co., as a master mechanic. Ruth E's hobby is baking and selling ceramics.

CARL HAFFNER b. 31 Dec 1921
RUTH (KARNES) b. 6 Aug 1923
Married 25 Nov 1939, Nebraska. Children: 1) BEVERLY JEAN, 2) MARY GERALDINE.

BEVERLY JEAN HAFFNER married CHARLES WARD PUTNAM of Bayard, Nebraska 25 Nov 1959. Charles was born 16 Nov 1940. They have lived in Mississippi, Idaho, and at present in California. Their children: 1) CHARA LEIGH, 2) CONNIE CARL. --(p. 152)

MARY GERALDINE HAFFNER was born and raised in Scottsbluff, Nebraska, where she met and married ROBERT ALLEN SCHWARTZKOFF 1 Apr 1962. They live on a farm near Bayard, Neb. Their children: 1) MARY MICHELLE, 2) TASHA RENEE, 3) HEIDI LYNN.

JAYNE ANN KARNES, daughter of STEPHEN EDWARD KARNES and MARY RICHTER, was born and grew to adulthood in Bayard, Nebraska, where she met and married #1 JOHN LUNDINE in Dec. of 1942. They had a child who lives in Denver, CO: STEPHEN LAWRENCE.

Jayne Ann Karnes married #2 GEORGE TRIPPLE in 1950, and lives in Colorado. Children: 1) GERALD EDWARD, 2) MARIE CHRISTINE.

MARY LOUISE KARNES, daughter of STEPHEN EDWARD KARNES and MARY RICHTER, was born in Bayard, Neb., where she met and married ALBERT MILES MONK, a semi-trailer driver. They live where ever his job takes him.

ALBERT MILES MONK b. 21 Aug 1923
MARY LOUISE (KARNES) b. 12 Sep 1926
Married 6 Dec 1945, Nebraska. Children:

1. ALBERT GLENN
2. RONALD LEE
3. MARK STEPHEN
4. EVA MARIE
5. ROBERT ELDEN

ALBERT GLENN is a heavy-steel welder in Memphis, Tennessee. He married LINDA RUTH WILLIAMS 10 Jul 1948. They have one child, DAVID ANDREW.

DeLOMA MAE KARNES, daughter of STEPHEN EDWARD KARNES and MARY RICHTER, was born, grew to adulthood, met HENRY SCHMICK in Bayard, Nebraska and married him in August 1950. They separated in a few years, but have the following children: 1) SINDY LUE, 2) JAMES HENRY, 3) ROBERT WILLIAM.

DeLoma Mae married #2, RICHARD GOOD. They moved from Nebraska to Pennsylvania, where their children were born, and now live in Brighton, Colorado. Their children: 1) DIXIE JANE, 2) DEBRA ELLEN, 3) SUSAN CAMILLE.

BESSIE EVA MAE, 3rd child of WILLIAM H. & SARAH KARNES, p. 151, was born in Studley, Kansas and went wither parents to Bayard, Nebraska, where she grew to adulthood, met and married CHIROSTPHER LLOYD JEFFERS. He was a teamster, horse farmer, and auto mechanic. Tragically, both of their daughters were killed in an auto accident. In 1947 the family moved to Ridgecrest, CA, where Chris died. Bessie was in a rest home in 1976.

CHRISTOPHER JEFFERS b. 15 Mar 1900
BESSIE EVA MAE (KARNES) b. 26 Jan 1902
Married 16 Sep 1920, Nebraska. Children:

1. WILLIAM LLOYD b. 6 Sep 1921
2. NINA LOUISE b. 17 Feb 1926 d. 29 Aug 1941
3. LILA JANE b. 14 Mar 1927 d. 29 Aug 1941

WILLIAM LLOYD JEFFERS was born in Bayard, Nebraska, where he grew to manhood and joined the Army in WWII and served in Europe. Returning home, he joined his parents in the move to Ridgecrest, CA. Here he met and married BETTY JEAN CLARK, and their children were born. He is a heavy-duty mechanic who also built his own home.

William married Betty J. 10 Dec 1949. Their children: 1) GARY EUGENE, 2) DONNA JEAN, 3) MICHAEL LLOYD, 4) DAVID ALLEN, 5) BARBARA LYNN.

MATTIE MAE, 2nd child of CHARLES & CLARISSA FOSTER, was born and lived out her life in northwest Kansas. Here she met and married HERBERT DONALD KARNES, brother of WILLIAM KARNES who married SARAH JANE FOSTER (dau. of Charles and Clarissa Foster). Mattie and Herbert married 1 Feb 1905. Two children were born to this union: 1) STELLA, who died as a youth, 2) ANNA CLARISIS, who was born and still lives in Hoxie, Kansas, where she still works in a jewelry store. Here, too, she met and married HOWARD ALBERT CURRIER. Howard is buried in the Hoxie, KS Cemetery.

HOWARD CURRIER b. 23 Mar 1911 d. 22 Feb 1971
ANNA (KARNES) b. 6 Feb 1910
Married 17 May 1931, Kansas. Children: 1) DONALD ALBERT Jr., 2) EDWARD GUY

DONALD ALBERT CURRIER married MARCILLE MADDEN 15 Sep 1957. Their children: 1) DONALD JAMES, 2) EDWARD EUGENE, 3) BRIAN KEITH, 4) KAREN LYNN.

EDWARD GUY CURRIER married KATHYN TREU 9 Jun 1957. Their children: 1) PATRICIA KATHYN, 2) PAULETTE LYNN.

SHANNIE BURT, 3rd child of CHARLES & CLARISSA FOSTER, was born in Kansas and grew to adulthood in the old Solomon River settlement. He married a relative, LuELLEN FOSTER, p. 99 (dau. of Sampson L. Foster and Jeanette Turnipseed and granddaughter of George Archie Foster and Tabitha Hutson. I don't know where Shannie Burt is buried, but LuEllen was living in a rest home in late 1971 in California. They had a son which I have been unable to trace: LESLIE FRANKLIN.

Note: More info on them was provided by Julie Richards, a direct descendant.
SHANNIE BURT FOSTER b. 10 Sep 1883 Solomon River Settlement, KS d. Place, CA
LUELLEN or LUELLA FOSTER b. 11 Nov 1877 Haddam, Washington KS d. in Sacramento, CA.
Son: LESLIE FRANKLIN FOSTER b. 18 Dec 1913 Nebraska d. 27 Dec 1931 Placer, CA and buried in Sylvan Cemetery, Citrus Heights, Sacramento, California, United States. He died of diabetes. Chart p. 150

GUY WILBER FOSTER, 4th child of CHARLES & CLARISSA FOSTER, married CHARLOTTE SEXTON 3 Oct 1913. She was born 25 Nov 1896.

BERTHA ELLEN FOSTER, 6th child of CHARLES & CLARISSA Foster, born in Kansas, married #1 JOHN F. McMAHAN, 23 May 1910. Later she married #2 MR. SHARPE. To the last union were born: 1) MARY JANE b. 1911, 2) CLARISSA b. 1912, 3) CHARLES FRANKLIN b. 22 Mar 1917.

LOLA BELLE FOSTER, 8th child of CHARLES & CLARISSA FOSTER, married ELMER RAY LOVE 7 Feb 1915. Elmer was born 17 May 1895. To this union was born LILLIAN IRENE 14 Dec 1914.

ALICE FLORENCE, 9th child of CHARLES & CLARISSA FOSTER, married FRANK EDWIN RICH, and moved to Fresno, California. Some of their children live in that area, but I have failed to contact any of them. Both Alice and Frank Rich are buried in Fresno, Calif.

FRANK EDWIN RICH b. 1895 d. 26 Jul 1976
ALICE (FOSTER) b. 26 Jul 1898 d. 11 Jun 1964
Married 24 Apr 1917 Kansas. Children:

1. CHESTER E. b. 15 Aug 1918 m. MARTHA DANIELS
2. VIVIAN FLORENCE b. 4 Jan 1920 d. 9 Jul 1940 m. RAY P. RICE
3. DONALD FRANKLIN b. 20 Jun 1921 m. MARY COWAN
4. ANNA MAE CLARA b. 23 Jan 1924 m. CLIFTON COWAN
5. EDWARD CHARLES b. 12 Jul 1926 m. COROTHY SCHWARZ
6. IRENE MINNIE b. 11 May 1928 m. GENE L. NUTT
7. ALBERT WILLIAM m. MARY J. NOVER
8. JAUNITA JUNE m. RONALD DeGRAW
9. IONO BELLE m. WESLEY DELVIN

MALISSA JANE, 3rd child of AARON BLUEFORD and ELIZA JANE FOSTER, was born in McLean Co., Illinois, and came to Kansas with her parents. Later the family moved to Missouri, returned and settled near Haddam, Kansas. Here, Malissa met and married MELVILLE LORENZO DAVIS, brother to Henry Davis who married Sarah Brown and had a one-year-old son in 1900. (p. 127, p. 188)

In the early 1880s Melville moved his family to the old Solomon River settlement, where their daughter, Eliza was born. Later the Davis family moved to Oklahoma. I don't know where Malissa is buried but Melville is buried in Buffalo, Oklahoma.

MELVILLE LORENZO DAVIS b. 7 Mar 1854 d. 26 Oct 1911
MALISSA (FOSTER) b. 18 Sep 1856 d. 27 Mar 1929
Married 7 Nov 1875 Kansas. Children:

1. CORA MAY b. 21 Oct 1879 d. 16 Feb 1968 m. Wm VAN-NYE

2. ELVIRA FRANCES b. 1 Nov 1886 d. 1977

Four other children died in infancy.

ELVIRA FRANCES DAVIS was born on the Davis homestead on the bank of the old sand draw mentioned in the Sod Shanty chapter. She called it, "the old sand Haller." Later, the family moved to Oklahoma.

In 1891 the Davis family returned to Haddam, Kansas, where Elvira grew to adulthood, met and married CHARLES EDWARD GREGORY. The year before this marriage took place, Charles had homesteaded in Woodward Co., Oklahoma, where they now set up housekeeping. In 1917 the family moved to California but didn't like the country. They then loaded all their belongings, including horses, hogs and chickens on a railroad immigrant car, and with their white cat, Chocolate, took off for Portland, Oregon. The Gregory's took up land in Rainier, a few miles northwest of Portland, which their son, Milford L. still farmed in 1971.

Marie, my wife and I visited Elvira in the fall of 1971, while she was living in Albany, Oregon with her son, Albert. Elvira's memory of her younger days was still keen, and I learned much history from her.

CHARLES GREGORY b. 14 Dec 1883 d. 5 Oct 1965
ELVIRA (DAVIS) b. 1 Nov 1886
Married 29 Apr 1905 Kansas. Children:

1. MILFRED L. b. 29 Mar 1907
2. HAROLD JAMES b. 3 Mar 1908 d. 16 Feb 1967
3. RUTH MAE b. 10 Nov 1911
4. ALBERT LLOYD b. 11 Jul 1913
5. LOREN EUGENE b. 16 Mar 1926
6. GENEVEE JOYCE died in infancy

MILFRED L., born in Oklahoma, made the swing to the homestead near Rainier, Oregon, where he now lives. In Portland he married AGNES MARIE LOFTESNESS.

MILFRED L. GREGORY b. 29 Mar 1907
AGNES MARIE LOFTESNESS b. 21 Jan1917
Married 19 Jun 1934, Oregon. Children: 1) KENNETH LEE, 2) CHARLES LOFTENESS.

KENNETH LEE GREGORY married LINDA LEE PATCH in Rainier, Oregon, 10 Sep 1960. Their children: 1) TODD KEOIN, 2) TORY LEE, 3) TAMERA LYN, 4) TYRON TAB EDWARD.

CHARLES LOFTENESS GREGORY married #1 NANCY ELIZABETH DANCHOK. Their children: 1) TONY LEE, 2) TIMOTHY FRANK, 3) TERRY JOHN.

CHARLES (above) MARRIED 32 CHERYL FAYE HAMILTON, a widow with one child. No children were born to this union. Her child: ANGELA MARIE (GRANERI).

HAROLD JAMES GREGORY, son of CHARLES & ELVIRA GREGORY, married NINA LORRAINE ROBISON. He too, was born in Oklahoma and made the swing to the homestead near Rainier, Oregon. After attaining adulthood he went to Seattle, Washington, where he met and married NINA ROBISON.

HAROLD JAMES GREGORY b. 3 Mar 1908 d. 16 Feb 1967
NINA ROBISON b. 24 Jun 1911
Married 21 Dec 1930, Washington. Children: 1) JAMES EDWARD , 2) JOHN LESLIE, 3) JOYCE LORRAINE, 4) JOEL WAYNE.

JAMES EDWARD GREGORY, a veteran of the Korean War, is a high school principal in Roseburg, Oregon. He married SHARON LEIGH POWELL in Carson City, Nevada 22 Feb 1954. Children: 1) ROBERT JAMES, 2) RICHARD POWELL, 3) WILLIAM JOHN, 4) CHERYL LEIGH.

JOHN LESLIE GREGORY (2nd son of Harold and Nina Gregory), married GINGER HARING in Portland, Oregon 27 Aug 1967. Their child: MARK EDWARD.

JOYCE LORRAINE GREGORY (dau. of Harold and Nina Gregory), married a Presbyterian minister, JOHN CLINTON EVANS, in Portland, Oregon 27 Aug 1967. According to the place and date, this must have been a brother-sister double wedding. Children: 1) JOHN CLINTON III, 2) DAVID GREGORY.

JOEL WAYNE GREGORY married RONA MADALYN HEIMOFF in Teaneck, New Jersey 20 Jul 1971. Joel graduated from Harvard, received a master's degree at Cornell, and is now studying for his Ph. D. in Africa. (1971)
* * * * *

RUTH MAE GREGORY, 3rd child of CHARLES and ELVIRA (DAVIS) GREGORY, married EARL PERRY FRAZER in Vancouver, Washington, 8 Apr 1833. He served as a Captain in the Marine Corps during WWII, and is now retired from the service and living in Fresno, California. Their children: 1) GERALD NATHAN, 2) RODNEY ALLEN, 3) FRANCIS RUTH.

GERALD NATHAN (#1 above para.), a Korean War veteran, married CENA DEASON in Edmonds, Washington 6 Sep 1969. Their children: 1) CHERI, 2) JEFFERY, 3) MARIE.

FRANCES RUTH (3rd child of Ruth Mae Gregory and Earl Frazer), married ROBERT M. CUNNINGHAM in Fresno, CA 29 May 1971.

ALBERT LLOYD GREGORY, an air force veteran of WWII, is now a deputy sheriff of Lynn Co., Oregon, living in Albany. He married a widow, ELIZABETH JONES BEUGLI, with two sons: 1) DAVID SCOTT (BEUGLI), 2) STEPHEN DOUGLAS (BEUGLI).

ALBERT LLOYD & ELIZABETH JONES (BEUGLI) GREGORY married in Reno, NV 9 Jun 1955 and had: 1) THOMAS EDWARD.

LOREN E. GREGORY, 5th child of CHARLES and ELVIRA (DAVIS) GREGORY, a navy veteran of WWII, is now employed by the Dept. of Indian Affairs in Sacramento, CA. In Rainier, Washington he met and married SHERLEY MARIE HALYETERIN 23 Sep 1946. She was born 20 Aug. 1928. Their children: 1) MICHAEL DEAN, a Vietnam veteran, 2) KATHLEEN MARIE, 3) DOUGLAS WAYNE. Family chart p. 149

ANDREW JACKSON, last child of AARON BLUEFORD & ELIZA JANE FOSTER, was born near Frankfort, Kansas and went with his parents to the homestead near Haddam. After attaining manhood, Andrew J. immigrated to the old Solomon River settlement, where he met and married LaVINA ROSELLA SPILLMAN. Her family is on p. 229.

This and other inter-related marriages has lead to a lot of confusion regarding relationship of the offspring. Andrew Jackson & Rosella Foster are buried in the old Adell Cemetery.

ANDREW JACKSON FOSTER b. 19 Jan 1862 d. 12 Jan 1936
ROSELLA (SPILLMAN) b. 1 Nov 1870 d. 7 May 1947
Married 1 Nov 1887, Kansas. Children:

1. ELMER M. b. 14 Dec 1888 d. 14 Jan 1970
2. WALTER RAY b. 4 Jun 1890 d. 7 Jan 1951
3. NELIE PEARL b. 11 Dec 1891 d. 16 Sep 1893
4. ELSIE MAE b. 23 Jun 1894 d. 1 Sep 1968
5. ROBERT b. 13 Oct 1896 d. 2 Oct 1924
6. RICHARD FRANKLIN b. 23 Sep 1901
7. WESLEY AARON b. 24 Jul 1906 d. 5 May 1962

ELMER M. (#1 above) married AMAND REED, who was born 6 Nov 1894 d. 14 Jul 1949. There were four REED sisters, three of whom married into the family of Andrew J. Foster, and the other married Eliphlet Foster, half-brother of Andrew J's wife. Elmer & Amanda Foster had no children but adopted KENNETH, who now lives in Oberlin, Kansas.

WALTER RAY FOSTER (#2 above), married ROSIE ANN REED in Hoxie, Kansas in a double wedding with his sister, Elsie Mae Foster (Spillman). For many years Walter lived on a farm, given him by his father, and homesteaded by his father's cousin, Robert Foster, pg. 40. In the 1940's oil was discovered on this land and Walter retired to Jennings, Kansas. Walter and Rosie are buried in the Jennings Cemetery.

WALTER FOSTER b. 4 Jun 1890 d. 7 Jan 1951
ROSIE (REED) b. 16 Jun 1891 d. 16 Sep 1968
Married 2 Jun 1910 Kansas. Children:

1. RAY WILLIAM b. 7 Feb 1912
2. LETHA MAY b. 5 Sep 1914
3. ANDREW JACKSON b. 31 Aug 1917

LETHA MAY (#2 above) was born on the farm in the old Solomon River settlement, 6 miles due south of the Jennings, Kansas. Here she grew to adulthood, met and married MORRIS LOGUE of Lenora, KS. Letha May died after giving birth t her 2nd child, De LOMA, who also died. Their first child: DONALD RAY.

RAY WILLIAM (#1 above) married MARIE KOERPERICH, and lives in a new house they built in 1972 near where he was born in the old Solomon River settlement.

RAY WILLIAM b. 7 Feb 1912
MARIE (KOERPERICH) b. 7 Mar 1914
Married 19 Jan 1938, Kansas. Their son: DELMAR, who married PARTICIA WAGNER.

DELMAR WILLIAM
PARTICIA (WAGNER)
Married 20 Aug 1959, Kansas. Children: 1) MICHAEL RAY, 2) COLEEN MARIE, 3) CHAD DEE.

ANDREW JACKSON FOSTER (the younger, b. 1917), son of WALTER & ROSIE (REED) FOSTER, was born in the old Solomon River settlement, where he got his elementary schooling. My sister, Irene, taught three terms at this old school, and on one occasion when my sister was sick our mother filled in for her. So both of them had a hand in teaching Andrew his A-B-C's. Andrew Jackson married EDITH ELAIN SHAFER, and lives about five miles from his old home. In season, Andrew farms and during the fall and winters he works for the Great Western Sugar Company near Goodland, Kansas.

ANDREW JACKSON FOSTER b. 31 Aug 1917
EDITH (SHAFER) b. 17 Feb 1922
Were married 3 Aug 1947, Kansas. Children: 1) MORRIS RAY, 2) JACK DeLANE, 3) LINDA ELAINE, 4) JOYCE KAY, 5) JANA SUE, 6) CARL LESLIE, 7) JERRY LYNN, 8) DONNA GLEE, 9) RICKY LEE.

* * * * *

ROBERT FOSTER (Note: I think he means Hobart William Foster), son of Andrew Jackson and Lavina Rose (Spillman) Foster, married VEVA GIBBINS, and soon died. He is buried in the Adell Cemetery.

RICHARD FRANKLIN FOSTER, son of Andrew Jackson and Lavina Rose (Spillman) Foster, was born in the old Solomon River homestead and farmed for several years northwest of Jennings, Kansas. He retired to Hoxie, where he spent most of his time fishing until his death. He married and divorced HATTIE REED, one of the four REED sisters. When Eliphalet Foster slipped in and married one of the sisters, it led Andy Foster to say, "If Liffee had stayed away I'd have all the Reed girls in my family.

Hattie still lives in Hoxie, Kansas. Richard is buried in the old Adell Cemetery.

RICHARD FRANKLIN FOSTER b. 21 Sep 1901 d. 16 Apr 1974
HATTIE (REED) b. 23 Aug 1906
Married 12 Sep 1922 Kansas. Children:

1. MELVIN b. 15 Jun 1923
2. MARVIN b. 17 Mar 1926
3. CHARLES

MELVIN (#1 above) married VIOLET DODSON and lives in Ft. Morgan, Colorado. They had a son and two daughters.

MARVIN (#2 above) married No. 1, MILDRED KATHKA and had two daughters and a son. He married No. 2, ADA TRECE, who bore him a daughter and a son.

CHARLES (#3 above) married No. 1, MARTHA ADAMS and had two daughters and a son. He married No. 2, ELSIE. That's all the material I have on this family.

* * * * *

Now hear this! Andrew Jackson Foster and Lorenzo Milton (Tack) Foster were 1st cousins. Lorenzo married Almira, mother of Rosella--I think he means LaVina Rosa Spillman--by her first husband Westunion Spillman. Rosella, i.e. LaVina Rosa, was Andrew Jackson Foster's wife. Eliphalet, Lorenzo's son, married one of the Reed sisters and Andrew Jackson's sons married the other three Reed girls. This makes Eliphalet a half-brother, brother-in-law, half-uncle, 2nd generation cousin, and half-cousin to Andrew Jackson Foster and his family. (I can't believe Flavius figured all that out without a PAF program)

ELSIE MAE FOSTER, 4th child of Andrew Jackson and LaVina Rosa (Spillman) Foster, was born and grew to adulthood on the old Solomon River homestead. Here too, she met and married MILAN WILBER SPILLMAN. Milan (Mike) Spillman was section boson the Rock Island railroad until retirement. during his long service Mike worked on many sections of the railroad. For a time Mike lived in Dresden, Kansas, but retired to Wichita.

Elsie Foster and Milan were married in a double ceremony with her brother, Walter in Hoxie, Kansas. Elsie & Milan are buried in Wichita, Kansas.

MILAN WILBER SPILLMAN b. 22 Oct 1881 d. 31 Jul 1958
ELSIE MAE (FOSTER) b. 23 Jun 1894 d. 1 Sep 1968
Married 2 Jun 1910, Kansas. Children:

1. JANIE ELMIRA b. 17 Mar 1911
2. IVA ROSELLA b. 22 Mar 1913
3. FORD FOSTER b. 14 May 1914 d. 7 Apr 1965
4. ROY ANDREW b. 27 Sep (abt 1916) d. 4 Mar 1944 killed in Italy WWII
5. RUTH ELAIN b. 12 Oct (abt 1917)
6. CHESTER WILBER b. 18 Jun1919 d. 3 Jul 1965
7. MARY ELLEN b. 23 Dec 1923
8. EVERETT GLENN died in infancy

JANE ELMIRA (#1 above) was born in Jennings, Kansas and got her schooling in Philipsburg and Dresden, KS. She married ARTHUR RAYMOND HALLENBECK in Farrington, Wyoming. They lived awhile in Denver, then moved to Buena, Colorado, where Arthur was engaged in the sawmill and lumber business till his retirement. In 1971 they visited all their children.

ARTHUR RAYMOND HALLENBECK b. 14 Aug 1908
JANE ELMIRA (SPILLMAN) b. 17 Mar 1911
Married 20 Oct 1934, Wyoming. Children:

1. DONALD RAYMOND
2. DENNIS EUGENE
3. DALE LeROY
4. DARWIN LESLIE

DONALD RAYMOND (#1 above) was born in Denver, Colorado and now lives in Buena Vista, Colorado, where he manages a grocery store. He married VIRGINIA LEE GROSE in Cripple Creek, Colorado on 4 Jan 1959. They have two children, but again, no data.

DALE LEROY,(#3 above) a Navy veteran, was born in Englewood, CO and now lives in Hacienda Heights, CA, where he is a foreman in a machine shop. He married SALLY ANN LINDON in Whittier, Calif. 18 Nov 1961. They have two children.

DARWIN LESLIE (#4 above) was born in Englewood, CO and is now a Machinist's Mate in the Navy. He married ETHEL PAULAS in Waukegan, Illinois 5 Nov 1966.
* * * * *

IVA ROSELLA SPILLMAN, 2nd child of MILAN and ELSIE (FOSTER) SPILLMAN, was born in Ruskin, Nebraska. She was quite sickly during the first few months of her life, and went through two rough sieges of illness when her parents felt sure she was a goner. She has outlived this period to become a grandmother and today lives in Wichita, Kansas with her second husband. The first marriage took place in Hoxie,

Kansas, and he was killed in a motorcycle accident, but they were separated before his death.

1st marriage:
ORLIE DALE PENBERTON G. 2 Mar 1910 d. 12 Aug 1956
IVA ROSELLA (SPILLMAN) b. 22 Mar 1913
Married 3 Dec 1932, Kansas. Children:

1. ROBERT DEE
2. JIMMIE JOE b. 15 Sep 1937 d. 16 Feb 1960

ROBERT DEE was born in Denver, Colorado. He lives in Richmond, Indiana, where he is employed as an electrician. He married PHYLLIS PETERSON, 5 Aug 1957. Their child: LISA DEMISE (Denise?).

2nd marriage:
EARL THOMAS THURMAN b. 8 Oct 1915
IVA ROSELLA (SPILLMAN) b. 22 Mar 1913
Married 16 Oct 1948, Kansas. Children:

1. TRUDY EARLENE
2. MICHAEL ROY

TRUDY EARLENE married JERRY DALE EATON 14 Dec 1968.

Iva Rosella and Earl Thomas Thurman were married El Dorado, Kansas. They live in Wichita, where Earl works for the Yellow Transit Trucking Company, but expects to retire in a few months.

FORD FOSTER SPILLMAN, son of Milan and Elsie (Foster) Spillman, born in Rushin (Ruskin?), Nebraska, moved with his parents to the Dresden, Kansas area. Here on a farm he grew to manhood and went to Wyoming, where he got a job on a cattle ranch. While working on this job Ford met VIOLA PACHON, and they were married in Scottsbluff, Nebraska. Soon after, Ford and Viola moved to Borger, Texas, where he got a job with a big oil company. Ford died of a heart attack and is buried in the Borger, Texas Cemetery.

FORD FOSTER SPILLMAN b. 14 May 1914 d. 14 Apr 1965
VIOLA (PACHON) b. 25 Nov 1921
Married 24 Sep 1939, Nebraska. Children:

1. JAMES PATRICK
2. PHYLLIS JUNE
3. JUDITH ANN
4. JERRI FORD

JAMES PATRICK SPILLMAN (#1), a career serviceman, is a dental assistant in the Army. He married KAREN SUE FINLEY 15 Aug 1954. Their daughter: JACQUE LYNN.

PHYLLIS JUNE (#2 above) married a career army man, BENJAMIN R. HASTINGS 15 Oct 1962. Their children: 1) ROCKY FORD, 2) SANDRA JUNE, 3) SHARON ANN, 4) FRANCES RENEE.

JUDITH ANN (#3 above) married a storekeeper in Borger, Texas, BOBBY RICHARD TRAMMRILL 8 Sep 1959. Their children: 1) GARY DON, 2) VICKIE LYNN.

RUTH ELAIN SPILLMAN, daughter of Milan and Elsie (Foster) Spillman, was born in Lanham, Kansas, and made the many moves with her family until she landed in Dresden, KS. Here she finished high school. During the depression days the merchants of Dresden tried to drum up business by giving free movies (keep in mind—these were the silent picture days). I don't know how much good these free movies did the merchants, but it was during one of these showings that Ruth met her "future."

Soon after this meeting RUTH ELAIN and ERNEST W. RANDOLPH, who was born and raised in the old Solomon River settlement, were married. They made their home in the old Solomon River settlement, where Ernest was employed by the Continental Oil Co. as an oil field pumper. He held this job for 25 years when Ruth's uncle, Wesley Foster, died. At that time Ernest was transferred to Ness City, Kansas, to take over the job Wesley had with the same company. Later Ernest transferred to Hennessey, Oklahoma, where they still live.

Hennessey has a long history beginning in the mid-1800's when an old trapper (of the same name) was burned to death by Indians. The town was later a watering place along the old Texas Cattle Trail that came through Dodge City, Kansas and ended in Ogallala, Nebraska. It was this trail that the Indians mentioned in the Sod Shanty chapter took in their effort to reach their old home in Montana. Hennessey, being rich in western lore, has many antique shops, a hobby Ernest is very much interested in, and which he expects to occupy him in his retirement due to start in a few months.

ERNEST W. RANDOLPH b. 5 Aug 1911
RUTH (SPILLMAN)
Married 31 Jul 1937, Kansas. Children:

1. DOROTHY LOUISE
2. DeLOMA JEAN
3. DALE DUANE

DOROTHY LOUISE RANDOLPH lives in Hoxie, Kansas, with her husband, DELBERT EUGENE LEWIS, married 21 Jul 1956. Their children: 1) DEBRA JEAN, 2) DEANNA LYNN, died in infancy, 3) DAYLENE KAY, 4) DARLETTA SUE, 5) DOUGLAS DEAN, 6) DERESA RUTH. (Teresa?)

DeLOMA JEAN RANDOLPH married MARVIN FOLEY in Hennessey, Oklahoma 19 Jun 1968. Marvin is employed by the Otis Engineers Oil Co. in Perryton, Texas. Their children: 1) PAMELA KAY, 2) ERNEST JAMES.

DALE DUANE RANDOLPH works for an oil company in Ness City, Kansas. He married ROSE MARY ANDERSON 18 Jan 1964. Children: 1) DELBERT DUANE, 2) DANA MARIE.

* * * * *

CHESTER WILBER SPILLMAN, son of Milan and Elsie (Foster) Spillman, was born in Lanham, Nebraska, and grew to manhood in the Dresden, Kansas area. He served in the Army in Italy during WWII. After the war he settled in Wichita, KS, where he was employed by the Duo Bed factory. He too, died of a heart attack, and is buried in Wichita, KS.

In a double wedding with his brother Ford in Scottsbluff, Nebraska, Chester W. married LORRAIN POCHON 24 Sep 1939. Lorrain was born 9 Oct 1919. Their children: 1) NANCY ANN, who married LEONARD DODGE and has two children, PHILLIP and PATTY, 2) ELSIE LORRINE, 3) JEAN.

MARY ELLEN SPILLMAN, daughter of Milan and Elsie (Foster) Spillman, was born and grew to adulthood in the Dresden, KS area, where she finished high school. On 28 Oct 1942 MARY ELLEN married EDWIN WALDO COOK. They live in Oklahoma, where Edwin deals in fertilizer – P-uu! They have a daughter, JUDY KAY.

JUDY KAY SPILLMAN (directly above) married RALPH KANE Jr. 4 May 1962. Their children: 1) JIMMIE E., 2) TIMMIE W. 3) TOMMY W., 4) TAMMY KAY (I hope these are nick-names. A name like Timmie for a boy would be hard to carry throughout life. Note: No doubt it became "Tim" as he grew older, a common name these days) Family chart pg. 159.

WESLEY AARON, last child of ANDREW & ROSELLA (LaVina Rosa) FOSTER, was born on the old home place on the Solomon River. Here he grew to manhood, met and married ETHEL N. HINES, and farmed in the district until 1947. At that time, Wesley Aaron moved to Ness City, Kansas, where he was employed in the oil fields. Wesley A's widow lives in Hoxie, Kansas, where Wesley A. is buried.

WESLEY FOSTER b. 24 Jul 1906 d. 5 May 1962
ETHEL (HINES) b. 26 Aug 19100
Married 26 Apr 1928, Kansas. Children:

1. OPAL MAE b. 3 Aug 1928
2. DORIS JEAN b. 10 Dec 1930

Both of Wesley and Ethel Foster's children married into the Johnson-Spillman family. The daughter's families are given in the Johnson-Spillman chapter, pg. 230.

SILAS JACKSON FOSTER, 5th child of AARON & SARAH ROYSTON (PATTON) FOSTER, has his own chapter. Chart p. 146.

SARAH ANN, 6th child of AARON & SARAH ROYSTON (PATTON) FOSTER, was born in McLean Co., Illinois, where she grew to adulthood, met and married JAMES W. SMITH. In 1852 they immigrated to Oregon Territory, where both died. Grandpa F.J. Foster wrote of them, "they moved across the plains in an early day, and in a few years we lost track of them. But we did learn that both Sarah-Ann and James died after a few years in the far west."

JAMES W. SMITH
SARAH ANN (FOSTER) b. 22 Sep 1835 d. 1857
Were married 23 Feb 1850, Illinois. Children:

1. EVALINE
2. EMMA
3. SILAS NEWTON
4. JASPER MILTON

Chart p. 146

NEWTON JASPER, 7TH child of AARON & SARAH FOSTER, was born in McLean Co., Illinois, and immigrated with his parents to Kansas Territory, in 1857. They settled in Jackson County, near Circleville. By an act of Congress, whether Kansas would enter the union as a free or a slave state would be settled by a vote of the people. This caused much bitterness between the two elements.
Some of the bonafide settlers were pro-slavery people, as were most of the anti-slavery forces. But there was a hard case element of pro-slavery people, who resorted to all kinds of tricks, hoping to win the election. These people lived in Missouri, and only entered Kansas to vote, and then return home. When this failed, they resorted to looting and burning the possessions of the free-state settlers. This, in turn, led the anti-slavery people to organize defense units. History tells us that this situation led to minor civil war, the pro-slave "Border Ruffians" against the anti-slave "Jayhawkers". Newton Jasper Foster joined one of the Jayhawker units under James Lane, who was a big wheel in the political life of Kansas for many years, later on.

During the Civil War, Newton J. joined the 11th Kansas Volunteer Cavalry, and was in the battle of the Little Blue, near Independence, Missouri. This battle, as seen by his brother, is described on pgs. 208-209.
*** ***** ***
NEWTON J. met and married MARY CHAPMAN in Circleville. Mary was a widow, whose married name had been BLACKERBY, and had two children: -- a son called,

BUDDY, and a daughter, SARAH ELIZABETH BLACKERBY, who married Newton J's half-brother, JAMES MONROE FOSTER. (See pg. 206.)

Newton J. and Mary Foster spent their married lives in the Circleville, Kansas area. But, as I get the picture, they moved in with, or near, descendants living in Wilsey, Kansas, a short time before their deaths. Both are buried in the Wilsey Cemetery, but there is no grave marker, except a bronze GAR emblem. I have been jolting some of Newton J's descendants into seeking a government marker for his grave, as a war veteran. (Good for you Flavius!)

NEWTON FOSTER b. 28 Jul 1837 d. 16 Jan 1921
MARY (CHAPMAN) b. 25 Apr 1937 d. 25 Mar 1918\
Married 1859, Kansas. Children:

1. AARON CHAPMAN b. 24 Sep 1860
2. ROBERT MILTON b. 7 Mar 1862
3. GEORGE DRAKE b. 4 Dec 1863
4. MIRANDA MAY Twin to George Drake, died 4 days after birth.
5. ARMINTA ELLEN B. 9 Jun 1866
6. MARTHA JANE b. 2 Dec 1867 d. 30 Oct 1938
7. JULIE ANN b. 20 Mar 1870 d. 24 Sep 1927
8. MARY MALINDA b. 29 Feb 1872 d. 4 Aug 1906
9. JOHN WILLIAM b. 24 Oct 1873

AARON CHAPMAN FOSTER (#1 above) married ANGELINE HINDS. I haven't learned the why-for, but Grandpa mentioned a "step-son," but this couldn't be the case. The child Angeline raised belonged to Aaron C's brother, George D. Foster. However, Angeline could have been married to George D. before becoming Aaron C's wife, and it is well-known that George D. was married several times, so the child could have been by a former marriage. I hope you are good at riddles. (DNA will tell)

Aaron Chapman and Angeline Foster's children were: 1) ANNA MARY, 2) ARTHUR, 3) AARON FRANKLIN, 4) ANDREW JAMES, 5) ADDIE, 6) ARMINTA ELLEN, 7) NEWTON JASPER, 8) ALICE.

AARON FRANKLIN FOSTER (#3 in above sentence) married ETHEL, who bore: 1) LAWRENCE and 2) EDITH LOVINA.

ANDREW JAMES (#4 above) married LOLA, who bore: 1) DEE EMERSON, 2) JEANETTE, 3) HARLEY.

ARMINTA, 6th child of Aaron and Angeline Foster, married MR. LICKLITER, and bore: 1) RUBY FRANCIS, 2) HARRY WAYNE, 3) GUY MARION.

* * * * *

ROBERT MILTON FOSTER, 2nd child of NEWTON and MARY (CHAPMAN) FOSTER, married MARTHA ELLEN HARRISON, a widow. Her children: 1) WILLIAM WINFIELD

(MAYOU) who died 29 Aug 1936, 2) ETTA MAE (MAYOU) d. 4 Aug 1936, who married and had 3 children: 1) MARGARET, 2) MARIE, 3) FRANCIS (McINTYRE).

ROBERT MILTON FOSTER b. 7 Mar 1862 d. 1 Mar 1939
MARTHA (HARRISON) b. 4 May 1857 d. 14 Apr 1937
Married 16 Mar 1889, Kansas. Children:

1. ROBERT THOMAS b. 21 Nov 1890 d. June 1944
2. ETHEL ELLEN b. 15 Sep 1893
3. WALTER WILLIAM b. 24 Feb 1895 d. at birth
4. RENA BELLE b. 26 Mar 1897
5. NEWTON JAMES b. 8 Aug 1900 d. May 1927

ROBERT THOMAS FOSTER (#1 above) married INEZ DANIEL in 1920 and had: 1) MARTHA ROSE b. 30 Oct 1920, 2) ROBERT b. 29 Mar 1922 d. Nov 1944

ETHEL ELEN FOSTER married GEORGE E. COTT and lived in Topeka and other Kansas towns, where he worked on farms for many years. They then moved to California where George took up the building trade. They built a nice home where they still live in South Gate, CA.

GEORGE E. COTT b. 13 Sep 1892
ETHEL (FOSTER) b. 15 Sep 1893
Married 24 Dec 1912, Kansas. Children:

1. ROBERT THEODORE b. 14 Mar 1914 d. 20 Aug 1950
2. MARY ELLEN b. 7 Mar 1916
3. OLIVER GEORGE b. 29 Feb 1920
4. HOWARD NEWTON b. 1 Sep 1921 d. 17 Sep 1944 WWII
5. PAUL WILLIAM b. 23 Dec 1923 d. 8 Jan 1924

ROBERT THEODORE COTT (#1 above) was born in Herington, Kansas, and died in auto accident.

We can't finish this family tonight, so let's hit the day, and start fresh on Robert's family Monday forenoon.

ROBERT THEODORE COTT b. 14 Mar 1914 d. 20 Aug 1950
ESTHER (CAMPBELL)
Married 16 Jun 1938, Kansas. Children: 1) LINDA LEE, 2) JANIS LEE.

LINDA LEE is married but I have no data, except that she has a daughter: LAURA LEE.

JANIS LEE unknowingly married a man who married her in a fruitless effort to dodge the draft. When he was called into the army in spite of his marriage, this man deserted both her and their son, ROBERT HOWARD. Janis L. is now happily married and living

in Texas with her second husband. Their children: 1) ROBERT HOWARD (adopted I assume), 2) JAMES STEVENS.
* * * *

MARY ELLEN COTT, daughter of GEORGE E. and ETHEL (FOSTER) COTT, was born Herington, Kansas and married ROLAND WILSON in Apr 1934. They had one child: ETHEL JOSEPHINE, who married DONALD D. SIESSER 22 May 1957. Their children: 1) DONALD DOUGLAS, 2) GEORGE EDWARD, STEVEN HOWARD.

OLIVER GEORGE COTT son of GEORGE E. and ETHEL (FOSTER) COTT, was born in Wilsey, Kansas, and is a veteran of WWII. He was on the high seas bound for France when his parents were notified that his brother, Howard H., had been killed in action. Oliver too, had a war-time marriage that failed. His ex-wife got custody of their daughter, whom Oliver hasn't seen in 23 years. This child: DELIA DOANA.

Oliver G's second marriage:
OLIVER G. COTT b. 29 Feb 1920
MADGE (HARMAN)
Married 7 Jan 1947 California. Children: 1) GEORGIA NELLIE, 2) DONNA MARIE, 3) JOAN YVONNE.

GEORGIE NELLIE COTT (#1) married DAVID KIRK 12 Oct 1967. Their child: GREGORY SEAN.

DONNA MARIE COTT (#2) married ALLAN COOKE 5 Oct 1969. Their child: ANGIE RENEE.

JOAN YVONNE COTT (#3) married TERRY PERKINS 18 Dec 1971.

Note: Rena Belle below is mistakenly called Rena Belle Cott on p. 171 of "Seedlings."
RENA BELLE FOSTER, 4th child of ROBERT MILTON and MARTHA (HARRISON) FOSTER, was born in eastern Kansas, where she grew to adulthood, met and married HARVEY M. ANDERSON. They now live in South Gate, California. Rena Belle isn't in very good health, and the death of her son hasn't helped any.

HARVEY ANDERSON b. 13 Sep 1895 d. 12 Oct 1972
RENA BELLE (FOSTER) b. 26 Mar 1897
Married 4 May 1916, Kansas. Children:

1. RAYMOND MARVIN b. 18 Jun 1917 d. 12 Oct 1972
2. EDWIN HARVEY b. 10 Jan 1919
3. ETHEL LaVERN b. 13 Oct 1920

GEORGE DRAKE FOSTER, 3rd child of NEWTON JASPER & MARY FOSTER, was born and raised in Jackson Co., Kansas. He married several times, but none of the marriages seem to have stuck. There seems to have been a son, p. 168. (the mother was ANGELINE HINDS, who married George's brother Aaron.) And, Grandpa F. J.

Foster knew of a wife and a daughter who lived in Sabetha, Kansas. This wife: EMELIE had a daughter: JULIE MAE FOSTER.

My wife and I went to Sabetha in1971. Here, we located two of George's great-granddaughters. However, since their grandmother was quite young when her parents separated they knew very little about George. The great-granddaughters thought George was buried in Sabetha cemetery. If so, the caretaker didn't know where.

EMELIE FOSTER'S daughter, JULIE MAE FOSTER, married JOHN BEER and fore: 1) ALVA, 2) RUTH, 3) HELEN, 4) NORMA, 5) FRED, 6) EMMA MAE, mother of the above-mentioned granddaughters.

* * * * *

ARMINTA ELLEN, 5th child of NEWTON JASPER & MARY FOSTER, was born in Jackson Co., Kansas. She married WILLIAM MEEKS and lived in Wichita, KS. Their children: 1) FRED, 2) CLARENCE, 3) MABEL, 4) LAWRENCE, 5) FREDERICK.
Chart p. 168

* * * * *

MARTHA JANE FOSTER, 6th child of NEWTON JASPER & MARY FOSTER, was born in Jackson , Kansas. Here she grew to adulthood, met and married JOHN HENRY HARRISON, brother to MARTHA (pg. 169) who married ROBERT MILTON FOSTER (son of Newton Jasper and Mary Foster). There are other parallels and a mystery I wish to present here.

Their father, James Harrison, came to America from London, England and settled first in Indiana, where he took up the building trade and made a lot of money. Later James moved to Jackson Co., Kansas, where he was a well-to-do building contractor, owning a fine brick home in Holton. His pride and joy was the fine draft horses he had imported from England. To go with this team James had a nice, well-painted wagon, and a set of very ornate harnesses.

On March 5, 1883, James Harrison set out from his Holton home for the contract job he had on the railroad, which was building a new spur from Kansas City to Emporia, Kansas. He made a business stop in Topeka, Kansas, where had made a six-month's payment on his insurance policy. He had enough money left to pay his crew's salaries after finishing the business. James then climbed to the seat of his freshly-painted wagon, clucked to his high-stepping, gilded team of imported horses, and rode out of the lives of friend and family, never to be heard of again.

MARTHA JANE (she is listed as Martha Tilly on p. 172—probably a typo by a tired hand) was born in the same Kentucky county as Aaron Foster. James Harrison and Martha Jane were married in the same Illinois county in which Aaron's half-uncle lived, by a Rev. R. V. Foster – no relation to our line. James and Martha Harrison then came to Jackson Co., Kansas, where, for the first time, the two families became acquainted and their children inter-married.

JOHN & MARTHA JANE (FOSTER) HARRISON lived in Jackson Co., KS for many years, then moved to Woodward Co., Oklahoma. In the spring of 1898 John loaded his wife and children in two covered wagons and set out for Washington state. Their daughters, Ardella and Lottie, trailed behind the wagons collecting dried cow chips for their campfire. The weather was hot, the trail-like roads dusty, and the sacks grew heavier and bulkier as the girls trudged along gathering their "fuel." During the earlier days in the nearly treeless prairie states every sod house had its forked stick to feed chips into the kitchen stove. Later Grandpa Foster referred to the chips as "grassoline," but I couldn't help thinking, 'Mom, are those brown specks in the pancakes wheat hulls???

Their first attempt to reach Washington state ended near the Rocky Mountains, when the children came down with fever, and one of their horses died. By the time the children were well John had almost run out of money, so he decided to return to Oklahoma. The next day one of the horses kicked John into the creek where he was watering them. Watermelon season was in full swing by the time the family drove back into their old yard, to be met by the girls' grandmother, smoking her old clay pipe.

When I read this part of Ardella's diary, I dug out my most prized possession: my Great-Grandmother Rachel Foster's old clay pipe, with its bamboo, teeth-marked stem. Forked "grassoline" sticks, a supply of clay pipes and tobacco for friend and neighbor, and a chamber pot, which Grandpa Foster later referred to as "Jerusalem's thunder mugs," were more a part of frontier life than apple pie.

In the summer of 1899 John loaded his family onto a railroad train bound for Portland, Oregon. After working here for a year, John left his family in Portland and took up a government claim 30 miles south of Tacoma, Washington. After building a cabin on his claim John went to Puyallup, Wash., and picked up his family, who had arrived by rail. John and the older children walked the 25 miles to his claim, while Martha J. and the baby rode their only horse. Today, their old homestead is under man-made Alder Lake.

JOHN HENRY & MARTHA JANE (FOSTER) HARRISON spent their last days in Tacoma, Washington, and are buried in Mountain View Cemetery. Here, too are buried some of their children, LOTTIE L., ARDELLA M., ORA O., and TRESSA L. Their daughter, Arminto E. is buried in Pioneer, Washington. Their son, Clarence A. is buried in Yakima, Washington.

Let's rest here, beside the trail, eat, then finish this family.

JOHN HENRY HARRISON b. 18 Mar 1865 d. 4 Dec 1930
MARTHA (FOSTER) b. 2 Dec 1867 d. 30 Oct 1939
Married 28 Mar 1886 Kansas. Children:

1. LOTTIE LUEABLE b. 21 Jan 1887 d. 3 Nov 1955
2. ARDELLA MAE b. 2 Oct 1888 d. 12 Apr 1966
3. ARMINTA ELLEN b. 6 May 1890 d. 7 Oct 1967
4. JESSIE FLORENCE b. 28 Mar 1892 d. 12 Aug 1905
5. CLARENCE ALONZO b. 27 Feb 1894 d. 19 Jan 1921
6. LEE MONROE b. 7 Jun 1899 d. 1972
7. ORA OREGON b. 11 Aug 1901 d. 27 Jul 1943
8. TRESSA LATONA b. 30 Oct 1904 d. 14 Oct 1969

All these children married but only three had children. Lee M's wife, Bectel, supplied most of the material on the above family.

ARDELLA MAE was born in Soldier, Jackson Co., Kansas, and came to Alder, Washington with her parents. Here, she grew to adulthood, met and married #1 GLENN FLEMING. Glenn was a shingle weaver in a Tacoma, Washington mill. I don't know where they got the term, but to you prairie rats, a shingle "weaver" makes the shingles for your houses from cedar bolts—4-foot logs. Whenever you see an old lumber millworker with one or more fingers missing, you will know, "there goes a shingle weaver."

After their children were born, Ardella divorced Glenn and married #2 GRAYSON P. MURRY. No children were born to #2, but Grayson had a child from an earlier marriage, BETTY.

GLEN E. FLEMING b. 2 Aug 1887 d. 1968
ARDELLA (HARRISON) b. 2 Oct 1888 d. 12 Apr 1966
Married 12 Oct 1906, Washington. Children:

1. EUGENE RICHARD b. 15 Jan 1912
2. JULIA MAE b. 28 May 1915 (or ALICE V. MURRAY)

EUGENE RICHARD FLEMING was born about 20 miles east of Seattle, Washington. Here, he grew to manhood, met and married MARTHA FRANCES PLATT. Eugene & Martha live in Morton, Washington, where he is now retired. The last I heard from them, Martha was driving 150 miles into western Oregon to a piano-playing job. Now I wonder, will she wait until she is old enough to retire, then move closer to her job?

EUGENE FLEMING b. 15 Jan. 1912
MARTHA (PLATT) b. 2 Jul 1911
Married 7 Mar 1935, Washington. Children:

1. DONALD EUGENE
2. RICHARD STEPHEN
3. MARTHA LATONA
4. JULIA MAE
5. LAWRENCE FRANKLIN

6. LINDA LOU
7. FRANCES DeLENE
8. GLENN HENRY
9. DANIEL ALAN

JULIA MAE FLEMING b. 1915, daughter of Glen E. and Ardella (Harrison) Fleming, prefers to be called ALYCE V. MURRAY. There seems to have been some irritation between Eugene and his step-father, that did not extend to his sister. It is thought by relatives that Julia was adopted by Grayson Murray, and she adopted a completely new name. She married WILBER S. BEATY in California, and they now live in Portland, Oregon.

WILBER S. BEATY b. 27 May 1916
JULIA MAE (FLEMING, OR ALYCE V. MURRAY) b. 28 May 1914
Married 14 Feb 1935, California. Children:

1. CHARLES LELAND
2. ARLENE MAE

CHARLES LELAND BEATY married SANDRA LOUISE McLEAN in Pasadena, Calif. 11 Nov. 1961. Their children: 1) LYNN LOUISE, 2) LANCE WILBER, 3) SHAUNIE LEE.

ARLENE MAE BEATY married JAMES DAVID QUANCKENBUSH 2 Jul 1959 and has a child: SCOTT.

ARMINTA ELLEN HARRISON, daughter of JOHN and MARTHA (FOSTER) HARRISON, was born in Washington Co., Kansas, and made the swing to Oklahoma, then to Alder, Washington. She grew to adulthood in that area, and married in Everett, Wash. to JOHN FRANCIS PATRICK WALKER.

JOHN FRANCIS PATRICK WALKER b. 21 Jul 1885 d. 31 Oct 1966
ARMINTA (HARRISON) b. 6 May 1890 d. 7 Oct 1967
Married 3 Jul 1910, Washington. Children:

1. MARCEL BERNARD b. 22 Aug 1912
2. MELVIN JOHN b. 3 Oct 1914 d. 19 Dec 1914

MARCEL BERNARD WALKER married and divorced #1 EDITH VIVAN TOTTEN in Everett, Washington. He then married #2 ELEANOR COMBS, 31 Jul 1966. They live in Umatilla, Oregon, where Marcel B. works for Umatilla Ordinance Depot. They have no children.

MARCEL BERNARD b. 22 Aug 1912
EDITH (TOTTEN) b. 8 Mar 1913
Married 26 Nov 1935, Washington. Children:

1. ELLEN FRANCIS
2. JOHN PATRICK
3. SHANNON MARCELLA

ELLEN FRANCIS BERNARD married JOHN H. TALBOTT 5 Jan 1958 and has two children: 1) JEANNIE, 2) JOHNNY.

* * * * *

ORA OREGON, 7th child of JOHN & MARTHA (FOSTER) HARRISON, was born in Portland, Oregon. Her parents liked the ring of the name, but for the daughter it was a source of many jests from friends, and she tried to change her middle name to Elizabeth. Ora O. grew to adulthood on the old family homestead in Washington state and married CARL KIMBEL in Tacoma. They separated in the 1930's and Carl took a job in Mayo Yukon Territory, Canada. Carl is buried in Shelton, Wash. and Ora O. is buried in Mountain View Cemetery, Tacoma, Washington.

CARL KIMBEL b. 8 Feb 1895 d. 28 Sep 1963
ORA OREGON (HARRISON) b. 11 Aug 1901 d. 27 Jul 1943
Married 22 Mar 1917, Washington. Children:

1. PEARL LORRAINE b. 22 Feb 1918
2. ERLINE CECILIA b. 15 Jul 1921

PEARL LORRAINE KIMBEL was born in Tacoma, Washington, and in 1932, joined her father in Mayo, Yukon Territory, Canada. Here she met and married GEORGE BERNARD KAZINSKY, who was born there. Three of their children were born in Canada, the youngest in the US. The family now lives in South Lake Tahoe, California, by the lake of that name.

GEORGE KAZINSKY b. 26 Sep 1911
PEARL LORRAINE (KIMBEL) b. 22 Feb 1918
Married 28 May 1936, Mayo, Canada. Children:

1. GEORGIA
2. CARL
3. EDWARD
4. BETTY

GEORGIA, born in Mayo, Y.T. Canada, married in Shelton, Washington to FRANK ROGERS in 1954. They live in Sitka, Alaska, where Frank is foreman in a lumber mill. Their children: 1) DONNY, 2) DEBBIE, 3) FRANK Jr., 4) DEANNA, 5) JOELLE, 6) HALLY.

CARL KAZINSKY (#2 above), was born in Mayo, Canada and married in Bremerton Washington to GLORIA SCHEIBER in 1961. They live in Portland, Oregon, where Carl is a new and used car dealer. Their children: 1) JENNY, 2) JEFF, 3) JASON.

EDWARD KAZINSKY (#3 above) was born in Mayo, Canada and married in Aberdeen, Wash., to JANE POTTS in 1966. They now live in Puyallup, Washington, where Edward teaches music in a local school. They have one child: ANGELIA.

BETTY KAZINSKY (#4 above) was born in Whitehorse, Canada, where she married her first husband, but I have no name for him. The first child on the list below was born to this marriage. Betty then married #2, WILLIAM VAUGHN, who was the father of the next two children in the list by a previous marriage.

Betty and Bill Vaughn live in Sitka, Alaska, where he is employed as a master mechanic in the same lumber mill as Betty's brother-in-law, Frank Rogers. They now have her child, my children, and our child: 1) JERRY (hers), 2) SHELLY and 3) WILLIAM Jr. (his), and 4) BRENDA (theirs.)

ERLINE C. KIMBEL, born in Shelton, Washington, married in Tacoma to #1 RAY HASH. They had a daughter: DONNA LeRAY. In 1951 Erline C., as she put it, "ran away from a tyrant." In Fresno, California she married #2 GEORGE EMERY HANCOCK in 1953. No children were born to this union but George has two children from a former marriage. I have no names.

DONNA LeREA HASH married LESLIE ALLISON 1956 and later divorced him. Their children: 1) DEBBIE LEE, 2) KATHRYNE MARIE.

Erline, her sister Pearl and Pearl's daughter, Donna, and their families all live in South Lake Tahoe, California. Here, Erline & George manage a 90-unit low-rent project. Family chart p. 168.

* * * * *

JULIE-ANN, 7th child of NEWTON JASPER and MARY FOSTER, was born near Circleville, Kansas. Here she grew to adulthood, met and married, EDWARD WILLARD ARNOLD. All their children were born in Kansas . Here too, Julia Ann is buried in Sunset Hill Cemetery, Herington, Kansas. After her death, Edward Arnold moved to southern California, where he died and is buried in Fair Haven Cemetery, Orange, California.

EDWARD W. ARNOLD b. 27 Jul 1866 d. 26 Jan 1952
JULIA ANN (FOSTER) b. 20 Mar 1870 d. 24 Sep 1927
Married 16 Aug 1891, Kansas. Children:

1. COILA MAY b. 14 Apr 1892 d. 6 Mar 1970
2. CHARLES LESTER b. 24 Mar 1894
3. JOHN WILLIAM b. 28 Aug 1895 d. 23 Jan 1965
4. PERCY HAMMON b. 10 Nov 1899 d. 30 Jan 1919
5. HAROLD JESSIE b. 12 Aug 1904 d. 1974

COILA MAY ARNOLD was born near Circleville, Kansas. Here she grew to adulthood, met and married WILLIAM HENRY ASLING 24 Dec 1911. He was born 3 Dec 1891 d. 11 Dec 1959. Soon after marriage, Coila and William Asling moved to California, where their only child was born, and they still live. Their child: JULIE LUCILE b. 5 Sep 1915.

Coila May is buried in Fair Haven Cemetery, Orange, California.

JULIA LUCILE ASLING married RANO HENRY LUEKER 11 Sep 1930. He was born 10 Jul 1911. They now live in the Los Angeles area of Cal. To this union were born 1) RANO EUGENE, 2) WENDELL HOWARD, RONNIE ILENE.

CHARLES LESTER ARNOLD, son of EDWARD W. and JULIA ANN (FOSTER) ARNOLD, was born in, met and married in Kansas, and ended up today in Ft. Collins, Colorado. He married FAYE EGGLESTON 27 Oct 1915. She was born 16 Jul 1895. Their children: 1) GERALD LAMONT b. 1 Aug 1916, 2) DON KEITH b. 17 Apr 1918.

Charles was supposed to send me data on the family of DON KEITH ARNOLD, but has failed to do so.

GERALD LAMONT ARNOLD married VIRGINIA OSBORN 5 Apr 1936. She was born 4 Oct 1917. Their children: 1) DARREL EUGENE, 2 DEAN LAMONT.

DARREL EUGENE ARNOLD married PATRICIA ANN TOWLES 4 Oct 1957. Their children: 1) DEBRA, 2) DON EUGENE.

DEAN LAMONT ARNOLD (son of GERALD and VIRGINIA two paragraphs above) married CAROLYN JEAN GALYARDT 27 Jul 1958 Both Dean and Darrell were married in Ft. Collins, Colorado. Dean and Carolyn's children: 1) CHARLES LAMONT, 2) LEE SCOTT.

* * * * *

JOHN WILLIAM ARNOLD, son of EDWARD W. and JULIA ANN (FOSTER) ARNOLD, married and divorced #1 NELLIE THELMA GEORGE. He then married her sister, GEORGIA ANN GEORGE. All three were dead by 1967. No children were born to either marriage.

HAROLD JESSIE ARNOLD, son of EDWARD W. and JULIA ANN (FOSTER) ARNOLD, like all of Julia Ann's children, was born, grew to adulthood, and married in Kansas. Harold J. married in Meriden, Kansas to CLARA EVELYN BROWN 4 Jul 1926. Later the family moved west, settling in Pomona, California, where they reside today. To this union was born: 1) CHARLES LeROY in Topeka, KS.

In California CHARLES LeROY married #1 FLORENA DeALVA STEVENSON 25 Mar 1961(?). She was born in Durango, Colorado, died and is buried in Covina, California. To this union were born: 1) CURTIS WAYNE.

CHARLES LeROY married #2, JOYCE CHAPMAN. She was a divorcee with two children, born in Hannibal, Missouri, bearing the surname, MORGAN. Her children: 1) BRETON CHARLES, JAY ALLEN.

Charles and Joyce's child: JEFFREY DEAN.
Family chart p. 168.

* * * * *

MARY MALINDA, 8th child of NEWTON JASPER & MARY FOSTER, was born and grew to adulthood in the Circleville, Kansas area. Here too, she met and married MILTON LESLIE SPIKER. They later moved to a farm near Wilsey, Kansas, where both are buried.

MILTON SPIKER b. 12 May 1866 d. 26 Jan 1942
MARY (FOSTER) b. 29 Feb 1872 d. 6 Aug 1906
Married 17 Jan 1892, Kansas, where both are buried. Children:

1. LULA MAUDE b. 13 Dec 1892 d. 28 Mar 1951
2. JOSEPH NEWTON b. 26 Nov 1894 d. 1 Jan 1968
3. ANNA MARIE b. 3 Aug 1902

LULA MAUDE married GEORGE JOHN PAIGE. In 1972, some of their children lived in Topeka, Kansas, but my letters went unanswered.

GEORGE JOHN PAIGE b. 2 Feb 1886
LULA (SPIKER) b. 13 Dec 1892 d. 28 Mar 1951
Married 24 Dec 1912, Kansas. Children:

1. GEORGE NATHAN b. 10 Dec 1913
2. ORVILLE L. b. 29 Oct 1916
3. HAZEL MARY b. 15 Feb 1922
4. GLADYS b. 3 Jun 1924
5. VELMA b. 19 Oct 1928
6. WILBER b. 1930

JOSEPH NEWTON SPIKER, son of Milton and Mary (Foster) Spiker, was born in Holton, Kansas, and grew to manhood in Jackson County, where he met and married OLIVE LEONA WORDEN. They lived in several towns mid-central Kansas, before ending up in Wilsey, where Olive Leona still lives. Joseph N. is buried in the Wilsey, Ks. Cemetery.

JOSEPH N. SPIKER b. 16 Nov 1894 d. 1 Jan 1968
OLIVE LEONA (WORDEN) b. 6 Oct 1900
Married 29 Oct 1918, Kansas. Children:

1. DOROTHY MALINDA b. 23 Nov 1919

2. MILDRED ELOISE b. 23 Feb 1921
3. PERCY LeROY b. 18 May 1922
4. BETTY JO b. 3 Jun

DOROTHY MALINDA and MILDRED ELOISE were born in mid-central Kansas (different towns) and ended up in Wilsey, Kansas. Here they grew to adulthood, met and married brothers in a ceremony that took place in the first buoyant minutes of the new year. Dorothy M. married JOYCE ROBERT FILKIN, and Mildred E. married GLEN L. FILKIN.

J. ROBERT FILKIN b. 12 Dec 1920
DOROTHY (SPIKER) b. 23 Nov 1919
Married 1 Jan 1940, Kansas. Children: 1) DONNA JUNE, 2) GERRY LEE, 3) BONNIE SUE.

DONNA JUNE, born in Wilsey, KS, married VERLIN ORA CROWE, 2 2Jul 1962 in Wichita, KS. Their children: 1) BRIAN KEITH, 2) PAULA JUNE, 3) GREGORY ALLAN.

GERRY LEE, born in Wilsey, KS, married SUSAN KAY HEWITT, in Wichita, KS 2 Apr 1966. Children: 1) BRADLEY WAYNE, JENA SHALENE.

BONNIE S. born in Council Grove, KS, married ROBERT ANDREW McELROY II in Wichita, KS 10 Jun 1966. Children: 1) ROBERT ANDREW III, 2) TRACY ANN.

The second half of this double wedding: Mildred ELOISE SPIKER married GLENN LENTELL FILKIN.

GLENN L. FILKIN b. 23 Mar 1916
MILDRED (SPIKER) b. 23 Feb 1921
Married 1 Jan. 1940, Kansas. Children:

"What will be, will be." But why do so many families "Will be" cut in the middle of a listing, when I wish to keep each family listing as a unite, so no one will get lost??

1. CHARLOTTE MAY
2. DENNIS LYNN
3. PATSY KAYE
4. RHONDA RAYE
5. JOHN GLENN

DENNIS LYNN FILKIN married JO LANE POWELL 15 Jul 1967. Jo was born in Norfolk, VA. Children: 1) DAWN MICHELLE, 2) SHELLY ANN.

PATSY KAYE FILKIN married CHARLES McNEESE 24 Jul 1967. They separated after the birth of KATHY ANN.

* * * * *

PERCY LeROY SPIKER, son of JOSEPH N. and OLIVE LEONA (WORDEN) SPIKER, married MILDRED PAULINE BROOKS 5 Nov 1945, and separated in 1954. Their children: 1) CONNIE DIANE, 2) ROBERT LeROY, 3) CLYDE NEWTON.

CLYDE NEWTON SPIKER married PAMELA in Port Orchard, Washington. They had one daughter: SUZANNE CHRISTINE.

BETTY JO SPIKER, daughter of JOSEPH N. and OLIVE LEONA (WORDEN) SPIKER, married #1, RICHARD LEE ALBIN in Georgia, and separated from him in Kansas.

RICHARD ALBIN
BETTY JO (SPIKER)
Married 24 Aug 1953, Georgia. Children: 1) SHERYL KAYE, 2) STEVEN LEE & MICHAEL RAY (twins), 3) JEFFREY DALE.

BETTY JO married #2, WILLIAM ROBERT MARKLEY, and lives on a farm 3 miles west of Wilsey, Kansas. It was Betty Jo who have me this material on the Spiker family.

WILLIAM MARKLEY b. 12 Jun 1926
BETTY (SPICER)
Married 20 Feb 1966, Kansas. Child: JULIE ELIZABETH.

ANNA MARIE SPIKER, youngest child of MILTON & MARY (FOSTER) SPIKER, was born near Circleville, Kansas, where she grew to adulthood, met and married ERNEST SAMUEL SANFORD, 7 Aug 1941. The family moved to Montana, and later to California. While living in Montana, their son, Eugene enlisted in the US Marine Corps. In the Pacific Arena he was killed in action and buried at sea. Ernest died of a heart attack and is buried in Montecito Park near San Bernardino, CA.

Anna Marie married #2, MANLY WILLIAMS, who died in a boating accident. She married #3, EVERETT W. SMITH, who died of a heart attack in 1970. After this last death Ann Marie resigned herself to widowhood, and now lives in a unit of the housing project ran by her daughter in Desert Hot Springs, California. No children were born to marriages #2 and #3.

ERNEST SANFORD b. 20 Nov 1899 d. 25 Mar 1951
ANNA MARIE (SPIKER) b. 3 Aug 1902
Married 17 Jan 1920, Kansas. Children:

1. EUGENE WILLIAM b. 23 Dec 1920, d. 17 Sep 1944 WWII
2. MAXINE MAY b. 23 May 1927
3. DELORES FAY b. 15 Nov 1929

MAXINE May SANFORD married and annulled it to #1, MR. PARMETER, 22 Dec 1945. A child born to this marriage took his step-father's name. (Below)

Maxine May married #2 CLAUDE SCOTT, 5 Jun 1948. Children: 1) LARRY GENE (PARMETER), 2) MILTON LESLIE, 3) GLENN ANTHONY, 4) BEVERLY ELAINE.

LARRY GENE PARMETER SANFORD married SUSAN, 13 Aug 1966. Their son: VICTOR.

DELORES FAY SANFORD married and divorced #1, JOHN A. DeNARDI. She married #2, KENNETH WALKER, and lives in Desert Hot Springs, CA, where they are assistant managers of a housing project. Delores' mother lives in one of these units. No children were born to marriage #2.

JOHN A. DeNARDI
DELORES FAY (SANFORD)
Married 19 Sep 1946, California. A bit more peckin' and we'll have the Spiker family salted down.
To this union were born:

1. ANN SANFORD married PATRICK DeRITO 3 Jul 1970. Their child: ANN MARIE.
2. BILLE GENE married BARBARA 9 Apr 1969 and had 1) CHROSTOPHER, 2) BILLIE GENE (Jr.).
3. JAY A.

* * * * *

JOHN WILLIAM FOSTER, youngest child of NEWTON JASPER and MARY FOSTER, was born in Jackson Co., KS. As a young man he moved to Dresden, KS, where he worked in the general store owned by his cousins, Hilbert and Mary-Etta Johnson (p. 211). Here he met and married a young school teacher from Shweyville, Ohio, IVA BOCK.

In 1904 JOHN WILLIAM FOSTER took his family by train to Alder, Washington. By mistake, they got off the train a town short of their planned destination. After a meal and a look at the local hotel, they decided to go on even if they had to walk. They were saved the walk by a railroad employee, who loaded them onto a handcar and pumped them to Alder.

John W. found a job in a general store and moved his family to Elbe, Washington. Here he built a house that is still standing, and lived many years. When he retired, John and Iva Foster did a lot of moving around until his death. Today, Iva, despite her 92 years, is as active as many people in their 60's, and lives with son in Federal Way, Washington. John W. is buried in Carnation, WA. (1971)

JOHN WILLIAM FOSTER b. 24 Oct 1873 d. 1947
IVA (BOCK) b. 24 Sep 1879 d. 1973
Married 5 Jul 1901, Kansas. Children:

1. TRUMAN LeROY b. 25 Sep 1903
2. ROBERTA MADELINE b. 24 Sep 1905 d. 28 Jul 1971
3. LOIS FLORENCE b. 11 Oct 1907
4. ELMER ALBERT b. 1 Jan 1913 d. Sep 1928
5. DOROTHY MARGARET b. 1 Jul 1916
6. RAYMOND SCOTT b. 7 Apr 1918

As welcome as spring flowers may mean daffodils, hyacinths, or skunk cabbage.

TRUMAN L., who lives in Federal Way, Washington, married MARGARET ANN ____, 12 Nov 1929. She was a widow with a child: GEORGIA LEE b. 12 Sep 1926, married HOWARD DERING.

TRUMAN and MARGARET'S children:

1. NANCY ANN who married RAY DURGON and had: 1) CRAIG, 2) JANIS, 3) IVA, 4) LAUREL ANN.
2. DAVID who married MARTHA LEE and had: 1) DARLENE, 2) DANIEL.
3. NELDA who married LARRY WOOD and had 2) JEFFREY, 2) DAVID MARK.

ROBERT MADELINE FOSTER, daughter of JOHN WILLIAM and IVA (BOCK) FOSTER, married MR. ALTON, and had:

1. CLYDE LeROY, who married and has a son: CLYDE LeROY II.
2. RAYMOND SCOTT, who married and has a son: RAYMOND SCOTT II.
3. DOROTHY FRANCES, who married #1 MR. LEDFORD and had: 1) DAVID MICHAEL, 2) GENE PAUL. She married #2 MR. KING and had: DENNIS ALBERT.

DOROTHY MARGARET, daughter of JOHN WILLIAM and IVA (BOCK) FOSTER, married but I have no husband's name. She had: 1) JOHN PETER III, 2) DANIEL, 3) WILLIAM FOSTER _____. JOHN PETER married and had a son: ANDREW J. (Sorry, this is all I have).

RAYMOND SCOTT FOSTER, son of JOHN WILLIAM and IVA (BOCK) FOSTER, married GERALDINE MARY CASSIDY 14 Apr 1943. She was born 26 Oct 1923. Their adopted children: 1) JOANN MARIE, 2) MYEA ANN, who married RONALD DAVIS in 1966.

The families of NEWTON JASPER and MARY ANN (CHAPMAN) FOSTER end here.

* * * * * * *

MARY CASSANDRA, 10th child of AARON & SARAH ROYSTON (PATTON) FOSTER, was born in McLean Co., Illinois. Here she grew to adulthood, met and married JOHN WILLIAM ECTON. The same year, the newlyweds joined her father Aaron Foster, in his migration to Kansas Territory, settling in Leavenworth, Kansas, where they remained when the rest of the Foster family moved on to Jackson County, Kansas. Both are buried in a cemetery in the Leavenworth, Kansas, area.

Except for what I have here, all I know about the children of John and Mary C. Ecton is that most, if not all of them, settled in Montana. I would liked to have had much more on this family but in all my searching I failed to located a single descendant.

JOHN WILLIAM ECTON b. ? d. 25 Mar 1917
MARY CASSANDRA (FOSTER) B. 14 Jan 1841 d. 10 Mar 1871
Married 26 Mar 1856, Illinois. Children:

1. SARAH ELIZABETH b. 7 May 1857 d. 4 Jul 1887
2. ELVIRA FRANCIS b. 1 Jan 1859
3. JOHN MILTON died in infancy
4. AARON SMITH b. 4 Jan 1863
5. EDGAR WILLIAM b. 16 Feb 1866
6. ISAAC NEWTON b. 15 Sep 1868 m. MANDIE WRIGHT
7. MARTHA JOSEPHINE b. 30 Mar 1870

SARAH ELIZABETH ECTON (#1 above) married SAMUEL H. HILL 20 Dec 1882. Their children: 1) WILLIAM BENONA, 2) ORIA ELVIRA.

ELVIRA FRANCIS ECTON (#2 above) married JOHN P. HAYDEN 26 Mar 1889 and had RALPH EDGAR b. 17 Mar 1890. They had no children.

EDGAR WILLIAM ECTON (#5 above)
WINNIE ELIZABETH MORGAN
Married 26 Mar 1889, Leavenworth, Kansas. Their son: RALPH EDGAR ECTON.

RALPH EDGAR ECTON b. 17 Mar 1890
AMANDA E. WILSON b. 1899 d. 1969
Married 1923. Children:

1. RALPH FREDERICK ECTON b. 2 Aug 1924 in Whittier, Los Angeles Co., California, d. 11 Apr 1992 Oxnard, Ventura Co., California
2. LEOLA b. 1928

AARON SMITH ECTON (#4 above) married DOLPHIA McVAY 2 May 1893. Their children: 1) WILLIAM BRYANT b. 1 Apr 1898, 2) ROY DEAN b. 8 May 1900.

Grandpa F. J. Foster, from whose notes this data is taken, was able to give me more help with this family, but let's move (forward) for it.

ISAAC NEWTON ECTON (#6 above) B. 15 Sep 1868
MANDIE (WRIGHT)
Married 28 Dec 1893, Kansas. Children:

1. HAZEL IRENE b. 30 Sep 1894

2. FLOSSIE FLORA b. 26 Jul 1898
3. BEULAH GERALDINE b. 22 Aug 1900
4. ERNEST b. 31 Jul 1904

MARTHA JOSEPHINE ECTON, 7th child of JOHN W. and MARY (FOSTER) ECTON, married GEORGE W. METIER and moved to Montana.

GEORGE W. METIER b. 1863 d. 1928
MARTHA (ECTON) b. 30 Mar 1870 d. 1937
Married 7 Mar 1888, Kansas. Children:

1. EARL CHESTER b. 25 Jul 1891 d. 10 Sep 1981
2. CLAUDE ECTON b. 1 May 1893 Kansas d. 27 Dec 1972 Montana
3. ONA MAY b. 20 Sep 1902 d. 1988

EARL CHESTER METIER married CLARA WALTON 16 Feb 1916 (b. 1895 d. 1973). They had at least one child but I have no name. (Note: www.findagrave.com gives the child's name and ancestry.com gives another son) 1) Walton T b. 16 Aug 1917 Idaho d. 2002, 2) Tom J. b. 1921 Idaho. The 1940 Census lists Clara Walton Metier's mother as Edith C. Walton b. 1870 Minnesota.

CLAUDE ECTON METIER married REBA SHAY, 28 Feb 1915. Their children: 1) GEORGE WILLIAM b. 28 Dec 1915, 2) LOIS M. b. Sep 1917. (Flavius wrote that Lois was Lewis M., a male child, but in the census she is listed as Lois, a female.)

ONA MAY METIER married HAROLD F. WRIGHT b. 5 Apr 1896 Belmont, Dawes, Nebraska. He is a possible relation of Mandie Wright who married Isaac Newton Ecton, Ona's uncle. Ona and Harold had a daughter, Martha J. b. 1927 Montana, and one other child who is still living (2016).

* * * * * *

MILTON SMITH, 10th child of AARON & SARAH ROYSTON (PATTON) FOSTER, was born in McLean Co., Illinois, and came to Kansas with his parents. Milton Smith Foster grew to manhood in the Circleville, Kansas area, where he met and married MARY JANE BROWN. The two children in the family list were born and died in Circleville, Kansas. Their children, Aaron B. and Silas N., were born on the farm south of Haddam, Kansas.

During the Civil War Milton Smith Foster served with Company A, 5th Kansas Cavalry, and was in the battle of the Little Blue near Independence, Missouri. While pursuing the fleeing Rebel forces Milton was taken prisoner. He was interned in the infamous Tyler, Texas prison. The contaminated water and hog-slop-type food served the prisoners caused a stomach ailment that finally caused Milton Smith's death. A family story tells of hunger so desperate that the prisoners caught and ate many of the rats that infested their prison encampment. (Note pgs. 208-209.)

In 1868 Milton S. took his family to Washington Co., Kansas, where he took up land on Mulberry Creek, 2 miles south of Haddam. Here, he farmed until his death, at which time his wife took over the farm. In the Spring of 1878 Mary Jane (Brown) Foster joined her nieces and nephews in a move westward, landing in the old Solomon River Settlement.

On the north fork of the Solomon River, in Sheridan Co., Kansas, Mary Jane took out an 80-acre homestead. Despite Indian raids, droughts, and plagues of grasshoppers, Mary Jane ran her farm and cared for her family when many men gave up in defeat (note: like she had a choice?). Thus, Mary Jane won the respect of all who knew her.

Mary Jane was one of three sisters. Sarah, who married HENRY DAVIS and had a son, CHARLES b. 1899; and MARGARET ANN who married MADISON COX, pg. 127. In later life, Mary Jane lived with Margaret & Madison Cox near Haddam, Kansas. Both Milton S. and Mary Jane Foster are buried 3 miles south of Haddam, Kansas in unmarked graves.

MILTON S. FOSTER b. 20 Jun 1843 d. 10 Dec 1872
MARY JANE (BROWN) b. 1843 Iowa d. 1903
Married 15 Jun 1865, Kansas. Children:

1. AARON BROWN b. 25 May 1869 d. 20 Apr 1895
2. SILAS NEWTON b. 8 Oct 1871
3. Two daughters died in infancy, buried in Circleville, Kansas Cemetery.
4. RUSS LYNDON b. 21 May 1878

SILAS NEWTON FOSTER, born near Circleville, Kansas, grew to manhood in the old Solomon River settlement. Here, too met and married ADDIE EDITH McMULLEN, sister to Lincoln Foster's wife, pg. 217. Later Silas & Addie lived in Dresden, Kansas, where he helped to build many of the homes, and did other carpentry work.

Silas Newton & Addie Foster lived many years in Colorado Springs, Colorado, where he continued his carpenter work. Here, Silas Newton Foster died. Addie E. spend her last days in a nursing home in Pueblo, Colorado. Both are buried in the McMullen plot, in unmarked graves, two miles north of Fomoso, Kansas on the south side of Highway 36. They had no children of their own, but raised several nephews and nieces.

AARON BROWN FOSTER, (#1 above) born in Washington Co., Kansas, went with his mother to the Solomon River settlement homestead. He took over the farm from adulthood until his death. Soon after Aaron B. died his wife married Franklin Spillman, who took over the farm. Later Aaron's wife sold the farm and moved to Lenora with her new husband.

While living on the Solomon River homestead, Aaron B. met and married MARGARET ANN PETERS. All their children were born there. Aaron B. is buried in the Adell

Cemetery. Margaret A. died and is buried in the furthermost south cemetery in Lenora, Kansas.

AARON BROWN FOSTER b. 25 May 1869 d. 20 Apr 1895
MARGARET ANN (PETERS) b. 5 Nov 1871 d. 10 Oct 1951.
Married 16 Jul 1889, Kansas. Children:

1. MYRTLE MAY b. 27 May 1891 d. 10 Mar 1964
2. CLARENCE ALFRED b. 23 Jul 1893 d. 2 Jan 1966
3. FLOYD LORENZO b. 21 Jan 1895
4. MARY JANE died in infancy 1889

FLOYD LORENZE (#3 above) MARRIED #1 MARIE CARPENTER 12 Aug 1917. They parted after the birth of their only child. Today, Marie lives in California with this child. Floyd Lorenzo is remarried, his 2nd wife living in Craig, Colorado, and Floyd spends the summers with his Colorado wife, and the winters with his daughter and ex-wife in California. Floyd L's daughter: EVELYN F.

MYRTLE MAY (#1 above) married NATHAN HUDSON AUMILLER in Adell Kansas. He and Myrtle Fern (Aumiller) Spillman, pg. 232, are first cousins. Nathan H. and Myrtle farmed in northwest Kansas for several years, then moved to Missouri, where he ran a sawmill for some time. Later they moved to Hugo, Colorado, where Nathan H. worded for the Colorado Highway Department until he retired. Both are buried in the Hugo Colorado Cemetery.

NATHAN AUMILLER b. 12 Jun 1890 d. 7 Apr 1964
MYRTLE (FOSTER) b. 27 May 1891 d. 10 Mar 1964
Married 18 Aug 1909, Kansas. Children:

1. EDITH ANNA b. 26 Jun 1910
2. DELLA FAY b. 19 May 1913
3. GRANT FLOYD b. 9 Jan 1915
4. MINA BELLE b. 26 Nov 1916
5. EPH C. (probably short for Eliphalet) b. 2 Jul 1919
6. LILLIE VIRGINIA b. 15 Oct 1921
7. NATHAN JERRY b. 25 Apr 1923
8. MABLE MARIE b. 15 Mar 1925
9. MYRTLE MAY b. 26 May 1926
10. EDNA BLANCH b. 6 Jul 1927
11. JOYCE PEARL b. 23 Dec 1928

    Two children died in infancy

EDITH ANNA (#1 above) married ELMER CLAYTON BEDKER, in Sharon Springs, Kansas. They made their home in Lubbock, Texas, where he is a salesman.

ELMER CLAYTON BEDKER

EDITH (AUMILLER) b. 26 Jun 1910
Married 26 Oct 1930, Kansas. Children:

1. DELORES JOAN
2. PHYLLIS NADINE
3. PATRICIA ANN

DELORES JOAN BEDKER married BLUFORD DOUGLAS HOFFMAN 20 Jan 1947. Their children: 1) CLAYTON DOUGLAS, who married BRENDA RIGA 27 Mar 1971, 2) PHYLLIA ANN (Phyllis?—this could be a typo—we all make those), who married RANDAL S. BURGESS 19 Dec 1970 and had: 1) DAVID PAUL , 2) DANIEL DWIGHT.

PHYLLIS NADINE BEDKER (#2 above) married SAMUEL H. ALLEN 21 Feb 1953 and had: 1) RODNEY B., 2) RANDEL JOHN, 3) RUSSELL WAYNE.
* * * * *
DELLA FAY AUMILLER, 2nd child of NATHAN and MYRTLE (FOSTER) AUMILLER, married in Goodland, Kansas: --

CHARLES JOHNSON b. 15 May 1911
DELLA FAY (AUMILLER) b. 19 May 1913
Married 26 Oct 26, 1932, Kansas. Children:

1. CHARLENE
2. CHARLES Jr.
3. GARY

CHARLENE JOHNSON married in Colorado to ELLIS WORLEY 26 Aug 1967.

CHARLES JOHNSON Jr. married MARILYN COHEN 16 Jan 1970.

GARY married CARMEN PRESKITT 24 Sep 1964. Their child: GARY Jr.

GRANT FLOYD AUMILLER, 3nd child of NATHAN and MYRTLE (FOSTER) AUMILLER, was taken to a farm near Sharon Springs, where he and his sisters walked 2 ½ miles each way to a country school. In 1930 he quit school to work for a big farm combine, driving a Caterpillar tractor. Later he held many jobs in Colorado, where he met and married HELEN JOHANNA MEIS.

GRANT AUMILLER b. 9 Jan 1915
HELEN J. (MEIS) b. 28 Jul 1913
Married 7 Nov 1931, Colorado. Children:

1. HELEN MERITA b. 10 Jul 1932 d. in infancy
2. DONALD GRANT
3. NATHAN JOHN

DONALD GRANT AUMILLER (#2 above) married in Hays, KS to ELEANOR L. BRENTON 10 Jul 1953. Their children: 1) SHERYL KAY, 2) LINDA SUE, 3) MICHAEL GRANT.

NATHAN JOHN AUMILLER (#3 above) married #1 THERESA RODRIGUEZ 7 Jan 1959 and she died the following year. No children. Nathan J. married #2, PATRICIA ANN EHMEN 24 Oct 1964. Their children: 1) THERESA ANN, 2) TIMOTHY ALLEN.
* * * * *
MINA BELLE, 4th child of NATHAN and MYRTLE (FOSTER) AUMILLER, married in Burlington, Colorado to ORVAL WELTON, and have two children who were born in Colorado: 1) VIRGINIA BELLE, 2) MINA EILEEN.

VIRGINIA (#1 in preceding para.), born in Colorado, married in Laramie, Wyoming to LEO ANTHONY MALONEY 10 May 1969. They have one child (so far): LEO ANTHONY Jr.

MINA E. (#2 in preceding para.) was born and married ANDREW ANTHONY FRANEK in Hugo, Colorado.

ANDREW FRANEK
MINA E. WELTON
Were married 31 Dec 1960, Colorado. Children:

1. DEBRA LYNN
2. CHARESE ANN
3. ROBERT JOSEPH

EPH C. AUMILLER, 5th child of NATHAN and MYRTLE (FOSTER) AUMILLER, was born in Raymondville, Missouri, and came to Kansas as a youth. Here he met and married in Goodland to DOROTHY L. STEPHENS 23 Mar 1942. Their child: GLORIA B.

LILLIE VIRGINIA, 6th child of NATHAN and MYRTLE (FOSTER) AUMILLER, was born in Hoxie, Kansas, and married in Goodland to RALPH WALTER JAMES. For a time, they lived in Lamar, Colorado, then moved to Wilshire, Ohio, where Ralph W. James is buried.

RALPH WALTER JAMES b. 15 Feb 1907 d. 1 Jan 1964
LILLIE VIRGINIA (AUMILLER) b. 15 Oct 1921
Were married 26 Jul 1938, Kansas. Children:

1. RALPH WALTER Jr.
2. FRED LeROY
3. JIMMIE LEON

RALPH Jr. (#1 above) was born in Lamar, Colorado and married in Ohio to CAROL ANN THOMAS 1 Jul 1961. They now live in Ft. Wayne, Indiana, where their children were born. Their children: 1) MARK ANTHONY, 2) NICKLAS PATRICK, 3) PHILLYS (Phyllis?) BRADLEY, 4) ANDREA CANDICE.
That's it for today!!!

FRED LeROY JAMES (#2 above) married JANET MARILYN GOODWIN 22 Jul 1961. Their children were all born in Indiana: 1) DAVID ERIC, 2) DAREN LEE, 3) DANNY STEWART, 4) DION MARTIN.

JIMMIE LEON (#2 above) married FLORENCE JOAN HAGGERTY 7 Oct 1962. Jimmie L. is a regular in the US Air Force, and is now stationed in England. Their children, all born in Indiana: 1) JOETTA DEAN, 2) JEANETTA RENEE.
* * *
NATHAN JERRY, 7th child of NATHAN and MYRTLE (FOSTER) AUMILLER, was born in Sharon Springs, Kansas. He married FLORENCE MULLEN in Goodland, Kansas.

NATHAN JERRY AUMILLER b. 25 Apr 1923
FLORENCE (MULLEN) b. 14 Nov 1930
Married 9 May 1948, Kansas. Children: 1) CONNIE, 2) MARILYN.

CONNIE AUMILLER, #1 in preceding paragraph, born in Goodland, Kansas, married ROBIN FOSTER, 3 Jul 1968. She and Robin, who is no known member of our family, were married in his home town of Laramie, Wyoming. Their child: WENDY.

MARILYN AUMILLER, #2 above, born in Goodland, Kansas, married in Laramie to PERRY CLARK 17 Aug 1968. Child: RAYMOND.
* * *
MABLE MARIE, 8th child of NATHAN and MYRTLE (FOSTER) AUMILLER, was born in Sharon Springs, Kansas. She married KESTER ELWOOD RICE in Goodland, KS.

KESTER ELWOOD RICE b. 19 Oct 1920
MABLE MARIE (AUMILLER) b. 15 Mar 1925
Married 28 May 1942, Kansas. Children:

1. ELIZABETH HELEN
2. NINA JEAN
3. KATHERYN MAE

Soon after marriage the Rice Family moved to Anaconda, Montana, then returned to Kansas. During their sojourn in Montana Elizabeth Helen was born. In Goodland, Kansas she met and married WILLIAM LeROY BAYSINGER and their children were born.

WILLIAM LeROY BAYSINGER
ELIZABETH HELEN (RICE)

Married 7 Jan 1960, Kansas. Children: 1) LYNDA SUE, 2) CHERI LANETTE.

NINA JEAN RICE (#2 above) was born in Goodland, Kansas, where she met and married MICHAEL MARVIN MERSCH, m.1 May 1967. They have no children but adopted SHARONA LYNN, who was born in Belleview, Washington.

KATHERYN MAE RICE (#3 above) was born in Goodland, Kansas, where she met and married RICHARD RAY HUNT, m. 30 Aug 1969. Family chart p. 190.

* * * * *

MYRTLE MAE, 9th child of NATHAN and MYRTLE (FOSTER) AUMILLER, was born in Sharon Springs, Kansas, and went with her parents to Goodland, Kansas, where she met and married DALE HERBERT MURPHY. They now live in Colorado.

DALE HERBERT MURPHY b. 11 Oct 1925
MYRTLE MAE (AUMILLER) b. 26 May 1926
Married 21 Dec 1945, Kansas. Children:

1. NORMAL DALE
2. LEATHA MAE
3. DOUGLAS CHARLES

LEATHA MAE MURPHY (#2 above) married and later divorced #1 LONIE GREGORY YARGER, 23 Mar 1968. Their child: CINDY LYNN.

LEATHA MAE MURPHY married #2, STEWART ALAN GILDER, 4 Nov 1969. They have children, but I have no names. Family chart p. 190.

I think I'll take the afternoon off and go to the turkey shoot, and see if I can win a prize or two with my rifle. See you tomorrow.

EDNA BLANCHE, 10th child of NATHAN and MYRTLE (FOSTER) AUMILLER, was born in Sharon Springs, Kansas. She married #1, DONALD AKINS, but I don't if this marriage ended in death or divorce. Their child: DONNA LEE.

EDNA B. married #2, GERALD E DUNCAN, in La Junta, Colorado 4 Oct 1960. Their children: 1) SHARON KAY, 2) MAY ELLEN.

* * *

JOYCE PEARL, last child of NATHAN and MYRTLE (FOSTER) AUMILLER, was also born in Sharon Springs, Kansas. In Stratton, Colorado, she met and married ROBERT LELAND AUSTIN.

ROBERT LELAND AUSTIN b. 25 Jun 1927
JOYCE PEARL AUMILLER b. 23 Dec 1928
Married 15 Feb 1948, Colorado. Children: 1) DANIEL LEE, 2) PAMELA JEAN.

DANIEL LEE AUSTIN was born in Denver, Colorado, and married MARGARET IRENE BIRDSALL 3 Apr 1971.

This brings to an end the Aumiller family. Now we'd better gallop back, and bring up the family of:--

* * *

CLARENCE ALFRED, 2nd child of AARON BROWN & MARGARET (FOSTER), was born in the Old Solomon River Settlement, and never strayed far from that area. After the death of his father, Clarence was raised by his step-father, Franklin Spillman, p. 232. For many years Clarence A. drilled water wells and did plumbing work in the Hoxie, Kansas area.

In Hoxie, KS, CLARENCE A. married LEA ELDA ALLEN. All their children were born in the Hoxie area, and after retiring the family moved to Lenora, Kansas. For many years, the Foster and allied families held family reunions on Uncle Tack Foster's place. Since his death the reunions have been held in Lenora, with Clarence A's children making up the bulk of those attending.

Clarence A. and Lea E. Foster are buried in the Lenora, KS, Cemetery.

CLARENCE ALFRED FOSTER b. 23 Jul 1893 d. 2 Jan 1966
LEA ELDA ALLEN b. 19 No 1908 d. 3 Jan1971
Married 21 Jul 1928, Kansas. Children: possibly still living—so no dates.

1. LYLE ALRED
2. LAWRENCE EDWARD
3. ROBERT MILTON
4. GORDON VICTOR
5. THELMA LEA
6. ELEANOR ELAINE
7. ERMA JUNE
8. VERNON WESLEY
9. FLOYD ERWIN
10. HELEN IONE
11. CLARENCE AARON
12. HOWARD MARION
13. DOROTHY ANN
14. MARILYN MAY
15. GLORIA GLEE

LYLE ALRED FOSTER (#1 above) married ROSALIE ALICE ARMSTRONG in Hoxie, KS. They live on a 40-acre hog ranch a mile north of Lenora, KS. Lyle A. is also in the well-drilling and plumbing business with his brother, Lawrence E, who lives in the old family home in Lenora, KS. Lawrence E. never married. Lyle A. and Rosalie are proud of their twin sons, the first twins in their family in 125 years!

LYLE ALRED FOSTER
ROSALIE ARMSTRONG
Married 29 Oct 1954, Kansas. Children:

1. EDWARD LEE
2. DOLE EUGENE
3. RONALD DEAN
4. JACKIE JO
5. DAVID WAYNE
6. JOHN ALAN
7. JAMES DARWIN

* * *

ROBERT MILTON FOSTER, 3rd child of CLARENCE and LEA E. (ALLEN) FOSTER, born in Hoxie, KS, married BEVERLY JANE McGREGOR, in Wichita Falls, Texas. They live in Hill City, Kansas.

ROBERT MILTON FOSTER
BEVERLY (McGREGOR)
Were married 8 Apr 1955, Texas. Children:

1. MARGARET ANN
2. ROBERTA INEZ
3. ROBERT MILTON II
4. LISLIE BROOKS
5. WILLIAM ALFRED

* * *

GORDON VICTOR FOSTER, 4th child of CLARENCE and LEA E. (ALLEN) FOSTER, was born in Hoxie, KS and married in Portland, Oregon to HELEN YVONNE McGUIRE. They live in Lake Oswego, Oregon.

GORDON VICTOR FOSTER
HELEN YVONNE (McGUIRE)
Married 23 Sep 1955, Oregon. Children: 1) GORDON VICTOR Jr., 2) LUANNE MARIE.

THELMA LEA, 5th child of CLARENCE and LEA E. (ALLEN) FOSTER, was born in Hoxie, KS and married MARVIN LEE BEAGLEY in Norton, KS. They live in Gladstone, Missouri, and her sister, Gloria Glee, lives with them.

MARVIN LEE BEAGLEY
THELMA LEA (FOSTER)
Were married 11 Jul 1952, Kansas. Children:

1. ROBERT LEE
2. STEPHEN DEE
3. DAWNA GLEE

* * *

ELEANOR ELAINE 6th child of CLARENCE and LEA E. (ALLEN) FOSTER, was born in Hoxie, KS and married in Norton, KS to RICHARD NICHOLAS ESSLINGER. They live in Bellville, Kansas, where he owns a service station.

Looks like it's time to move again.

RICHARD NICHOLAS ESSLINGER
ELEANOR (FOSTER)
Married 31 Dec 1959, Kansas. Children: 1) SHARON RENE, 2) TIMOTHY ALAN.
* * *

ERMA JUNE, 7th child of CLARENCE and LEA (ALLEN) FOSTER, born in Hoxie, married in Norton, Kansas to ROBERT MORGAN ALLISON.

ROBERT MORGAN ALLISON
ERMA (FOSTER)
Married 29 Jun 1958, Kansas. Children:

1. TODD FOSTER
2. DON NOEL
3. ROBERT ELLIS
4. TOM M. EARL
5. DEBRA LYNN
6. JOE MORGAN

VERNON WESLEY FOSTER 8th child of CLARENCE and LEA (ALLEN) FOSTER, was born in Hoxie, Kansas and married in Beatrice, Nebraska to CAROL LEE LUHRING. They live in Hays, Kansas.

VERNON WESLEY FOSTER
CAROL (LUHRING)
Married 28 Jun 1959, Nebraska. Children:

1. NORMAN ALFRED
2. CONNIE LYNN
3. RUSSELL ALLEN
4. RODGER

HELEN IONE, 10th child of CLARENCE and LEA (ALLEN) FOSTER, was born in Hoxie, Kansas and married in Norton, Kansas to KENNETH WAYNE BIVENS. They live in Ft. Collins, Colorado.

KENNETH WAYNE BIVENS
HELEN (FOSTER)
Married 26 Nov 1958, Kansas. Children: 1) AARON LYNN, 2) COLETTE RENEE.

HOWARD MARION, 12th child of CLARENCE and LEA (ALLEN) FOSTER, was born in Hoxie, KS and married JANET KAYE MATTISON. They were married and live in Menden, Nebraska. Janet was a divorcee with 2 children, top of family list below.

HOWARD MARION FOSTER
JANET KAYE (MATTISON)
Married 14 May 1969, Nebraska. Children:

1. CARMA MARIE (PETERSEN)
2. TRACY LYNN (PETERSEN)
3. MOLLIE KAYE (FOSTER)

* * *

DOROTHY ANN, 13th child of CLARENCE and LEA (ALLEN) FOSTER, was born in Colby, Kansas and married HARRY CARL JOSLYN. They were married and live in Kansas City, Missouri.

HARRY CAROL JOSLYN
DOROTHY (FOSTER)
Married 16, 1966, Missouri. Children:

1. LEE ELDON
2. HARRY CARL, Jr.
3. MICHAEL ALEXANDER

* * *

MARILYN MAY, 14th child of CLARENCE and LEA (ALLEN) FOSTER, was born south of Lenora just over the line in Graham Co., Kansas, and married and divorced TERRY CHARLES MILES. Both still live in Norton, Kansas.

TERRY CHARLES MILES
MARILYN MAY (FOSTER)
Married 26 Feb 1966, Kansas. Children:

1. RENEE SUE
2. CHARLES ALFRED
3. TERRY Jr.

* * * (chart p. 188)

ROSS LYNDON FOSTER (listed on p. 188 as RUSS), the youngest child of MARY JANE (BROWN) FOSTER, who married MILTON S. FOSTER (11th child of AARON and SARAH ROYSTON PATTON FOSTER), was just a few weeks old when his mother took him to western Kansas, where she homesteaded in the old Solomon River settlement. Here he grew to manhood, met and married #1, MISS McMULLEN, sister to the wife of Ross' brother Silas Newton Foster.

Ross then moved to Colorado Springs, Colorado, where he divorced his wife. At that time, the children went to live with their uncle Silas Newton Foster. Ross' children: 1) CECIL, 2) ARCHIE.

In 1911 Ross L. married #2 FRANCES MARY BREEN, who was born in New York City, 6 Mar 1891. They lived in several places in Colorado and western Kansas until they ended up in Colorado Springs, where Ross abandoned his family. He was last heard of in Pasadena, California, where he made a living painting landscapes.

Ross & Frances' children: 1) LYNDON AARON b. 4 Jul 1912 d. 13 Oct 1932 (suicide), 2) JOHN MILTON b. 10 Jul 1915, 3) ROBERT ANTHONY b. 6 Aug 1917 d. 13 Oct 1962 (also suicide), 4) FLORENCE MARIE B. 1 Jun 1921. (Ross and his families sure had more than their share of tragedies)

JOHN MILTON FOSTER (#1 in preceding para.), an Air Force retiree, was born in Colorado Springs, Colorado. In 1939 he met and married MARY ELLEN SMITH of Pawnee
Rock, Kansas, where they now live.
ROBERT ANTHONY FOSTER, 3rd child of ROSS & FRANCES (BREEN) FOSTER, went with his parents to Colorado Springs, CO. Here he grew to adulthood and met and married LELA FERN HEMPHILL, m. 18 Nov 1938. Lela F. was born in Purdy, Missouri 20 May 1919. They made their home in Las Animas, Colorado, where they finally divorced on 7 May 1962, and where Lela still lives.
Their children: 1) ROBERT, 2) RANDY, 3) GARY, 4) STEVE, 5) JOE, 6) PATRICIA, 7) CHERYL, 8) another daughter.

FLORENCE M. FOSTER, 4th child of ROSS & FRANCES (BREEN) FOSTER, was born in Colorado Springs and married LYNN HODGE CAMPBELL in 1940. They have a son and a daughter, but I have no names.

* * * * * *

AARON FOSTER, 3rd child of HARRISON and ANNA MARGARET (BARTLETT) FOSTER, married #2 ELENOR TAYLOR in McLean Co., Illinois after his first wife, Sarah Royston Patton, died in 1845. In 1856, nine years later, Aaron sold his land holdings and his interest in the firm of Enoch & Foster, and left his Pleasant Hill homestead. The family spent the first winter in Leavenworth, Kansas, later moving to Jackson Co. and settling ½ mile southwest of Circleville, Kansas.

In 1857 Circleville was just a community of frontier shacks with a store, blacksmith shop, and a sawmill under construction. It was a time of bitterness between the pro and anti-slavery forces. It was also a time of looting, burning and killing by outlaw gangs on both sides of the argument. Things got so bad that the settlers had to organize for protection. When one of Aaron's best horses was stolen his eldest son joined one of these Kansas home guard units called "Jayhawkers." He served under James (Jim) Lane, who in later years was very active in Kansas politics.

Aaron Foster, always a strong Christian, soon was helping to organize a Methodist Church in the settlement. He took over the adult class and taught it until his death. Aaron & Elenor Foster and 2 of his granddaughters are buried side-by-side in the Circleville, Kansas Cemetery.

AARON FOSTER b. 31 Mar 1804 d. 6 Aug 1864
ELENOR (TAYLOR) b. 29 Jan 1816 d. Sep 1888
Married 19 Oct 1847, Illinois. Children:

1. SAMUEL COLUMBUS b. 29 Jan 1849 d. 26 Jul 1851
2. ELIZABETH ALMEDA b. 22 Aug 1850 d. 9 Aug 1876
3. JAMES MONROE b. 23 Apr 1854 d. 8 Apr 1913
4. MARTHA JANE b. 13 Jan 1858 d. 1912
5. ALICE ELENOR b. 20 Mar 1862 d. 26 Jul 1864

ELIZABETH ALMEDA FOSTER (#2 above), born in McLean Co., Illinois, went with her parents to Circleville, Kansas. Here she grew to adulthood, met and married OSCAR LAMB, who was born 24 Aug. 1844. They moved to California, where Elizabeth died in childbirth.

JAMES MONROE FOSTER (#3 above), born in McLean Co., Illinois, came with his parents to Circleville, Kansas. Here he grew to manhood, met and married SARAH ELIZABETH BLACKERBY. She was the daughter of MARY CHAPMAN BLACKERBY, who married James' half-brother, Newton Jasper Foster (p. 168). James Monroe set up farming near Silver Lake, a few miles northwest of Topeka, Kansas.

While breaking a blind horse, the animal became frightened and crushed James against the corral fence. He died after suffering from broken ribs and severe chest pains (probably a punctured lung). His half-brother and son, Silas J. and Flavius J. Foster, were at his bedside, and Grandpa F. J. Foster preached at James M.'s funeral.

JAMES MONROE FOSTER b. 23 Apr 1854 d. 8 Apr 1913
SARAH JANE (BLACKERBY) b. 31 Aug 1854 d. 1946
Married 11 May 1873, Kansas. Children:

1. DAISY MAY b. 5 Jan 1878 d. 1952
2. VIRA FRANCIS b. 12 Feb 1885 d. 28 Mar 1971
3. LULA MAUDE b. 13 Mar 1886 d. Apr 1974
4. OTHA MONROE b. 28 Mar 1895
5. 3 more babies died as infants

DAISY MAY was born in Jackson Co., Kansas and grew to adulthood on the Silver Lake Farm. She married JAMES SUTTON. He was an orphan, and I do not know if this name was his birthright or adopted. The Suttons moved to Topeka, and later Kansas City, Kansas. Two children still live in Kansas, and I have visited one of them and got a lot or promises but no material on the Sutton family.

JAMES SUTTON b. 1874 d. 1959
DAISY MAY (SUTTON) b. 5 Jan 1878 d. 1952
Married 4 Nov 1904, Kansas. Children:

1. FLOYD MONROE b. 25 Apr 1904
2. CARL FREDERICK b. 8 Jul 1906
3. LOLA MAY b. 22 Feb 1910 m. MR. McQUIRK
4. GOLDIE b. Nov 1911
5. RUTH b. Oct 1914 m. Mr. GARRETT
6. CHARLES MARVIN b. 3 Dec 1918

VIRA FRANCIS FOSTER, 2nd child of JAMES MONROE & SARAH (BLACKERBY) FOSTER, married #1, CHARLES MELLOISH, who was part Indian, and got hooked on the bottle. As time went on his sober periods became so short Vira divorced him. Marriage #2 soon ended in divorce. Vera then married #3, F.J. TURNER, a milk inspector for the city of Topeka, Kansas. After his death Vira F. moved in with her daughter and lived out her life in Topeka. Her daughter: SOPHIA JAUNITA MELLOISH b. 5 Nov 1903, married ELBERN M. BEAL (b. 1895 d. 1966). Sophia and Elber's children: 1) JEAN, 2) ELIZABETH, 3) FRANCIS.

* * *

LULA MAUDE, 3rd child of JAMES MONROE & SARAH (BLACKERBY) FOSTER, married ERNEST TOWLES, and lived many years in the Kansas City area. I don't have a thing on Ernest, but Lula M. died in a nursing home in Los Angeles, Calif. Their children: 1) FRED b. 12 Jul 1904, 2) ERNEST Jr., 3) ERNESTINE & FERN (twins) b. 10 Jul 1906.

* * *

OTHA MONROE FOSTER, 4th child of JAMES MONROE & SARAH (BLACKERBY) FOSTER, married MARY FRANCES MOHLER of Circleville, KS and later moved to Picher, Oklahoma. Here, in 1927, Otha deserted his wife and family. While visiting his aunt Lula in Kansas City his son, Dale James, saw Otha there. This was in 1934. One rumor has it that Otha died in a truck accident while in Colorado with the old CCC (Civilian Conservation Corps), and Dale J. has heard that he was killed in a bar in Fort Scott, KS. But none of the children knows for sure what happened to their father. It is entirely possible that he is still living (in 1971). Note: On ancestry.com we find the following death record. I haven't verified that this is the same Otha but the name and age match nicely:

Kentucky Death Index 1911-2000
Otha M Foster:
Death date: 25 Jun 1946
Age: 51
Residence: Jefferson

OTHA M. FOSTER b. 27 Mar 1895 d. probably 25 Jun 1946
MARY (MOHLER) b. 21 Nov 1894 d. 25 Jul 1965
Married 15 Jun 1915, Kansas. Children:

1. ALFRED MONROE b. 19 Apr 1916 d. 19 Aug 1969
2. MARY LUCILLE b. 22 Jul 1918
3. DALE JAMES b. 19 Dec 1920

4. NOMA MAXINE b. 1 Apr 1924
5. WANDA LEE b. 21 Feb 1927

ALFRED M. married MARIE SMITH. He died and is buried in Topeka, KS, where Marie still lives. They had no children but adopted: JANET SUE.

MARY LUCILLE (#2 above) married and divorced #1 JOSEPH LeVON McCULLEN and had: 1) NORMAN LeVON, 2) FRANCIS DEAN, 3) ROGER DALE. Mary L. married #2, FLOYD CLOUD 5 Aug 1946, who died 26 Feb 1959. Their children: 1) DARA GAY, 2) SANDRA LUE (Lou or Sue?), 3) FLOYD F. Jr. Mary L. married #3, W. F. CHILDREY, and lives in Topeka, Kansas.

DALE JAMES (#3 above) married and divorced #1, LELA ADKINS in Topeka, KS. They had a son: JAMES DALE (JIM), who married #1 SHIRLEY WELCH of Riverside, California in 1960 and now lives in Lawrence, KS. She was a widow with a child: GINA LYNN. They have no children, but Jim adopted Gina L.

DALE JAMES married #2 IRENE ESPINOSA, in Topeka, KS, and in 1956 moved to Ontario, California. Here they own a stereo and allied electronics business, aided by their sons, Richard and Galen.

DALE JAMES FOSTER b. 19 Dec 1920
IRENE (ESPINOSA) b. 6 Jul 1932
Married 12 Mar 1949, Kansas. Children:

1. RICHARD DEAN
2. VIRGINIA DIANE
3. GALEN LEE
4. GALA SUE
5. STACEY IRENE

RICHARD DEAN married RITA E. SNODGRASS in Topeka, KS 3 Jan 1967. They live in California where Richard is in business with his father. Their children: 1) RICHARD GUY, 2) LAURITA RACHELLE.

VIRGINIA DIANE (#2 above list) married DAVID MICHAEL MORGAN in Pomona, California and now lives in Ravenna, Ohio, where he works for Rotek Inc. Their children: 1) DAVID MICHAEL II, 2) DUSTIN MATHIS.

GALEN LEE (#3 above list), twin to GALA SUE, married DONNA MAYE MURPHY in Pomona, Calif., 6 Feb 1971. Their child: JACOB LEE.

GALA SUE, Galen's twin, married WILLIAM C. DOKOS of Salt Lake City, Utah 2 May 1970. They have: 1) MORIAH MOREH, 2) JUDAH WAYNE.

* * *

NOMA MAXINE, 4th child of OTHA MONROE and MARY (MOHLER) FOSTER, married JAMES EDWARD KRALLMAN of Scranton, Kansas. They live in Topeka where he is half-owner of a body and fender shop.

JAMES R. KRALLMAN b. 23 Sep 1921
NOMA MAXINE FOSTER b. 1 Apr 1924
Married 10 Sep 1943, Kansas. Children:

1. JAMES EDWARD II
2. GARY LEE
3. MICHAEL KEVIN
4. RANDALL LINN

JAMES EDWARD II married THELMA BRUGARDT 27 Feb 1965 in Topeka, KS, where they now live. Children: 1) STACEY CHARLENE, 2) SUSAN DIANE.

* * *
WANDA LEE FOSTER, 5th child of OTHA MONROE and MARY (MOHLER) FOSTER, married NEAL PHILLIPS in Topeka, where he works for the Santa Fe Railroad.

NEAL PHILLIPS b. 20 Oct 1926
WANDA LEE FOSTER B. 21 Feb 1927
Married 25 Aug 1945, Kansas. Children:

1. SHARON – married JOHN HASLETT II and has: 1) JEFFERY, 2) STANLEY.
2. LINDA – married and divorced GID DYCHE and has: 1) TAMMY, 2) TINA.
3. CONNIE – married DENNIS WARNOCK. They had no children in 1974

* * * * *
MARTHA JANE FOSTER, last child of AARON & ELENOR FOSTER, was born and grew to adulthood near Circleville, KS. She married HESS HENRY FREEMAN and moved to Washington State, where they became "lost" as far as the rest of her family were concerned. He was born 16 Dec 1857. Their children: 1) ROY b. 20 Dec 1879, 2) HERBERT b. 2 Aug 1882, 3) HOPE B. 11 Mar 1885.
* * * Family chart pg. 151* * *

Here we bid a fond, reluctant farewell to the families of AARON & SARAH, and AARON & ELENOR FOSTER, except his son, Silas J.
* * * * * *

SILAS JACKSON FOSTER

SILAS JACKSON FOSTER, 5th child of AARON & SARAH (PATTON) FOSTER, was born in McLean Co., Illinois. He grew to manhood in the now-gone town of Pleasant Hill, which was laid out on his father's claim. For a time, Silas tried farming, and ended up as a carpenter and cabinet maker. His favorite pastimes were knitting, which he could do as well as any woman, and hunting. At an early age, Silas J. became a minister of the Gospel. When age forced him to hang up his gun and lay aside his hammer and saw, Silas still kept his covenant with the Lord.

(The following is about the parents of Rachel Bills, Silas' wife)
Mary Enoch and Ephraim Bills were married in Ohio; date unknown. He was Pennsylvania Dutch, whose mother was still living in Cincinnati Ohio as late as 1840. Mary was a sister of Absalom Enoch, who was Aaron Foster's business pardner, pg. 146. To the union of Ephraim and Mary Bills were born at least two children, then the father died. Mary married #2, _______Burge, and moved to Peoria, Illinois in 1840, where they are buried. To this last union was born:--Isachar.

In the mid-1840's, Margaret and Rachel, children of Ephraim & Mary Bills, joined their uncle, Absalom Enoch in Pleasant Hill, Illinois. Soon after, Margaret and Constantine Patton were married, pg. 135, and Rachel Bills moved in with them. A year or two later, Silas J. Foster came courting Rachel.

Silas Jackson Foster and Rachel Bills were married in the home of his uncle, Aaron Patton, the ceremony being performed by Rev. Samuel Smith. They set up housekeeping on a farm near Pleasant Hill, and doing carpentering on the side, till 1858. The preceding year, Silas J's father had gone to help make Kansas a slave-free state, and Silas J. decided to follow him there.

Silas got as far as Knox Co., Missouri, when the coming of a child and a shortage of money forced him to squat till he could get a new grubstake. Silas J. was still working toward a grubstake when the last phase of events leading up to the Civil War caught up with him. However, earlier events had sent out their grim warnings, and Silas J. had his answer ready.

Silas J. was one of the 79 local voters, out of 1,497 men, who cast his ballot for Abraham Lincoln, whom he knew personally. During his practice of law, Mr. Lincoln had often visited Pleasant Hill on court business. When Mr. Lincoln was nominated as President of the U.S., the pro-slavery people began gathering arms for the upcoming revolt. Silas J. wrote of the times:--"As Pat put it, it was dangerous to be safe." (I love that line!)

On July 22, 1861, Silas J. joined the local home guard unit, to protect the public buildings of Knox Co., Missouri against raids by pro-slavery forces. Quote: "Thirty men with a few squirrel rifles."

Silas J. made haste to move his family to Clark Co., Missouri, where there were fewer pro-slavery people. The little pro-government home-guard unit was chased from pillar to post, by a pro-slavery unit of 1,500 men under Col. Green. Then Silas J's little unit was joined by a larger unit, at Novelty, southeast of Knoxville, the 1st Regiment of Home guards under Col. David Moore. Now, it was their turn to chase the rebels - all the way to Canton, Missouri. Here the 1st Regiment joined the 2nd Regiment of Home guards, and were mustered into the Union Army as the 21st Missouri Volunteers, commanded by Col. David Moore under General Prentiss.

Silas J. served with Company D, 21st Missouri Volunteers till April 23, 1863. At that time, he was discharged with a stomach ailment that bothered him the rest of his life. In the spring of 1862, Silas J. had taken furlough and moved his family to Circleville, Kansas, near his parents, where he now joined them.

Soon after getting settled in his new home, Silas J. joined the 20th Volunteer Regiment, a militia unit, as captain of Infantry. His three eldest brothers also belonged to this unit, for the protection of Kansas from invasion. Milton S. Foster, 5th Kansas Volunteer Cavalry, Aaron B. Foster, Co. G, 13th Ks. Vo.. Cavalry, Newton J. Foster, Co. B 11th Ks. Vo. Cavalry. All four of them served in the Union Army at the battle of, "The Little Blue," Independence, Missouri. (The following description was taken from his writings.)

BATTLE OF THE LITTLE BLUE

On Sept 27, 1864, Gen. Price, with his Confederate Army, invaded Missouri from the south, advancing almost to St. Lewis, where he made a westward turn. At first sign of invasion, the Kansas forces, under Gen. Blunt, were called out to help in the defense of Missouri. The union units, to which the Foster brothers belonged, set up a defense line just east of Lexington, Missouri, where the Rebel forces attacked them.

After a short, sharp engagement, the Rebel force outflanked this position, and the Union Militia retired to the west bank of the Little Blue River. They had gotten a few reinforcements, but, again, the confederates outflanked their position. The Union force retired still further westward and set up a defense position bordering Independence Missouri. More reinforcements arrived during the night, under Gen. Curtis, who out-ranked Gen. Blunt.

All during October 22, Gen. Price's forces attacked the Union troops with infantry, cannon and cavalry. This time, the reinforced Kansas Militia was able to beat off each assault, although the Confederates did capture a portion of Independence. During the night, however, Union Army units that had been dogging Gen. Price's trail, arrived on the scene. Again the opposing forces battled long and hard, until finally a Union cavalry charge pushed the Rebels out of Independence. Soon thereafter, Gen. Price decided he had urgent business in the state of Arkansas, and took off, with the Union troops in hot pursuit. It was during this pursuit that Milton S. Foster was taken prisoner and confined in the infamous prison at Tyler, Texas.

This is the way Silas J. Foster described the battle of October 23, 1864:-- "After a cool, damp night, we lay in the 'brash' along the Little Blue and traded shots with the Rebels. Early in the fight, one of my men was hit by a sharpshooter, the Minis ball lodging under the skin near his elbow. While he was removing the ball with his knife, a second ball entered just above the elbow, drove upward under the skin, and lodged near his shoulder.

The damp air 'helt' the smoke from our muskets and cannon close to the ground, so thick we often had to hold our fire till it cleared enough so we could see targets to shoot at. We would have at it again, but after a few rounds from our cannon, and musket volleys, the smoke would be as thick as before., But we were doing pretty well, for the Rebs had had enough after taking our lead for three hours. They headed south, with us on their tails. We hiked our boots off, but were unable to catch 'em, and we were very willin' to let the horse soldier take over the job at evening of the second day. (In his every day speech, like most of his age group, Silas J. (Silas Jackson Foster) used see'd for saw, Brash for brush, and fought was always, fit.)

After the battle, Silas J. rejoined his family for good. It was at that time in Circleville, Ks., shortly after his father's death, that Silas J. made his final Covenant with the Lord. He became a local minister in the Methodist Church, a position he held till the church abandoned local ministers. At that time, Silas J. joined the United Brethren in Christ Church, and worked with them until his death.

In 1869 Silas J. moved his family to Washington County, south of present-day Haddam, Kansas. Until mid-1878, he plied his trade in that part of Kansas and Nebraska, building homes and furnishings. At this time, Silas J. joined his son F.J. in the westward move to the Solomon River settlement. It was he who led the settlers up river when the Indiana came, to meet any attack on their homes. Later in 1878 he took up a claim on the river, remaining there until the railroad passed four miles north of the settlement. In 1895, Silas J. made his last move to the home he built in Dresden, Kansas.

At the age of 82 years, 11 months and 13 days, Silas J. (Sile) Foster went to meet his maker, escorted to his grave by the band and parade of Civil War Veterans. Six years later, at the age of 87, his wife Rachel, joined him. Both rest in the cemetery at Dresden, Kansas, where are buried many of their descendants." Flavius Foster

I live at Dresden, Decatur Co., Kans., N. J. Foster lives at Holton, Jackson Co., Kans., James M. lives at Silver Lake, Kans., and Martha J. lives in Tacoma, Wash. Mr. (Aaron) Foster was an old-time Methodist and officiated as class leader as long as he lives.--Silas Jackson Foster

SILAS JACKSON FOSTER b. 14 Jan 1834 d. 27 Dec 1916
RACHEL (BILLS) b. 27 Aug 1835 d. 3 Oct 1922
Married 15 Jul 1852, Illinois. Children:

1. MARY-ETTA b. 26 Mar 1854 d. 7 Nov 1938
2. FLAVIUS JOSEPHUS b. 8 Apr 1856 d. 8 Jul 1938
3. LORENZO MILTON b. 2 Feb 1858 d. 21 Apr 1944
4. ABRAHAM LINCOLN b. 28 Apr 1861 d. 1 Jun 1917
5. ANNA ARIZONA b. 26 Jun 1865 d. 29 Apr 1858
6. EMMA FLORENCE b. 22 Jan 1868 d. 2 Dec 1927
7. WILLIAM JASPER b. 26 Sep 1870 d. 5 Mar 1907
8. SARAH MARGARET b. 26 Jan 1873 d. 13 Oct 1918
9. RUDOLPHUS DORCAS b. 25 Jan 1876 d. 1 Oct 1963

MARY-ETTA FOSTER, eldest child of Rev. SILAS & RACHEL FOSTER, was born in McLean Co., IL, and went with her parents to Kansas via Knox Co., Missouri. The family settled on the southwest edge of Circleville, Ks., where Mary-Etta got her schooling - all 4 years of it. Here, too she again saw her father dress in Blue, don his sword and march off to war.

In 1869 the family moved to Washington County, settling near present-day Haddam, Ks. Here, Mary-Etta met and married Hilbert Johnson, and their two eldest children were born. In the spring of 1878 Hilbert and Mary-Etta moved to the old Solomon River settlement, where Hilbert traded a mare for 80 acres of bottom land. A few years later, Hilbert became the proud owner of a general store in Adell.

In 1896 Hilbert and Mary-Etta made their last move, to Dresden, KS. Here they started another general store, later taking in their son-in-law Henry Law as pardner. Hilbert and Mary-Etta spent their remaining years in Dresden, and are buried in the Adell Cemetery, a short distance from their old homestead."

For more on the lives of Hilbert & Mary-Etta see the Johnson-Spillman and Sod Shanty chapters."

HILBERT JOHNSON b. 1 Jun 1847 d. 18 Nov 1933
MARY-ETTA (FOSTER) b. 26 Mar 1854 d. 7 Nov 1938
Married 1 Jan 1870, Kansas. Children:

1. ISAAC NEWTON b. 10 Mar 1874 d. 25 Jun 1887
2. MARTHA JANE b. 22 Nov 1876 d. 31 Jan 1966
3. IRA V. b. 8 Jan 1881 d. 26 Jul 1902

MARTHA JANE, born in Haddam, KS, came with her parents to the homestead, then to Dresden, Ks. Here, she met and married CHARLES HENRY LAW, and their children were born. Henry was a pardner in the store with Martha's father, till it was sold. At that time, Henry became a director in the old Dresden State Bank. When death called, Henry and Martha were buried near her Foster relatives in Dresden, Kansas.

CHARLES HENRY LAW b. 18 Apr 1869 d. 29 Dec 1941
MARTHA JANE b. 22 Nov 1876 d. 31 Jan 1966
Married 12 Jan 1897, Kansas. Children:

1. ETHEL MAE b. 14 Apr 1898 d. 28 Nov 1965
2. CHESTER IVAN b. 14 Nov 1901
3. NORMAN WILLIS b. 28 May 1911 d. 26 Aug 1959

Two other children died in infancy

ETHEL MAE LAW was born in Dresden, KA where she finished high school, married ELMER UFFORD of nearby Oberlin, KA. They made their home in Dresden, living in the old home built by Ethel's Gr. Grandfather, Silas J. Foster. Elmer, a WWI veteran was carpenter, and had one of the largest bird's egg collections in the country. I have often wondered what became of that collection, which contained over 300 eggs from huge ostrich to tiny hummingbirds from all over the world.

For the last four or five years of their lives Ethel and Elmer suffered the crippling pain of rheumatoid arthritis together. The ailment sent them to a nursing home, and finally to the grave. Elmer and Ethel Ufford are buried in the Foster section of the Dresden, Kansas cemetery.

ELMER UFFORD b. 22 Jan 1895 d. 8 Dec 1962

ETHEL MAE (LAW) b. 14 Apr 1898 d. 28 Nov 1965
Married 22 Apr 1920, Kansas. Children:

1. CLINTON MAX b. 15 May 1921
2. LESTER WARNER b. 8 Jun 1926

CLINTON MAX UFFORD was born, went to school and grew to manhood in Dresden, KS. During WWII, he was a military photographer. Clinton M. married JENNIE ELIZABETH SPILLMAN, adopted a daughter of Roy & Naomi Spillman, pg. 230, in Hoxie, KS. Today they lived in Kansas City, KS. Their children were born in the Hoxie area, where Clinton and Jennie lived for several years.

CLINTON MAX UFFORD b. 15 May 1920
JENNIE ELIZABETH (SPILLMAN) b. 3 Nov 1923
Married 18 Sep 1944, Kansas. Children:

1. MAXINE ELIZABETH
2. MILDRED KATHLEEN

MAXINE ELIZABETH UFFORD married LARRY GENE ARNOLD 26 Oct 1963 and divorced him 18 months later. Their child: LESA ANN.

MILDRED KATHLEEN UFFORD married and divorced #1 WILLIAM M. NEWHOUSE m. 1 Aug. 1964. Their children: 1) MICHELLE DENESE, 2) WENDEE KATHLEEN.

MILDRED KATHLEEN married #2 LeROY BAXTER 28 Jul 1969.

* * *

LESTER WARNER UFFORD, 2nd son of ELMER & ETHEL (LAW) UFFORD, was born and got his schooling in Dresden, Kansas. He too, was in the armed forces during WWII. He married somewhere in Kansas and now lives in the Kansas City area. Lester W. married LaJUNE DEINES, who was born 5 Oct 1930. They had at least one child: GREGG.

* * *

CHESTER IVAN, 2nd son of HENRY & MARTHA (JOHNSON) LAW, was born and finished high school in Dresden, KS. Chester I. married ADELE MARIE OLSEN, who was born in Ulefass, Telemark, Norway. For many years, Chester worked for the Foster Lumberyards Inc., first in Jennings, KS, and finally in Chappell, Neb. He retired as a manager and still lives in Chappell, Neb. with his wife.

During his life, Chester has seen his home town, Dresden, build up from near nothing to a population of around 200, then decline to a mere shell. He grew up and worked with the Foster Lumberyards, from the beginning, till, they too have almost disappeared. He, too has another distinction, if you can call it that.

Gr. Grandmother Rachel Bills Foster inherited an indescribable inflection of speech from her Pennsylvania Dutch father. That inflection of speech has been carried to this day, through her Gr. Grandson, Chester. And, on occasions can be noted in the voice of his nephew Larry Law.

So, ends another day of hunt'n and peckin'.

CHESTER IVAN LAW b. 14 Nov 1901
ADELE MARIE (OLSEN) b. 24 Apr 1904
Married 1928, Kansas. Children:

1. JOAN ADELE b. 20 Nov 1929 d. 18 Jul 1966 never married
2. FREDERICK EUGENE b. 22 Aug 1931

FREDERICK EUGENE LAW married CAROL JOYCE McDONALD 6 Jun 1952 in Honolulu, Hawaii. They now live in Denver, CO, where their children were born: 1) LISA LEILANE, 2) THOMAS RAY.

* * *

NORMAN WILLIS LAW, last child of HENRY & MARTHA LAW, married his second-generation cousin, OLIVE IRENE FOSTER. Their family is given on p. 272.

* * * Family chart pg. 210 * * *

FLAVIUS JOSEPHUS FOSTER's family is given in the upcoming chapter.

* * *

LORENZO MILTON FOSTER (Uncle Tack), 3rd child of SILAS J. & RACHEL (BILLS) FOSTER was born in Knox, Missouri, and went with his parents to Circleville, Kansas. In 1869 the family moved to Washington Co., where Lorenzo grew to manhood. It was during this time, that he acquired the handle, "Tack" due to his very slim build. This nickname stuck so tight, and was so universally used most of his neighbors and some of his grandchildren never learned his true given name.

In early 1878 Lorenzo joined his brother-in-law Hilbert Johnson and his aunt, Mary Jane Foster, when they immigrated to the Solomon River settlement. The other two took out homesteads, but Lorenzo was not of age, and by the time he was, the best land had been taken up. However, since he wasn't married he didn't worry until he married Almira, sister of Hilbert Johnson. She had an 80-acre farm, to which they later added another 40 acres.

Breaking sod by the crude methods of the day, using "horse" power was not exactly a bowl of cherries. Then spiced with hot winds, invasions of grasshoppers and Indian raids, it was discouraging. In later years, Lorenzo wrote many words on homesteading along the Solomon River. Some of these I have given herein, others are in the possession of his grandson, Leonard Foster. I have tried unsuccessfully to contact this grandson, regarding this material. However, I too, have some and have made use of it in "Sod Shanty."

As noted, Lorenzo M. married Almira Johnson. She was the widow of Westunion Spillman, and her first family is given on pg. 229. After the tragic death of her first husband, Almira joined her brother, Hilbert in the old Solomon River settlement. Here she took out an 80-acre homestead, to which they later added other acreage.

Together Lorenzo and Almira Foster saw the land fill with settlers and went through good times and times not so good, including the "Dirty 30's." They saw swarms of grasshoppers devouring every plant, including the onion bulbs underground. They saw winds so hot, every green plant curled up and died within a week's time, and raging prairie fires leaping 20 feet high, as they swept across miles of prairie, including a woman and her two girls who were trying to save their farm stock.

At family reunions, held year after year at Uncle Tack's home, they could laugh at these disasters. They would dwell for hours on the good things of those lean days of their youth, with relish. After 66 years of life on their Solomon River claim, they were laid to rest just a mile from their old home, in the Adell Cemetery.

LORENZO MILTON FOSTER b. 2 Feb 1858 d. 21 Apr 1944
ALMIRA (JOHNSON) b. 17 Aug 1850 d. 24 Aug 1941
Married 19 Feb 1885, Kansas. Child: ELIPHLET JACKSON b. 9 Mar 1887 d. 14 Oct 1868.
ELIPHLET JACKSON (Liffee) FOSTER married CINDA ELLEN REED, sister to the girls who married Andrew J. Foster's sons, pgs. 159 & 161. These marriages created one of those situations stories are told of. (Note pg. 161) For many years, Eliphlet J. farmed along the Solomon, later inheriting the home place, which he then sold and moved into Oberlin, Kansas, where both are buried.

Eliphlet J., like his father, was interested in the doings of those old timers along the Solomon River, and his notes are being kept by some of his children, mainly, Leonard Foster."

Seedlings pg. 160 – to save you the trouble of back-tracking:
"Richard Foster was born on the old Solomon River homestead, and farmed several years northwest of Jennings, Kansas. He retired to Hoxie, where he spent his time fishing, till his death. He married and divorced Hattie Reed, one of the four (Reed) sisters. When Eliphalet Foster slipped in and married one of the sisters, it led Andy Foster to say, "If Liffee had stayed, I'd have all the Reed girls in the family." Hattie still lives in Hoxie, Ks. Richard is buried in the old Adell Cemetery.

ELIPHLET JACKSON (Liffee) FOSTER b. 9 Mar 1887 d. 14 Oct 1968
CINDA ELLEN (REED) b. 11 Dec 1892 d. 24 Dec 1956
Married 7 Sep 1910, Kansas. Children:

1. LORENZO FRANK b. 17 Jul 1911
2. LORETTA MAY b. 27 Sep 1915
3. LYMAN LEONARD b. 3 Oct 1922

LORENZO FRANK (RENNIE) married IDELLA MAE MATHENY. For several years he worked at various jobs, and is now employed by the city of Oberlin, Kansas as a cemetery caretaker. Idella is also employed by the city, but both are due to retire soon.

LORENZO FOSTER b. 7 Jul 1911
IDELLA MAE (MATHENY) b. 1 Apr 1919
Married 28 Sep 1934, Kansas. Children:

1. HAROLD MELTON
2. NORMAN DALE
3. RAYMOND DUANE

HAROLD MELTON FOSTER is married, has a family and lives in Kansas City, KS.

NORMAN DALE FOSTER married MARIE ______ 27 Mar 1971. They both work for the Lakeside hospital in Kansas City, Missouri as medical technologists.

RAYMOND DUANE FOSTER (#3 above) married LINDA BUTLER in Stanton, CA 23 May 1969. They still live in California.

* * *

LORETTA MAY, 2nd child of ELIPHLET & CINDA E. (REED) FOSTER, married ARTHUR NELSON. For many years they owned a service station on Highway 36 in Oberlin, KS. At that time, Loretta worked as a receptionist for a dentist. They are now retired and a son-in-law bought the service station. However, their home is only a few yards from the station, so, when they are not traveling they can be found at the station – just can't keep away.

ARTHUR NELSON b. 26 Dec 1909
LORETTA MAY FOSTER b. 27 Sep 1915
Married 17 Aug 1934, Kansas. Children:

1. JANETTE
2. IDELLA
3. PATRICIA

JANETTE NELSON married HOWARD VOTAPKA 3 Aug 1958. They live north of Oberlin, KS and have: 1) DONNA JO, 2) LYNDA LEA, 3) WARD EUGENE.

IDELLA NELSON married LeMOIN RUSH 1 Jun 1958. Their children: 1) CINDIA ELLEN, 2) TERRY ALLEN, 3) KEVAN RAY.

PATRICIA NELSON (#3 in the list above) married ROBERT BOWEN, 1 Feb 1963. Children: 1) STEPHEN, 2) TRACY.

* * *

LYMAN LEONARD FOSTER, 3rd child of ELIPHLET and CINDA (REED) FOSTER, married more than once and had children. He lives in Grand Junction, Colorado, but I have no further data.

ABRAHAM LINCOLN FOSTER, Uncle Link, 4th child of SILAS J. & RACHEL (BILLS) FOSTER, was born in Knox Co., Missouri. He went to Circleville, Kansas with his parents, then to Haddam, and later to the old Solomon River settlement. In the old Adell area, he met and married #1, FANNIE KRESSLER. She took whooping cough during childbirth and both mother and child died.

ABRAHAM LINCOLN FOSTER married #2, HANNAH J. McMULLEN in Hoxie, KS. He farmed, built a lot of homes and ran a livery stable while living on the Solomon. Uncle Link, like all his brothers, was very handy with tools, being especially good at finish carpenter work.

Dad has told of the time when his father had moved to Dresden, KS in 1895, and his Uncle Link came over to help build their new home. One night Dad and his brothers were sleeping on a pile of lumber. It was the morning of 4th of July, and Uncle Link decided to awaken the boys with a giant firecracker. When Uncle Link tossed the firecracker it hit a tree branch over the bed, and fell on the boy's bedding. Uncle Link made a grab for the firecracker and it exploded before he could let go of it. Due to firecracker burns, Uncle Link handled his hammer and saws very tenderly for the next few days, and took a lot of ribbing from family and friends.

Lincoln ran his livery stable and did carpentering in Adell, until the promised railroad ended in Lenora, Kansas, twelve miles to the east. Lincoln moved to La Crosse, KS, where he finished out his live. Lincoln & Hannah Foster are buried one mile east of La Crosse, Kansas.

ABRAHAM LINCOLN FOSTER b. 28 Apr 1861 d. 1 Jun 1917
HANNAH (McMULLEN) b. 11 Oct 1865 d. 2 Feb 1941
Married 23 Feb 1884, Kansas. Children:

1. LULA GRACE b. 23 Jan 1885 d. 28 Apr 1941
2. LAWRENCE HAROLD b. 21 Nov 1888 d. Mar 1961
3. LeROY BENTON b. 29 Jul 1890 d. 1972
4. ADDIE RUDOLPHUS b. 17 Mar 1892
5. MILDRED MALINDA b. 19 Jun 1894 d. 8 Dec 1958
6. DELLA MAE b. 21 May 1899
7. one child died as an infant

LULA GRACE FOSTER married WILLIAM E. HALL 24 Dec 1914. Their children: 1) WILLIAM EDWARD Jr., 2) VENITA MAE, who married a Mr. POLLYARD.

LAWRENCE HAROLD FOSTER (#2 above) married ANNA LeVAN. They lived in Independence, Missouri, where Lawrence worked for a railroad Co. They had a son: ROBERT E.

LeROY BENTON FOSTER MARRIED MARIE ZIMMERMAN, who was born in 1892. They lived in La Crosse, KS until his death in a Wichita hospital. In 1972 I was unable to contact Marie, so I don't know where she now lives, nor where LeRoy is buried, but probably in La Crosse, KS.

Once LeRoy told me of a visit he made to his grandfather in Dresden, KS, when he lived with his parents on the Solomon River. It was a Sunday and LeRoy, while knowing better, decided to target a shotgun. At the blast his Grandfather Silas J. Foster came boiling out of the house and read the riot act. Silas J. enjoyed guns and hunting as much as anyone, but Sunday belonged to the Lord. LeRoy didn't wait for his dinner, but hiked the 9 miles home at once. But he eventually got over his hurt feelings, long before he told me the story.

MILDRED MALINDA FOSTER, 5th child of ABRAHAM LINCOLN & HANNAH (McMULLEN) FOSTER, married FREDERICK H. BARNES and lived in Wichita, Kansas, where their daughter Marjorie still lives. Mildred's sister, ADDIE RUDOLPHUS, also lives there in a rest home. She never married.

FREDERICK BARNES b. 26 Jan 1888
MILDRED (FOSTER) b. 19 Jun 1894 d. 8 Dec 1958
Were married 17 May 1916, Kansas. Children:

1. MARJORIE EDITH who married Mr. SPIVEY
2. DOROTHY ADDIE who married Mr. DREBENSTEDT

* * *

DELLA MAE FOSTER, 6th child of ABRAHAM LINCOLN & HANNAH (McMULLEN) FOSTER, married ALVA CARSON 29 Aug 1920. Their children: 1) DONALD MERLE, 2) MARJORIE MARIE, who married MR. BROWN and had DORIS MAE who married a Mr. PUCKETT. Chart p. 210

* * *

ANNA ARIZONA (Aunt Zona), 5th child of SILAS JACKSON & RACHEL (BILLS) FOSTER, was born near Circleville, KS. She went with her parents to Haddam, and later to the old Solomon River settlement. Here she grew to adulthood and married Rev. GEORGE WASHINGTON ROWLAND. As noted in the Sod Shanty chapter, they knew one another in Haddam, Kansas, and George had come to the Solomon River settlement with her family.

George was a United Brethren minister, in the same conference as his brother-in-law F. J. Foster. George's first assignment was in Sheridan and Graham Co., Kansas. Later he was assigned to Burlington, Colorado. In those days preaching was a non-paying job, but I don't what George did for a living. (Note: the 1900 US Federal Census for

Lyon, Decatur, Kansas lists George Rowland as a farmer who was born in New York, along with both of his parents.) George died and is buried in the Burlington, Colorado Cemetery.

GEORGE ROWLAND b. 5 Feb 1853 d. 11 Apr 1916
ANNA ARIZONA (FOSTER) b. 26 Jun 1865 d. 29 Apr 1958
Married 26 Jun 1883, Kansas. Child: JAMES ARTHUR b. 18 Apr 1898 d. 1972.

JAMES ARTHUR ROWLAND was born and grew to manhood on his father's Solomon River homestead. In Norton, Kansas, he met and married MINNIE GEORGIA UPHOFF. As noted in the birthplaces of their children they did a lot of moving about, ending up in Colorado Springs. During WWII they lived in Boone, Colorado, where Arthur worked for the US Army. Arthur died in a Colorado Springs rest home, and both he and Minnie are buried in the Evergreen Cemetery, Colorado Springs, Colorado.

JAMES ARTHUR ROWLAND b. 18 Apr 1898 d. 1972
MINNIE GEORGIA (UPHOFF) b. 8 Dec 1897 d. 12 Feb 1959
Married 22 Dec 1916, Kansas. Children:

1. GEORGE WASHINGTON b. 6 Dec 1917
2. CLEO EILEEN b. 15 Sep 1919
3. GAIL ARTHUR b. 20 Oct 1921 d. 4 Sep 1950
4. LORAINE AGNES b. 16 Feb 1924
5. EDWIN LYLE b. 3 Mar 1926
6. WYNONA MAY b. 12 Sep 1927
7. MERLE GENE b. 19 Jun 1931 (twin)
8. EARL DEAN b. 19 Jun 1931 (twin)
9. GLENN and EDNA FLORENCE died in infancy.

GEORGE WASHINGTON ROWLAND was born in Dresden, KS, and went with his parents to Colorado Springs, where he met and married IRENE WYBLE in April 1940. She was born 26 Sep 1921. They live in Huntington Beach, California, and have three children.

* * *

CLEO EILEEN ROWLAND (#2 above) was born in Fairbury, Nebraska and married ERAL RAY MURR 12 May 1940. They have a daughter.

* * *

GAIL ARTHUR ROWLAND (#3 above) was born in Mundon, Kansas and married in Las Vegas, New Mexico to BETTY JEAN ALEXANDER. During WWII he served in the Air Force. After the birth of a daughter eh and Betty divorced. He died in Mesa, Arizona, and is buried in the military lot, Evergreen Cemetery, Colorado Springs, Colorado.

* * *

LORAINE AGNES ROWLAND (#4 above) was born in Colorado Springs and married in Castle Rock, CO to EDWARD BUFMACK on 4 May 1942. He was born in Colorado Springs 20 Dec 1920. Edwards was a C.S. employee at the Ordinance Depot, Pueblo, Colorado. They have a daughter.

* * *

EDWIN LYLE ROWLAN (#5 above) was born in Silida, CO and served in the Marines during WWII, and now lives a bachelor's life in Colorado Springs. He married #1, MARJORIE JANE RANDALL and they separated after the birth of a son. Edwin L. married #2, BILLIE ANN BOLTON in 1948 and this marriage also ended in divorce after the birth of a son.

* * *

WYNOMA MAY was born in Colorado Springs, CO and married #1, RICHARD DALE BUNCH. They too, divorced after the birth of a son. Wynoma M. married #2, RICHARD ELMER BROWN. This marriage – yes, you have guessed it – also ended in divorce after the birth of a son. Today Wynoma lives in Washington, D.C. with her two sons. (1972)

* * *

MERLE GENE ROWLAND, 7th child of JAMES ARTHUR and MINNIE G. (UPHOFF) ROWLAND, was born in Penrose, a suburb of Colorado Springs and served in the US Army during the Korean conflict. In Boone, Colorado, he married DOROTHY JEAN STICE 5 Jun 1953. They live-in Portland, Oregon, and had 3 sons and a daughter.

* * *

EARL DEAN ROWLAND, 8th child of JAMES ARTHUR and MINNIE G. (UPHOFF) ROWLAND, the twin of Merle Gene above, also served in the Army during Korea. He married GEORGIA ANN SCHAFFER in Pueblo, Colorado 14 Sep 1952. They live-in Colorado Springs and have a son and two daughters.
(All the above data was correct in 1972. I have no names of children.) Family chart p. 210.

* * * * *

EMMA FLORENCE FOSTER, 6th child of SILAS JACKSON & RACHEL (BILLS) FOSTER, was born near Circleville, Kansas, made the swing to Haddam, then to the old Solomon River settlement. In now-gone Adell, KS, Emma met and –much to her sorrow—married WILLIAM ALVA COLEMAN.

William Alva, half-brother of Rev. James Arthur Rowland, but here the similarity ended. While J. Arthur was an honest, quiet family man, William A. liked to roam around the country doing nothing, yet at the same time expecting a work-free living. This attitude drove him through at least four marriages, mainly because William took out his frustrations on his family. By his first wife, unnamed, who died, William A. had: 1) EDNA, 2) FRANCES.

EMMA F. and William hadn't been married long when she discovered that he did slight-of-hand tricks with other people's property. This habit soon soured their neighbors wherever they moved – to Montana, back to Kansas, several places in Kansas, Nebraska, then back to Kansas. After this last return, Emma, who liked friendly neighbors, church services and a permanent home, had had it. She gave William the word, "No more gallivantin' around the country for her and the children."

For about 18 months things went along, then one Sunday Emma and her children went to church with her father, S. J. Foster. During the service all the harnesses from the teams disappeared –and William too. In 1914 William's son Maurice was visiting his uncle Rowland in Burlington, Colo., when he learned his father had just left. Hurrying out on the prairie, Maurice, the last of the family to see William, had a short visit with his father.

EMMA F. married #2, FRANK LEE DALLY, and moved to Colorado Springs, where she died. Frank died and is buried in Blue Rapids, Kansas. Emma F. is buried with her parents and relatives in the Dresden, KS, Cemetery. They had no children.

WILLIAM ALVA COLEMAN b. 17 Dec 1860
EMMA FLORENCE (FOSTER) b. 22 Jan 1868 d. 2 Dec 1927
Were married 20 Dec 1887, KS. To this union were born:

1. ALVA WILLIAM b. 10 Dec 1888 d. 29 Jul 1978
2. MAURICE CLINTON b. 28 Dec 1893 d. 17 Jun 1973

ALVA WILLIAM COLEMAN was born in Kalispell, Montana, and spent his early years shifting from one place to another with his parents until his mother settled them in the old Solomon River settlement. Here Alva W. met and married NEVA BLACK. For many years they lived in Allison, Kansas, where Alva owned and ran a blacksmith shop. In 1950 Alva & Neva retired in Oberlin, KS, where both died and are buried in the Foster section of the Dresden, KS, Cemetery.

During his last years Alva made small concrete markers and placed them old neighbor's unmarked graves in the old Adell and the Dresden, Kansas cemeteries.

ALVA COLEMAN b. 10 Dec 1888 d. 29 Jul 1978 – the last of Dad's generation.
NEVA (BLACK) b. 1 Apr 1893 d. 17 Apr 1969
Married 30 Aug 1911, Kansas. Child: ROBERT b. 28 Oct 1914.

ROBERT COLEMAN (child above) was born in Allison, Kansas, married a neighborhood girl, #1 GEORGIA L. RHODES. In a few years Robert got to hitting the bottle so strong that Georgia finally left him. Both have since remarried but I have no information on either of them.

ROBERT COLEMAN b. 27 Oct 1914
GEORGIA (RHODES) b. 8 Jun 1923
Married 1939, Hoxie, Kansas. Children: 1) VIRGINIA LEA, 2) ROBERT Jr., 3) JERRY WAYNE.

* * *

MAURICE CLINTON, 2nd child of WILLIAM & EMMA (FOSTER) COLEMAN, was born in North Platte, Nebraska and came with his parents to the old Solomon River settlement. Here Maurice grew to manhood, and at the age of 28 ran off with another man's wife. The other man didn't seem to have been too put-out, but freed his wife and let him keep their daughter. Maurice then married her, #1 ELIZABETH RANDLE, formerly BLACK, sister to Alva W.'s wife, Neva Black.

For many years Maurice farmed along the Solomon River valley, then retired to Oberlin, Kansas Here they divorced and Maurice remarried, and his second wife still lives in Oberlin's low-rent project. Maurice and Elizabeth (Black) Coleman are buried in Oberlin, Kansas, side-by-side.

MAURICE CLINTON COLEMAN b. 28 Dec 1893 d. 17 Jun 1973
ELIZABETH (BLACK) b. 1893 d. 1941
Married 22 Sep 1922, Kansas. Children:

1. DOROTHY M. b 18 May 1923, who married ROBERT HANSON and has at least two children.
2. DeLORES MAXINE b. 26 Feb 1925, married CLAYTON MANROE, and has at least two children but I have no names for either family.

Leaning back in my chair, taking a few puffs from a fresh cigar, I had a thought. Since our introduction to WILLIAM the Elder and HANNAH FOSTER we have become acquainted with a whole host of their descendants. I wonder! If we were put head-to-toe, would we span the United States from their Virginia foothold to California's shore and beyond, where their descendants have trod?
* * * * *
SARAH MARGARET (Aunt Sade) FOSTER, 7th child of Rev. SILAS J. & RACHEL (BILLS) FOSTER, was born on a farm near Haddam, Kansas. She was just a toddler when her parents loaded her into a covered wagon and headed west. They stopped off on the north fork of the Solomon River, where he uncle and aunt, Hilbert & Mary-Etta Johnson had homesteaded. After looking the country over her father selected a likely-looking piece of land, which he homesteaded.

While quite young, Sarah and two of her younger nieces wandered off onto the prairie, giving their parents quite a scare. The land was still wild, and memory of the last Indian raid still fresh in every one's mind. Luckily, her father found Sarah's tracks in a fresh mole hill, and the children were found just after sundown.

Sarah M. grew to adulthood in the old Solomon River settlement, where she met and married Franklin W. McLure, and their children were born. Franklin was a farmer and well digger, and found plenty of work for several years, before moving to Marshall Co., Kansas.

Later Sarah M. and Franklin divorced, and he disappeared. Sarah got the children and continued to live in Marshall Co., till her death. Sarah M. and her son Morrill are buried in the Foster section of the Dresden, Kansas, Cemetery. Her son, Glenn died at his son's home in Texas, where he is buried

FRANKLIN McLURE b. 30 Apr 1873
SARAH (FOSTER) b. 26 Jan 1873 d. 13 Oct 1918
Married 21 Nov 1891, Kansas. Children:

1. MORRILL EDMUND b. 27 Nov 1894 d. 8 Jan 1927
2. GLENN b. 25 Jul 1898

Let's finish this family on the next page.

MORRILL EDMUND McLURE married BESSIE GERTRUDE SMITH and lived in east Kansas. In mind-January of 1927 they were visiting in Dresden, Kansas. In the afternoon of the 8th, Morrill and his cousin, Alf Foster decided to go coyote hunting. They loaded Alf's coyote dogs into his Model T-Ford pickup, and with a bottle to ward off the numbing cold, they set out.

They were driving across a wheat field when they saw a coyote too far for the dogs to see. Alf opened the old Ford up and was bouncing and racing across the snow-covered ground when suddenly they hit a weed-overgrown ditch. The Model T-Ford flipped, trapping them under the car, but contact with the frozen ground had put both to sleep. When Alf came to he found that his faithful dogs had almost freed him, and he was soon out, and freed Morrill. But for Morrill E. it was too late. Gas from the under-seat tank had penetrated his clothing, and Morrill E. froze to death.

MORRILL EDMUND McLURE B. 27 Nov 1894 d. 8 Jan 1927
BESSIE GERTRUDE (SMITH) b. 26 Apr 1900
Married 20 Nov 1916, Kansas.

They had children but after Morrill's death it seems Bessie chose to avoid any contact with her Foster relatives, so I have no data.
* * *
GLENN McLURE, 2nd child of FRANKLIN and SARAH (FOSTER) McLURE, married DIXIE JONES of Dresden, Kansas, and made his home in Colorado for many years. He finally retired to a home in Texas with his son, where he died. I have no data on his family either, and none of those I have contacted know anything about him.
Chart pgs. 210-211
* * * * *
RUDOLPHUS DORCAS JANE (Aunt Dolph), youngest child of SILAS J. & RACHEL (BILLS) FOSTER, was born near Haddam, Kansas, and went with her parents to the Solomon River settlement. Here she grew to adulthood, met and married CLARENCE ALBERT LOWRY, in Dresden, Kansas.

They lived first in Brown Valley, Minnesoto, then South Dakota, then back to Kansas, then to California, then to Buhl, Idaho. Aunt Dolph lived her last years near her daughter Ruby in Buhl, Idaho, where she died of a heart attack. Clarence died in San Bernadino, Calif. and both buried in the Buhl, Idaho, Cemetery.

CLARENCE ALBERT LOWRY b. 17 Sep 1874 d. 13 Nov 1946
RUDOLPHUS DORCAS (FOSTER) b. 25 Jan 1876 d. 14 Oct 1963
Married 20 May 1900, Kansas. Children:

1. CLYDE MELVIN b. 9 Sep 1902 m. EDNA BLANCH
2. CASSEL HERMAN b. 18 Nov 1904 m. VIOLA HEJTMANEK
3. ORVILL HARLEY b. 9 May 1907 d. 18 Dec 1973
4. RACHEL ANN b. 28 Sep 1913 d. 13 May 1920 (drowned)
5. RUBY GRACE B. 20 May 1919

ORVILL HERMAN LOWRY married LOUISE, and had: 1) KENT, who married and divorced #1? and had a son, MARK. KENT married #2, IRENE, and had: 1) DAVID, 2) TERESA. (They may be her children by a previous marriage.)

RUBY GRACE LOWRY (#5 above) married WESLEY RAY HAGDORN. They live in Buhl, Idaho, where their children were born.

WESLEY RAY HAGDORN
RUBY GRACE (LOWRY) b. 20 May 1919
Married 20 May 1937, Idaho. Children: 1) NONA JEAN, 2) FONTAINE RAY.

NORMA JEAN HAGDORN married PAUL J. JONES 13 Jul 1957. They live in Norriston, PA, and have: 1) RONALD ALLEN, 2) RICHARD BRIAN.

FONTAINE R. married ELIZABETH OLSON 20 Jun 1969 in Minnesota. They live in Portland, Oregon, and have: 1) AMY KATE, 2) AARON ALEXANDER. This family now lives in Twin Falls, Idaho.

Except for their son Flavius J. whose chapter begins on p. 249. this ends my material on the families of SILAS J. & RACHEL (BILLS) FOSTER.

* * * * *THE JOHNSON-SPILLMAN FAMILY * * * * *

ELIPHLET CUTTING JOHNSON married LAURA H. TYRRELL in Ohio, where he engaged in farming. In 1864 the family moved to Kansas and settled in Republic County, a few miles west of Haddam, KS. In 1877 Laura's brother, Henry Tyrell, took up a homestead in western Kansas, to be joined a year later by their son, Hilbert Johnson (who married Mary-Etta Foster, dau. of Silas and Rachel Foster). On September 27, 1887, Eliphlet joined them in the Solomon River settlement. As noted in the Sod Shanty chapter, the Johnson family arrived the day before the Indians came. It was their wagon, loaded with seed oats, that was used to take the women and children to the safety of the stockade in Spring City (Lenora) Kansas.

Their six eldest children were born in Ohio, the others in Kansas. Eliphalet C. and Laura H. Johnson are buried in the old Adell Cemetery.

ELIPHLET CUTTING JOHNSON b. 5 Apr 1816 NY d. 20 Jan 1914
LAURA H. (TYRELL) b. 2 Feb 1826 d. 27 Apr 1882
Married 16 Mar 1845, Ohio. Children:

1. HILBERT b. 1 Jun 1847 d. 18 Nov 1833
2. LOUISA b. 18 Dec 1848
3. ALMIRA b. 17 Aug 1850 d. 24 Aug 1941
4. AMELIA b. 11 Aug 1853
5. MULVINA b. 21 Dec 1854
6. MALINDA b. 27 Jan 1859
7. ELIJAH b. 29 Sep 1860 d. 10 Aug 1926
8. NEWTON b. 23 Apr 1862
9. JANE b. 11 Nov 1864 d. 8 Dec 1935
10. ELLEN b. 3 Jul 1866 d. 31 Dec 1907
11. JOB b. 10 May 1868
12. ANNA b. 30 Apr 1870 d. 9 Mar 1962

HILBERT JOHNSON married MARRY-ETTA FOSTER, p. 213.
* * *

AMELIA JOHNSON (#4 above) married JOHN OLIVER in Haddam, Kansas, and had at least two children: 1) ELIPHLET, 2) GUY. Both were born in Haddam, Kansas, and went with their parents to the old Solomon River settlement. I don't know where Eliphlet (Lifee) Johnson is buried, but both spent their lives around old Adell. In his last years, Guy returned to Haddam, KS, where he is buried.

ALMIRA JOHNSON married #1, WESTUNION SPILLMAN, whose family is given on p. 225. Almira married #2, LORENZO M. FOSTER, p. 215.

ANNA JOHNSON (#12 above) married JACOB (JAKE) SPALL b. 1851 d. 1924. After the death of her husband, Anna lived with a man who I knew only as ISSARY. ANNA & JACOB SPALL are buried in the old Adell Cemetery. To this union was born a daughter: PEARL, who married WESLEY CONAGA and had two daughters.

ELIJAH JOHNSON (#7 above) married MARY A. GILBERT, and lived in the old Solomon River settlement, where all their children were born. All these children, except the one noted are still living. Elijah was struck on the head by lightening. The blast was so great his shoes were torn from his feet, and lay 25 feet from his body. Yet the man lived for 36 hours after being struck. I don't know where (unless it would be in the Adell Cemetery) Elijah and Mary Johnson are buried. But there are no stones for them in this cemetery.

ELIJAH JOHNSON b. 29 Sep 1860 d. 10 Aug 1926
MARY (GILBERT) b. 15 Mar 1866 d. 23 Mar 1947
Married 1885 Kansas. Children:

1. JESSIE MILTON b. 26 May 1886
2. ERNEST WARNER b. 29 Feb 1888
3. MAUDIE MAY b. 6 Jan 1890
4. NETTIE AMELIA b. 9 Feb 1892

5. CHARLES HILBERT b. 12 Jan 1894
6. GOLDIE JOSEPHINE b. 27 May 1897 d. 21 Jul 1958
7. GLADYS ANNA b. 18 Dec 1901
8. MYRTLE JOAN b. 23 Sep 1905

ERNEST WARNER JOHNSON (# 2 above) never married and now lives in Hoxie, KS. They have children who could be traced if one so desires.

CHARLES HILBERT (# 5 above) married and lives in Gove, Kansas. They too have children who could be traced.

* * * * *

WESTUNIO SPILLMAN was born in Indiana, and Immigrated to Kansas, settling just over the county line in Republic County, west of where Haddam now stands. Her he met and married Almira Johnson, who was born in Ohio (daughter of Eliphalet Cutting and Laura (Tyrell) Johnson.

On Christmas Eve, 1880, the family were gathered in the living room of their log cabin. A gentle snowfall blanketed the Spillman homestead, and the only window in the cabin, a hinged chunk cut from the logs, was closed against the cold-- A family at peace with world. Suddenly the log window was pushed aside, a shot rang out, and Westunion fell dead.

Footprints were later found in the new snow, leading to the window, then retreating through a cornfield. The size and shape of the tracks, and the direction of their coming and going, plus the fact there had been hard feelings between the two men, led to a man named Slover being accused of the crime. Some of those now living way that he was never brought to trial, but others say Slover spent time in the Pen.

Later, Almira took her family to the Solomon River settlement. Here she met and married #2, Lorenzo Milton Foster. This second family is given on page 215. Due to this second marriage, and intermarriage of the two families, some interesting relationships resulted.

Westunion Spillman is buried in Washington Co., KS. Almira is buried in the Adell, KS Cemetery with her 2nd husband.

WESTUNION SPILLMAN b. Mar 1845 d. 24 Dec 1880
ALMIRA (JOHNSON) b. 17 Aug 1850 d. 24 Aug 1941
Were married 1 Jan 1866, Kansas. Children:

1. JAMES RICHARD b. 26 Nov 1866 d. 20 Jul 1941
2. LaVINA ROSELLA b. 1 Nov 1870 d. 7 May 1947
3. FRANKLIN ELKANAH b. 11 Nov 1875 d. 24 May 1956

JAMES RICHARD SPILLMAN was born near Haddam, KS and went with his mother to the Solomon River settlement. Her he met and married LYDIA E., the daughter of

JAMES M. & SARAH PETERS. Both are buried in the Adell, KS Cemetery, in fact all four of them are.

JAMES RICHARD SPILLMAN b. 26 Nov 1866 d. 20 Jul 1941
LYDIA E. (PETERS) b. 19 Jan 1870 d. 7 Nov 1949
Married 11 Dec 1887, Kansas. Children:

1. ROY F. b. 27 Aug 1895 d. 27 Oct 1970
2. RAY E. b. 16 Mar 1898

ROY F. SPILLMAN married NAOMI TOWNSEND in Hoxie, Kansas 5 Sep 1917. No children were born to this union but they adopted a daughter:-- JENNIE ELIZABETH, who married CLINTON UFFORD (see p. 212). Naomi Spillman lives with the Ufford family in Kansas City, KS. Roy F. is buried in the Hoxie, Kansas, Cemetery.

RAY E. SPILLMAN (#2 above) married MERNA BATCHELDER, but they have since separated. Both live in Hoxie, Kansas. For many years they farmed land about a mile south of the north fork of the Solomon River, and 1 mile east of today's Highway #23. The old red brick house still stands and their son Doren likes to show his friends the old home he grew up in.

RAY E. SPILLMAN b. 16 Mar 1898
MERNA (BATCHELDER) b. 1 Sep 1902
Married 19 Apr 1922, Kansas. Children:

1. LLOYD RAY b. 26 May 1923
2. ARLAN B. b. 14 Feb 1925
3. DOREN ARTHUR b. 18 Nov 1926
4. LOIS EVELYN b. 27 Feb 1935
5. WILMA NADINE b. 15 Mar 1938

ARLAN B. (#2 above) married OPAL MAE FOSTER (p. 166), daughter of WESLEY & ETHEL (HINES) FOSTER, and granddaughter of ANDREW JACKSON & LaVINA ROSA (SPILLMAN) FOSTER. They live in Hoxie, Kansas where Opal is a hospital dietician.

ARLAN B. SPILLMAN b. 14 Feb 1925
OPAL MAY (FOSTER) b. 3 Aug 1928
Were married 8 Jan 1948, Kansas. Children:

This family of Spillmans have spilled over onto pg. 231. – see 'em.

1. SHIRLEY JEAN b. 4 Dec 1948
2. SHARON KAY b. 22 Nov 1949
3. RICHARD ARLAN b. 19 Aug 1952

* * *

DOREN ARTHUR SPILLMAN, son of RAY E. & MERNA (BATCHELDER) SPILLMAN, was born, raised, and has lived most of his life in the Hoxie, Kansas area. He is a WWII veteran and now owns and runs a Phillips 66 service station in Hoxie on Highway #24. He is married to DORIS JEAN FOSTER, p. 166, daughter of WESLEY and ETHEL (HINES) FOSTER.

Doris Jean and Opal May Foster are sisters. They were born in Lucerne, Kansas and got their elementary schooling in the old Adell area. The school and community is known as McGraw. The old school building was used by Grandpa F. J. Foster as a church. My sister, Irene taught school there, and one 3-day period when she was sick, during the "Dirty Thirties," our mother, Pearl Foster taught her last time there. This old school is now a community hall, still serving people, as it did in the old days.

DOREN ARTHUR SPILLMAN b. 18 Nov 1926
DORIS JEAN (FOSTER) b. 10 Dec 1930
Married 15 Feb 1947, Kansas. Children:

1. NORA MAE
2. WESLEY RAY
3. PAULA FAY
4. JEFFRY ALAN

NORA MAE (#1 above) has been married and divorced and is living in Oklahoma City with her two children.
WESLEY RAY (#2 above) married in June of 1971. He served his time in Viet Nam
* * * * *
LaVINA ROSELLA SPILLMAN married ANDREW JACKSON FOSTER, son of Aaron Blueford and Eliza Jane (Foster) Foster, and their family is given on p. 158.

* * * * *
FRANKLIN ELKENAH SPILLMAN, 3rd child of Westunion and Almira (Johnson) Spillman, was born in the old log cabin in Republic Co., and came to the Solomon River Settlement with his mother. Here he met and married MARGARET ANN PETERS. She is the sister of Lydia E. Peters and the widow of Aaron Brown Foster, p. 189. Franklin and Margaret made their homes in old Adell and Hoxie, KS, and finally in Craig, Colorado. Here Franklin died and both he and Margaret Spillman are buried in Lenora, Kansas.

FRANKLIN SPILLMAN b. 11 Nov 1875 d. 24 May 1956
MARGARET (PETERS) B. 5 Nov 1871 d. 10 Oct 1951
Married 27 Apr 1897, Kansas. Children:

1. AMOS J. 15 Mar 1903 d. 29 Oct 1959
2. GLENN R. b. 6 Aug 1904 d. 24 Jul 1968

AMOS J. SPILLMAN married and divorced. The wife, name unknown, got their child and moved to Waterloo, Iowa. The child: LOIS.

AMOS J. married #2 FLORA, a widow with a child. To this union were born: 1) AARON, 2) MARGARET, 3) FRANKLIN, 4) MYRA, 5) GLENN.

During a family argument Amos killed both his wife and himself. The children were split up, the girls going to one home, two of the boys to another, and the youngest boy to still a third home. They were raised by three different families.

The stupidity, childishness, and bitter arguments of parents, and drunkenness in the home, have caused more anguish among children than can ever be told. These parents don't deserve children!!

* * *

GLENN R. SPILLMAN, 2nd son of FRANKLIN and MARGARET (PETERS) SPILLMAN, was born and grew to adulthood in the Hoxie, Kansas area. Here too, he met and married MYRTLE FERN AUMILLER. In the 1940's Glenn R. moved his family to Hutchinson, KS. Here Glenn R. worked for the Kansas Oxygen Inc. for over 20 years. Myrtle Fern and least one daughter still live in Hutchinson, KS, where Glenn R. is buried in the Fairlawn Cemetery.

Myrtle Fern gave the material on Franklin & Margaret's family.

GLENN R. SPILLMAN b. 6 Aug 1904 d. 24 Jun 1968
MYRTLE (FERN) AUMILLER b. 19 Dec 1905
Married 3 Sep 1924, KS. Children:

Again the Spillman family has spilled over onto another page.

1. CORA FERN
2. NORMAN GLENN
3. FRANKLIN UDELL
4. ARDITH ANNIE
5. RONALD CLAY
6. CAROLYN GWEN
7. STANTON BOYD

CORA FERN married #1 PAUL E. STAPLETON, whom she divorced. On 4 Oct 1961 she married #2 WARREN FORREST RUDE in Miami, Oklahoma. They live in Wichita, KS, where Warren runs a nation-wide mobile home transportation service, with Cora F. acting as flagman. Warren was born 10 Jun 1927. They have no children.

PAUL E. STAPLETON b. 26 May 1920
CORA F. (SPILLMAN) b. 30 Sep 1925
Married 24 May 1941, KS. Children:

1. LANDRA JOY
2. CORA JEAN
3. DENNY PAUL
4. LARRY LYNN

LANDRA JOY married GARY L. McKENNA in Raton, New Mexico 12 Jun 1961. Landra J. all her children were born in Hutchinson, KS, where Gary L. is employed by the Kelly Flour Mill Co. Their children: 1) JERRY D., 2) MARK ALLEN, 3) GAYLA SUE, 4) LISA JOLENE.

CORA JEAN STAPLETON (#2 above) married WILLIAM HENRY BROOMER, 23 Sep 1943. He is route man for Dolly Madison Pastries, in Valley Center, a suburb of Wichita, Kansas. Their children: 1) DIANA, 2) DAVID PAUL, 3) AMY KATHLEEN.

* * *

NORMAN GLENN SPILLMAN, 2nd child of GLENN R. and MARGARET FERN (AUMILLER) SPILLMAN, was born in Selden and married in Newton, KS to DOROTHY MAE SMITH. He is a master sergeant in the Air National Guard, and has done his time in Vietnam. During his spare time he is building a sporting aircraft from the ground up, which he hopes to enter in air shows.

NORMAN GLENN SPILLMAN B. 5 Mar 1927
DOROTHY MAE SMITH b. 25 Mar 1927
Married 16 Dec 1944, Kansas. Children:

1. ANNETA LEE
2. STARR LYNN
3. KERVIN GLENN
4. MARIE ANN, died at birth.

ANNETA LEE SPILLMAN married NEIL EUGENE BONHAM 19 Dec 1964. They live in Hutchinson, Kansas, where Neil is plant superintendant for McDonald's Golden Arches Co. Anneta L. is a receptionist in the North Hospital in Hutchinson. Their children: 1) BRET EUGENE, 2) GARRETT NEIL, 3) DUSTIN LEE.

* * *

FRANKLIN UDELL SPILLMAN, 3rd child of GLENN R. and MARGARET FERN (AUMILLER) SPILLMAN, was born in Selden, Kansas and went to Hutchinson, where he met, married, and divorced #1, WILMA FAYE GILMORE, 27 Dec 1948. They had: DONALD UDELL.

DONALD UDELL SPILLMAN married DIANA LYN HUDNELL in California 3 Oct 1969. They now live in Wichita, Kansas, where Donald is employed by the Coleman Col. They have at least one child: DAWN ANGENETTA.

FRANKLIN UDELL SPILLMAN married #2, CAROL SUE LAWRENCE 30 Jul 1962 in Mulvane, Kansas. For over 20 years Franklin has been an employee of the Fleming Co. of Valley Falls, Kansas. To this union were born: 1) MICHAEL ALAN, 2) DERRIN JAMES, 3) TRACEY KYLE.

ARDITH ANNIE SPILLMAN 4th child of GLENN R. and MARGARET FERN (AUMILLER) SPILLMAN, married KENNETH RICHARD MARCUM in Hutchinson, Kansas, where all their children were born. Kenneth is employed by the Kansas Oxygen Co. of Hutchinson.

KENNETH RICHARD MARCUM b. 31 Apr 1925
ARDITH ANNIE SPILLMAN
Married 25 Nov 1948, Kansas. Children:

1. RONALD LEE
2. SHERLYN ANN
3. LARRY CRAIG
4. LORELEI DAWN
5. KENNETH SHAWN

RONALE LEE MARCUM (#1 above), an employee of Barton Salt Co. of Hutchinson, KS, married ANNA LOU SPENCER 15 Mar 1969.

* * *

RONALD CLAY SPILLMAN, 5th child of GLENN R. and MARGARET FERN (AUMILLER) SPILLMAN,
was born and raised in Hoxie, Kansas. He now lives in Hutchinson, where he is a route supervisor for Jackson Ice Cream Co., Here, he met and married GOLDIE BERNICE ORTNER 19 Mar 1955, Kansas. Children: 1) RANDY CLAY, 2) JANET RENEE.

* * *

CAROLYN GWEN SPILLMAN, 6th child of GLENN R. and MARGARET FERN (AUMILLER) SPILLMAN, born in Hoxie, KS, also ended up in Hutchinson. She has been married three times at least. Number one:

ARLEN DALE WHITFORD
CAROLYN GWEN (SPILLMAN)
Married 30 Sep 1954, Kansas. Children:

1. TERRY LYNN
2. ARLENE GWEN
3. LARRY CORDELL
4. STANTON COLE
5. CAROL LaFERN
6. DENISE LaVONNA

CAROLYN GWEN married #2, DeWAYNE CALDWELL in 1964. They had a child: ALLEN RAY.

CAROLYN GWEN married #3, CHARLES V. MILLER, in Miami, Oklahoma. They live in Hutchinson, KS, where Charles owns a string of taxicabs. All nine of Carolyn's children were born in Hutchinson, KS.

CHARLES V. MILLER b. 3 Apr 1921
CAROLYN GWENN (SPILLMAN)
Married 4 Oct 1966, Oklahoma. Children:

1. VERNON GLENN
2. CHRISTINE LYNNETTE

* * *

STANTON BOYD SPILLMAN, last child of GLENN & MARGARET FERN SPILLMAN, was born in Hoxie, KS. He later went to Hutchinson, KS, where he is employed with his brother Ronald by the Jackson Ice Cream Co., Here, he met and married LENORA LEE SPELLMAN (No! I did not hit the wrong key. Her maiden name is spelled with an 'E'). I know of no children being born to this union.

At this time and at this place I'll end the Johnson-Spillman family. Perhaps some future descendant will update this family.

* * * * * SOD SHANTY SAGA * * * * *

I WENT TO THE HILLS TODAY. – There is high ground overlooking that section of the Solomon River where Flavius Josephus Foster (F. J.) carved out his first home, and to which he brought his young wife, Margaret, "MAGGIE" to view the scenes of our childhood, where stood the sod house he had built, the cool spring from which they drank, and the sand draw where they and their children swam. All have long since gone to decay. The spring is no more, the sand draw where river water had backed up has filled with silt, and the old soddy has gone back to the earth from which it was built.

But "footprints in the sand" are not the exclusive property of great men alone. The Fosters, Johnsons, and other pioneers of the old Solomon River settlement have departed for greener pastures. But as long as there are sketches such as this, their successful challenge of this untamed land will never be completely forgotten. It was a raw land when they came, where large herds of wild beasts fed and clothed a few wandering tribes. It was their aching backs and scarred hands that turned this same land into homes and towns supporting many thousands of people.

This sketch of homesteading in northwest Kansas is a very short composite of the numerous writings of Flavius Josephus and Lorenzo Milton Foster, and of their niece, Martha (Johnson) Law. I have tried to include the most pertinent parts of their combined stories, leaving out much meaningful material. For instance, the many invasions of grasshoppers which stripped the land bare, and the many fires that swept 50 feet high over the prairie, one of which surrounded a home, killing a mother and her two daughters.

Reason Oliver, F. J. Foster's father-in-law, left Washington County to take up a homestead in newly opened Norton Co., Kansas. Their glowing accounts of their new home struck a responsive chord in the heart of F. J., who had no home for his family. He and Alonzo Mapes, who had married F. J.'s wife's sister, decided in late summer of 1877 to visit the "west" and take up land. At this time 160 acres of upland of 80 acres of bottom land could be had for improving and living on the land for three years.

Arriving at the Oliver homestead, 7 miles north of present-day Norcatur, Kansas, on Long Branch of the Sappa River, Alonzo and F. J. soon found suitable land, and set about preparing the soil for a spring crop. First, F. J. Bought a load of hard-to-find lumber and repaired an old trapper cabin for his family's new home. He then began breaking sod for his crops. Breaking sod by horse power is never easy, and the dryness of the late summer made his task doubly so, and F. J.'s breaking job left a lot to be desired.

After making as good a breaking job as possible, F. J. and Alonzo returned to their Washington County homes. Alonzo lost no time in loading his family up for the move to his claim. F. J., however, had a corn crop to harvest, and before he had completed this task a messenger arrived telling him a squatter had moved into his cabin.

So many settlers would take up a piece of land, only to abandon it for another piece, that the government made a ruling. A settler, if he wished to keep a piece of land had, to live on it for most of his 3-year contract. If he was gone longer than a short visit and a squatter moved onto the land, the settle would have to prove his claim in a court of law. Soon after this ruling a shady lawyer-squatter combine moved in. The squatter would wait until a settler had done a lot of work on a claim, then move in while the settler was absent. Then the lawyer would defend the squatter in court, and if lucky, would divide the spoils when the claim was sold. It was then that this phrase was coined, "Possession is 90% of the law."

Few settlers had money for lawsuits, most of their dealings being done by the barter system before the coming of the railroads. They just cursed and moved to another claim. Later, as free land became scarce, some claim-jumping ended in gun smoke. In 1880, '81, and '82, hot winds, drought, and an invasion of grasshoppers forced the upland settlers off their land. Then a devastating prairie fire shooting flames 50 feet high swept down both sides of the Solomon River, sending still more families fleeing. These families needed homes, and jobs to support their children.

Most of the displaced settlers returned to their old homes in eastern states, where they had friends or relatives who could help them. Many planned on returning to their claims once the long drought had subsided. But with the first rains the squatters moved in, and before the original settlers returned, they had squatted on the most improved claims.

Due to the conditions under which the settlers had left their claims, the government made another ruling.

If a settler could prove he had lived on a claim on or before June of 1880, he could reclaim his land. For those settlers whose old neighbors had returned, this proof was easy to get, but others were not so lucky. Their old neighbors never returned and they had no other proof, so they lost their land and improvements to squatters, and another phrase was coined, "June 80-proof."

In the spring of 1878, Hilbert Johnson, who had married F. J.'s sister, Mary-Etta, decided to seek free land in Western Kansas. With him went F. J.'s brothers, Leonard Milton (Tack) Foster, and their aunt, Mary Jane Foster and her children. They had planned to go to Norton County, but once underway, they decided to join Hilbert's uncle on the north fork of the Solomon River.

F.J. Foster had a preaching assignment in Washington Co., so he took over his aunt's farm on Mulberry Creek. It has been agreed that a supply of farm produce would come in handy in case the first crops failed on the hoped-for homesteads, or land could not be found. If claims were found, F. J. would join the others later in the year.

In due time the Johnson party arrived on the north fork of the Solomon River, where a small settlement had been started. Here, in the northeast corner of Sheridan County, Hilbert traded a mare to a Mr. Evans for his 80-acre claim. The Johnson family crowded into the one-man dugout where Mr. Evans had lived, while Hilbert and L.M. Foster were building a larger cabin.

In past winters, Indians had felled trees so their horses could eat the tender twigs. The Johnsons stripped the bark from the old stumps for cooking fuel, learning too late that the space between the stumps and bark was the home of numberless bedbugs. It was many moons before they were rid of the bedbugs, and years before they were able to eliminate the fleas that inhabited the area. (AAH!! Those good old days before bug sprays.)

We'd better move to page 240 before we get eaten alive.

While Hilbert and the others were building a cabin L.M. (Tack) Foster broke out ground for a garden. Here he planted watermelons, black-eye peas, and other vegetables, including squash. These were a variety of squash with hull so tough they had to be opened with an axe, but made delicious pies and were very tasty when baked. Plans were made for breaking more sod for gain in the fall, but events prevented this.

After his corn on Mulberry Creek was "laid-by," "grown too tall to cultivate," F.J. Foster decided to visit the Solomon River settlement and see what his relatives were up to. Grandpa F. J. wrote, "George Rowland, Link (his brother Lincoln), and myself took a load of ear corn to Clifton (KS), and got money we thought we would need for the trip.

Then I drove to Fairbury, Nebraska and got S. J. Foster, my father, and we were soon on the road for the far west."

"I shall never forget when we came to the big bend of the Solomon River. Father had liked the country until we reached this place. Here we got into deep sand, and he said, 'Now boys, if it is the rest of the way like this, I'm ready t turn homeward right now.'

I told him that it was only a short way through this, then we would come to solid dirt again.

Grandpa F. J.'s party arrived at the Hilbert Johnson homestead in time for a late noon meal. Next day, Hilbert took them on a land inspection trip. They traveled south as far as Bow Creek, where the land was as level as a table top, but there was no wood for building or fuel and the creek was dry half of each year. These two points decided Flavius. J. and his father Silas. J. to take out land in the Solomon River settlement.

Flavius J. Foster took out his claim in Range 27, Twp 6, Section 4 on August 4, 1878. Silas J. Foster took his homestead rights out later in the year. Grandpa Flavius' was the first homestead taken out in Sheridan County, Kansas, none of which were upland, or prairie claims. One and a half years later the county was divided into 80 and 160 acre lots with a house on each plot.

Doesn't this vivid description just send shivers up your spine? Flavius. J. and his brother Lincoln returned to Washington County to bring out his and Silas.J.'s families, but Grandpa Silas had found the prairie alive with game: rabbits, coyotes, antelope, and deer—his version of heaven on earth, which decided S. J. to remain behind.

Flavius J. got his wife and young child, Lincoln, his mother, brothers, and sisters, and in three wagons they set out for the Solomon River settlement. On their return trip they met a wagon loaded with ex-settlers. They had found homesteading too tough and with the rumor of Indian trouble they were running.

By mid-September the settlement consisted of: (by Leonard Milton Foster's count) L.H. Tyrell, H.H. Carlton, Oliver and Ira Taylor, George Miller, and Mr. Decker. These were east, or downriver from Hilbert Johnson's homestead. Upriver were: Oliver Evans, Aunt Mary Jane, F. J. Foster—who had not yet built on his claim—John Kim, Joe and Newt Lytle, Henry Bolster, Jack Leatherman, George Kious, and last, Joe Bayless. Joe ran a small store and post office known as Sheridan, Kansas. Beyond this claim there were no homes closer than the Rocky Mountains. Joe Bayless' claim was 12 miles upriver from the Hilbert Johnson homestead, and 4 miles east and ¾ of a mile south of present-day Selden, Kansas.

The settlement's nearest trading post was at Buffalo Station on the Kansas Pacific (UPRR), 30 miles south of Hilbert Johnson's place. It is today's "Park, Kansas." Their trail lay across Bow Creek to the south fork of the Solomon, where they "nooned" at Willow Grove, (now Pasco). From here they crossed the head of Saline River, and on to Buffalo Station, where they would do their trading and load their wagons for the return trip on the following day – two dawn-to-dusk days for each round-trip.

The old Texas Cattle trail came north to Buffalo Station, crossed the north fork of the Solomon River just west of Joe Bayless' place, and on north to Ogallala, Nebraska. During the spring months droves of cattle would be strung along this trail as far as the eye could see. During the dry season these drives fell to a trickle and were mostly local ranchers.

On Friday, September 26, 1878, Silas J. Foster and Hilbert Johnson arrived in Buffalo Station with a load of buffalo bones for sale. It had been rumored for a day or two that there was Indian trouble in Oklahoma. Now the men learned that a band of Cheyennes had left their Oklahoma reservation and was following the Texas Cattle Trail northward. A few hours before Hilbert and S. J. arrived word had been received that the Indians and soldiers had collided, with losses on both sides, about 30 miles southeast of Dodge City.

Although Silas and Hilbert were a little uneasy they felt sure the Indians would pass to the west of the Solomon River settlement, especially as they were paralleling the cattle trail. But they also knew that there was no guarantee that the Indians would continue on their present course. So the two men were anxious to get back home with their families in the case the Indians decided to come that way.

On arriving home on Saturday Hilbert was glad to learn that his father, Eliphlet Johnson had arrived from Republic County, Kansas, with his family. The next morning Hilbert, his brother Elijah, Leonard (Tack) Foster, and Grandpa Flavius J. decided to drive to Slab City for the mail. Slab City was on the Prairie Dog Creek, about half a mile or so east of present-day Jennings, KS.

September 28, 1878 was a Sunday, and the men were pleased to learn that a Reverend Harvey, a circuit-riding preacher, was holding a meeting in a grove of trees nearby. Grandpa Flavius J. later wrote, "We thought it quite a treat to hear a sermon in the Far West."

Of a later meeting, in old Adell, Grandpa wrote, "The meeting took place in a grove of trees. In those days, we wore our 'Sunday clothes' seven days a week. On this Sunday I had left my shoes at home. They were so shabby, I thought I'd look better without them. When the preacher asked me to take over the meeting I tried to wiggle out of it, but had to give in to his urging. I bet I was the first and maybe the last man to preach a sermon barefooted in western Kansas.

The men headed for home after the sermon, letting their team choose its own pace. Grandpa said they were singing, joking, and having a good time in the warm fall sunshine. They were within 2 miles of home when they saw a rider coming toward them waving his rifle. Thinking it was a hunter after the nine antelope feeding beside the trail, Flavius J. pulled the team to a stop. But the rider passed the herd at a full gallop and they saw that it was Hilbert's father. He yelled at them that 400 to 500 Indians were on the upper part of the river killing and looting (according to a later count, there were 89 braves and 129 women and children.)

Martha Johnson, Hilbert's daughter, described the events leading up to this time thus: "Grandpa Johnson had heard the postmaster of Sheridan (Joe Bayless) say that if the Indians were coming his way the government would let him know. He was 30 miles from the telegraph office and must have been pretty ignorant to thing a warning could reach him before the Indians could. While Grandfather was telling this, a man raced into the yard on a lathered horse. Our women folk were cooking squash and antelope meat for dinner when all was forgotten in the excitement caused by this man's message. He told that hundreds of Indians were at the Bayless claim, killing livestock and people alike. While Grandfather Johnson and the women got a team of horses hitched up for a retreat downriver, Grandpa Silas J. Foster went looking for the children, who were found at the Old Sand Draw baptizing weeds in a mock-revival meeting. Everything was in an uproar and everyone was all thumbs. First we hitched the team to a disabled wagon left at the house for repairs. We then hitched the team to Grandfather Johnson's wagon, but the horses refused to pull. It was then we learned that we had put their collars on wrong. Finally we got going. We went downriver to Uncle Tyrell's claim, where the men folk who had gone to Slab City met us."

Contrary to popular belief, not all the men who moved into a frontier settlement carried firearms. The man who gave the Johnsons warning of the Indians' presence begged them for a gun for protection, as he had none. The man who left the wagon at the Johnsons for repair was killed by the Indians when they raided the Prairie Dog Creek homesteads.

Because Grandma Margaret was carrying her second child it was decided that Grandpa Flavius J. Foster would take the women and children to Spring City (Lenora, Kansas). Once on the road the team seemed to be pulling unusually hard. Digging through the blankets, they found the wagon loaded with seed oats that Grandfather Johnson had brought west to sell to the settlers. The horses were to eat well, but the noon meal had been left uneaten on the stove and there was only bread and coffee for the human cargo.

Most of the men left in the settlement mounted horses and set off upriver to keep an eye on the Indians. They advanced slowly westward under the leadership of Silas J. Foster, who had been a captain of Militia during the Civil War, until they came to a north-south ridge that changed the course of the river to the south, then back west. From this ridge they had a sweeping view of the valley for two miles to the west. They could see the Indians looting the Bayless homestead. They had killed a calf and some chickens which the squaws were cooking over a big fire.

Meanwhile, L.M. Tack Foster was on his way to the Prairie Dog settlements to warn the settlers there. Uncle Tack relates, "I met Oliver and Ira Taylor a few miles north of the Solomon. There I let them convince me that the Indians would be on the Prairie Dog long before I could get there. So I was returning with them when we sighted a moving mass of animals against the tree line. I felt sure they were loose cattle, but the Taylor boys insisted they were Indians. They took to the east, leaving me alone.

The "moving" was cattle, which I learned later had been abandoned by the cowboys when they learned that Indians were in the area. I crossed the Solomon and followed the south ridge west until I came to a dugout (home). Here, I re-crossed the river to the north bank due south of Dresden, Kansas. Soon after crossing the river I heard some shots. I stopped a bit, then continued my ride, but very carefully. Soon I saw a group of men about a mile away. I stopped and waited to see if they were white, or the noble Redman. One of the men walked to one side of the group and waved me in. The first man I met was father (Silas. J. Foster). I asked, "Are there any Indians beyond the ridge?"

"Yes, you can see them yonder. They shot at something a few minutes ago, but we don't know what. We learned later that two land seekers had ridden up on the Indians, unaware of their presence. Before they could turn their buggy and get out of range one of the Indians shots had hit a Mr. Young. The buggy escaped but Mr. Young died that night on the Prairie Dog."

Joe Bayless gave the following description of the Indians' arrival on his homestead, where they were entertaining:

> "It was the noon hour and one of the Bayless boys was looking out the door.
> "Daddy, there are some little boys up the draw."
> "Get back to the table," his father ordered. "There are no boys out there."
> "I know there are some boys up the draw," the boy insisted, "and they have some things that are shining."
> Then Joe remembered the Indian rumors. Looking where his son pointed Joe saw a band of Indians watering their horses in an old buffalo wallow about half a mile away. There was a mad scramble as the family and visitors loaded up and fled upriver. Joe remained behind until the Indians were less than 200 yards from his home, then he fled." (Note: Thank heavens for kids who stand their ground when adults ignore them)

After they had eaten, the Indians moved downriver, where they looted the homes of Jack Leatherman and George Kious. The latter claim was less than a half-mile from the ridge where the settlers were forted up, but the Indians seemed satisfied to remain where they were. During the late evening some of the settlers advanced nearer to the Indians' camp. A scout decided that the Indians would remain where they were during the night.

Feeling that the Indians would continue their northward march, the settlers decided to return to their homes and care for their livestock. Returning to his claim, Silas J. Foster lit a lantern so he could see to milk his cow. A man who had remained in the area—not knowing the situation—thought the light meant Indians and set off afoot downriver. By daylight he had arrived in Spring City, but his walk was for nothing. The Indians were well on their way north by that time.

The settlers' families returned home the next day, but in a few days another Indian alert sent them scurrying to the protection of Spring City. This alert proved to be false, as did two later ones. The Indian raid and the false alerts caused much distress in the ranks of the settlers, especially the women and children. Then it was learned that the false alerts were being sent out by a rancher who wanted the settler's land. A delegation of settlers paid this rancher a visit: "Any more false reports and someone would hang." (This rancher's name was Mr. Bacon)

It was during this period that Grandpa Flavius J. Foster was cutting fire wood one day. Frost had killed the leaves, which fell thickly on the ground, covering a long branch. In moving about, Grandpa stepped on one end of this branch. The other end sprang out of its leafy cover with a sinister rustle. "I thought of Indians. I must have jumped higher that time than I was able to jump before or since."

Later the country filled with settlers but hard times continued to plague them. The Fosters and Johnsons had a hard first winter because they had not had time to prepare for it. They made several trips to Buffalo Park with buffalo bones or wood for sale, as well as two trips back to Washington County, where they had some grain crops. Most of these trips were made in zero temperature weather, when they had to walk beside their wagons to keep from freezing. Many days their families subsided on cornmeal gravy and potatoes, with whole wheat bread and no meat or fruit.

In listening to their tales of hardship, I can only marvel at their perseverance. When drought, prairie fire, or grasshopper plagues hit and sent other settlers scurrying, the Fosters and Johnsons held on by grit alone. Their tales and writings took me beyond the grey hair and flowing beards, their work-bent backs and gnarled hands. Instead, I saw young supple bodies, strong, bronze faces that look on the world from eyes that feared no man nor the rigors of nature, and lips that were ready to break into a smile. They were restless young men, ready for adventure, and took great pride in wrestling homes from a reluctant wilderness.

The Fosters and Johnsons were no different than most of their neighbors, all being a product of the place and times. But since this is the Foster history, naturally theirs is the story I'm telling here.

Silas J. and his son Flavius J. Foster were preachers in the local Methodist Church, later taking up with the United Brethren in Christ Church. So too, was S. J.'s son-in-law George W. Rowlands. Beach held regular Sunday meetings, as well as revival meetings, but there was no payment for this work, so each had their living to make. Silas J. was a carpenter by trade, and many of the homes he built are still being lived in.

In 1886 F.J. Foster gave up farming to start a store in old Adell. In its heyday Adell had a general store, blacksmith shop, livery stable, and a school. It also had 3 saloons and a Temperance Hall where the church and revival meetings were held. But the fate of the town was sealed when the promised railroad ended its tracks in Spring City, now Lenora, Kansas, 12 miles to the east.

A year after starting the general store, F. J. took in his brother-in-law, Hilbert Johnson. Still later he grew tired of storekeeping and sold out to his pardner, Hilbert. F. J. then started a blacksmith shop, which he ran until 1895, at which time he moved his family to Dresden, Kansas, which had been started on what was then the new Rock Island Railroad.

A short time later Hilbert sold out the store and moved to Dresden also. Silas J. Foster had moved to Dresden when it was being built and had worked on many of the homes and shops going up. Maybe these rolling stones gathered a little moss along their tumbling paths, but they did take great pride in what they were doing.

* * * * * FLAVIUS JOSEPHUS FOSTER * * * * *

FLAVIUS JOSEPHUS, son of Rev. SILAS JACKSON & RACHEL (BILLS) FOSTER, was born in McLean Co., Illinois. At the time, his father was reading a history of the Jewish nation, written by Flavius Josephus. (Nuff said.) In 1858 Silas J. started out for Kansas territory but ran out of money in Know Co. Missouri. Before a new grubstake could be earned Silas J. was caught up in the coils of the Civil War, and it was in April of 1862 before the family arrive in Kansas.

Silas J. lived on a farm southwest of Circleville, Kansas until the spring of 1869. At that time the family moved to Washington County, settling south of present-day Haddam. KS. Here, Flavius J. grew to manhood and left his mark on a limestone rock overhanging Mulberry Creek: "F. Josephus Foster, 1872."

Here Flavius J. took up preaching and met and married MARGARET ALICE OLIVER. In the spring of 1877 Flavius J. and Margaret's brother-in-law, Alonzo Mapes, visited her parents in Norton Co., KS, where Flavius took up and lost a homestead. The following year, Flavius J., his wife, and child immigrated to the Solomon River settlement, where he took out a homestead. (Note Sod Shanty Chapter.)

Flavius J. & Margaret's home on the Solomon consisted of a half-dugout, half-sod cabin built on a slight slope. Here, their last seven children were born. During the birthing of one child a gully-washing rain swept over the prairie. Soon the sod-covered rook began leaking in several places. The two-room soddy was so small and crowded the bed could not be moved, even if a dryer place could have been found. So Flavius J. held cooking pans under the worst drips over the bed while his new son was being born.

Around 1885 Flavius J. and some of his neighbors started the town of Adell, 15 miles west of Lenora. Here Flavius owned a store and took in his brother-in-law, Hilbert Johnson as a pardner, later selling out to him. Flavius J. then built a sod blacksmith shop, which he soon outgrew, and built a larger one of lumber. He kept the old sod shop with a few tools for his sons to play with—all this in anticipation of the promised railroad.

The fate of Adell was settled when the promised rail line ended in Lenora, KS. However, a few miles north, a new railroad had already reached the Colorado line. Soon Flavius J. & Margaret Foster arrived in the new town of Dresden, Kansas in March of 1895, along with other Foster families. Here, they all built homes.

Flavius J. built a home and blacksmith shop one block west of main street in Dresden. Later, he sold these and moved catty-corner across the street when he built new ones. Flavius J. spent the rest of his working days in the new blacksmith shop, and he and Margaret spent their remaining days in the new house they built.

Many other homes in Dresden were built by Flavius J's father and brothers, as well as a general store for brother-in-law Hilbert Johnson. Five generation of Fosters have lived and many were born in the little town of Dresden, Kansas.

When 19 years old Flavius J. became a minister of the Gospel in Haddam, Kansas. Later, he joined the United Brethren Church and continued to preach until nearing the age of 80. Many times when the roads were impassable Flavius would walk eight to ten miles to hold promised services. Flavius J. held many revival meetings and funerals in schoolhouses and homes throughout western Kansas. In his earlier years Flavius drove horses, but toward the last he drove—I guess one could call it driving—a Model T. Ford.

When his son Ralph gave him a 1926 Model T Flavius J. would get one of his grandsons to drive him to his preaching assignments. But –sorry to say now—we soon tired of driving him around and found places to be busy. It was then Flavius J. decided he would learn to drive, and did. With his small granddaughter Lucile sitting on her knees so she could see out the rear window of the coupe and warn him when a car wished to pass, Flavius J. would drive down the middle of the dirt roads.

It was this determination to succeed, to learn to drive a car at 72 years old. that prompted his whole life. Whether it was preaching, building a new home in a wild land, learning a trade, or making a living for his large family, Flavius J. always drove himself to do his very best. In his diary he often wrote of preaching or working when he was sick.

Flavius J. wasn't a hunter but he loved Civil War and Indian histories, and had a large collection of old muskets and cap lock rifles. Another hobby was writing songs and poems on Indians, homesteading, and religious subjects, many of which are now in the possession of his many grandchildren.

Every sign, except a tombstone, that Flavius J. and Margaret Foster existed are gone from their old haunts. Of all their descendants, only an unmarried grandson remains. The rest have died or moved away. The old soddy, both frame houses and all three blacksmith shops are gone. Their last frame house went up in flames in 1948, and with it, all of his old study books on religion and many other valuable items. Flavius J. & Margaret Foster are buried in the Foster plot, Dresden, Kansas.

FLAVIUS JOSEPHUS FOSTER b. 8 Apr 1856 d. 8 Jul 1938
MARGARET ALICE (OLIVER) b. 9 Apr 1858 d. 16 Oct 1938
Married 11 Mar 1876, Kansas. Children:

1. ANNA MARY-ETTA b. 27 Jan 1877 d. 4 Oct 1936
2. R.S. JACKSON b. 3 Dec 1878 d. 7 Nov 1879
3. DOUGLAS H. J. b. 7 Oct 1880 d. 29 Mar 1969
4. ALFRED HIMAN b. 12 Aug 1883 d. 18 May 1970
5. ELFERD LIMAN b. 12 Aug 1883 d. 21 Jul 1964
6. EMMA GERTRUDE or BESSIE b. 23 Dec 1885 d. 19 Dec 1948
7. OLIVE MARGARET b. 27 Jan 1888 d. 3 Feb 1945
8. WILLIAM RALPH b. 23 Feb 1892 d. 4 Feb 1953

ANNA MARY-ETTA, (Aunt Annie) was born on Mulberry Creek in Washington County, just south of Haddam, Kansas. In the summer of 1878 a few days before the Indian raid described in the Sod Shanty Chapter, her parents took her to the old Solomon River settlement. In 1895 the family moved to Dresden, Kansas, where Anna met and eloped with Dr. ALFRED LeROY WASHINGTON ELY.

Alfred Ely was born in Mason City, West Virginia and went with his parents to Sandusky, Ohio. Here he grew to manhood and attended the Stiles School of Medicine. In 1897 Alfred hung up his shingle in Dresden, KS, only to elope with Annie Foster a year later. They were married in Washington, D.C.

In Washington Alfred met a classmate, Dr. Robertson and wife. In 1903 or 1904 the doctors took up a contract with the Mexican government to set up a clinic I the leper colony at Casa Grandes, Chihuahua. After his contract expired Alfred and Annie moved to Buenaventura, Chihuahua, Mexico and set up a hospital.

All went well with them until the Mexican government was overthrown in 1911. For over three years revolution and counter-revolution swept the country, but only once was there an attack on their town. For several days the fighting kept their hospital full of wounded, but Alfred treated all alike and both sides respected the flag flying over the hospital. Because of his neutrality in caring for the wounded on both sides, Alfred's property remained intact.

Alfred died in 1913. At that time the American government offered Annie safe conduct our of Mexico but she refused. She could make a living there, and didn't want to leave her husband's grave and her property. But decreed otherwise. In December of that year death took a son, and a few weeks later one of her daughters. She telegraphed her parents for help.

Annie's father waited in El Paso, Texas, while her brother Elferd and a U.S. agent went by wagon to bring Annie and the children back. Annie arrived in the United States with only $5 to her name, never expecting to get a dime from her Mexican Property. But fate swung full circle. In 1935 when her daughter Margaret became of age the Mexican government honored Alfred's will and paid for the property. Margaret also has the red-cross flag that flew over her father's hospital during the siege.

Anna Mary-Etta married #2, CHARLES HENLINE 5 Jul 1916. They lived in Dresden, KS, for awhile, where a child was born and died a few days later. They then moved to Great Bend, Kansas, where both are buried. Alfred still remains in Old Mexico with their children, Helen F. and Joseph B.

Dr. ALFRED LeROY WASHINGTON ELY b. 25 Dec 1866 d. 16 Jul 1913
ANNA MARY-ETTA FOSTER b. 27 Jan 1877 d. 4 Oct 1936
Married 30 Mar 1898, Washington, D.C. Children:

1. HELEN FRANCIS b. 23 Jan 1902 d. 3 Jan 1914
2. ALFRED FLAVIUS STILES b. 1 Jul 1904
3. JOSEPH BRYAN b. 2 Apr 1909 d. 14 Dec 1913
4. MARGARET ANN LYMAN b. 6 Jan 1914

ALFRED FLAVIUS ELY (#1 above) was born in the Eastern part of the United States and went with his parents to Old Mexico. When he came back to the US he was more Mexican than American and could speak the language like a native. I haven't seen him in 40 years, but I bet he can still rattle it off.

Alfred F. married #1, BELLZADA ELLEN YAHANE and for many years made his home in Great Bend, Kansas, where he was employed by the City Light Company. Sometime during or just after WWII the family moved to Jasper, Missouri. There Bellzada died during childbirth, as did the baby. Both are buried there.

Alfred F. married #2, OLLIE WHEAT, and again lives in Great Bend, Kansas, where he is retired. I hear he is in poor health, but he hasn't seen fit to answer my letters, so I don't know. There were no children born to this union.

ALFRED FLAVIUS STILES ELY b. 1 Jul 1904
BELLZADA ELLEN (YAHANE) b. 15 Jul 1910 d. 2 Mar 1947
Married 2 Sep 1928, Kansas. Children:

1. BERTHA ANN
2. ARUELLA BELLE
3. ALICE MARIE
4. ALFREDIA LORRAINE
5. ALFRED EDWARD
6. ALANA

MARGARET ANNA LYMAN, 4th child or Dr. ALFRED and ANNA (FOSTER) ELY, married FRANKLIN FREDERICK BATHMAN in Great Bend, KS, and they made their first home in Alexander, Kansas, where their first child was born. They now live in Wichita, Kansas, where Margaret owns a Bakery. Franklin is now retired.

FRANKLIN FREDERICK BATCHMAN b. 7 Oct 1903
MARGARET ANN LYMAN (ELY) b. 6 Jan 1914
Married 12 Sep 1934, Kansas. Children:

1. DUANE OTIS
2. JANICE ROBERTA
3. FRANKLIN ROBERT
4. JONETHA LOUIS

DUANE OTIS BATCHMAN (#1 above) married SHIRLEY VIRGINIA HENDERSON in Kansas City, 2 Dec 1961. Children: 1) DIANA LYNN, 2) DAVID DUANE.

JANICE ROBERT BATCHMAN (#2 above) married RALPH EDWARD BRUCE 19 Jun 1962. Children: 1) JANICE ANN, 2) TONIA JENEICE.

FRANKLIN ROBERT BATCHMAN, a twice-wounded veteran of Vietnam, married a Puerta Ricoan, ELISE REVERIA 7 Nov 1970.
* * *Family Chart p. 251 * * *
Douglas Foster's slot, but I'm reserving an entire chapter for him.

ELFERD LIMAN FOSTER, 4th or 5th child of FLAVIUS J. & MARGARET FOSTER, was born in the same old soddy with his twin brother (naturally). Uncle Elf came to Dresden, Kansas, with his parents in 1895. Here he grew to manhood and became the "son" in "F.J. Foster & Son, Blacksmithing." After the death of his father Elferd took over the shop until the bleak days of the "Dirty 30's." At that time, he became a tool shop mechanic on a WPA project. When things began to pick up during WWI Elferd got a job with the Kansas Highway Department.

ELFERD L. had an unproductive marriage. He then married #2, BESSIE JEANETTE BOARDMAN. The newlyweds moved into the home Elferd had built on land given him by his father, a hundred yards southwest of the old blacksmith shop. Here all their children were born, and his wife and son, Kenneth still live (in 1978). Elferd L. is buried with his father in the Foster plot, Dresden, Kansas, Cemetery.

ELFERD LIMAN FOSTER b. 12 Aug 1883 d. 21 Jul 1964
BESSIE JEANETTE (BOARDMAN) b. 14 Oct 1890 d. 10 Apr 1981
Married 29 Dec 1916, Kansas. Children:

1. KENNETH LYMAN b. 5 Oct 1917
2. FRANCES EFFIE b. 21 Nov 1918
3. MARY MARGARET b. 23 May 1920

4. LAWRENCE HIMAN b. 13 Jan 1922
5. REX RAY b. 8 Nov 1924 d. 1 May 1975
6. GERTRUDE BESSIE b. 26 Jun 1926
7. ALICE MILDRED b. 2 Nov 1927

KENNETH LYMAN FOSTER (#1 above) never married and lives in the old home caring for his mother. He is a 155MM Howitzer veteran of the Pacific, WWII.

FRANCES EFFIE FOSTER (#2 above) married #1 LLOYD YAHANE, brother of Alferd Ely's wife, p. 253 (Bellzada Yahane). They were married in Great Bend, Kansas, and made their home in Dodge City, where Lloyd was employed in the oil fields. In the early 1950's Lloyd was killed in an auto accident while on the way to work. Frances is now married to #2, WILLIAM WILLIAMS, and lives in Louisiana near her daughter. They have no children.

LLOYD LEE YAHANE
FRANCES EFFIE (FOSTER) b. 21 Nov 1918
Married 4 Dec 1936, Kansas. Children:

1. RAYMOND LEE
2. EDWARD
3. THAINE
4. JEANETTE

MARY MARGARET FOSTER, 3rd child of ELFERD L. and BESSIE (BOARDMAN) FOSTER, married #1, RAYMOND LaPORTE in 1937 and had a child: BONNIE LOU, who married JOHN J. LAUGHLIN 16 Jun 1957. They have children but I have no names.

MARY MARGARET FOSTER married #2 FRANCIS LEON BROUGHARD, in Dresden, Kansas. Later they moved to Smith Center, Kansas, where he owns a bulk oil and service business.

FRANCIS LEON BROUGHARD b. 6 Jun 1920
MARY MARGARET FOSTER b. 26 May 1920
Married 25 Dec 1947, Kansas. Children: 1) CONNIE LOU, 2) RONALD LEON.

CONNIE LOU BROUGHARD married JAMES HUENERGARDE 29 Dec 1968.
* * *
LAWRENCE HIMAN FOSTER, 4th child of ELFERD L. and BESSIE (BOARDMAN) FOSTER, married SHIRLEY (no last name), an Australian, while serving in the Pacific in WWII. Shortly after his bride joined him in the U.S. he began hitting the bottle so hard that she left him. At present Shirley and their son live in Australia. Their son: KENNETH RAY.

GERTRUDE BESSIE FOSTER, 5th child of ELFERD L. and BESSIE (BOARDMAN) FOSTER, married twice, but the first one, a WWII marriage, didn't last. She then married #2 REX MUSICK, and lives in Dodge City, KS. Their children: 1) GARY LYNN, 2) RODNEY, 3) LARRY, 4) REXIENE, 5) JAMES.
* * *
ALICE MILDRED FOSTER, 6th child of ELFERD L. and BESSIE (BOARDMAN) FOSTER, married IRA KOLSKY, my wife's brother, in Jennings, Kansas. In 1957 they divorced, with Alice getting the children. She lives in Dodge City, Kansas. Ira has remarried and owns a Kentucky Fried Chicken place in Harrisburg, Missouri. Alice has also remarried.
IRA ELWOOD KOLSKY b. 11 Apr 1927
ALICE MILDRED FOSTER b. 2 Nov 1927
Married 14 Aug 1946, Kansas. Children:

1. PAULA DIANE
2. CHARLES EUGENE
3. ROBERT WAYNE

* * * Family chart pg. 251 * * *

EMMA GERTRUDE FOSTER, 6th child of FLAVIUS J. & MARGARET FOSTER, was born in the old Solomon River settlement and came to Dresden, Kansas with her parents. Here she met and married ERNEST ROBY CADWALLDER. He was a barber who plied his trade in Dresden, Clayton, and Biglow, Kansas. They ended up in Colorado Springs, Colorado, where both are buried. Biglow, Kansas, is on the Blue River, and had some fine fishing spots, and Dad, who could never pass up a chance to hunt or fish, spent many weekends there. On one of these visits to his sister and brother-in-law I slipped from their living quarters into the attached barber shop. When found, I had cut my face with a straight edge razor. My mother threw a fit when she saw her 3-year-old pride and joy holding a razor and blood running down his face. But according to the story I was only disgusted, "Dammit! Daddy don't cut his face when he shaves."

Aunt Bessie, Emma G., was a very fine oil painter, and put some fine oils on cedar slabs and on velvet.

ERNEST ROBY CADWALLDER b. 19 Mar 1880 d. 19 Oct 1943
EMMA GERTRUDE (FOSTER) b. 23 Dec 1885 d. 19 Dec 1948
Married 1904, Kansas. Children:

1. LAWRENCE RAYMOND b. 24 Aug 1905 d. 12 Jun 1956
2. REVILLE MARGARET b. 10 Jul 1907 d. 3 Nov 1931
3. RILLA MAE b. 16 Jul 1909
4. EVELYN ROBY b. 13 Sep 1911
5. WILLIAM LINN b. 8 Dec 1918

REVILLE MARGARET CADWALLDER (#1 above) was born in Clayton, Kansas and went with her parents to Colorado Springs. Here she grew to adulthood, met and married JAMES THOMAS STREENAN, and their children were born. Jim was coal miner. One morning while on her way home after taking Jim to work Reville drove off a cliff and was killed.

At Reville's death her mother moved into the home to care for the children. When Jim died too this became a full-time job. Both Reville and James are buried in Colorado Springs, CO.

JAMES THOMAS STREENAN b. 29 Jun 1903 d. 26 Aug 1935
REVILLE MARGARET (CADWALLDER) b. 10 Jul 1907 d. 3 Nov 1931
Married 16 Nov 1924, Colorado. Children:

1. JAMES THOMAS b. 13 Oct 1925
2. IMOGENE b. 23 May 1927

JAMES THOMAS STREENAN Jr. was born and married in Colorado Springs, CO and now lives in San Diego, CA, where all of his children were born. He married LEONA MAE WEIDE 23 Jun 1946. Their children: 1) THOMAS WESLEY, 2) DONNA RAY, 3) LORA LEE, 4) MICHAEL JAMES.

IMOGENE STREENAN (#2 above) was born, raised, and married in Colorado Springs, CO to RALPH CARE HALE, 30 Jun 1946. Their child: CARLENE.

* * *

RILLA MAE CADWALLDER, 3rd child of ERNEST & EMMA G. (FOSTER) CADWALLDER, was born in Clayton, Kansas, just four months before I was in the same town. She went with her parents to Biglow, Kansas, then to Colorado Springs, CO. Here she met and married JAMES EDWARD McPHILLIAMY, and their children were born. For years, they had a beer distributorship before they retired in El Cajon, Calif. Here James died and is buried in Colorado Springs, CO.

JAMES EDWARD McPHILLIAMY b. 19 Feb 1906 d. 9 Sep 1972
RILLA MAE (CADWALLDER) b. 16 Jul 1909
Married 29 Sep 1928, Raton, New Mexico. Children: 1) JAMES EDWARD, 2) MARY KATHLEEN.

JAMES EDWARD McPHILLIAMY Jr. was born, raised, and later married in Colorado Springs, now lives in San Diego, Calif.

JAMES EDWARD McPHILLIAMY Jr.
VIRGINIA LEE (JONES)
Married 25 Apr 1948, Colorado. Children:

1. SANDRA LEE, who married LEONARD L. BURTON and had TAMIRA LYNN.
2. LY-ANN

MARY KATHLEEN McPHILLIAMY, 2nd child of JAMES & RILLA MAE McPHILLIAMY, married at least 3 times and still lives in Colorado Springs. She married #4, MR. ANDREWS, 13 May 1971 in Raton, New Mexico. Their children were born to two marriages. Note para. #2 pg. 259.

JACK MILTON TIMMERMAN
MARY KATHLEEN McPHILLIAMY
Married 26 Oct 1947, New Mexico. Children:

1. DEBORAH KATHLEEN
2. JACK MILTON Jr.
3. CHERYL RAE

DEBORAH KATHLEEN TIMMERMAN was born in Colorado Springs, Colo., where she met and married MICHAEL DENNIS CONWAR 28 Jan 1967. Children: 1) MICHAEL GREGORY, 2) AMY KATHLEEN.

MARY KATHLEEN McPHILLIAMY married in Colorado Springs, Colo. to OTIS DeLEE MOORE. They had one child JAMES DeLEE.

* * *

EVELYN RUBY CADWALLDER, 4th child of ERNEST & EMMA G. (FOSTER) CADWALLDER,
was born in Dresden, Kansas and went with her parents to Colorado Springs, Colorado. Here she grew to adulthood and took a job as waitress in cafes. While doing this work she met JAMES VINCENT VARRONE, and after a long delay, finally married him. James (Jim) worked as a coal miner for many years, but quit to become a welder for A&P Steel Company.

James was born and raised in Colorado Springs, where they still live. He was born 17 Mar 1913 and married Evelyn R. 27 Jun 1942.

WILLIAM LINN CADWALLDER, 5th child of ERNEST & EMMA G. (FOSTER) CADWALLDER, was born in Dresden, Kansas and went with her parents to Colorado Springs, Colorado, where he grew to adulthood. William Linn always liked the selling end of business and worked as a salesman for several companies. Linn married twice, but the first one didn't take, and no children were born.

WILLIAM LINN married #2, NORMA VIRGINIA MOSHER in Raton, New Mexico. I was there twice during the 1930's and could see nothing in Raton that looked like a honeymoon paradise, but many of my cousins were married there. Linn and Norma made their home in Colorado Springs until mid-WWII, when they moved to San Diego, California. They still live there, where Linn is employed as route man for the Weber Bread Company.

WILLIAM LINN CADWALLDER b. 8 Dec 1917

NORMA VIRGINIA (MOSHER) b. 15 Jul 1917
Married 15 Mar 1941, New Mexico. Children:

1. BARBARA RAY
2. WILLIAM LINN Jr.
3. NORMA VIRGINIA

BARBARA RAY CADWALLDER (#1 above) was born and lives in San Diego, California. She married HAROLD DEAN NELLIS.

HAROLD DEAN NELLIS
BARBARA RAY (CADWALLDER)
Married 30 Apr 1960, California. Children:

1. LAWRENCE WILLIAM
2. COREY DEAN

WILLIAM LINN CADWALLDER Jr., 2nd child of WILLIAM LINN & NORMA VIRGINIA CADWALLDER, was born in San Diego, CA. He married SALLIE RAY HENDRICKS.

WILLIAM LINN CADWALLDER Jr.
SALLIE RAY HENDRICKS
Married 30 May 1963, California. Children:

1. ROBERT EDWARD
2. NORMAN LENN

NORMA VIRGINIA, 3rd child of WILLIAM LINN & NORMA VIRGINIA CADWALLDER, married CHARLES ALAN BOWERS in San Diego, California. He was born in Ohonaneb, Germany. Charles is in the US Air Force, and most of their children were born on different Air Bases in Wiesbaden, Germany (1st child) and in the U.S. Charles had a daughter born to a previous marriage, KATHY LEE.
CHARLES ALAN BOWERS
NORMA VIRGINIA (CADWALLDER)
Married 4 Feb 1962, California. Children:

1. CHARLES ALAN Jr.
2. RONALD LENN
3. REBEKAH JOY
4. SHELLY RUTH

* * * chart pg. 251 * * *

OLIVE MARGARET (Aunt Ollie) FOSTER, 7th child of FLAVIUS J. & MARGARET (OLIVER) FOSTER, was born in the Solomon River settlement in a frame house that had replaced the old soddy. In 1895 she moved to Dresden, Kansas with her parents, where she finished her schooling. Here she met and married WALTER TOBIS (TOBE) HAROLD.

They spent all their married lives on a farm five miles southeast of Dresden, Kansas. Aunt Ollie suffered many years with diabetes, which cost her a leg and finally her life. Tobe & Ollie struggled hard to make a living during the "dirty 30's" (the Great Depression) and just when things were looking up she passed away. Tobe sold the farm and moved to Missouri near his daughter. Olive & Tobis Harold are buried in the Foster section of the Dresden, Kansas, Cemetery.

WALTER TOBIAS HAROLD b. 5 Jan 1881 d. 29 Sep 1968
OLIVE MARGARET (FOSTER) b. 27 Jan 1888 d. 3 Feb 1945
Married 21 Jun 1915, Kansas. Children:

1. MILDRED B. b. 11 Dec 1917 d. 8 Dec 1970
2. BASIL

Grandpa & Grandma Foster liked to hold large Sunday dinners during the summer months At one of these dinners we children were playing near Uncle Tobe's car. About mid-afternoon Uncle Tobe came out and searched all through the old Model T Ford, then went back into the house. A few minutes later, out he came a second time, and again did some searching. I asked him what he was looking for. "I've lost my pipe," he said. He had it in his mouth all the time.

MILDRED B. HAROLD (#1 above) was born and grew to adulthood on the family farm, and married JAMES D. TOWBRIDGE in Hoxie, Kansas. They farmed in western Kansas until 1946, when they moved to Bloomfield, Missouri. Jim, a heavy duty mechanic, works for a heavy equipment repair shop. After a series of crippling strokes Mildred passed away and is buried in the Baptist Church Cemetery, New Bloomfield, Missouri.

JAMES D. TOWBRIDGE b. 19 Jan 1912
MILDRED B. HAROLD b. 11 Dec 1917 d. 8 Dec 1970
Married 30 Jul 1938, Kansas. Children:

1. CAROL B.
2. ARNOLD H.

CAROL B. TOWBRIDGE was born in Oberlin, KS and went with her parents to New Bloomfield, Missouri, where she met and married LIONEL D. GRAY 14 Aug. 1960. Their children: 1) JEFFREY WAYNE, 2) RHONDA.
ARNOLD H. TOWBRIDGE (#2 above) was born in Norton, Kansas and went with his parents to New Bloomfield, Missouri. Here he grew to manhood and met and married SUSAN KAY LYNES 9 Jul 1966. Susan K. Their child: 1) CHRISTINA KAY.
* * *

All of Flavius J. and Margaret Foster's children are now gone. Except for Aunt Annie and Aunt Bessie (Emma G.), all of their children repose at their side in the Dresden, Kansas Cemetery. Of their sons and daughters-in-law, only Aunt Bessie, widow of Elferd L. Foster remains among us, and she is now past 88 years of age.

With the passing of Alva W. Coleman (p. 222) went our last link with our father's generation. We can no longer look back, but must look forward toward upcoming generations, until it is our time to depart.

Except for their son, DOUGLAS, this ends the families of Flavius J. & Margaret (Oliver) Foster. If your family isn't listed or you are not on the pages ahead, then you are "lost," or a different breed of Fosters, or you haven't been born yet (9 Aug. 1978).

*** * * * * THE OLIVERS – THE BOBBITTS – THE KOLSKYS * * * * ***

PIONEER WOMEN! Without them and their fortitude this nation would never have been settled. From coast to water-washed coast, in log cabins of the forest or sod shanties of the prairies they stuck by their men like the proverbial rib from which they came. They taught their children, washed, cooked and sewed for their families, and often became field hands during rush harvest seasons.

REASON OLIVER married #1, LOIS WILSON in Ohio, and in 1869 migrated to Kansas. They first settled just west of Haddam, but seven years later moved to Norton County, where they homesteaded on Long Branch north and east of present-day Norcatur, Kansas. Here they remained until death overtook them.

Lois died some years before Reason, and he married a second time but due to circumstances I have been unable to get any dates. (Note: Poor Flavius. He worked so hard and sent so many letters, and many went unanswered. Be satisfied with the amazing work you did Cousin.) There were two children born to this second marriage. The second wife, whose name I have never heard, was murdered by an axe under hush-hush circumstances, and the children adopted by a Jones family.

Reason, Lois and the unnamed wife are all buried in an old cemetery near their homestead northeast of Norcatur, Kansas.

REASON OLIVER b. 24 Jun 1833 d. 28 Sep 1898
LOIS (WILSON) b. 14 Sep 1833
Married 14 Nov 1850, Ohio. Children:

1. JAMES HENRY b. 17 Aug 1851
2. SARAH ELIZABEH b. 26 Sep 1853 d. 13 Feb 1900
3. JOHN GOSET b. 8 Jan 1856
4. MARGARET ALICE b. 9 Apr 1858 d. 16 Oct 1938 m. F. J. Foster
5. WILLIAM SHARP b. 5 Mar 1861
6. LUCY JANE b. 8 Nov 1863 d. 7 May 1900

7. GEORGE WASHINGTON b. 11 May 1866 d. 22 Nov 1938
8. ROBERT SAYMORE b. 7 Sep 1868
9. ULYSSES GRANT b. 14 Mar 1872
10. LANT F. died in infancy
11. FRANKLIN B. died in infancy
12. FRANCIS A. died in infancy

* * *

SARAH ELIZABETH OLIVER married ALONZO MAPES in Haddam, KS in 1875 and later joined her father in Norton County, where they took up land. After proving up on this land they sold their claim and joined her sister and brother-in-law in the old Solomon River settlement. Their children: 1) JOHN b. 23 Sep 1879, d. 25 Feb 1929; 2) FRANKLIN b. 2 Apr 1883 d. 16 Jul 1943; 3) BENJAMIN b. 21 Jul 1889 d. 21 Jul 1975. The first two sons are buried in the Dresden, Kansas Cemetery.

BENJAMIN MAPES, 3rd child of ALONZO & SARAH (OLIVER) MAPES, married MARY, and spent the last days with his daughter in Lebanon, Kansas, where both he and Mary are buried. Their children: 1) FLOYD, 2) LETHA, 3) IVAN, 40 IMOGENE.

* * *

GEORGE WASHINGTON OLIVER, 7th child of REASON and LOIS (WILSON) OLIVER, married SARAH, who was born 18 Aug. 1855 d. 20 Mar 1949. Both are buried in the Norcatur, KS Cemetery.

MARGARET ALICE, 4th child of REASON & LOIS (WILSON) OLIVER, was born in Ohio and came to Kansas with her parents. Here she grew to adulthood, met and married Rev. FLAVIUS JOSEPHUS FOSTER. During that period a preacher could expect very little for his services except possibly a meal and a little garden produce. Since F. J. had no land or money with which to buy some he was soon looking westward toward free land.

Early in the spring of 1878 some of F. J.'s relatives had settled on land in the old Solomon River settlement. After putting in a crop of corn on his aunt's place south of Haddam, Flavius J. and Margaret decided to join these relatives. Their first child was only 18 months old and there was another on the way. Although "homesteading in the far west" was far from the romance they first thought, Flavius J. and Margaret felt that they had bettered themselves by the move.

Like chickens, the Foster males did a lot of crowing, but Grandma Margaret had her "Huh!" Like and Indian's "Ugh," this exclamation covered a lot of ground, from doubt to agreement, from sadness to enjoyment. In later life Grandma Margaret would sit in her old rocker before the wood stove, while Grandpa Flavius J. told and retold of their old homesteading ways. During the telling of the Indian episode her old rocker would really vibrate. May times during these tales Grandma's "Huh" could be heard, yet all the while she was comfortable in the knowledge that they had met and overcome every obstacle. Yet, why my sister Lucile was reading her "Little Orphan Annie" episodes from the local newspaper, Grandma Margaret would wipe tears of pity from her eyes with the apron she always wore.

* * *

THE BOBBITTS: Only an outline of my Bobbitt line will be given here. Mr. John Bobbitt, 2502 I St. NW, Washington, D.C. is doing very extensive research on the entire Bobbitt genealogy.

In 1673 WILLIAM & ANNA BOBBITT emigrated from Wales and were given 100 acres of land in Prince George Co., Virginia, where their son JOHN was born. JOHN (2) married SARAH GREEN and moved to Chowan District, North Carolina where their son, WILLIAM was born. WILLIAM (3) married AMY BENNETT and lived in Warren Co., NC, where their son JOHN RICHARD was born. JOHN RICHARD (4) married AMY ALSTON in Warren Co., where their son ISHAM was born.

ISHAM BOBBITT (5), a Revolutionary War veteran, was born in Warren Co., NC where he met and married ELIZABETH JAMES, and their son STEPHEN was born. STEPHEN (6) married BARBARA CHRISMAN, and moved to Christian Co., KY where their son DRURY ALLEN was born 19 May 1822 d. 1892. Later Isham, Stephen, and Drury A. moved to Scott Co., Illinois.

In Illinois DRURY ALLEN BOBBITT (7) married MARY MORRISON, 14 Sep 1947. Mary b. 8 Aug 1821 d. 26 Mar 1897, was the widow of LeROY GILLIHAM, by whom she had 3 sons: 1) JOHN NEWTON, 2) JAMES C., 3) ROBERT CLARK.

DRURY A. & MARY BOBBITT'S children: 1) JOSEPHINE, 2) RICHARD, 3) SARAH, 4) MATTIE, 5) JESSIE, 6) HENRY M.

* * *

HENRY M. BOBBITT (8) married PHOEBE CAROLINE JACKSON in Lincoln, Illinois. Her father was CHARLES DUNCAN JACKSON, who married MARY BROWN in Warrick Co., Indiana, and later moved to Illinois. They had several children, but I have only the one who married Henry Bobbitt.

Some of the children of Henry and Phoebe Bobbitt were born in Illinois. Later the family moved to Callaway, Nebraska, then to Brown Co., Kansas and finally to a farm 4 miles south and 3 miles east of Seneca, Kansas. Here they finished out their lives and are buried in concrete vaults in the Sabetha, Kansas, Cemetery, with five of their children. Only two members of this family are still living, and they too, will be buried with their parents.

Henry M. & Phoebe Bobbitt's daughter, Grace Pearl, is buried with her husband, Douglas H. Foster in Dresden, Kansas. (See next chapter.)

HENRY M. BOBBITT b. 18 Sep 1857 d. 9 Aug 1945
PHOEBE (JACKSON) b. 9 May1856 e. 10 Oct 1947
Married 6 Feb 1879, Illinois. Children:

1. CHARLES E. b. 24 Jan 1880 d. 18 May 1973
2. LEFFA M. b. 11 Dec 1881 d. 22 Sep 1947
3. ROSCO (ROSS) b. 11 Nov 1883 d. 24 Oct 1969

4. MYRTLE b. 14 Mar 1885 d. 5 Jan 1941 m. JOHN HEINEN
5. GRACE PEARL b. 8 Aug 1887 d. 6 Jun 1978
6. BERT b. 30 Mar 1891 d. 4 Apr 1968
7. ARTHUR b. 14 Jan 1895 m. ALTHA DAVIS
8. LUCILE b. 25 Jul 1900 m. CECIL HAYDEN

CHARLES E. BOBBITT (#1 above) married ELIZABETH HEINEN, and lived in Sidney, Iowa, where he owned an oil distributorship. Their son, Gilbert married a widow with two children, but had none of his own. Gilbert was born 24 Dec 1910, but was killed at a Railroad crossing in 1966.

DONALD BOBBITT, (apparently Elizabeth Heinen's other son—adopted by Charles Bobbitt above) was born 12 Oct 1913 and married MABLE MYERS 2 Nov 1936. The was born 19 Nov 1914. They live in Sidney, Iowa, where Donald inherited the oil business. Their son GARY married DEBORAH MARIE BOWMAN 22 Dec 1973. Gary is the only chance this Bobbitt family name has to remain on the census rolls of the future.

* * *

LEFFA M. BOBBITT, 2nd child of HENRY and PHOEBE (JACKSON) BOBBITT, married WILLIAM BROADHURST and lived in Kansas City, MO, where William ran a hardware store. He is buried in California with their daughter. Their daughter, CAROLINE b. 17 Aug 1909 d. 12 May 1970, was married three times and had no children.

* * * * * THE KOLSKYS * * * * *

JOSEPH, son of GEORGE & BARBARA KOLSKY, was born on a homestead six miles northwest of Jennings, Kansas. Both parents and some of their children were born in Bohemia province, Czechoslovakia, then a part of the old Austria-Hungarian Empire. Joseph grew to manhood and married on the old homestead, which he later inherited.

On a nearby homestead, GRACE ALVERNA, daughter of ROBERT & NELLIE SPIRES was born in a sod house. On reaching adulthood JOSEPH & GRACE were marred by his brother, Rev. Charles Kolsky. They set up housekeeping on the old Kolsky homestead, where Joseph died, and is buried in the Jennings, Kansas Cemetery.

At Joseph's death, Grace Alverna and the children continued to run the farm, until their son Dallas returned from the army at the end of WWII. At that time he took over the farm, buying out the other heirs. With her share, Grace A. bought a home in Oberlin, Kansas, where she set up a seamstress business in1947. When Dallas' first wife (Dorothy, see below) was killed Grace A. returned to the farm to care for his children until he remarried. At that time Grace returned to her home-seamstress business, where she is now semi-retired, doing only off-the cuff jobs.

JOSEPH KOLSKY b.23 Feb 1890 d. 28 Apr 1941
GRACE (SPIRES) b. 7 Jul 1901
Married 25 May 1919, Kansas. Children:

1. GOLDIE MAE b. 12 Mar 1920
2. DALLAS EUGENE b. 13 Sep 1921
3. GERALD JOSEPH b. 22 Sep 1923
4. MARIE VIOLET 15 Jul 1925
5. IRA ELWOOD b. 11 Apr 1927
6. BETTY LEE b. 28 Dec 1928

GOLDIE MAE KOLSKY (#1 above) married DONALD STAPP and for several years lived on his farm northwest of Norcatur, Kansas. In 1969 they sold the farm and moved into Oberlin, where Goldie M. is employed in a dry goods store. Donald has held many jobs in Oberlin and is now in the employ of the city. They have three sons, all married: 1) RODNEY, 2) GARRY & LARRY (twins).

* * *

DALLAS EUGENE KOLSKY (#2 above) married #1, DOROTHY CONNORS in El Paso, Texas, just after WWII. Back from the Air Corps, Dallas bought out the other heirs to the home place. On the afternoon of 4 Apr 1953, Dorothy went to Jennings for groceries and was killed by a train. It was at that time Dallas' mother returned to the farm. Dorothy is buried in the Jennings, Kansas Cemetery. Their children: 1) JOSEPH, 2) MARILEN.

DALLAS EUGENE KOLSKY married #2, JOYCE NORRIS, a local school teacher in 1960. They live in Sedalia, Missouri, where they are engaged in the Kentucky Fried Chicken Business, owning several establishments. Here too, they own two farms in addition to the old home place. Their children: 1) LEE, 2) NANCY JO.

Joseph, 1st son of Dallas and Dorothy (Connors) Kolsky, manages one of the Kentucky Fried Chicken Outlets, with Marilyn (his sister) and Lee (his half-brother) helping him.

GERALD JOSEPH KOLSKY (#3 above), married #1, DOREEN BOUTS, and has four children. They divorced and she got the children and lives in Bellville, Kansas. Their children: 1) GREGG, 2) GINIA, 3) EVAN, 4) LINET.

GERALD JOSEPH KOLSKY married #2, LUCILLE in 1971, a divorcee with a married daughter. They have no children. Lucille works in a motel and Gerald works in an Oberlin, Kansas, grain elevator and farms on the side.

MARIE V. KOLSKY, 4th child of JOSEPH and GRACE (SPIRES) KOLSKY, married FLAVIUS M. FOSTER, p. 282. (Me! Ain't she the lucky one???)

* * *

IRA ELWOOD KOLSKY, 5th child of JOSEPH and GRACE (SPIRES) KOLSKY, married #1, ALICE MILDRED FOSTER, daughter of ELFERD L. and BESSIE (BOARDMAN) FOSTER. (Their family is given on p. 255 & 256). They divorced and both have remarried. IRA E. married #2, LEONA SMITH, a widow with two daughters. Ira E. Leona live in Harrisburg, Missouri, where they own a Kentucky Fried Chicken Business.

* * *

BETTY LEE, 6th child of JOSEPH & GRACE (SPIRES) KOLSKY, married ROLLY THOMPSON, a travelling clothing salesman. They lived in Kansas, Nebraska and lastly, Iowa. Rolly died of suicide. Betty L. lives in Storm Lake, Iowa, where she is employed as a private secretary. Near her live two adopted children: 1) VANCE, 2) ANN.

* * * * *

This brings to an end the end of the In-law families. As noted, both the Bobbitt and Kolsky families are being extensively researched by a member of the respective family.

* * * * * DOUGLAS HILBERT JASPER FOSTER * * * * *

DOUGLAS H. J., 2nd child of FLAVIUS J. & MARGARET (OLIVER) FOSTER, was born in the old soddy in the Solomon River settlement, later going with his parents to Dresden, Kansas. Here he grew to manhood, during which time he helped build the old home and blacksmith shop. Later he worked as a section hand on the Rock Island Railroad.

One day his father gave Doug an old mare, which in due time bore a colt, palomino in color, which he named Babe. Soon after Doug had broken Babe to harness he got a mail contract to old Shebaleth. It was one of those old-time winters when snow drifted 10 feet deep and the temperature often dropped to 25 below, and Babe earned his keep. With some of the money from the mail contract Doug bought a new buggy, which outlasted Babe by 10 years. However Babe outlasted 3 mates, living to be 26 years old. May tears were shed at his passing.

Now to back-track a little (you'll see why in a minute), GRACE PEARL, 5th child of HENRY M. & PHOEBE (JACKSON) BOBBITT was born in Callaway, Nebraska, and went with her parents to their farm southeast of Seneca, Kansas. Here she started her schooling: 2 years of high school in Seneca and the last two in Lincoln, Nebraska, and then she took up teaching. Grace Pearl's first job was in Tobias, Nebraska. In 1907 she took a job with the now-defunct Fairview school 5 miles southeast of Dresden, Kansas.

Until the 1940's there many of these one-teacher, 1-8-grade schools dotting the countryside. In these, the teacher not only had to teach, but was also janitor and all around handyperson. Except for these 3 previous years Peal did only three days teaching in 1933, when her teacher-daughter, Irene, was sick. It was during her two terms at Fairview school that she met and married.

DOUGLAS H. J. FOSTER and PEARL BOBBITT were married in her home southeast of Seneca, KS. They made their home in Dresden, where Pearl finished her second year of teaching and Douglas worked on the railroad. In 1909 they moved to Clayton, where Douglas ran a blacksmith shop, and their 1st child was born. In 1910 Douglas sold this shop and moved to Corning, Kansas, where he bought another shop from Clyde Cooke, which he ran for 11 years. He sold this blacksmith shop to C.O. Sever in early 1921.

In the spring of 1922, Dad decided to try his hand at farming, and moved his family to a farm four miles southwest of Corning, KS. From here it was a 2 ½ mile hike to an 8-grades, one-room, country school. Each evening after school Mom would meet us with a supply of pumpkin pie, which we ate one-handed while doing the chores.

During winter evenings before a roaring fire Mom would aloud a Zane Grey book while Dad glued pith from corn stalks together. While listening to the story Dad would carve the pith into the shape of ranch stock and horsemen, and pin the pealed corn stalks into log cabins. Not surprising, the riders and their mounts were given names from characters for these books. Some of these carvings are in the Indian Raid Museum in Oberlin, Kansas.

In March of 1924 Dad moved to another farm one mile further west, where the one-room school was only 1 ½ miles away. Here we had two small ponds where we trapped muskrats to help the budget, and wild grapes and elderberries for jelly. Dad, always a fine shot gunner, kept our table supplied with wild game. When hunting the myriads of rabbits we children would bird-dog the weed patches for Dad, at the same picking off setting game with our .22's.

On March 22, 1927, Dad set his family on the trail back to western Kansas. The farm had been sold from under him and he could not get another, so he sold everything he couldn't get into two wagons. Dad drove the lead covered wagon, and Mom and I the other one, while my brothers in the old buggy brought up the rear of our "wagon train." Babe, now grown old, was one of the team on the buggy.

Our first day's haul was a short one to set a pattern for the trip and to wait for Mom, who was taking a last visit with her folks. The first day of the 8-day trip it rained, hailed, and rested up to start all over again during the last seven days. Most of the trip was over the same ground covered by our grandparents when they headed west to homestead, so our trip held a romantic flavor for us boys.

The third day out, we had a little excitement when a band of Gypsies took us for some of their own. Luckily we got away without losing a things to their sticky fingers. A romantic trip? Not until later did we realize what a miserable time Mom had, standing at the tailgate of her wagon, trying to get enough heat from a stove full of damp wood to cook our meals.

In western Kansas Dad kept things on an even keel, working on county roads until the blight of the "Dirty 30's". At that time he joined the WPA as a stone mason. Many of the stones he cut are now a part of the city hall in Jennings, Kansas. With the advent of WWII, Dad went back to his old forge, making hunting-type knives for servicemen, which were carried on every American fighting front.

At age 84-plus Dad's heart warned him to quit his fishing trips. For 20 years he and two cronies had slept on the ground from March until October on weekends of cat-fishing.

He died of cancer of the bladder. The before he died, Dad awoke from his hospital bed saying, "Mom, I dreamed that I was fishing from an "airoplane."

Mom had a sense of humor that could break through the clouds of trouble or disappointment like rays of sunshine. Mom could put in a day of housework, do chores, and still have energy left to skip rope with her children, until her mid-40's. She cooked, sewed, baked, canned for family of eight, and still found time to go to quilting parties.

Until age 85 Mom kept her own home, but then failing eyesight and a heart condition demanded that she moved closer to a doctor, 20 miles away. Mom moved into the Oberlin, Kansas, nursing home, where she continued to work her beloved cross-word puzzles with a magnifying glass until even that wasn't enough. For the last year of her life Mom just faded away. Douglas & Pearl are buried with his relatives in the Dresden, Kansas Cemetery.

DOUGLAS HILBERT JASPER FOSTER b. 7 Oct 1880 d. 29 Mar 1967
PEARL (BOBBITT) b. 8 Aug 1887 d. 6 Jun 1978
Married 26 Nov 1908, Kansas. Children:

1. **FLAVIUS MILTON** (the original author of this book) b. 7 Nov 1909 d. 20 Mar 2006
2. OLIVE IRENE b. 11 Sep 1911
3. MAURICE LYNN b. 15 Nov 1913 d. 11 Oct 1973
4. ELFERD JACKSON b. 14 Feb 1916
5. BLANCH LUCILE b. 23 Sep 1920
6. DOROTHY MARIE b. 17 Jan 1926

FLAVIUS MILTON FOSTER – I'm going to hog a whole chapter for my family (later).
* * *
OLIVE IRENE FOSTER, 2nd child of DOUGLAS & PEARL FOSTER, was born in a school-house converted into a home, in Corning, Kansas, one block east of Main Street. She was taken by her parents to the two farms southwest of Corning, mentioned in the preceding chapter, then to Dresden, Kansas, where she finished high school. After high school Irene taught four terms of school in the now-defunct Solomon Valley school.

OLIVE IRENE married #1, NORMAN WILLIS LAW, her second-generation cousin (p. 212), son of CHARLES HENRY & MARTHA (JOHNSON) LAW and grandson of HILBERT & MARY-ETTA (FOSTER) JOHNSON). Norman had finished high school in their home town of Dresden, and while Irene taught her last term of school, he started at Hays Teacher's college. They then moved to Hays, Kansas, where Norman finished his 4-year course, but due to the depression he was only able to teach school one term. Norman then got a job as timekeeper on a WPA project until WWII, when he got a job with the Kansas Highway Department.

When Norman got his highway job the family moved to Oberlin, Kansas, were Irene was elected County Treasurer, a job she kept until voted out of office in 1970. Norman Law died in the Oberlin, KS hospital and is buried in the Foster section of the Dresden, KS Cemetery.

NORMAN WILLIS LAW b. 28 May 1911 d. 25 Aug 1959
OLIVE IRENE FOSTER b. 11 Sep 1911
Married 25 Aug 1933, Kansas. Children:

1. PHILLIP EUGENE
2. LARRY LaVERNE

PHILLIP EUGENE was born in Dresden, Kansas, and finished high school in Oberlin, where the family had moved. He then majored in music at Hays, Kansas, while doing summer jobs to help pay his way. While still in college, PHILLIP met and married MARJORIE MAY JORDAN, who lived in Oberlin, KS. They now live in Arvada, a suburb of Denver, Colorado, where Phillip teaches music in the local school.

PHILLIP EUGENE LAW
MARJORIE (JORDAN)
Married 10 Jun 1956, Kansas. Children:

1. MACHELLE GAE
2. CYNTHIA SUSAN
3. LORI JILL

LARRY LaVERNE LAW, 2nd son of NORMAN W. & IRENE (FOSTER) LAW, never married. After finishing school Larry joined the army. Returning from service, Larry moved to the Denver, Colorado area, where he is a building contractor.

OLIVE IRENE married #2, EDWIN MARTLEY 5 Aug 1967, who has three children by a former marriage that ended in divorce. Edwin went to Hays College with Norman on an exchange ride basis. Edwin was born southwest of Jennings, KS and joined the army in 1942, transferred to the Air Corps and retired as Sgt. Major in 1966. Irene and Edwin live in Oberlin, Kansas.

* * * * *

MAURICE LYNN FOSTER, 3rd child of DOUGLAS & PEARL FOSTER, was born in the converted school-home in Corning, Kansas, and went to Dresden, Kansas with his parents. Here he finished high school and entered the army during WWII, and served in the 85th Infantry Division in Europe. After the war, Maurice tried the contracting business until the Korean conflict broke out, when he moved in with his brother, Flavius, in Poulsbo, Washington. Here he worked in the Bangor Ammo Depot until he retired, and died a few months later.

* * * * *

ELFERD JACKSON FOSTER, 4th child of DOUGLAS & PEARL FOSTER, was also born in the converted school-home. Like the other children of this family, Elferd lived and went to school on the two farms southwest of Corning, Kansas, and finished high school in Dresden, Kansas. In making the latter move, he rode with his brother Maurice in the old buggy.

Elferd worked on a cattle ranch in northwest Nebraska until WWII. At that time he was assigned to Btry. D, 116th Anti-Aircraft Regiment, and was assigned to the Los Angeles area. Later his unit went to England. Three days after the Normandy invasion, Elferd's unit went to France and followed the retreating Germans into their homeland.

After the war Elferd married ROBERTA LOUIS DUNNING of Ontario, California, whom he had met during the war. They made their first home in California, the moved back to Dresden, Kansas in 1951. At that time, Elferd moved to Bremerton, Washington and took a job in the Navy shipyard. In 1974 Elferd retired from civil service with a heart condition, requiring a pace-maker. Roberta also worked for the Civil Service.

Until the mid-1960's Elferd lived in the Port Orchard area, then he moved to a 20-acre plot four miles southwest of Poulsbo, Washington and raised beef cattle on the side. In June of 1980 he sold this land and moved to Benson, Arizona.

ELFERD JACKSON FOSTER b. 14 Feb 1916
ROBERTA (DUNNING) b. 16 Sep 1925
Married 16 Nov 1945, Kansas. Children: 1) JO-DEAN, 2) BETTY-LOU.

JO-DEAN FOSTER was born in Upland, California and made the tour to Kansas, then to Washington State, where she finished high school, met and married JERRY LEE GREENLEE, a navy man. Later, they moved to Houston, Texas, where they now live. Douglas Foster's only sight of a great-grandchild, just before he died, was when he was shown Jo Dean's son Brian through the hospital window. Dad's last request to my mother was, "Mom, get the little feller a present."

JERRY LEE GREENLEE
JO-DEAN (FOSTER)
Married 10 Apr 1965, Washington. Children: 1) BRIAN CLINTON, 2) DAVIE WAYNE.

BETTY LOU FOSTER, 2nd child of ELFERD J. & ROBERT (DUNNING) FOSTER, was born in Upland, California and made the tour to Kansas, then to Washington State, where she grew to adulthood and met and married STEPHEN ROBERT KADLECEK, a marine. They too, moved to Houston, Texas, where their son was born: PAUL E.
* * * * Family chart p. 271

BLANCH LUCILE FOSTER, 5th child of DOUGLAS & PEARL FOSTER, was born in the southeast part of Corning, Kansas. At the age of two years Lucile went with her parents to the two farms southwest of Corning, where she started school. When the family moved to Dresden, Kansas, Lucile finished high school and got a job in nearby Norton, Kansas. Here Lucile met and married HOWARD ALBIN, and their eldest child was born.

Later the family moved to Elbert, Colorado, where Howard was engaged in the bulk oil business, and the other children were born. In 1959 the family moved to Pasco, Washington, where they got an improved farm. After several years of hard labor, most of it done by Lucile and the children, much of this land was brought under water. Howard was working in a service station during the improving of the land and helped only on Sundays and time off. The "pay-off" came when Howard got involved with the bottle and another woman, and the marriage ended in divorce.

With more guts than most women, Lucile bore her children through caesarian operation. Today Lucile lives in Pasco, Washington, near her children, and works in a dry-cleaning establishment.

HOWARD ALBIN b. 8 May 1921
LUCILE (FOSTER) b. 23 Sep 1920
Married 28 Jun 1941, Kansas. Children:

1. STEPHEN EARL
2. KENNY RAY
3. TERRI LYNN

STEPHEN EARL ALBIN, born in Norton, Kansas, went with his parents to Colorado, then to Washington state, where he finished high school. During school he bought an FHA pig and set himself up in the show-pig business, which he ran until he enlisted in the Air Corps in 1968. After six years of service, during which he got married, Stephen set himself up in the farming business north of Pasco, Washington, where he now lives.

STEPHEN EARL ALBIN married PATRICIA ANN PEARSON, while in the service, and their child was born in Pasco, Washington.

STEPHEN EARL ALBIN
PATRICIA ANN (PEARSON)
Married 15 Jun 1968, Washington. Children:

1. BETH ANN
2. KENNY R.

KENNY R. ALBIN, born in Denver Colorado, went with his parents to Pasco, Washington, where he finished high school, and took up auto mechanics. Kenny R. married VICHI LYNN WEANER in Pasco, where their children were born. For selfish reasons Vichie divorced Kenny R., taking their child, car, and furniture. Everything except the debts. Child: DARIN RICHARD.

* * *

TERRI LYNN ALBIN, 3rd child of HOWARD & LUCILE (FOSTER) ALBIN, was born in Colorado and went with her parents to Pasco, Washington, where she finished high school. Here she met and married THOMAS BROWN and their children were born.

THOMAS BROWN
TERRI LYNN (ALBINI)
Married 3 Feb 1973, Washington. Children:

1. ERICA MARIE
2. ROBERT

Family chart p. 271.

* * * * *

DOROTHY MARIE FOSTER, last child of DOUGLAS & PEARL FOSTER, was born on a farm, five miles southwest of Corning, Kansas, and went with her parents to Dresden. Here, she finished high school and moved in with her sister Lucile in Norton, Kansas, where Dorothy got a job as a soda jerk. Here she met and married JOHN JOE LAWN, who was an infantryman in the Pacific during WWII.

Dorothy and J. J. Lawn spent the first few years of their married life on his adoptive parents' farm southwest of Norton, KS, which he inherited. Just when things were going good for Dorothy and J.J. the government condemned the farm for a dam site.

After the sale of the farm, Dorothy and John-Joe moved to Norcatur, Kansas, where they bought a large home for their large family on six acres of land. At that time John-Joe got a job with the Kansas Highway Department, where he still works. Dorothy works in the local café. They have a huge garden, where they grow most of their food, freezing, canning, and preserving the produce. In their "spare" time Dorothy and John Joe babysit their many grandchildren.

They come from haunt and hoot and hurn, they dilly and they dally,
They sparkle through the ferns of life, then fade down the valley.

JOHN-JOE LAWN b. 23 Aug 1923
DOROTHY (FOSTER) b. 17 Jan 1926
Married 29 Jul 1948, Kansas. Children:

1. PRISCILLA ANN
2. PATRICIA JO
3. MARLINA KAY
4. JOHN RICHARD
5. JAMES DOUGLAS
6. DONA MARIE
7. LARETTA LEA
8. BRENDA SUE
9. KERWIN MICHAEL

Today, as I bring to a close the latest data on the Douglas & Pearl Foster family, it is 90 degrees and sticky, after a high of 100 yesterday. Tuesday, Aug. 14, 1978, setting at the table in the kitchen of my parent's old home in Dresden, Kansas, I find it hard to concentrate on my "families." Tomorrow, I'll start on my own chapter.

* * * * * FLAVIUS MILTON FOSTER * * * * *

I warned you many pages back that I was going to hog a whole chapter for my family. Well, here it is.

From WILLIAM Sr. AND HANNAH (unknown) FOSTER
To – GEORGE & MARGARET (GRIGSBY) FOSTER
To – WILLIAM W. & SALLIE (SLADE) FOSTER
To - HARRISON & ANN (BARTLETT) FOSTER
To – AARON & SARAH (PATTON) FOSTER
To – SILAS & RACHEL (BILLS) FOSTER
To – FLAVIUS J. & MARGARET (OLIVER) FOSTER
To – DOUGLAS & PEARL (BOBBITT) FOSTER
To – FLAVIUS M. & MARIE (KOLSKY) FOSTER, and their children's families.

I, Flavius M. (Flave), was born to Douglas & Pearl (Bobbitt) Foster in Clayton, Norton, Kansas. I was born in the bedroom of a house which stood a block east of main street and 100 yards south of the railroad. At that time, Dad was employed in a blacksmith shop, but the following spring, he took his family to Corning, in Nemaha Co., Kansas. Here, after working for Clyde Cook, Dad bought the blacksmith shop from him, in 1912, and sold it 10 years later to C.O. Seaver.

Dad then moved to a farm 3 miles southwest of Corning, where we children had to walk 2 1/2 miles to and from old Greenwood school. In that neighborhood the neighbors were always having "surprise" parties on some family. Word would be passed regarding what goodies each family was to bring, then we would drop in on the victim. Mom always furnished the homemade buns and mince meat pies, with MEAT in them.

On Dad's 42nd birthday, he was ready for his "surprise party," with a 20-foot square-dance platform. Despite the lack of liquor, which never appeared at these parties, but, which so many people insist they must have for a good time, the dancing and merry-making lasted till 4 am. By the time the last car, and horse-drawn wagon had gone, it was getting light in the east.

In 1924, Dad moved one mile west to another farm, where I finished the 8th grade and started high school. It was 5 miles to school with 1 to 1 1/2 hours of chores to do, morning and night, but I kept at it till winter winds began to bite, then quit.

Those years on the farm were my version of "the good old days." We had a bountiful crop of rabbits, squirrel and quail that lived off our corn fields, and we in turn enjoyed the hunting. Dad would surround a weed patch with his shotgun, while we children would bird-dog for him. He would catch the running game, and we would pick off the setting game with our .22 rifles.

We moved to Dresden, Ks., in 1926, where I finished my growing up. On Labor Day 1931, I took a train to Colorado Springs hoping to enlist in the Navy, but found a 3-page waiting list. For the next 5 months I sponged off my Aunt Bessie Cadwallader while I bugged the recruiter. On Feb. 6 1932 he finally broke down and sent me out with a batch of recruits bound for San Diego, CA.

After all my bugging and high hopes I found Navy life at sea hard on my stomach muscles. However, one aspect of Navy life was right up my alley, when I got on the battlewagon USS Maryland's rifle and pistol team. I never made master marksman, but I was better than most men on the teams.

I was discharged Jan 29, 1936 and boarded with the parents of a Navy buddy, in Sedro Wooley, Wash., where I found a job in a garage. This job lasted for 2 1/2 years, at which time I returned to Dresden, Kansas. This was the middle of the "dirty thirties," and jobs were like hen's teeth, hard to find. During the entire summer of 1939, I found only 12 days work. For the "tidy" sum of $1.50 I put in an 11-hour day on the tired end of a pitchfork. I also got my noon meal, and had to walk 4 miles to and from work.

Those were mighty bleak days, but far worse than better, a light was beginning to gleam in Europe. A madman who was destined to go out in a blaze of gasoline was himself, setting the world afire.

In Sept. of 1939 Hitler's Nazi armies invaded Poland and I felt it in my bones that the world was in for another war. I was all "het up," and soon boarded a truck-load of hogs bound for market, ending up in Ft. Leavenworth, Kansas. Here, I enlisted in the 10th Field Artillery of the 3rd Infantry Division. I was stationed in Ft. Lewis, Washington on December 7, 1941, when Japanese forces bombed Pearl Harbor. On November 8, 1942, aged 32 years and one day, I was in the invasion of North Africa. In "pardnership" with a battery of 105mm howitzers, I paraded through North Africa, Sicily, Italy, Anzio, France, the German Fatherland, and to Salzburg, Austria. Thirty-one months of combat and the 3rd Division's 34,000 casualties later, I was on my way back home.

Work in Dresden, Ks. was now plentiful and the pay good. Ant it wasn't long till I met and married Marie Violet Kolsky. We built a house and two sons were born there. We felt sure Kansas would be our home till we were called to that greener pasture, but, again, war changed our way of life. Korea was afire with war, and I felt I should be in the service of my country, but I was 40 years old, and had a family.

I would be no good on a battlefield, but I could help in the war effort, so I loaded my family into our old 1937 Ford, and headed west. We landed in Bremerton, Washington, where I got a job with the Navy as an auto mechanic at the Bangor Ammunition Depot on Aug. 23, 1950. On May 17, 1970, I finished my 30 years of service with the government and retired.

Our first home in Washington was in the old Sheridan Park Housing project. In 1953 we moved to a rental near Poulsbo, Washington, and on June of 1955 we bought a 6-acre farm north of Poulsbo. Here, the children finished high school and departed on their own life's paths. It was in in1955 that I realized my life's ambition, the ownership of a new car.

War is a terrible thing but it has brought me from the depths of depression to a way of life I never expected to enjoy. My retirement income will provide a home, food, and many miles of travel for Marie and me the rest of our days. The Lord, in his mysterious way, had been extremely kind and generous to me and mine, and I thank Him with every fiber of my being.

Now wasn't that description of my life thrilling, embracing and a refreshing bit of mish-mash??...

FLAVIUS MILTON FOSTER b. 7 Nov 1909
MARIE V. (KOLSKY) b. 15 Jul 1925
Married 2 Sep 1946, Kansas. Children:

1. THOMAS GRANT
2. MAURICE EUGENE
3. LINDA MARIE
4. DOUGLAS JACKSON

Thomas Grant (Grant) was named for my two favorite Civil War generals, George Thomas – the “rock of Chickamauga,” and Ulysses S. Grant.

Maurice Eugene (Eugene) was named for his uncles, Maurice L. Foster and Dallas Eugene Kolsky.

Linda Marie’s (Linda) first name was tacked on for effect, her middle name for her mother.

Douglas Jackson (Jack) was named for his grandfather, Douglas H. Foster, and his uncle, Elferd Jackson, Foster.

WOW!! Am I ever glad this history has finally jolted to an end!! If any additions are made to it, the work will be done in the form of supplements. Despite my best efforts I doubt if there is another person who is less qualified to do this type of work. I'm very poor at spelling, grammar, punctuation, English and paragraph building. I type hunt & peck, erase, and start over again and again.

During my struggle to make a history out of the large amount material I had accumulated over 15 years, I often lost pages, old photos, and erasers. I would fly off the handle, swearing to burn the whole damned mess, only to cool off and return to the typewriter.

Every tale must end, and this is the tail-end of this tale, which started over three and a half centuries ago on a tiny beachhead on the shores of Colonial Virginia."--by Flavius Milton Foster

THOMAS GRANT, eldest child of FLAVIUS M. & MARIE (KOLSKY) FOSTER, was born in the hospital at Oberlin, Kansas, while the family lived in Dresden, Kansas. In mid-August of 1950 the family piled into a 1937 Ford and headed for Bremerton, Washington. They moved into the old Sheridan Park rental, the site of which is now under the north approach of the Warren Ave. Bridge.

Grant's father got a civil service job at the Naval Ammunition Depot, Bangor. In 1954, the family moved into a rental a mile south of Poulsbo, Washington, where Grant started school. In 1956 the family made its last move to a 6-acre plot north of Poulsbo, where Grant finished high school.

During his last year of high school Grant met BARBARA A. CHRISTOPHERSON, whom he married. But passion will never replace love, honor and respect, so this marriage was doomed to fail, although Grand did all he could to save it. During the last four and half years that the marriage lasted, Grant worked at Bangor Ammo Depot.

Grant married 4 Mar 1967 to BARBARA. To this union were born: 1) ROBERT CURTIS, 2) ZOE ANN.

Grant and Barbara were divorced in March of 1972, and she got the children. She soon remarried and now lives south of Poulsbo.

In March or 1972 Grant joined the army and took 1 ½ years of electronics courses at Ft. Huachacha, Arizona. Later he was stationed in Ft. Lewis, Washington until Thanksgiving Day in 1975, which saw him winging his way to a new duty station near Soeul, Korea. Here he met and married #3, HYE SUK CHOE (PENNY), who has a son named TRAVIS.

On January 8, 1977 Grant and his new family arrived in the U.S. and spent 6 weeks with his parents. In March of that year, they loaded into Grant's Plymouth Duster and took off for Ft. Belvoir, Virginia, through that year's record-breaking blizzard. Here, their son Timothy was born.

From June to July 10 of 1978 Grant spent visiting his parents, who had inherited the old Foster home in Dresden, Kansas, and were spending the summer there. Grant's brother, Eugene and family soon arrived, and for the next few days the old home hummed with activity as the 12 occupants scurried hither and thither, visiting relatives and holding a family reunion in Oberlin, Kansas, where both grandmothers were then residing. The Foster family visit ended with a fireworks display on the lawn of the old

Foster home. (Due to the families' interests elsewhere and the shifting sands of time, it is doubtful that the old home will ever again witness such Foster activity.)

July 10, 1978, Grant, Eugene and their 10-member family loaded into Eugene's Plymouth station wagon and headed back home to Poulsbo, Washington, and soon Grant and family were back in Korea. In January of 1981 Grant said goodbye to army life and returned to the U.S. A few weeks later he got a civil service job in the navy shipyard, Bremerton, Washington. He is now living four miles northwest of Poulsbo, Washington (Nov. 3, 1981).

T. GRANT FOSTER
HYE SUK (CHOE)
Married 8 Nov 1976. Children:

1. TRAVIS
2. TIMOTHY GREG

*** * * * * MAURICE EUGENE FOSTER * * * * ***

MAURICE EUGENE, 2nd child of FLAVIUS M. & MARIE (KOLSKY) FOSTER, was born in the hospital at Norton, Kansas. At that time the family was living in the home built by his father in Dresden, Kansas. In August of 1950 the family moved to Bremerton, Washington, where his father got a job at the old Bangor Ammunition Depot. In June of 1956 the family moved to a 6-acre plot a mile north of Poulsbo, Washington where Eugene started school and finished high school.

From April 22, 1969 to April 23, 1971 Eugene was a draftee with the 25th Infantry Division's artillery. In Vietnam he, like his father during WWII, served as an artillery observer with an infantry unit. His largest action was the invasion of Cambodia, where the Viet Cong North Vietnamese forces had extensive bases, in the mistaken belief that the American/South Vietnamese troops would not invade.

Little did Eugene and hundreds of other American troops realize that the Democrat administration in power was sending them into a deadly no-win war. A stupid, stupid, sacrifice of young bodies, because those in power refused to let them win battles, then traded those American bodies for thousands of Vietnamese refugees. (Wow! You said it, Flave.)

Back home, Eugene took a job at Keyport Torpedo Station and received schooling in electronics. A year later her married DIANE MARIE FOREMAN, a widow with two young daughters.

DIANE MARIE, daughter of WARREN (BUD) & VIOLA FOREMAN, was born in Portland, Oregon, and came with her parents to Keyport, Washington. Here she attended school and met and married #1) ROBERT DAVID PECKHAM, 19 Jul 1968.

Robert was born 4 Jul 1950 and died 25 Jul 1971 while on a fishing trip in Puget Sound. His body was never found.

Eugene and Diane's first home was in a trailer Diane had bought, 3 miles south of Poulsbo, Washington. Here their two sons were born. Diane's daughter, KIMBERLY K., was born in Bremerton, Washington and her daughter, CARI A. was born in Edmonds, Washington. In point of fact, the oldest daughter and both sons were born in the Harrison Hospital, Bremerton.

In 1975 Eugene's parents gave him 5 acres of the old homestead with the provision that he pay his sister and two brothers one fourth of the appraised-for-tax-purposes value of the land. Here, about 50 yards from his old childhood home, Eugene built his house. On the land, which is very rich and well-watered, Eugene has a garden, calves, and pigs for meat, and chickens for eggs and meat. There too, they have planted apple, cherry, plum, and pear trees, a regular farm though small in size.

MAURICE EUGENE FOSTER
DIANE (FOREMAN)
Married 10 Mar 1972, Washington. Children:

1. KIMBERY KAY PECKHAM
2. CARI ANN PECKHAM
3. MICHAEL AARON FOSTER
4. NATHANIEL LEE FOSTER

Notified that his grandmother, Pearl Foster, wasn't expected to live, Eugene's parents had hurried back to Kansas. Here the reopened the old Foster homestead in May of 1978. On June 23rd, Eugene loaded his family in their station wagon and headed for Kansas, via Disneyland, California. They arrived in Kansas June 28th, where they joined Eugene's parents and brother Grant, and his family, who had arrived two weeks earlier.

From June 28th to July 10th, Eugene, Diane, their four children, Grant, Penny, their two children, and Eugene's parents flitted hither and thither, visiting relatives. On July 2nd Eugene's parents held a Kolsky-Foster reunion in Oberlin, Kansas's Sappa Manor, a community center, attended by 68 close relatives. July 4th was celebrated on the lawn of the old Foster home in Dresden, Kansas, where Eugene and Grant's families shot off fireworks.

Due to the death of the grandparents and the shifting of interests elsewhere it is doubtful the old Foster home will ever again see such a Foster family gathering. Although their parents remained in Kansas until September, Eugene, his family, and Grant with his family loaded into Eugene's station wagon and headed back home July 10, 1978.

*** * * * * LINDA MARIE FOSTER * * * * ***

LINDA MARIE, 3[d] child of FLAVIUS M. & MARIE (KOLSKY) FOSTER, was born in the 1st Harrison hospital in Bremerton, Washington, while her parents were living in the rental now covered by the north approach of the Warren Ave. Bridge. She went with her parents to the rental south of Poulsbo, then to the family home north of that town, where she finished high school. In June of 1970 Linda, her parents and brother, Jack, took a summer-long tour of mid-America.

Linda took a live-in babysitting job in Bremerton, where she met MICHAEL JOHN BINGAMAN, a navy man. When Mike's ship moved to San Diego, Calif., Linda joined him there, and they were married. A short time later Mike's ship went to Vietnam for a second tour of duty and Linda returned to the home of her parents.

It is 18 miles from Linda's home to the naval hospital in Bremerton, Washington. The night Linda's daughter chose to make her squalling way into this world was just after a slushy snow had fallen and had turned to ice. Her father thought he had made his last birthing run twenty years earlier with the birth of his last child. Yet, here he was slipping sliding all over the road to the tune of grunts and groans from the rear seat of his car.

Lower-income families that wish to stay off relief have just about been priced out of having children. But, if Democrat presidents continue to start no-win wars, we can fill in the void of unborn American children by refugees and unwanted people from other nations and be taxed to support them.

In the fall of 1977 Mike divorced Linda. Today, 1981, she is working in a nursing home in Moses Lake, Washington, and fighting to keep her children. If Mike has his way it is doubtful my wife and I will see much of them in the years to come, perhaps nothing.

MICHAEL BINGAMAN and LINDA FOSTER were married in California 24 Jul 1971 and had:

1) JESSICA MARIE, 2) JEROD LEE.

*** * * * * DOUGLAS JACKSON FOSTER * * * * ***

DOUGLAS JACKSON, last child of FLAVIUS M. & MARIE (KOLSKY) FOSTER, was born in the old Harrison Hospital, Bremerton, Washington and taken to the rental, now under the north approach of the Warren Avenue Bridge. In 1956 Jack went with his parents to the 6-acre plot north of Poulsbo, Washington. Here he finished high school 5 Jun 1970 and went with his parents and sister on a summer-long tour of mid-America.

Jack worked a year in a seafood processing plant, and in October of 1971, he joined the army. A year later Jack was in Vietnam as a helicopter crew chief. His unit was the last American troops to leave Vietnam, after carting north Vietnamese generals into the south on their phony peace mission. In 1973, Jack returned home and was stationed at Ft. Campbell, Kentucky, where he reenlisted for Alaska. His first assignment was Fairbanks, then Anchorage.

In Anchorage, Alaska, Jack met DIANE ROXIE, daughter of DOUGLAS X. & MILDRED MARGARITE (YOUNG) WOMER. In parts of the deep south, male children are given only one name, a carryover of colonial days. Douglas was one of these cases, the X. being added later.

DIANE R. was born and started school in Dundalk, Maryland. Later the family moved to Hereford, MD, where she finished high school. Diane then met and married #1 HARRY FRITZ, a soldier stationed near Williamsburg, Virginia. Their daughter was born here, a short time before Harry transferred to Anchorage, Alaska, a short time before transferred to Anchorage, Alaska, where their son was born. Until the divorce, Diane worked as a civil service secretary in Ft. Richardson, where Harry and Jack Foster were stationed.

In April 14, 1977, Jack, Diane, and her children arrived in Poulsbo, Washington, where she visited Jack's parents for four days before returning to Maryland. Jack spent two weeks with his parents, then went to Maryland to meet Diane's family before reporting to his new duty station at Ft. Riley, Kansas.

On July 5, 1977, Diane, her children and sister, Deborah joined Jack at Ft. Riley, Kansas. On the 14th, all of them arrived in Dresden, where Jack's parents were spending the summer in the old Foster home. The next day, an army buddy of Jack's joined the party, and on the third day Jack and Diane were married in the Methodist Church, Dresden, Kansas. A wedding reception was held in Sappa Manor, Oberlin, Kansas, so that the groom's parents could attend.

Diane, her children and sister returned to the home of her parents in Butler, Maryland, where on Sept. 23, 1977, Jack joined them, and their son was born. Later Jack and Diane got a house in nearby Dundalk, MD. When Jack's brother Grant remarried we got a free grandson. Eugene's marriage gave us two "free" granddaughters, and Jack's marriage gave us two more "free' grandchildren.

DOUGLAS J. FOSTER
DIANE R. (WOMER)
Married 16 Jul 1977, Kansas. Children:

1. DAWN MARIE (FRITZ)
2. DWIGHT EUGENE (FRITZ)
3. FLAVIUS JACKSON (FOSTER)

The name Flavius was first born by a Foster in 1856, was handed down by his grandson, and from this grandson, to his grandson. It is an old Roman name, worn by many well-known men in the Roman Senate, but Flavius Josephus, the author of the Jewish history during the time of Christ, is the god-father of our Foster usage of the name. One thing is for sure, when the name is called, we who bear it know we are a select few. ? ? ? ?